Elaine Showalter was born in Cambridge, Massachusetts in 1941, and was educated at Bryn Mawr College and the University of California. From 1967 to 1984 she taught English and Women's Studies at Rutgers University, and is now Avalon Professor of the Humanities and chair of the department of English at Princeton University. She has written and edited many books, including, *The Female Malady: Women, Madness and English Culture, 1830–1980* (Virago, 1987), *Sexual Anarchy: Gender and Culture at the Fin de Siècle, The New Feminist Criticism: Essays on Women, Literature and Theory* (Virago, 1986) and *Daughters of Decadence: Women Writers of the Fin de Siècle* (Virago, 1993).

A Literature of Their Own

FROM CHARLOTTE BRONTË TO DORIS LESSING

Elaine Showalter

REVISED AND EXPANDED EDITION

Virago

VIRAGO

Published by Virago Press 1999
Reprinted 2003

First published by Virago Press 1978
Reprinted 1979, 1984, 1988, 1991, 1993, 1995, 1999, 2003, 2007

First published in the UK by Princeton University Press 1977

A CIP catalogue record for this book
is available from the British Library

ISBN 978-0-86068-285-1

Papers used by Virago are natural, recyclable products made from
wood grown in sustainable forests and certified in accordance with
the rules of the Forest Stewardship Council.

Printed and bound in Great Britain by
Clays Ltd, St Ives plc
Paper supplied by Hellefoss AS, Norway

Virago
An imprint of
Little, Brown Book Group
Brettenham House
Lancaster Place
London WC2E 7EN

A Member of the Hachette Livre Group of Companies

www.virago.co.uk

Contents

Acknowledgments to the Expanded Edition

THE PREPARATION of this corrected and updated edition of *A Literature of Their Own* would not have been possible without the research and editorial help of Jane Eldridge Miller, herself a distinguished scholar of Victorian women's writing. The Princeton University Council for Research in the Humanities and Social Sciences provided a grant to support Jane's work on this new edition. Mary Murrell at Princeton University Press has been a sensitive and extremely efficient editor. Over the past twenty years, my thinking about women's writing has been shaped most of all by wonderful students at Rutgers, Princeton, and the School of Criticism and Theory, many of whom have gone on to make their own important contributions to the field: Elizabeth Constable, Wayne Koestenbaum, Ellis Hanson, Maggie Debelius, Sue Basalla, Tracy Brown, Richard Kaye, Sarah E. Maier, Andrew Miller, Hyungji Park, John Perry, Matt Potolsky, Renata Kobetts, Jennie Kassanoff, Jane Eldridge Miller, Catherine St. Louis, Siobhan Kilfeather, Jayne Lewis, Carol Barash, Celeste Woodridge, Jeslyn Medoff, Jacqueline Osherow, Dennis Denisoff, and Diane Elam.

Acknowledgments

IN the atlas of the English novel, women's territory is usually depicted as desert bounded by mountains on four sides: the Austen peaks, the Brontë cliffs, the Eliot range, and the Woolf hills. This book is an attempt to fill in the terrain between these literary landmarks and to construct a more reliable map from which to explore the achievements of English women novelists.

Many people have helped me during the preparation of this book, and I would like to thank them here. I am indebted to the Rutgers University Faculty Research Council, whose fellowship enabled me to spend 1972–73 in London. My Rutgers University colleagues, Carol Smith, Alice Crozier, Alicia Ostriker, Katherine Ellis, Richard Poirier, Mary S. Hartman, and Judith Walkowitz, read sections of the manuscript in preparation and offered advice and support, as did Florence Howe, Tillie Olsen, Carol Ohmann, Erica Jong, and Wendy Martin. Nancy Paxton and Leslie Clark assisted me in compiling the bibliography and the biographical appendix. I owe special thanks to Gwendolyn B. Needham, whose enthusiasm for women writers encouraged me in the early stages of this research, to Ann Douglas and U. C. Knoepflmacher, whose criticism aided me in the final stages, and to Carol Orr and Connie Martin of Princeton University Press for continued interest and expert help. In London, Leonore Davidoff, Jean L'Esperance, Alice Prochaska, Mildred Surry, Anna Davin, Andrew Rosen, Patricia Thane, Patricia Caplan, and Ann Oakley helped me locate materials on the social history of Victorian women. For illuminating discussions of the English woman novelist, I am grateful to Marie Seton Hesson, Jennifer Stern, Margaret Walters, and Margaret Drabble.

ACKNOWLEDGMENTS

The following libraries have kindly granted permission to quote from manuscripts in their possession: the Beinecke Library, Yale University; the Morris L. Parrish Collection of Victorian Novelists, Firestone Library, Princeton University; the Fawcett Library, London; the Fales Collection, Elmer Holmes Bobst Library, New York University; the Bath Reference Library, Avon County Library, England; the Henry W. and Albert A. Berg Collection, New York Public Library, Astor, Lenox and Tilden Foundations; and the British Library. Permission to quote from unpublished letters has been granted by the following holders of literary rights: for Thomas Hardy, Lloyds Bank Ltd., Trustees of the Estate of Miss Eva Anne Dugdale; for Elizabeth Robins, Trekkie Parsons, Trustee of the Elizabeth Robins Estate; and for Dorothy Richardson, Mark Paterson.

Some of the material in Chapters II, III and VI appeared in a different form in "Women Writers and the Double Standard," *Woman in Sexist Society: Studies in Power and Powerlessness*, edited by Vivian Gornick and Barbara K. Moran, © 1971 by Basic Books, Inc., Publishers, New York; and in "Desperate Remedies," *Victorian Newsletter* (Spring 1976), 1-5.

Introduction

Twenty Years On: *A Literature of Their Own* Revisited

In 1965, when I began to do research for my Ph.D. dissertation on Victorian women writers, feminist criticism did not exist. Virginia Woolf's letters and diaries were scattered and unpublished. Scholars still called Elizabeth Gaskell "Mrs." and Frances Burney "Fanny." No one edited women's studies journals or compiled bibliographies of women's writing. At the University of California in Davis, where I was studying, "Theory" was not even a shadow on the sunny horizon, and the New Criticism, F. R. Leavis, Northrop Frye, and seven kinds of ambiguity marked the boundaries of my critical sophistication. I had chosen my thesis topic in part out of lingering anger at my undergraduate college, Bryn Mawr, where English majors were required to read every tenth-rate male Romantic poet and Elizabethan dramatist, but virtually no women; and in part out of my own devotion to the Victorian women writers.

Professional opportunities for academic women seemed so limited in the mid-1960s that I felt paradoxically freed to write about the books I liked, rather than the ones most likely to get me a job. Gwendolyn Needham, my thesis adviser at Davis, was sympathetic to my ideas and demanding about my scholarship, but my dissertation, "The Double Standard: Criticism of Women Writers in Victorian Periodicals, 1845–1880," was a hybrid, an attempt to write about women in an outmoded and inadequate critical vocabulary. Princeton University, where I actually wrote most of the dissertation as a faculty wife from 1966 on, did not hire women, but it had a fabulous collection of Victorian fiction, and all the Victorian journals were still on the open shelves, although only the first volume of the *Wellesley Index to Victorian Periodicals* was available to help me identify anonymous reviewers.

By 1970, when I received my Ph.D., the mood of the country had changed, and I had become an active member of the women's liberation movement. I had spent the summer of 1968 in Paris living in a communal household of French, English, and American students and professors in the aftermath of the politically transformative *événements* of May, and had been involved with the antiwar protests at the MLA. I had started writing for *Radical Feminism*, and I was editing an anthology called *Women's Liberation and Literature*. As the issues in my work and my life took on new meaning in the light of feminism, I began to envisage a much bolder critical undertaking than my thesis, and to imagine a literary criticism that would do for the history of women's writing what Northrop Frye had done for Canadian literature, or even what Perry Miller and F. O. Matthiessen had done for American literature.

At Douglass College, the women's college of Rutgers University, I had been promoted from part-time lecturer to assistant professor, and had started to teach courses on women writers. With the support of Richard Poirier and Frederick Main at Rutgers, I was awarded an English Department fellowship and spent a year in England doing research and using the dissertation as the basis of a book that would take the story up to the present. Traveling around chilly municipal libraries in England in quest of women writers' archives, I was often rewarded by becoming the first scholar to read a harrowing journal or open a box of letters. Victorian women writers, whom I thought of by their initials, CB, GE, EG, EBB, became my closest companions, more real to me than my own sister. And in the W.S.P.U. collection at the London Museum and the women's movement collection at the Fawcett Library, I found "free zones in the library world, newfound lands for scholars to explore."[1]

I had set myself the task of filling in the gaps between Austen and Lessing by reading as many novels by English women as I could find, and trying to understand the ways they related to each other. If there was a female literary tradition, I was sure, it came from imitation, literary convention, the marketplace, and critical reception, not from biology or psychology. My theoretical structure came from the sociology and ethnography of literature. Looking at such literary subcultures as African-American writing, Canadian writing, and Anglo-Indian writing, I attempted to define women's writing as the product of a subculture, evolving with relation to a dominant mainstream. In its evolution, I argued, women's writing moves "in the direction of an all-inclusive female realism, a broad, socially informed exploration of the daily lives and values of women within the family and the community."[2] But a mature women's literature ceases to be part of a subculture, and can move into "a seamless participation in the literary mainstream."[3] When I argued that "the ultimate room of one's own is the grave," I took a stance—*avant la lettre*—against theories of *écriture féminine*. "If the room of one's own becomes the destination," I concluded, "a feminine secession from the political world, from 'male' power, logic, and violence, it is a tomb, like Clarissa Dalloway's attic bedroom. But if contact with a female tradition and a female culture is a center; if women take strength in their independence to act in the world," women's literature could take any form, and deal with any subject.[4]

[1] Elaine Showalter and Jean L'Esperance, "Notes from London," *Women's Studies* 1, no. 2 (1973): 225.
[2] Elaine Showalter, *A Literature of Their Own*, Virago Press, 1978, p. 29.
[3] Ibid., p. 36.
[4] Ibid., p. 319.

My research raised many questions I didn't know how to solve, but I felt sure that there would be an audience for my book; and the writers themselves kept me going as I read about their hopes that all their struggles and failures would make a difference to the women who came after. They gave me the confidence to believe that even if I were not Northrop Frye's sister—the great feminist critic who would get everything right—it was enough to find the courage to write exactly what I thought, and to be willing to share my own struggles and errors in the faith that the critics who came after me would know more and do better.

I sent the manuscript to Princeton University Press, and they accepted it with some substantial cuts—half of the chapter on Virginia Woolf bit the dust. Their "Titles Committee" also changed my working title from "The Female Literary Tradition in the English Novel" to *A Literature of Their Own*, from a statement by John Stuart Mill, whom I quote on the first page and third sentence of the book: "If women lived in a different country from men, and had never read any of their writings, they would have a literature of their own."[5]

I liked the title, because this sentence from Mill's *The Subjection of Women* had been my point of departure: it raised the issues of nationality, subculture, literary influence, and literary autonomy I had attempted to theorize; and, in the word "their," rather than "our," it emphasized my own cultural distance, as an American, from the English women I discussed. The phrase "of their own," or "of our own," in the titles of feminist scholarly and popular books has certainly had quite a vogue in the past twenty years; but almost all reviewers of the book ignored my reference to Mill. They interpreted the title as a reference to Virginia Woolf, whom, some thought, I had treated with insufficient reverence. Toril Moi perceived hidden motives of appropriation and rejection: "A distinguished feminist critic like

[5] Ibid., p. 3.

xiv

Elaine Showalter, for example, signals her subtle swerve away from Virginia Woolf by taking over, yet changing, Woolf's title. Under Showalter's pen, *A Room of One's Own* becomes *A Literature of Their Own*, as if she wished to indicate her problematic distance from the tradition of women writers she lovingly uncovers in her book."[6] Janet Todd noted that "In *A Literature of Their Own*, already a snub, many thought, to the original Woolfian text, *A Room of One's Own*, Virginia Woolf was trounced for evading the problem of femaleness in her projection of the disturbing and dark aspects of a woman's psyche onto men."[7] Only the Australian critic K. K. Ruthven emphasized Mill, to take exception to the "separatism" of writing a book about women writers alone, for, he argued, "men and women inhabit the same countries and read each other's work habitually."[8]

Having a male critic like Ruthven comment on the book was already progress. Certainly women writers and critics must and do habitually read the work of men; until very recently, however, the reverse has not been the case. The critical reception of *A Literature of Their Own* by men has been generally respectful, but among women critics the book has been both imitated and reviled. On one hand, it helped create the new field of feminist literary history and gynocriticism, has been translated into several languages, and has influenced similar undertakings around the world. I've even been cited in an article on the evolution of women's rock music.[9] On the other hand, I have been attacked from virtually every point on the feminist hermeneutic circle, as a separatist, careerist, theoretical, antitheoreti-

[6] Toril Moi, *Sexual/Textual Politics*, London and New York: Methuen, 1985, p. 1.

[7] Janet Todd, *Feminist Literary History*, London and New York: Routledge, 1988, p. 36.

[8] K. K. Ruthven, *Feminist Literary Studies: An Introduction*, Cambridge: Cambridge University Press, 1984, p. 124.

[9] Elizabeth Wurtzel, "Girl Trouble," *The New Yorker*, June 29, 1992, pp. 63–70.

cal, racist, homophobic, politically correct, traditional, and noncanonical critic. For the past twenty years I've come to expect new critical studies of women's writing to point out how I have "failed," and in 1997, at the book exhibit at the MLA convention in Toronto, I picked up galleys of a new book that added that I had "notoriously failed."

Still, being notorious for failing is better than not being noticed at all; and I decided early on that I would not defend *A Literature of Their Own* against attack, but rather that I would try to let go of the book and allow intellectual debate in feminist criticism to follow its natural course. I've continued to work on women writers and on the theory of feminist criticism, and to move on to other subjects as well. I have followed the cycles of criticism and attack with attention and interest, and I have even had the good fortune to live long enough to receive a few apologies, in person or in print.

Most important, I've had the advantages of two decades of a fruitful and dazzling critical revolution in women's literary history and feminist criticism to broaden my understanding, deepen my knowledge, and sharpen my thinking. *A Literature of Their Own* appeared during the first wave of feminist literary criticism which focused on rediscovery. In the early 1970s, I found it important to write about continuities between generations of women writers, and I deliberately foregrounded women critics as well. But the emphasis on female literary lineage is partly rhetorical, for women's writing is always at least bitextual; as I wrote in "Feminist Criticism in the Wilderness," it is a double-voiced discourse influenced by both the dominant masculine literary tradition and the muted feminine one.[10]

By the end of the 1970s, in their magisterial study of women writers, *The Madwoman in the Attic* (1979), Sandra Gilbert and Susan Gubar set out a compelling theory of

[10] Elaine Showalter, "Feminist Criticism in the Wilderness," *Critical Inquiry* 8, no. 2 (Winter 1981): 179–205.

female literary history as a dialogue between women writers and a patriarchal tradition. Their own theory was a revision of Harold Bloom's "anxiety of influence," presenting the battle between the sexes as a linguistic and literary struggle that generated new genres and forms. Moreover, Gilbert and Gubar mapped out an anxiety-ridden terrain for nine-teenth-century women writers that seemed unconsciously to describe the psychodynamics of the contemporary feminist critic: feelings of alienation from male precursors, an urgent need for a female audience, dread of patriarchal authority, and internalized conflict about theoretical invention and imaginative autonomy. In their critical trilogy *No Man's Land*, Gilbert and Gubar moved into the twentieth century to describe the ways that women artists were not only enabled but also daunted by the example of great female precursors, and how they responded with "mingled feelings of rivalry and anxiety."[11]

In the 1990s, criticism of women's writing has to take the fullest possible account of the whole network of literary forces in which each text is enmeshed, and my hypothetical model of a chain of female literary influence needs to be understood as a historically specific strategy rather than a dogmatic absolute. The eve of a new century seems like the ideal time for stocktaking, and the prospect of a revised new edition of *A Literature of Their Own* gives me the opportunity to reflect on what has taken place and how I would want to change the book if I were writing it now.

THEORIES

In the 1980s, as European theoretical models came to dominate literary criticism, feminist critics of *A Literature of Their Own* pointed to my theoretical "naïveté" and my

[11] Sandra M. Gilbert and Susan Gubar, *The War of the Words*, vol. 1 of *No Man's Land: The Place of the Woman Writer in the Twentieth Century.* New Haven: Yale University Press, 1988, p. 199.

stubborn American pragmatism. Some critics identified theoretical contexts in my writing of which I myself had certainly been unaware. Patricia Waugh noted that "theories of ego-psychologists and the cognitive developmental models of Erikson, Piaget, and Kohlberg hover behind the pages . . . of feminist literary histories like Elaine Showalter's."[12] Gayle Greene and Coppelia Kahn argued that "implicit in Showalter's argument—as in much Anglo-American feminist criticism—is the assumption that the text, and language itself, are transparent media which reflect a pre-existent objective reality, rather than signifying systems which inscribe ideology and are actually constitutive of reality."[13]

The most substantial attack came from Toril Moi, in *Sexual/Textual Politics* (1985). Even before her book came out, I had heard rumors that it would be very critical of my work, and I had received a letter from Moi assuring me that her stringent critique came from deep sisterly respect. (This is the standard feminist academic formula for "Brace yourself.") Indeed, from the first page of the book, *Sexual/Textual Politics* used my work, along with that of Sandra Gilbert, Susan Gubar, and others, to exemplify the inadequacies of "Anglo-American" feminist criticism.

Moi's central argument is that my "theoretical framework is never made explicit." In her view, my implicit theory was that "a text should reflect the writer's experience, and that the more authentic the experience is felt to be by the reader, the more valuable the text." "Implicitly," she maintains, my position "strongly favours the form of writing commonly known as critical or bourgeois realism." Indeed, Moi declares, "there is detectable within her literary criticism a strong unquestioned belief in the

[12] Patricia Waugh, *Feminine Fictions: Revisiting the Postmodern*, London and New York: Routledge, 1989, p. 40.
[13] Gayle Greene and Coppelia Kahn, *Making a Difference: Feminist Literary Criticism*, London and New York: Methuen, 1985, p. 25.

INTRODUCTION

values, not of proletarian humanism, but of traditional bourgeois humanism of a liberal-individualist kind." In my "crypto-Lukacsian" realism, my "demand for a unitary vision," and my dependence on "traditional aesthetic categories,"[14] I am unable to appreciate the decentered writing of modernism and its feminist uses.

Moi returns to discuss *A Literature of Their Own* in two pages in her fourth chapter, "Women writing and writing about women," in which she reiterates her view that its flaws lie in "its unstated theoretical assumptions about the relationship between literature and reality and between feminist politics and literary evaluation." In contrast, she maintains, the poststructuralist theory of French feminism in general, and of Julia Kristeva in particular, is the most sophisticated and far-reaching form of feminist literary analysis. Rejecting biologism and essentialism, it deconstructs "the opposition between masculinity and femininity."[15]

Moi's analysis of feminist criticism has been very influential, and in the U.K., where *Sexual/Textual Politics* is a standard university text, many students take their views of *A Literature of Their Own* directly from it, without reading my work at all. Undisputably, I had not read or even heard of Cixous, Irigaray, or Kristeva, who were barely known in the U.S. when I finished the book in 1974. *New French Feminisms*, edited by Elaine Marks and Isabelle de Courtivron, which introduced American scholars to French feminist writing, did not come out until 1980. But as a literary historian, I would still have found little that was useful in their work. More significantly, in her own immersion in French and Marxist criticism, Moi missed the real theoretical assumptions of *A Literature of Their Own*, assumptions derived from a very different approach to literature, reality, gender, and canon. In Moi's view, the most important theoretical questions were philosophical: "What is interpretation? What

[14] *Sexual/Textual Politics*, pp. 4, 6, 8, and 17.
[15] Ibid., pp. 56 and 12.

does it mean to read? What is a text?"[16] My theoretical questions, however, were historical and cultural. What is the relationship between a dominant and a muted culture? Does a muted culture have a history and a literature of its own, or must it always be measured according to the chronology, standards, and values of the dominant? Can a minority criticism develop its own methods and theories through wide and careful reading of its own literary texts? How does a literary subculture evolve and change? The disciplines with answers for such questions were not philosophy and linguistics, but cultural anthropology and social history.

If I were writing *A Literature of Their Own* today, I would certainly have a broader comparative base in literary subcultures, and in the theories that have emerged around postcolonial studies. I would also make a stronger theoretical case for "realism" as a literary convention. As George Levine has demonstrated in *The Realistic Imagination*, Victorian narrative realism is far from being a simplistic mimetic rendering of "experience," male or female. It is a highly developed technique of representation, with its own theoretical underpinnings.[17] In addition, there is nothing inherently radical or subversive about antirealist literary conventions. Today's avant-garde is tomorrow's advertising. Despite its intellectual vogue, French feminist theory has still not come to terms with women's writing and literary history, and many of its leading figures have moved on to other subjects.

Meanwhile, gynocriticism, as I named the study of women's writing in 1979, has developed to offer a coherent narrative of women's literary history. In relation to the literary mainstream, women's writing has moved through phases of subordination, protest, and autonomy, phases connected by recurring images, metaphors, themes, and plots that emerge from women's social and literary experience, and from

[16] Ibid., pp. 76–77.
[17] See George Levine, *The Realistic Imagination: English Fiction from Frankenstein to Lady Chatterley*, Chicago: University of Chicago Press, 1981, pp. 131–228.

reading both male and female precursors. As Susan Wolfson notes in her excellent overview of feminist criticism and British literature, "by the early 1980s it was clear that feminist literary criticism and attention to female writers had gained institutional legitimacy. These achievements consolidated over the decade, their success evident in the curricula of English courses from junior high school through graduate school. . . . And the classroom anthologies . . . have evolved accordingly." Wolfson concludes that "the 1990s are shaping up as a decade in which women's writing is becoming increasingly available by force of new anthologies and reprints of long-out-of-print writing by women, and by the mergence of on-line texts and editions of women's writing, accessible on the internet through (among other websites) the University of Virginia's Electronic Text Center, the Brown University Women Writers Project, and the University of Pennsylvania Department of English home page."[18]

Literary History and the Canon

I had imagined *A Literature of Their Own* as a book that would challenge the traditional canon, going far beyond the handful of acceptable women writers to look at all the minor and forgotten figures whose careers and books had shaped a tradition. "It is only by considering them all—Millicent Grogan as well as Virginia Woolf," I wrote, "that we can begin to record new choices in a new literary history."[19] I wanted to demystify the process by which some women writers had been granted "greatness" and reveal the material contexts and circumstances in which women's writing was imagined, published, disseminated, and reviewed. Nevertheless, some critics have objected to

---

[18] Susan Wolfson, *British Literature: Discipline Analysis*, Baltimore: National Center for Curriculum Transformation Resources on Women, 1997, pp. 12–13 and 18.

[19] *A Literature of Their Own*, p. 36.

my choices and omissions, and some to the idea that literary history can be written at all.

Several scholars have argued that the female literary tradition in the novel begins much earlier than the 1840s, and that I neglect novelists of the eighteenth century. Marilyn Butler objects: "Showalter concludes that a continuous women's tradition can be spoken of only for writers born after 1800. She believes that women writers before that date did not consider themselves professionals and therefore (though the connection between these two propositions is not clear) could not relate to other women writers. Here it is hard to know quite what thinking has gone into Showalter's use of the term professional. . . . There was always a woman writer's network, though not all women writers belonged to it, and Austen herself did not."[20] Margaret J. Ezell blames my "evolutionary" model, which "leads in part to the relegating of earlier women to the earliest phase of the female tradition, not very high up on the evolutionary ladder."[21] Janet Todd protests that "Showalter can declare that women did not think of themselves as professional writers before 1800, when there are in fact hosts of professional novelists in the eighteenth century. . . . In this concentration on the Victorian period and on the mode of domestic realism, as well as in its ignoring of the problem of aesthetic judgment and language, *A Literature of Their Own* was typical of the early phase of feminist criticism on women. . . .[I]ts omissions skewed the understanding of the female past and encouraged premature generalization that did duty for specific history."[22]

Actually my initial research for the book had been on

[20] Marilyn Butler, *Jane Austen and the War of Ideas*, Oxford: Clarendon Press, 1988, p. xxviii.

[21] Margaret J. M. Ezell, "Re-Visioning the Restoration: Or, How to Stop Obscuring Early Women Writers," in *New Historical Study: Essays on Reproducing Texts, Representing History*, ed. Jeffrey N. Cox and Larry J. Reynolds, Princeton: Princeton University Press, 1993, p. 145.

[22] *Feminist Literary History*, p. 27.

eighteenth-century and earlier writers; and I have learned an enormous amount since from Butler, Ezell, Todd, Ruth Perry, Moira Ferguson, Claudia Johnson, Nancy Armstrong, Jane Spencer, Margaret Doody, Carol Barish, Susan Wolfson, Esther Schor, and my husband English Showalter, who has been editing the seventy volumes of manuscript letters of the eighteenth-century French woman novelist Madame de Graffigny almost as long as we have been married. But I continue to think that before the nineteenth century, as Ruth Perry points out in her splendid biography of Mary Astell, no British "woman planned a career as a writer; there was no such concept as a woman of letters."[23] Moreover, the appearance of the male pseudonym among British and European women writers—from "Ernst Ahlgren" (Victorian Benedictson) in Sweden, to George Sand in France, and "Fernando Caballero" (Cecilia Bohl) in Spain—was a clear historical marker of a new literary consciousness based on gender. It was to emphasize professionalism, marketing, and group awareness, rather than to ignore or disdain eighteenth-century women novelists, that I chose to begin in the 1840s. Kathleen Tillotson's great study of *Novels of the 1840s* (1956), which clearly delineated the major changes in the form and marketing of novels during the decade, influenced my choice as well.

Geoffrey Hartman, in his influential book *Criticism in the Wilderness* (1980), argues that every new literary theory is based on or generalizes from a particular text-milieu. In its first phase, feminist criticism developed out of a dialogue with the Victorian patriarchs (Mill, Carlyle, Arnold, Marx, Freud) and with a textual preference for Victorian women's novels. Moreover, Victorian studies was a field hospitable to a feminist presence early on, in its interdisciplinarity, its acceptance of women writers, and its friendliness toward women scholars and critics. Many young women graduate

[23] Ruth Perry, *The Celebrated Mary Astell: An Early English Feminist,* Chicago and London: University of Chicago Press, 1986, p. 5.

students in my generation were drawn to the Victorian period because it was the only literary period in which women were accepted as canonical writers. Kate Millett's *Sexual Politics* (1970) began as a dissertation in Victorian literature at Columbia; at the interdisciplinary journal *Victorian Studies* a feminist editor, Martha Vicinus, commissioned a special issue on women and edited a two-volume set of bibliographic essays, *Suffer and Be Still* and *A Widening Sphere*. Only later did the field of eighteenth-century studies become receptive to feminist analysis.

By the late 1970s, feminist criticism was debating differences of class and race, and my references to the development of a black literary subculture as "a precedent for feminist scholarship to use" offended Barbara Smith, who commented in her essay "Toward a Black Feminist Criticism" that "the idea of critics like Showalter *using* Black literature is chilling, a case of barely disguised cultural imperialism."[24] I reprinted the essay without comment when I edited *The New Feminist Criticism*, but I was chilled myself by Smith's response to my interdisciplinary efforts and her rage ("the final insult") at my citation in the book of a literary history of the African-American novel written by a white male scholar.

As late as 1994, a commentator indifferent to the fact that my book is about the English tradition remarked that "the absence of American black women" in *A Literature of Their Own* had been "much criticized," and that my "inability" to deal with them made my arguments "fundamentally flawed."[25] Nonetheless, I have yet to hear from anyone exactly which nineteenth-century and early-twentieth-century

[24] Elaine Showalter, "Literary Criticism," *Signs* 1, no. 2 (Winter 1975): 445; and Barbara Smith, "Toward a Black Feminist Criticism," *Conditions: Two* (October 1977): 29.

[25] Sara Mills, with Jane Goldman, Vassilike Kolcotroni, Pauline Polkey, Angie Sandhu, and Diana Wallace, "Feminist Theory," in *The Year's Work in Critical and Cultural Theory*, vol. 4, ed. Kate McGowan, London: Blackwell, 1994, p. 115.

black English women novelists I should have included. Of course, I have a much wider range of theoretical work on African-American writing to draw upon today; and in a new chapter bringing the history of women's writing up to the present, I deal with the work of contemporary black, Caribbean, and Asian women novelists in Britain.

Finally, for some critics in the 1970s and 1980s, I was still much too canonical, too unwilling to abandon altogether the idea of any coherent history or tradition or canon. According to Ruthven, the whole notion of "literary history" and a "literary tradition" was dead: "It first demarcates an arbitrary category called 'the literary' from other cultural phenomena for which a marxist would expect to find common materialistic explanations; and it then assumes that instances of it constitute a continuum on which literary historians are free to project those tripartite structures of development they are so fond of."[26] My tripartite structure—feminine, feminist, female—is the one he mainly has in mind.

Moi went further, arguing that work like mine aimed "to create a separate canon of women's writing, not to abolish all canons."[27] Yet, as Moi herself declared when she was attacking another Anglo-American feminist critic in a different context, claiming to "abolish" literary canon is a gesture of hollow rhetorical grandiosity: "To be against power is not to abolish it in a fine, post-1968 libertarian gesture, but to hand it over to someone else."[28] The construction of a literary canon is not a conspiracy, but a process determined by a large cultural network. Work by critics such as Richard Brodhead and John Guillory has shown that canon-formation, involving the reclamation of devalued writers, is an important part of critical revolutions, and that new canons "will not surface except through the force of someone's or

[26] *Feminist Literary Studies*, p. 126.
[27] *Sexual/Textual Politics*, p. 78.
[28] Ibid., p. 148.

some groups' interests. And whether they will stay above water on future maps of the literary continents is a question exactly *not* of their innate value (which never saved a past yet) but of whether those interests can successfully institutionalize themselves and win old ones to the cause of making theirs be the past worth remembering."[29]

In contrast to the claims of some careless readers, I was not advocating a simple Whig literary history. But I still remain committed to the idea, even the metaphor, of progress in English women's writing, if only in terms of range and freedom of expression. Moreover, I think it is necessary to evaluate the relative success and failure of women's writing, and I cannot agree with critics like Ann Ardis, who insists that feminist critics should reject all models of "literary hierarchies" as patriarchal, in the interests of a "noncanonical theory of value." "When asked if I have found any great works in all my reading," Ardis concludes in her study of New Woman's writing, "I usually respond by turning the question back on my interlocutor: does your interest in aesthetic value disguise anxiety about the feminist politics of these novels? What cultural values are you defending through an emphasis on the formal rather than the ideological pleasures of these texts?"[30]

Although the intent of these rhetorical questions is clearly both to avoid answering the issue of value and to induce guilt and shame in the hapless interlocutor, I confess to a shameless persistence in my heresy. After twenty-five years of feminist criticism, I do not think that feminists have exorcised all sense of literary hierarchies, however forcefully we may argue in public against them. And as I consider the development of English women's fiction from

[29] See Richard Brodhead, *The School of Hawthorne*, New York: Oxford University Press, 1896, p. 7; and John Guillory, "The Ideology of Canon-Formation: T. S. Eliot and Cleanth Brooks," *Critical Inquiry* 10 (September 1983): 173–98.

[30] Ann Ardis, *New Women, New Novels: Feminism and Early Modernism*, New Brunswick, N.J.: Rutgers University Press, 1990, p. 174.

the early 1970s to the present, I continue to believe that women's writing needs no apologies or special treatment, and can sustain the most rigorous tests of aesthetic judgement and literary quality.

New Women and Their Fiction

In 1990, as the approaching millennium kindled a new interest in women's fiction of the 1890s, *A Literature of Their Own* came under attack from a new generation of feminist literary critics. Some complained that I was too dismissive of the artistic importance of women novelists of the 1890s, or that I had underestimated the value of the women's suffrage novel. "Elaine Showalter, in *A Literature of Their Own*," wrote Shirley Peterson in 1993, "continues to validate canonical aesthetic standards at the expense of women's political writing. She hails the British women's suffrage movement as a historical and literary period that galvanized women writers in a uniquely political fashion. She praises them for the courageous rejection of Victorian reserve, yet she goes on to devalue the literary importance of their work."[31]

I would now be able to give much more emphasis to the 1890s as a transitional period for women's writing, thanks in large part to books like Jane Eldridge Miller's *Rebel Women: Feminism, Modernism, and The Edwardian Novel* (1994), Ann Ardis's *New Women, New Novels* (1990), Rita Felski's *The Gender of Modernity* (1995), and the work of Margaret D. Stetz, who edited the journal *Turn-of-the-Century Women*. There are now editions of the work of Amy Levy, Sarah Grand, George Egerton, and other important women writers of the 1890s. But when I was writing *A Literature of Their Own*, most of these women were

[31] Shirley Peterson, "The Politics of a Moral Crusade: Gertrude Colmore's *Suffragette Sally*," in *Discovering Forgotten Radicals: British Women Writers 1889–1939*, ed. Angela Ingram and Daphne Patai, Chapel Hill and London: University of North Carolina Press, 1993, p 102.

INTRODUCTION

completely unknown. In 1971, I went to Bath in search
of Sarah Grand, and, on a rainy winter day, opened the
cartons in the Municipal Library which had sat untouched
since her death. After the book was published, Gillian Kersley, an independent scholar living in Bath, decided to write
a full-length biography of Grand. The papers and novels of
the suffragettes were kept at Kensington Palace, and scholars had not yet analyzed the art of the suffrage movement.

Artistically and politically, the 1890s were a major period
for women writers. In contrast to the gloom of Hardy and
Gissing, Emmeline Pethick-Lawrence, the British suffragist
who was part of this generation, recalled the joy felt by
young women: "It was a wonderful thing at that period to
be young among young comrades, for the ninth decade of
the last century was a time of expansion and vision. . . . We
read, discussed, debated, and experimented and felt that all
life lay before us to be changed and moulded by our vision
and desire."[32] In the field of fiction, the 1890s seemed to
offer great opportunities to the young, with the demise of
the three-volume novel and lending-library system, and the
rise of the literary journal and the short story. With the collapse of the three-decker came the collapse of what Holbrook Jackson called "a type of novel: the old sentimental
lending-library novel of polite romantic atmosphere and
crudely happy endings . . . [the novel which] was calculated
to produce that downy state of mild peacefulness which
many people believe to be the end and aim of all good
literature."[33]

In place of the dowdy three-decker came the slim single
volume, exquisitely bound in shades of lemon or mauve
and hinting of the forbidden and perverse. *The Yellow Book*,
founded in April 1894, epitomized the shift from domesticity to art, and "represented wide-scale collaboration and

[32] Emmeline Pethick-Lawrence, *My Part in a Changing World*, London: Victor Gollancz Ltd., 1938, p. 88.
[33] Holbrook Jackson, *The Eighteen-Nineties*, New York: Alfred A.
Knopf, 1922, p. 218.

xxviii

cooperation across the boundaries of class, nationality, gender, sexual orientation, discipline and ideology."[34] It published works by many women poets, artists, and writers, two of whom also served as subeditors. Indeed, the term "New Woman" made its debut in May 1894, in an exchange between Sarah Grand and Ouida in the *North American Review*.

The year 1894 was an *annus mirabilis* for New Woman writing as well.[35] Among the novels published that year were Rhoda Broughton's *A Beginner*; Emma Frances Brooke's *A Superfluous Woman*; Sara Jeanette Duncan's *A Daughter of Today*; Rita's *A Husband of No Importance*; Sarah Grand's *Our Manifold Nature*; Edith Johnstone's *A Sunless Heart*; Mona Caird's *The Daughters of Danaus*; May Crommelin's *Dust before the Wind*; Annie Holdsworth's *Joanna Trail, Spinster*; "Iota"'s *A Yellow Aster*; Ella Hepworth Dixon's *The Story of a Modern Woman*; Dorothy Leighton's *Disillusion*; Florence Farr's *The Dancing Faun*; John Strange Winter's (Henrietta Stannard) *A Blameless Woman*; George Paston's (Emily Symonds) *A Modern Amazon*; George Egerton's *Discords*; and Elizabeth Robins's cruel satire on these pseudonymous female personae, *George Mandeville's Husband*.

Yet the heyday of the New Woman Novelist was pitifully brief. By 1895, the blaze of women's writing was reduced to sparks and ashes, and the death of the New Woman novel was widely proclaimed. Moreover, the writers themselves did not fare well. Many published little or nothing after their debuts; virtually all have disappeared from standard literary history.

In *A Literature of Their Own*, I placed most of the blame for the New Woman writers' demise on the women themselves. "In retrospect," I wrote then, "it looks as if all the feminists had but one story to tell, and exhausted them-

[34] Margaret Stetz and Mark Samuels Lasner, "Introduction," *The Yellow Book: A Centenary Exhibition*, Cambridge, Mass.: The Houghton Library, Harvard University, 1994, p. 12.

[35] Jane Eldridge Miller, *Rebel Women: Feminism, Modernism, and the Edwardian Novel*, London: Virago Press, 1994, p. 32.

selves in its narration. . . . Beginning with a sense of unity
and . . . an interest in the 'precious speciality' of the female
novelist, they ended . . . with the dream that by withdrawing
from the world they would find a higher female truth."[36]
But I have since tried to soften this harsh judgment, in introductions to Sarah Grand's *The Beth Book* (1981), Mary
Cholmondely's *Red Pottage* (1985), and Olive Schreiner's
Story of an African Farm (1993); in *Sexual Anarchy* (1990)
and especially in an anthology of women's short stories
from the 1890s, *Daughters of Decadence* (1995). Women's
novels in the 1890s often choose the woman artist, writer,
or intellectual as heroine, and explore the limits of feminist
aspiration for their generation; the tragic feminist intellectual is a nineties' heroine as significant as the tragic mulatto
in African-American fiction. If New Woman novelists with-
drew in frustration from social engagement, they had good
reason to do so and fought courageously against the conventions of the time.

Nevertheless, fascinating as I find the psychological twists
and turns of New Woman fiction, none of these British
novels are as aesthetically satisfying as Kate Chopin's *The
Awakening* (1899) or Rachilde's *The Juggler* (1900). The
novel was a problematic genre for fin-de-siècle English
women writers, as many of them realized. In their hands it
tended to be didactic, talky, episodic, and contrived. Following on the great achievements and reputation of George
Eliot, they suffered from the anxiety of influence; and they
had outgrown the plots of Victorian fiction without having
entirely reinvented their own. John Kucich argues that
New Woman novelists had difficulties "accommodating the
ambiguities of truth-telling within fiction itself to the demands of feminism, especially at a time when early modernist aesthetics was moving . . . away from the ideals of truth-
telling cherished by Victorian realism. It is because women
writers could not negotiate the truth dilemmas of post-Vic-

[36] *A Literature of Their Own*, p. 215.

torian literature, not because of their lack of talent or their ideological single-mindedness, that they made inevitable their own exile from a canonical tradition that had begun to treat honestly as an issue that could only be solved through aesthetic rarefaction."[37]

The best women's writing of the 1890s is in the short story rather than in the novel. Women writers found an appropriate form in the short story for the strong feminist themes of the decade: the rebellion of the muse, the exploration of a New Woman's language, and the protest against the appropriation, even theft, of women's stories by men. New Women had to rewrite aestheticism and decadence in order to include female creativity. They had to present female sexuality and reproduction as positive creative forces, rather than as biological traps or the binary opposite of artistic creation. They had also to deal with the relationship between aestheticism and commodification.

Their short stories, more than their novels, describe the struggle for new words and new forms. In Sarah Grand's "The Undefinable: A Fantasia," for example, a painter whose work has become sterile and conventional is agonizing over the loss of his powers. "There gradually took possession of me a great amazement, not to say alarm, as I forced myself to acknowledge that there must be some blunting of my faculties. . . . What could be the matter with me? Loss of nerve-power?" He is interrupted in these thoughts by an unexpected visit in his studio from a confident young woman offering herself as a model. At first he does not find her attractive; she had "eyes out of which an imperious spirit shone independently, not looking up, but meeting mine on the same level." Nonetheless, he paints her, and to his astonishment, the work is brilliant. He suddenly realizes who she is: "a free woman, a new creature, a source of inspiration the like of which no man has even

[37] John Kucich, *The Power of Lies: Transgression in Victorian Fiction*, Ithaca: Cornell University Press, 1994, p. 279.

imagined in art or literature." But before he can finish the painting she vanishes, and although he drives in his carriage through the streets, hoping to find her, he never sees her again. Until he himself changes and grows, the story concludes, she will never return.[38]

The Twenty-First Century

The themes and forms of contemporary women's writing have certainly changed since the 1970s, and there is now even a major literary award, the Orange Prize, for women novelists in English. Of the writers who have emerged since the first edition of *A Literature of Their Own*, at least one—Angela Carter—must be included in any female literary canon or tradition, and several—Hilary Mantel, Michele Roberts, Joanna Trollope, Fay Weldon, and Jeanette Winterson—deserve serious critical attention. But I would stand by the concerns I expressed in 1977, with one important modification. Then I warned that if "the room of one's own becomes the destination, a feminine secession from 'male' power, logic, and violence, it is a tomb." Disturbingly, even in 1998, the room of one's own, as the locus for chronic fatigue syndrome, female fantasy, or paralyzing anxiety, is still an isolated space in women's fiction. But there is also hopeful evidence that "contact with a female tradition and a female culture" has been a center, inspiring women writers to "take strength in their independence to act in the world."[39]

What seems different now is that the goal Virginia Woolf articulated at the end of *A Room of One's Own*, seventy years ago, to labor in poverty and obscurity for the coming of Shakespeare's sister, no longer seems mean-

[38] Sarah Grand, "The Undefinable: A Fantasia," in *Daughters of Decadence: Women Writers of the Fin-de-Siècle*, ed. Elaine Showalter, Virago Press, 1992, pp. 265 and 267.
[39] *A Literature of Their Own*, p. 319.

ingful or necessary. Feminist criticism and women's literary history do not depend on the discovery of a great unique genius, but on the establishment of the continuity and legitimacy of women's writing as a form of art. With the globalization of culture, moreover, the national boundaries of the novel are fading and disappearing. Was Sylvia Plath a British or an American writer? Can the influence of Toni Morrison fail to affect the novel in Europe? The distinctions of nationality and culture I meant to imply in the title of *A Literature of Their Own* are no longer as sharp as they were only twenty-five years ago. But if the distinctions of gender may also soon become matters of literary history, it will be because feminist criticism has succeeded in its task, and having played a part in that great collective effort has been a source of pride and delight to me that no theoretical debates can ever blur.

A Literature of Their Own

CHAPTER I

~~~~~~

The Female Tradition

> The advent of female literature promises woman's view of life, woman's experience: in other words, a new element. Make what distinctions you please in the social world, it still remains true that men and women have different organizations, consequently different experiences. . . . But hitherto . . . the literature of women has fallen short of its functions owing to a very natural and a very explicable weakness—it has been too much a literature of imitation. To write as men write is the aim and besetting sin of women; to write as women is the real task they have to perform.—G. H. LEWES, *"The Lady Novelists,"* 1852

ENGLISH women writers have never suffered from the lack of a reading audience, nor have they wanted for attention from scholars and critics. Yet we have never been sure what unites them as women, or, indeed, whether they share a common heritage connected to their womanhood at all. Writing about female creativity in *The Subjection of Women* (1869), John Stuart Mill argued that women would have a hard struggle to overcome the influence of male literary tradition, and to create an original, primary, and independent art. "If women lived in a different country from men," Mill thought, "and had never read any of their writings, they would have a literature of their own." Instead, he reasoned, they would always be imitators and never innovators. Paradoxically, Mill would never have raised this point had women not already claimed a very important literary place. To many of his contemporaries (and to many of ours), it seemed that the nineteenth century was the Age of the Female Novelist. With such stellar examples as Jane Austen, Charlotte Brontë, and George Eliot, the question of women's aptitude for fiction, at any rate, had been answered. But a larger question was whether women, excluded by custom and education from achieving distinction in poetry, history, or drama, had, in defining their literary culture in the novel, simply appropriated another masculine genre. Both George Henry Lewes and Mill, spokesmen for women's rights and Victorian liberalism in general, felt that, like the Romans in the shadow of Greece, women were overshadowed by male cultural imperialism: "If women's literature is destined to have a different collective character from that of men," wrote Mill, "much longer time is necessary than has yet elapsed before it can emancipate itself from the influence of accepted models, and guide itself by its own impulses."[1]

There is clearly a difference between books that happen to have been written by women, and a "female literature," as Lewes tried to define it, which purposefully and collectively concerns itself with the articulation of women's experience, and which guides itself "by its own impulses" to autonomous self-expression. As novelists, women have always been self-conscious, but only rarely self-defining. While they have been deeply and perennially aware of their individual identities and experiences, women writers have very infrequently considered whether these experiences might transcend the personal and local, assume a collective form in art, and reveal a history. During the intensely feminist period from 1880 to 1910, both British and American women writers explored the theme of an Amazon utopia, a country entirely populated by women and completely isolated from the male world. Yet even in these fantasies of autonomous female communities, there is no theory of female art. Feminist utopias were not visions of primary womanhood, free to define its own nature and culture, but flights from the male world to a culture defined in opposi-

[1] "The Subjection of Women," in John Stuart Mill and Harriet Taylor Mill, *Essays on Sex Equality*, ed. Alice S. Rossi, Chicago, 1970, ch. III, p. 207.

tion to the male tradition. Typically the feminist utopias are pastoral sanctuaries, where a population of prelapsarian Eves cultivate their organic gardens, cure water pollution, and run exemplary child care centers, but do not write books.

In contradiction to Mill, and in the absence, until very recently, of any feminist literary manifestoes, many readers of the novel over the past two centuries have nonetheless had the indistinct but persistent impression of a unifying voice in women's literature. In *The History of the English Novel*, Ernest Baker devotes a separate chapter to the women novelists, commenting that "the woman of letters has peculiarities that mark her off from the other sex as distinctly as peculiarities of race or of ancestral traditions. Whatever variety of talent, outlook or personal disposition may be discernible among any dozen women writers taken at random, it will be matched and probably outweighed by resemblances distinctively feminine."[2] Baker wisely does not attempt to present a taxonomy of these feminine "peculiarities"; most critics who have attempted to do so have quickly found themselves expressing their own cultural biases rather than explicating sexual structures. In 1852, Lewes thought he could identify the feminine literary traits as Sentiment and Observation; in 1904, William L. Courtney found that "the female author is at once self-conscious and didactic"; in 1965, Bernard Bergonzi explained that "women novelists . . . like to keep their focus narrow."[3] Women reading each other's books have also had difficulties in explaining their potential for what George Eliot called a "pre-

[2] "Some Women Novelists," *History of the English Novel*, x, London, 1939, p. 194.

[3] G. H. Lewes, "The Lady Novelists," *Westminster Review*, n.s. II (1852): 137; W. L. Courtney, *The Feminine Note in Fiction*, London, 1904, p. xiii; Bernard Bergonzi, *New York Review of Books*, June 3, 1965. In a review of Beryl Bainbridge's *The Bottle Factory Outing*, Anatole Broyard comments "that quite a few extremely attractive women write rather despairing books" (*New York Times*, May 26, 1975, p. 13).

cious speciality, lying quite apart from masculine aptitudes and experience." Eliot herself tried to locate the female speciality in the maternal affections.[4]

Statements about the personal and psychological qualities of the woman novelist have also flourished, and have been equally impressionistic and unreliable. The "lady novelist" is a composite of many stereotypes: to J. M. Ludlow, she is a creature with ink halfway up her fingers, dirty shawls, and frowsy hair; and to W. S. Gilbert, a "singular anomaly" who never would be missed.[5] To critics of the twentieth century, she is childless and, by implication, neurotic: "We remind ourselves," writes Carolyn Heilbrun, "that of the great women writers, most have been unmarried, and those who have written in the state of wedlock have done so in peaceful kingdoms guarded by devoted husbands. Few have had children."[6] Nancy Milford asks whether there were any women "who married in their youth and bore children and continued to write . . . think of the women who have written: the unmarried, the married and childless, the very few with a single child and that one observed as if it were a rock to be stubbed against."[7]

There are many reasons why discussion of women writers has been so inaccurate, fragmented, and partisan. First, women's literary history has suffered from an extreme form

[4] "Silly Novels by Lady Novelists," *Westminster Review* LXVI (1856); reprinted in *Essays of George Eliot*, ed. Thomas Pinney, London, 1963, p. 324.

[5] "Ruth," *North British Review* XIX (1853): 90–91; and "Ko-Ko's Song" in *The Mikado*. The stereotype of the woman novelist that emerges in the early nineteenth century conflates the popular images of the old maid and the bluestocking; see Vineta Colby, *Yesterday's Woman: Domestic Realism in the English Novel*, Princeton, 1974, pp. 115–116, and Katharine M. Rogers, *The Troublesome Helpmate: A History of Misogyny in Literature*, London, 1966, pp. 201–207.

[6] Introduction to May Sarton, *Mrs. Stevens Hears the Mermaids Singing*, New York, 1974, p. xvi.

[7] "This Woman's Movement" in *Adrienne Rich's Poetry*, ed. Barbara Charlesworth Gelpi and Albert Gelpi, New York, 1975, p. 189.

6

of what John Gross calls "residual Great Traditionalism,"[8] which has reduced and condensed the extraordinary range and diversity of English women novelists to a tiny band of the "great," and derived all theories from them. In practice, the concept of greatness for women novelists often turns out to mean four or five writers—Jane Austen, the Brontës, George Eliot, and Virginia Woolf—and even theoretical studies of "the woman novelist" turn out to be endless recyclings and recombinations of insights about "indispensable Jane and George."[9] Criticism of women novelists, while focusing on these happy few, has ignored those who are not "great," and left them out of anthologies, histories, textbooks, and theories. Having lost sight of the minor novelists, who were the links in the chain that bound one generation to the next, we have not had a very clear understanding of the continuities in women's writing, nor any reliable information about the relationships between the writers' lives and the changes in the legal, economic, and social status of women.

Second, it has been difficult for critics to consider women novelists and women's literature theoretically because of their tendency to project and expand their own culture-bound stereotypes of femininity, and to see in women's writing an eternal opposition of biological and aesthetic creativity. The Victorians expected women's novels to reflect the feminine values they exalted, although obviously the woman novelist herself had outgrown the constraining feminine role. "Come what will," Charlotte Brontë wrote to Lewes, "I cannot, when I write, think always of myself and what is elegant and charming in femininity; it is not on these terms, or with such ideas, that I ever took pen in hand."[10] Even if we ignore the excesses of what Mary Ell-

8 *The Rise and Fall of the Man of Letters*, London, 1969, p. 304.

9 Cynthia Ozick, "Women and Creativity," in *Woman in Sexist Society*, ed. Vivian Gornick and Barbara K. Moran, New York, 1971, p. 436.

10 Letter of November 1849, in Clement Shorter, *The Brontës: Life and Letters*, II, London, 1908, p. 80.

ann calls "phallic criticism" and what Cynthia Ozick calls the "ovarian theory of literature," much contemporary criticism of women writers is still prescriptive and circumscribed.[11] Given the difficulties of steering a precarious course between the Scylla of insufficient information and the Charybdis of abundant prejudice, it is not surprising that formalist-structuralist critics have evaded the issue of sexual identity entirely, or dismissed it as irrelevant and subjective. Finding it difficult to think intelligently about women writers, academic criticism has often overcompensated by desexing them.

Yet since the 1960s, and especially since the reemergence of a Women's Liberation Movement in England and in America around 1968, there has been renewed enthusiasm for the idea that "a special female self-awareness emerges through literature in every period."[12] The interest in establishing a more reliable critical vocabulary and a more accurate and systematic literary history for women writers is part of a larger interdisciplinary effort by psychologists, sociologists, social historians, and art historians to reconstruct the political, social, and cultural experience of women.

Scholarship generated by the contemporary feminist movement has increased our sensitivity to the problems of sexual bias or projection in literary history, and has also begun to provide us with the information we need to understand the evolution of a female literary tradition. One of the most significant contributions has been the unearthing and reinterpretation of "lost" works by women writers, and the documentation of their lives and careers.

In the past, investigations have been distorted by the emphasis on an elite group, not only because it has excluded from our attention great stretches of literary activity

---

[11] Mary Ellmann, *Thinking About Women*, London, 1979, pp. 28–54; and Ozick, "Women and Creativity," p. 436.

[12] Patricia Meyer Spacks, *The Female Imagination*, London, 1976, p. 3.

between, for example, George Eliot and Virginia Woolf, but also because it has rendered invisible the daily lives, the physical experiences, the personal strategies and conflicts of ordinary women. If we want to define the ways in which "female self-awareness" has expressed itself in the English novel, we need to see the woman novelist against the backdrop of the women of her time, as well as in relation to other writers in history. Virginia Woolf recognized that need:

> The extraordinary woman depends on the ordinary woman. It is only when we know what were the conditions of the average woman's life—the number of her children, whether she had money of her own, if she had a room to herself, whether she had help in bringing up her family, if she had servants, whether part of the housework was her task—it is only when we can measure the way of life and the experience of life made possible to the ordinary woman that we can account for the success or failure of the extraordinary woman as writer.[13]

As scholars have been persuaded that women's experience is important, they have begun to see it for the first time. With a new perceptual framework, material hitherto assumed to be nonexistent has suddenly leaped into focus. Interdisciplinary studies of Victorian women have opened up new areas of investigation in medicine, psychology, economics, political science, labor history, and art.[14] Questions of the "female imagination" have taken on intellectual weight in the contexts of theories of Karen Horney about feminine psychology, Erik Erikson about womanhood and

[13] "Women and Fiction," *Collected Essays*, London 1976, p. 142.
[14] See, for example, Sheila Rowbotham, *Hidden from History*, London, 1973; Martha Vicinus, ed., *Suffer and Be Still: Women in the Victorian Age*, London 1980; Mary S. Hartman and Lois N. Banner, eds., *Clio's Consciousness Raised: New Perspectives on the History of Women*, New York, 1974, and Françoise Basch, *Relative Creatures: Victorian Women in Society and the Novel*, London, 1974.

the inner space, and R. D. Laing about the divided self. Investigation of female iconography and imagery has been stimulated by the work of art historians like Linda Nochlin, Lise Vogel, and Helene Roberts.[15]

As the works of dozens of women writers have been rescued from what E. P. Thompson calls "the enormous condescension of posterity,"[16] and considered in relation to each other, the lost continent of the female tradition has risen like Atlantis from the sea of English literature. It is now becoming clear that, contrary to Mill's theory, women have had a literature of their own all along. The woman novelist, according to Vineta Colby, was "really neither single nor anomalous," but she was also more than a "register and a spokesman for her age."[17] She was part of a tradition that had its origins before her age, and has carried on through our own.

Many literary historians have begun to reinterpret and revise the study of women writers. Ellen Moers sees women's literature as an international movement, "apart from, but hardly subordinate to the mainstream: an undercurrent, rapid and powerful. This 'movement' began in the late eighteenth century, was multinational, and produced some of the greatest literary works of two centuries, as well as most of the lucrative pot-boilers."[18] Patricia Meyer Spacks, in *The Female Imagination*, finds that "for readily discernible historical reasons women have characteristically concerned themselves with matters more or less peripheral to male concerns, or at least slightly skewed from them. The

[15] Linda Nochlin, "Why Are There No Great Women Artists?" in *Woman in Sexist Society*; Lise Vogel, "Fine Arts and Feminism: The Awakening Consciousness," *Feminist Studies* II (1974): 3–37; Helene Roberts, "The Inside, the Surface, the Mass: Some Recurring Images of Women," *Women's Studies* II (1974): 289–308.

[16] *The Making of the English Working Class*, London, 1968, p. 13.

[17] Vineta Colby, *The Singular Anomaly: Women Novelists of the Nineteenth Century*, New York, 1970, p. 11.

[18] "Women's Lit: Profession and Tradition," *Columbia Forum* I (Fall 1972): 27.

differences between traditional female preoccupations and roles and male ones make a difference in female writing."[19] Many other critics are beginning to agree that when we look at women writers collectively we can see an imaginative continuum, the recurrence of certain patterns, themes, problems, and images from generation to generation.

This book is an effort to describe the female literary tradition in the English novel from the generation of the Brontës to the present day, and to show how the development of this tradition is similar to the development of any literary subculture. Women have generally been regarded as "sociological chameleons," taking on the class, lifestyle, and culture of their male relatives. It can, however, be argued that women themselves have constituted a subculture within the framework of a larger society, and have been unified by values, conventions, experiences, and behaviors impinging on each individual. It is important to see the female literary tradition in these broad terms, in relation to the wider evolution of women's self-awareness and to the ways in which any minority group finds its direction of self-expression relative to a dominant society, because we cannot show a pattern of deliberate progress and accumulation. It is true, as Ellen Moers writes, that "women studied with a special closeness the works written by their own sex";[20] in terms of influences, borrowings, and affinities, the tradition is strongly marked. But it is also full of holes and hiatuses, because of what Germaine Greer calls the "phenomenon of the transcience of female literary fame"; "almost uninterruptedly since the Interregnum, a small group of women have enjoyed dazzling literary prestige during their own lifetimes, only to vanish without trace from the records of posterity."[21] Thus each generation of women writers has found itself, in a sense, without a history, forced

[19] Spacks, p. 7.
[20] Moers, "Women's Lit," 28.
[21] "Flying Pigs and Double Standards," *Times Literary Supplement*, (July 26, 1974): 784.

11

to rediscover the past anew, forging again and again the consciousness of their sex. Given this perpetual disruption, and also the self-hatred that has alienated women writers from a sense of collective identity, it does not seem possible to speak of a "movement."

I am also uncomfortable with the notion of a "female imagination." The theory of a female sensibility revealing itself in an imagery and form specific to women always runs dangerously close to reiterating the familiar stereotypes. It also suggests permanence, a deep, basic, and inevitable difference between male and female ways of perceiving the world. I think that, instead, the female literary tradition comes from the still-evolving relationships between women writers and their society. Moreover, the "female imagination" cannot be treated by literary historians as a romantic or Freudian abstraction. It is the product of a delicate network of influences operating in time, and it must be analyzed as it expresses itself, in language and in a fixed arrangement of words on a page, a form that itself is subject to a network of influences and conventions, including the operations of the marketplace. In this investigation of the English novel, I am intentionally looking, not at an innate sexual attitude, but at the ways in which the self-awareness of the woman writer has translated itself into a literary form in a specific place and time-span, how this self-awareness has changed and developed, and where it might lead.

I am therefore concerned with the professional writer who wants pay and publication, not with the diarist or letter-writer. This emphasis has required careful consideration of the novelists, as well as the novels, chosen for discussion. When we turn from the overview of the literary tradition to look at the individuals who composed it, a different but interrelated set of motives, drives, and sources becomes prominent. I have needed to ask why women began to write for money and how they negotiated the activity of writing within their families. What was their professional self-image? How was their work received, and what effects did criticism have upon them? What were their experiences as women, and how were these reflected in their books? What was their understanding of womanhood? What were their relationships to other women, to men, and to their readers? How did changes in women's status affect their lives and careers? And how did the vocation of writing itself change the women who committed themselves to it? In looking at literary subcultures, such as black, Jewish, Canadian, Anglo-Indian, or even American, we can see that they all go through three major phases. First, there is a prolonged phase of *imitation* of the prevailing modes of the dominant tradition, and *internalization* of its standards of art and its views on social roles. Second, there is a phase of *protest* against these standards and values, and *advocacy* of minority rights and values, including a demand for autonomy. Finally, there is a phase of *self-discovery*, a turning inward freed from some of the dependency of opposition, a search for identity.[22] An appropriate terminology for women writers is to call these stages, *Feminine, Feminist,* and *Female.* These are obviously not rigid categories, distinctly separable in time, to which individual writers can be assigned with perfect assurance. The phases overlap; there are feminist elements in feminine writing, and vice versa. One might also find all three phases in the career of a single novelist. Nonetheless, it seems useful to point to periods of crisis when a shift of literary values occurred. In this book I identify the Feminine phase as the period from the appearance of the male pseudonym in the 1840s to the death of George Eliot in 1880; the Feminist phase as 1880 to 1920, or the winning of the vote; and the Female phase as 1920 to the present, but entering a new stage of self-awareness about 1960.

It is important to understand the female subculture not

---

[22] For helpful studies of literary subcultures, see Robert A. Bone, *The Negro Novel in America,* New York, 1958; and Northrop Frye, "Conclusion to *A Literary History of Canada,*" in *The Stubborn Structure: Essays on Criticism and Society,* London, 1970, pp. 278–312.

only as what Cynthia Ozick calls "custodial"[23]—a set of opinions, prejudices, tastes, and values prescribed for a subordinate group to perpetuate its subordination—but also as a thriving and positive entity. Most discussions of women as a subculture have come from historians describing Jacksonian America, but they apply equally well to the situation of early Victorian England. According to Nancy Cott, "we can view women's group consciousness as a subculture uniquely divided against itself by ties to the dominant culture. While the ties to the dominant culture are the informing and restricting ones, they provoke within the subculture certain strengths as well as weaknesses, enduring values as well as accommodations."[24] The middle-class ideology of the proper sphere of womanhood, which developed in post-industrial England and America, prescribed a woman who would be a Perfect Lady, an Angel in the House, contentedly submissive to men, but strong in her inner purity and religiosity, queen in her own realm of the Home.[25] Many observers have pointed out that the first professional activities of Victorian women, as social reformers, nurses, governesses, and novelists, either were based in the home or were extensions of the feminine role as teacher, helper, and mother of mankind. In describing the American situation, two historians have seen a subculture emerging from the doctrine of sexual spheres:

By "subculture" we mean simply "a habit of living" . . . of a minority group which is self-consciously distinct from the dominant activities, expectations, and values of a society. Historians have seen female church groups, reform

23 "Women and Creativity," p. 442.
24 Nancy F. Cott, introduction to *Root of Bitterness*, New York, 1972, pp. 3–4.
25 For the best discussions of the Victorian feminine ideal, see Françoise Basch, "Contemporary Ideologies," in *Relative Creatures*, pp. 3–15; Walter E. Houghton, *The Victorian Frame of Mind*, London, 1957, pp. 341–343; and Alexander Welsh's theory of the Angel in the House in *The City of Dickens*, London, 1971, pp. 164–195.

associations, and philanthropic activity as expressions of this subculture in actual behavior, while a large and rich body of writing by and for women articulated the subculture impulses on the ideational level. Both behavior and thought point to child-rearing, religious activity, education, home life, associationism, and female communality as components of women's subculture. Female friendships, strikingly intimate and deep in this period, formed the actual bonds.[26]

For women in England, the female subculture came first through a shared and increasingly secretive and ritualized physical experience. Puberty, menstruation, sexual initiation, pregnancy, childbirth, and menopause—the entire female sexual life cycle—constituted a habit of living that had to be concealed. Although these episodes could not be openly discussed or acknowledged, they were accompanied by elaborate rituals and lore, by external codes of fashion and etiquette, and by intense feelings of female solidarity.[27] Women writers were united by their roles as daughters, wives, and mothers; by the internalized doctrines of evangelicalism, with its suspicion of the imagination and its emphasis on duty; and by legal and economic constraints on their mobility. Sometimes they were united in a more immediate way, around a political cause. On the whole these are the implied unities of culture, rather than the active unities of consciousness.

From the beginning, however, women novelists' awareness of each other and of their female audience showed a kind of covert solidarity that sometimes amounted to a gen-

[26] Christine Stansell and Johnny Faragher, "Women and Their Families on the Overland Trail, 1842–1867," *Feminist Studies* II (1975): 152–153. For an overview of recent historical scholarship on the "two cultures," see Barbara Sicherman, "Review: American History," *Signs: Journal of Women in Culture and Society* I (Winter 1975): 470–484.

[27] For a sociological account of patterns of behavior for Victorian women, see Leonore Davidoff, *The Best Circles: Society, Etiquette and the Season*, London, 1973, esp. pp. 48–58, 85–100.

teel conspiracy. Advocating sisterhood, Sarah Ellis, one of the most conservative writers of the first Victorian generation, asked: "What should we think of a community of slaves, who betrayed each other's interests? of a little band of shipwrecked mariners upon a friendless shore who were false to each other? of the inhabitants of a defenceless nation, who would not unite together in earnestness and good faith against a common enemy?"[28] Mrs. Ellis felt the binding force of the minority experience for women strongly enough to hint, in the prefaces to her widely read treatises on English womanhood, that her female audience would both read the messages between her lines and refrain from betraying what they deciphered. As another conservative novelist, Dinah Mulock Craik, wrote, "The intricacies of female nature are incomprehensible except to a woman; and any biographer of real womanly feeling, if ever she discovered, would never dream of publishing them."[29] Few English women writers openly advocated the use of fiction as revenge against a patriarchal society (as did the American novelist Fanny Fern, for example), but many confessed to sentiments of "maternal feeling, sisterly affection, *esprit de corps*"[30] for their readers. Thus the clergyman's daughter, going to Mudie's for her three-decker novel by another clergyman's daughter, participated in a cultural exchange that had a special personal significance.

It is impossible to say when women began to write fiction. From about 1750 on, English women made steady inroads into the literary marketplace, mainly as novelists. As early as 1773, the *Monthly Review* noticed that "that branch of

[28] Sarah Ellis, *The Daughters of England*, London, 1845, ch. IX, p. 338.
[29] Dinah M. Craik, "Literary Ghouls," *Studies from Life*, New York, 1861, p. 13.
[30] Letter of October 6, 1851, in *Letters of E. Jewsbury to Jane Welsh Carlyle*, ed. Mrs. Alex Ireland, London, 1892, p. 426. For Fanny Fern, see Ann Douglas Wood, "The 'Scribbling Women' and Fanny Fern: Why Women Wrote," *American Quarterly* XXIII (Spring 1971): 1–24.

the literary trade" seemed "almost entirely engrossed by the ladies." J.M.S. Tompkins finds that most eighteenth-century epistolary novels were written by women; the Minerva Press published twice as many novels by women as by men; and Ian Watt simply says that the majority of all eighteenth-century novels came from the female pen.[31] At the same time, men were able to imitate, and even usurp, female experience. Oliver Goldsmith suspected that men were writing sentimental novels under female pseudonyms, and men did write books on childcare, midwifery, housekeeping, and cooking.[32]

Early women writers' relationship to their professional role was uneasy. Eighteenth-century women novelists exploited a stereotype of helpless femininity to win chivalrous protection from male reviewers and to minimize their unwomanly self-assertion. In 1791 Elizabeth Inchbald prefaced *A Simple Story* with the lie that she was a poor invalid who had written a novel despite "the utmost detestation to the fatigue of inventing."[33] At the turn of the century, women evaded the issue of professional identity by publishing anonymously. In 1810 Mary Brunton explained in a letter to a friend why she preferred anonymity to taking credit for her novels:

> I would rather, as you well know, glide through the world unknown, than have (I will not call it *enjoy*) fame, however brilliant, to be pointed at,—to be noticed and commented upon—to be suspected of literary airs—to be shunned, as literary women are, by the more unpretend-

31 J.M.S. Tompkins, *The Popular Novel in England 1770–1800*, London, 1932, pp. 119–121; Dorothy Blakey, *The Minerva Press 1790–1820*, London, 1939; and Ian Watt, *The Rise of the Novel*, London, 1963, pp. 298–299.

32 Myra Reynolds, *The Learned Lady in England 1650–1760*, New York, 1920, pp. 89–91.

33 William McKee, *Elizabeth Inchbald, Novelist*, Washington, D.C., 1935, p. 20.

ing of my own sex; and abhorred as literary women are, by the pretending of the other!—my dear, I would sooner exhibit as a rope-dancer.[34]

Here again we need to remember the distinction between the novel as a form, and the professional role of the novelist. Many of the most consistent themes and images of the feminine novel, from the mysterious interiors of Gothic romance to the balancing of duty and self-fulfillment in domestic fiction, can be traced back to the late eighteenth century. Certainly nineteenth-century women novelists had some familiarity with Burney, Edgeworth, Radcliffe, and Austen, as well as with scores of lesser writers such as Inchbald and Hofland. But almost no sense of communality and self-awareness is apparent among women writers before the 1840s, which Kathleen Tillotson sees as the decade in which the novel became the dominant form. Tillotson points out that, despite the respectful attention paid by mid-Victorian critics to Jane Austen (attention that had some negative impact on Victorian women novelists), there appears to have been relatively little direct influence by Austen on Mrs. Gaskell, Harriet Martineau, the Brontës, and several minor writers.[35] Even George Eliot's debt to Austen has been much exaggerated by the concept of the Great Tradition.[36] The works of Mary Wollstonecraft were not widely read by the Victorians due to the scandals surrounding her life.

More important than the question of direct literary influence, however, is the difference between the social and professional worlds inhabited by the eighteenth- and nineteenth-century women. The early women writers refused to deal with a professional role, or had a negative orientation toward it. "What is my life?" lamented the poet Laetitia

[34] "Memoirs of the Life of Mrs. Mary Brunton by Her Husband," preface to *Emmeline*, Edinburgh, 1819, p. xxxvi.

[35] Kathleen Tillotson, *Novels of the Eighteen-Forties*, London, 1956, pp. 142–145.

[36] For a refutation of Leavis's view of Austen and Eliot, see Gross, *Rise and Fall of the Man of Letters*, pp. 302–303.

Landon. "One day of drudgery after another; difficulties incurred for others, which have ever pressed upon me beyond health, which every year, in one severe illness after another, is taxed beyond its strength; envy, malice, and all uncharitableness—these are the fruits of a successful literary career for a woman."[37] These women may have been less than sincere in their insistence that literary success brought them only suffering, but they were not able to see themselves as involved in a vocation that brought responsibilities as well as conflicts, and opportunities as well as burdens. Moreover, they did not see their writing as an aspect of their female experience, or as an expression of it.

Thus, in talking about the situation of the feminine novelists, I have begun with the women born after 1800, who began to publish fiction during the 1840s when the job of the novelist was becoming a recognizable profession. One of the many indications that this generation saw the will to write as a vocation in direct conflict with their status as women is the appearance of the male pseudonym. Like Eve's fig leaf, the male pseudonym signals the loss of innocence. In its radical understanding of the role-playing required by women's effort to participate in the mainstream of literary culture, the pseudonym is a strong marker of the historical shift.

There were three generations of nineteenth-century feminine novelists. The first, born between 1800 and 1820, included all the women who are identified with the Golden Age of the Victorian authoress: the Brontës, Mrs. Gaskell, Elizabeth Barrett Browning, Harriet Martineau, and George Eliot. The members of this group, whose coevals were Florence Nightingale, Mary Carpenter, Angela Burdett, and other pioneer professionals, were what sociologists call "female role innovators"; they were breaking new ground and creating new possibilities. The second generation, born between 1820 and 1840, included Charlotte

[37] Quoted in S. C. Hall, *A Book of Memories of Great Men and Women of the Age*, London, 1877, p. 266.

Yonge, Dinah Mulock Craik, Margaret Oliphant, and Elizabeth Lynn Linton; these women followed in the footsteps of the great, consolidating their gains, but were less dedicated and original. The third generation, born between 1840 and 1860, included sensation novelists and children's book writers. They seemed to cope effortlessly with the double roles of woman and professional, and to enjoy sexual fulfillment as well as literary success. Businesslike, unconventional, efficient, and productive, they moved into editorial and publishing positions as well as writing.

By the time the women of the first generation had entered upon their careers, there was already a sense of what the "feminine" novel meant in terms of genres. By the 1840s women writers had adopted a variety of popular genres, and were specializing in novels of fashionable life, education, religion, and community, which Vineta Colby subsumes under the heading "domestic realism." In all these novels, according to Inga-Stina Ewbank, "the central preoccupation . . . is with the woman as an influence on others within her domestic and social circle. It was in this preoccupation that the typical woman novelist of the 1840s found her proper sphere: in using the novel to demonstrate (by assumption rather than exploration of standards of womanliness) *woman's* proper sphere."[38] A double standard of literary criticism had also developed, as I show in Chapter III, with a special set of terms and requirements for fiction by women.

There was a place for such fiction, but even the most conservative and devout women novelists, such as Charlotte Yonge and Dinah Craik, were aware that the "feminine" novel also stood for feebleness, ignorance, prudery, refinement, propriety, and sentimentality, while the feminine novelist was portrayed as vain, publicity-seeking, and self-assertive. At the same time that Victorian reviewers assumed that women readers and women writers were

[38] Inga-Stina Ewbank, *Their Proper Sphere: A Study of the Brontë Sisters as Early-Victorian Female Novelists,* London, 1966, p. 41.

dictating the content of fiction, they deplored the pettiness and narrowness implied by a feminine value system. "Surely it is very questionable," wrote Fitzjames Stephen, "whether it is desirable that no novels should be written except those fit for young ladies to read."[39]

Victorian feminine novelists thus found themselves in a double bind. They felt humiliated by the condescension of male critics and spoke intensely of their desire to avoid special treatment and achieve genuine excellence, but they were deeply anxious about the possibility of appearing unwomanly. Part of the conflict came from the fact that, rather than confronting the values of their society, these women novelists were competing for its rewards. For women, as for other subcultures, literature became a symbol of achievement.

In the face of this dilemma, women novelists developed several strategies, both personal and artistic. Among the personal reactions was a persistent self-deprecation of themselves as women, sometimes expressed as humility, sometimes as coy assurance-seeking, and sometimes as the purest self-hatred. In a letter to John Blackwood, Mrs. Oliphant expressed doubt about "whether in your most manly and masculine of magazines a womanish story-teller like myself may not become wearisome."[40] The novelists publicly proclaimed, and sincerely believed, their antifeminism. By working in the home, by preaching submission and self-sacrifice, and by denouncing female self-assertiveness, they worked to atone for their own will to write.

Vocation—the will to write—nonetheless required a genuine transcendence of female identity. Victorian women were not accustomed to *choosing* a vocation; womanhood was a vocation in itself. The evangelically inspired creed of work did affect women, even though it had not been pri-

[39] *Saturday Review* IV (July 11, 1857): 40–41. See also David Masson, *British Novelists and Their Styles*, Cambridge, 1859, p. 134.

[40] *Autobiography and Letters of Mrs. M.O.W. Oliphant*, ed., Mrs. Harry Coghill, London, 1899, p. 160.

marily directed toward them. Like men, women were urged to "bear their part in the *work* of life."[41] Yet for men, the gospel of work satisfied both self-interest and the public interest. In pursing their ambitions, they fulfilled social expectations.

For women, however, work meant labor for *others*. Work, in the sense of self-development, was in direct conflict with the subordination and repression inherent in the feminine ideal. The self-centeredness implicit in the act of writing made this career an especially threatening one; it required an engagement with feeling and a cultivation of the ego rather than its negation. The widely circulated treatises of Hannah More and Sarah Ellis translated the abstractions of "women's mission" into concrete programs of activity, which made writing appear selfish, unwomanly, and unchristian. " 'What shall I do to gratify myself—to be admired—or to vary the tenor of my existence?' " are not, according to Mrs. Ellis, "questions which a woman of right feelings asks on first awakening to the avocations of the day." Instead she recommends visiting the sick, fixing breakfast for anyone setting on a journey in order to spare the servant, or general "devotion to the good of the whole family." "Who can believe," she asks fervently, "that days, months, and years spent in a continual course of thought and action similar to this, will not produce a powerful effect upon the character?"[42] Of course it did; one notices first of all that feminine writers like Elizabeth Barrett, "Charlotte Elizabeth," Elizabeth M. Sewell, and Mrs. Ellis herself had to overcome deep-seated guilt about authorship. Many found it necessary to justify their work by recourse to some external stimulus or ideology. In their novels, the heroine's aspirations for a full, independent life are undermined, punished, or replaced by marriage.

Elizabeth Barrett Browning's *Aurora Leigh* (1857) is one

[41] "An Enquiry into the State of Girls' Fashionable Schools," *Fraser's* XXXI (1845): 703.

[42] Sarah Ellis, *The Women of England*, London, 1838, ch. I, p. 35.

of the few autobiographical discussions of feminine role conflict. Aurora's struggle to become an artist is complicated by the self-hatred in which she has been educated, by her internalized convictions of her weakness and narcissism, and by the gentle scorn of her suitor Romney. She defies him, however, and invokes divine authority to reject his proposal that she become his helpmeet:

> You misconceive the question like a man
> Who sees the woman as the complement
> Of his sex merely. You forget too much
> That every creature, female as the male,
> Stands single in responsible act and thought . . .
> I too have my vocation,—work to do,
> The heavens and earth have set me.
>
> (Book II, 460–466)

Aurora succeeds as a poet. But she marries Romney in the end, having learned that as a woman she cannot cope with the guilt of self-centered ambition. It is significant that Romney has been blinded in an accident before she marries him, not only because he has thereby received firsthand knowledge of being handicapped and can empathize with her, but also because he then needs her help and can provide her with suitably feminine work. When Aurora tells Romney that "No perfect artist is developed here / From any imperfect woman" (Book IX, 648–649) she means more than the perfection of love and motherhood; she means also the perfection of self-sacrifice. This conflict remains a significant one for English novelists up to the present; it is a major theme for women novelists from Charlotte Brontë to Penelope Mortimer. Male novelists like Thackeray, who came from an elite class, also felt uncomfortable with the aggressive self-promotion of the novelist's career. As Donald Stone points out:

> Thackeray's ambivalent feelings towards Becky Sharp indicate the degree to which he attempted to suppress or

23

make light of his own literary talents. The energies which make her (for a time) a social success are akin to those which made him a creative artist. In the hands of a major woman novelist, like Jane Austen or George Eliot, the destructive moral and social implications of Becky's behavior would have been defined more clearly and more urgently. Jane Austen's dissection of Lydia Bennet, and George Eliot's demolition of Rosamond Vincy, for example, indicate both how and why the defense of the status quo—insofar as women of the nineteenth century were concerned—was most earnestly and elaborately performed by women writers. Their heroines are hardly concerned with self-fulfillment in the modern sense of the term, and if they have severely limited possibilities in life it is because their authors saw great danger in, plus a higher alternative to, the practice of self-assertiveness.[43]

The dilemma is stated by George Eliot in *Romola* as the question of where "the duty of obedience ends and the duty of resistance begins."[44] Yet this was the question any Victorian woman with the will to write would have had to ask herself: what did God intend her to do with her life? Where did obedience to her father and husband end, and the responsibility of self-fulfillment become paramount? The problem of obedience and resistance that women had to solve in their own lives before they could begin to write crops up in their novels as the heroine's moral crisis. The forms that the crisis takes in feminine fiction are realistically mundane—should Margaret, in Mrs. Gaskell's *North and South*, lie to protect her brother? should Ethel May, in Charlotte Yonge's *Daisy Chain*, give up studying Greek to nurse her father?—but the sources were profound, and were connected to the women novelists' sense of epic life. At the same time that they recognized the modesty of their

[43] "Victorian Feminism and the Nineteenth-Century Novel," *Women's Studies* I (1972): 69.
[44] *Romola*, London, 1863, II, ch. XXIII.

own struggles, women writers recognized their heroism. "A new Theresa will hardly have the opportunity of reforming a conventual life," wrote George Eliot in *Middlemarch*, "any more than a new Antigone will spend her heroic piety in daring all for a brother's burial: the medium in which their ardent deeds took shape is forever gone. But we insignificant people with our daily words and acts are preparing the lives of many Dorotheas, some of which may present a far sadder sacrifice than that of the Dorothea whose story we know."[45]

The training of Victorian girls in repression, concealment, and self-censorship was deeply inhibiting, especially for those who wanted to write. As one novelist commented in 1860, "Women are greater dissemblers than men when they wish to conceal their own emotions. By habit, moral training, and modern education, they are obliged to do so. The very first lessons of infancy teach them to repress their feelings, control their very thoughts."[46] The verbal range permitted to English gentlewomen amounted almost to a special language. The verbal inhibitions that were part of the upbringing of a lady were reinforced by the critics' vigilance. "It is an immense loss," lamented Alice James, "to have all robust and sustaining expletives refined away from one."[47] "Coarseness" was the term Victorian readers used to rebuke unconventional language in women's literature. It could refer to the "damns" in *Jane Eyre*, the dialect in *Wuthering Heights*, the slang of Rhoda Broughton's heroines, the colloquialisms in *Aurora Leigh*, or more generally to the moral tone of a work, such as the "vein of perilous voluptuousness" one alert critic detected in *Adam Bede*.[48]

[45] *Middlemarch*, ed., W. J. Harvey, London, 1965, "Finale," p. 896.
[46] Jane Vaughan Pinckney, *Tacita Tacit*, II, p. 276; quoted in Myron Brightfield, *Victorian England in Its Novels*, IV, Los Angeles, 1968, p. 27.
[47] *The Diary of Alice James*, ed., Leon Edel, London, 1965, p. 66.
[48] *British Quarterly Review* XLV (1867): 164. On the term "coarseness," see Ewbank, *Their Proper Sphere*, pp. 46–47.

John Keble censored Charlotte Yonge's fiction, taking the greatest care "that no hint of 'coarseness' should sully the purity of Charlotte's writings. Thus he would not allow Theodora in *Heartsease* to say that 'really she had a heart, though some people thought it was only a machine for pumping blood.' He also transformed the 'circle' of the setting sun into an 'orb' and a 'coxcomb' into a 'jackanapes'."[49] While verbal force, wit, and originality in women was criticized, a bland and gelatinous prose won applause. "She writes as an English gentlewoman should write," the *North British Review* complimented Anne Marsh in 1849; "her pages are absolutely like green pastures."[50] Reduced to a pastoral flatness, deprived of a language in which to describe their bodies or the events of their bodies, denied the expression of pain as well as the expression of pleasure, women writers appeared deficient in passion.

It is easy to understand why many readers took the absence of expression for the absence of feeling. In "The False Morality of Lady Novelists," W. R. Greg argued that woman's sexual innocence would prevent her ever writing a great novel:

Many of the saddest and deepest truths in the strange science of sexual affection are to her mysteriously and mercifully veiled and can only be purchased at such a fearful cost that we cannot wish it otherwise. The inevitable consequence however is that in treating of that science she labours under all the disadvantages of partial study and superficial insight. She is describing a country of which she knows only the more frequented and the safer roads, with a few of the sweeter scenes and the prettier by-paths and more picturesque detours which be not far from the broad and beaten thoroughfares; while the rockier and loftier mountains, and more rugged

---

[49] Margaret Mare and Alicia C. Percival, *Victorian Best-Seller: The World of Charlotte Yonge*, London, 1947, p. 133.

[50] James Lorimer, "Noteworthy Novels," xi (1849): 257.

tracts, the more sombre valleys, and the darker and more dangerous chasms, are never trodden by her feet, and scarcely ever dreamed of by her fancy.[51]

The results of restrictive education and intensive conditioning were taken as innate evidence of natural preference. In an ironic twist, many reviewers who had paternally barred the way to the sombre valleys, the darker chasms, and the more rugged tracts also blamed women for the emasculation of male prose, finding, like the *Prospective Review*, that the "writing of men is in danger of being marked" by "the delicacy and even fastidiousness of expression which is *natural* to educated women" [my italics].[52] When G. H. Lewes complained in 1852 that the literature of women was "too much a literature of imitation" and demanded that women should express "what they have really known, felt and suffered,"[53] he was asking for something that Victorian society had made impossible. Feminine novelists had been deprived of the language and the consciousness for such an enterprise, and obviously their deprivation extended beyond Victoria's reign and into the twentieth century. The delicacy and verbal fastidiousness of Virginia Woolf is an extension of this feminized language.

Florence Nightingale thought the effort of repression itself drained off women's creative energy. "Give us back our suffering," she demanded in *Cassandra* (1852), "for out of nothing comes nothing. But out of suffering may come the cure. Better have pain than paralysis."[54] It does sometimes seem as if feminine writers are metaphorically paralyzed, as Alice James was literally paralyzed, by refinement and restraint, but the repression in which the feminine novel was situated also forced women to find innovative and co-

---

[51] "The False Morality of Lady Novelists," *National Review* VII, (1859): 149.

[52] "Puseyite Novels," VI (1850): 498.

[53] "The Lady Novelists," 132.

[54] "Cassandra," in *The Cause*, ed. Ray Strachey, London, 1978, p. 398.

vert ways to dramatize the inner life, and led to a fiction that was intense, compact, symbolic, and profound. There is Charlotte Brontë's extraordinary subversion of the Gothic in *Jane Eyre*, in which the mad wife locked in the attic symbolizes the passionate and sexual side of Jane's personality, an alter ego that her upbringing, her religion, and her society have commanded her to incarcerate. There is the crippled artist heroine of Dinah Craik's *Olive* (1850), who identifies with Byron, and whose deformity represents her very womanhood. There are the murderous little wives of Mary Braddon's sensation novels, golden-haired killers whose actions are a sardonic commentary on the real feelings of the Angel in the House.

Many of the fantasies of feminine novels are related to money, mobility, and power. Although feminine novelists punished assertive heroines, they dealt with personal ambition by projecting the ideology of success onto male characters, whose initiative, thrift, industry, and perseverance came straight from the woman author's experience. The "woman's man," discussed in Chapter iv, was often a more effective outlet for the "deviant" aspects of the author's personality than were her heroines, and thus male role-playing extended beyond the pseudonym to imaginative content.

Protest fiction represented another projection of female experience onto another group; it translated the felt pain and oppression of women into the championship of millworkers, child laborers, prostitutes, and slaves. Women were aware that protest fiction converted anger and frustration into an acceptable form of feminine and Christian expression. In the social novels of the 1840s and 1850s, and the problem novels of the 1860s and 1870s, women writers were pushing back the boundaries of their sphere, and presenting their profession as one that required not only freedom of language and thought, but also mobility and activity in the world. The sensation novelists of the 1870s, including Mary Braddon, Rhoda Broughton, and Florence Marryat, used this new freedom in a transitional literature that explored genuinely radical female protest against marriage and women's economic oppression, although still in the framework of feminine conventions that demanded the erring heroine's destruction.

From Jane Austen to George Eliot, the woman's novel had moved, despite its restrictions, in the direction of an all-inclusive female realism, a broad, socially informed exploration of the daily lives and values of women within the family and the community. By 1880, the three-decker had become flexible enough to accommodate many of the formerly unprintable aspects of female experience. Yet with the death of George Eliot and the appearance of a new generation of writers, the woman's novel moved into a Feminist phase, a confrontation with male society that elevated Victorian sexual stereotypes into a cult. The feminists challenged many of the restrictions on women's self-expression, denounced the gospel of self-sacrifice, attacked patriarchal religion, and constructed a theoretical model of female oppression, but their anger with society and their need for self-justification often led them away from realism into oversimplification, emotionalism, and fantasy. Making their fiction the vehicle for a dramatization of wronged womanhood, they demanded changes in the social and political systems that would grant women male privileges and require chastity and fidelity from men. The profound sense of injustice that the feminine novelists had represented as class struggle in their novels of factory life becomes an all-out war of the sexes in the novels of the feminists. Even their pseudonyms show their sense of feminist pride and of matriarchal mission to their sisters; one representative feminist called herself "Sarah Grand." In its extreme form, feminist literature advocated the sexual separatism of Amazon utopias and suffragette sisterhoods.

In the lives of the feminists, the bonds of the female subculture were particularly strong. The feminists were intensely devoted to each other and needed the support of close, emotional friendships with other women as well as the loving adulation of a female audience. In this generation, which mainly comprises women born between 1860 and 1880, one finds sympathetically attuned women writing in teams; Edith Somerville and Violet Martin were even said to have continued the collaboration beyond the grave.[55] Although· they preached individualism, their need for association led to a staggering number of clubs, activities, and causes, culminating in the militant groups and the almost terrifying collectivity of the suffrage movement. They glorified and idealized the womanly values of chastity and maternal love, and believed that those values must be forced upon a degenerate male society.

In their lives and in their books, most feminist writers expressed both an awareness of, and a revulsion from, sexuality. Like the feminine novelists, they projected many of their own experiences onto male characters, creating, for example, the Scarlet Pimpernels, "effeminate" fops by day and fearless heroes by night, semi-androgynous symbols of a generation in uneasy transition. To some degree these tactics were typical of the period in which they wrote; male novelists were creating "masculine" independent women who, as Donald Stone puts it, "could be used as a cover for those men who, for one reason or another, were anxious to proclaim their own standards and follow their own instincts."[56]

As the feminists themselves often seem neurotic and divided in their roles, less productive than earlier generations, and subject to paralyzing psychosomatic illnesses, so their fiction seems to break down in its form. In the 1890s the three-decker novel abruptly disappeared due to changes

[55] See Maurice Collis, *Somerville and Ross*, London, 1968, for an account of the careers of Edith Somerville and Violet Martin. After Martin's death in 1915,. the "collaboration" continued through psychic communications. Katherine Bradley and Edith Cooper wrote under the name of "Michael Field;" the sisters Emily and Dorothea Gerard used the name ·"E. D. Gerard" for such joint efforts as *Beggar My Neighbor* (1882).

[56] "Victorian Feminism and the Nineteenth-Century Novel," 79.

in its marketability, and women turned to short stories and fragments, which they called "dreams," "keynotes," and "fantasias." At the turn of the century came the purest examples of feminist literature, the novels, poems, and plays written as suffragette propaganda and distributed by the efficient and well-financed suffrage presses.

The feminist writers were not important artists. Yet in their insistence on exploring and defining womanhood, in their rejection of self-sacrifice, and even in their outspoken hostility to men, the feminist writers represented an important stage, a declaration of independence, in the female tradition. They did produce some interesting and original work, and they opened new subjects for other novelists. Sarah Grand's powerful studies of female psychology, George Egerton's bitter short stories, and Olive Schreiner's existential socialism were all best sellers in their own day and still hold attention. Through political campaigns for prostitutes and working women, and in the suffrage crusades, the feminists insisted on their right to use the male sexual vocabulary, and to use it forcefully and openly. The feminists also challenged the monopoly of male publishers and rebelled against the dictatorship of the male establishment. Men—John Chapman, John Blackwood, Henry Blackett, George Smith—had published the works of feminine novelists and had exerted direct and enormous power over their contents. Sarah Grand parodied the masculine critical hegemony by describing a literary journal she called the *Patriarch*, and feminist journalists, writing in their own magazines, argued against the judgments of the men of letters. In the 1860s the sensation novelists had begun to retain their copyrights, work with printers on a commission basis, and edit their own magazines. The feminists continued to expand this economic control of publishing outlets. Virginia Woolf, printing her own novels at the Hogarth Press, owed much of her independence to the feminists' insistence on the need for women writers to be free of patriarchal commercialism.

31

In its early stages feminist analysis was naive and incoherent, but by the turn of the century Mona Caird, Elizabeth Robins, and Olive Schreiner were producing cogent
theories of women's relationship to work and production,
to class structure, and to marriage and the family.[57] Robins
and other members of the Women Writers Suffrage League
were beginning to work out a theory of women's literature,
making connections between the demands of the male publishing industry, the socialization of women, and the heroines, plots, conventions, and images of women's fiction. Finally, the militant suffrage movement forced women writers
to confront their own beliefs about women's rights, and in
the process to reexamine their own self-hatred and inhibition.

English women (or at least those women who were over
thirty, householders, the wives of householders, occupiers
of property of £5 or more annual value, or university grad-
uates) were given the franchise in 1918 by a government
grateful for their patriotism during World War I.[58] Ironically, the death of many young male writers and poets during the war left English women writers with a poignant
sense of carrying on a national literary tradition that had,
at its heart, excluded them. Women felt a responsibility to
continue, to take the men's place, but they also felt a pitiful
lack of confidence. Alice Meynell's poem "A Father of
Women" conveys some of the anxiety, as well as the guilt,
of the survivors:

Our father works in us,
The daughters of his manhood. Not undone
Is he, not wasted, though transmuted thus,
    and though he left no son.

[57] Mona Caird, *The Morality of Marriage*, London, 1897; Elizabeth
Robins, *Way Stations*, London, 1913; Olive Schreiner, *Women and Labour*,
London, 1978.

[58] See Andrew Rosen, *Rise Up, Women!* London, 1974, p. 266.

Meynell calls upon her father's spirit in the poem to arm her "delicate mind," give her "courage to die," and to crush in her nature "the ungenerous art of the inferior."

The literature of the last generation of Victorian women writers, born between 1880 and 1900, moved beyond feminism to a Female phase of courageous self-exploration, but it carried with it the double legacy of feminine self-hatred and feminist withdrawal. In their rejection of male society and masculine culture, feminist writers had retreated more and more toward a separatist literature of inner space. Psychologically rather than socially focussed, this literature sought refuge from the harsh realities and vicious practices of the male world. Its favorite symbol, the enclosed and secret room, had been a potent image in women's novels since *Jane Eyre*, but by the end of the century it came to be identified with the womb and with female conflict. In children's books, such as Mrs. Molesworth's *The Tapestry Room* (1879) and Dinah Craik's *The Little Lone Prince* (1875), women writers had explored and extended these fantasies of enclosure. After 1900, in dozens of novels from Frances Hodgson Burnett's *A Secret Garden* (1911) to May Sinclair's *The Tree of Heaven* (1917), the secret room, the attic hideaway, the suffragette cell came to stand for a separate world, a flight from men and from adult sexuality.

The fiction of Dorothy Richardson, Katherine Mansfield, and Virginia Woolf created a deliberate female aesthetic, which transformed the feminine code of self-sacrifice into an annihilation of the narrative self, and applied the cultural analysis of the feminists to words, sentences, and structures of language in the novel. Their version of modernism was a determined response to the material culture of male Edwardian novelists like Arnold Bennett and H. G. Wells, but, like D. H. Lawrence, the female aestheticists saw the world as mystically and totally polarized by sex. For them, female sensibility took on a sacred quality, and its exercise became a holy, exhausting, and ultimately self-destructive rite, since woman's receptivity led inevitably to suicidal vulnerability.

Paradoxically, the more female this literature became in the formal and theoretical sense, the farther it moved from exploring the physical experience of women. Sexuality hovers on the fringes of the aestheticists' novels and stories, disguised, veiled, and denied. Androgyny, the sexual ethic of Bloomsbury and an important concept of the period, provided an escape from the confrontation with the body. Erotically charged and drenched with sexual symbolism, female aestheticism is nonetheless oddly sexless in its content. Again, "a room of one's own," with its insistence on artistic autonomy and its implied disengagement from social and sexual involvement, was a favorite image.

After the death of Virginia Woolf in 1941, the English women's novel seemed adrift. The harsh criticism of Bloomsbury, of female aestheticism, and especially of Virginia Woolf by writers for *Scrutiny* in the 1930s had pointed out the problems of disengagement. In her late writings, *The Years* (1937) and *Three Guineas* (1938), Woolf herself had tried to move in the direction of social realism. During the 1940s and 1950s, however, women writers, many of an older generation, continued to work in conservative modes untouched by either modernism or a sense of personal experiment. The works of such novelists as Rose Macaulay and Ivy Compton-Burnett are closely connected to a female tradition in their themes and awareness, but they seem to represent a passive rather than an active continuity. This passivity is one aspect of the larger situation of the postwar English novel. Adrian Mitchell describes "the disease of the British artist since 1945" as "a compulsion to stay small, to create perfect miniatures, to take no major risks."[59]

In the 1960s the female novel entered a new and dynamic

[59] Quoted in Bernard Bergonzi, *The Situation of the Novel*, London, 1972, p. 79.

phase, which has been strongly influenced in the past ten years by the energy of the international women's movement. The contemporary women's novel observes the traditional forms of nineteenth-century realism, but it also operates in the contexts of twentieth-century Freudian and Marxist analysis. In the fiction of Iris Murdoch, Muriel Spark, and Doris Lessing, and the younger writers Margaret Drabble, A. S. Byatt, and Beryl Bainbridge, we are beginning to see a renaissance in women's writing that responds to the demands of Lewes and Mill for an authentically female literature, providing "woman's view of life, woman's experience." In drawing upon two centuries of the female tradition, these novelists have been able to incorporate many of the strengths of the past with a new range of language and experience. Like the feminine novelists, they are concerned with the conflicts between art and love, between self-fulfillment and duty. They have insisted upon the right to use vocabularies previously reserved for male writers and to describe formerly taboo areas of female experience. For the first time anger and sexuality are accepted not only as attributes of realistic characters but also, as in Murdoch's *The Severed Head*, Lessing's *The Golden Notebook*, and A. S. Byatt's *The Game*, as sources of female creative power. Like the feminist novelists, contemporary writers are aware of their place in a political system and their connectedness to other women. Like the novelists of the female aesthetic, women novelists today, Lessing and Drabble particularly, see themselves as trying to unify the fragments of female experience through artistic vision, and they are concerned with the definition of autonomy for the woman writer. As the women's movement takes on cohesive force, and as feminist critics examine their literary tradition, contemporary women novelists will have to face the problems that black, ethnic, and Marxist writers have faced in the past: whether to devote themselves to the forging of female mythologies and epics, or to move beyond the female tradition into a seamless participation in the literary mainstream that might be regarded either as equality or assimilation.

Feminine, feminist, or female, the woman's novel has always had to struggle against the cultural and historical forces that relegated women's experience to the second rank. In trying to outline the female tradition, I have looked beyond the famous novelists who have been found worthy, to the lives and works of many women who have long been excluded from literary history. I have tried to discover how they felt about themselves and their books, what choices and sacrifices they made, and how their relationship to their profession and their tradition evolved. "What is commonly called literary history," writes Louise Bernikow, "is actually a record of choices. Which writers have survived their time and which have not depends upon who noticed them and chose to record the notice.[60] If some of the writers I notice seem to us to be Teresas and Antigones, struggling with their overwhelming sense of vocation and repression, many more will seem only Dorotheas, prim, mistaken, irreparably minor. And yet it is only by considering them all—Millicent Grogan as well as Virginia Woolf—that we can begin to record new choices in a new literary history, and to understand why, despite prejudice, despite guilt, despite inhibition, women began to write.

[60] *The World Split Open: Four Centuries of Women Poets in England and America, 1552–1950*, New York, 1979, p. 3.

CHAPTER II

++

The Feminine Novelists and
the Will to Write

THE task of defining a subculture in relation to English women novelists is made surer by their remarkable social homogeneity over more than a century. This uniformity of social origin is true of English writers generally, but it is more extreme in the case of women, who were even less likely than men to be the children of the laboring poor. Women novelists were overwhelmingly the daughters of the upper middle class, the aristocracy, and the professions. Thus, while there were significant differences in the cultural outlook of the daughter of a member of Parliament and the daughter of an agricultural migrant laborer, these do not figure in the consideration of women writers; Tess Durbeyfield did not write fiction. Yet the comments of critics in Victorian journals give the impression that every woman in England was shouldering her pen. In 1859 W. R. Greg declared that "the number of youthful novelists, and of young-lady novelists, extant at this moment, passes calculation, and was unparalleled at any former epoch. Indeed, the supply of the fiction market has fallen mainly into their hands."[1]

To answer the question of whether women really did sweep into the market in the nineteenth century and monopolize the writing of fiction we must first concede the impossibility of establishing absolute lists and numbers. More than forty thousand titles in fiction were published during the Victorian period, and anyone who turns to the publish-

[1] "The False Morality of Lady Novelists," *National Review* VII (1859): 148.

ers' advertisements at the back of a Victorian novel will soon be aware that scores of books have disappeared along with their authors. For example, in the back of my copy of Mrs. Craik's *A Noble Life* (published by Hurst & Blackett, 1866) who are Mrs. G. Gretton, author of *The Englishwoman in Italy*; Beatrice Whitby, author of five novels; who are Mabel Hart, E. Frances Poynter, and Martha Walker Freer? They have all slipped through the literary historian's net, as have half of the women writers listed month by month in the *Englishwoman's Review* in the 1870s.[2]

If we go beyond the women who actually managed to publish something, to the number who completed a novel but could not get it accepted, the problem assumes mammoth proportions. Readers' reports for large publishing houses like Bentley and Macmillan show that a consistently high percentage of rejected manuscripts came from women. Similarly, John Murray recalled with some amusement the "lady-authoresses" who began to besiege him about 1869, including "M. M.," who begged him not to reveal her name, and "Rose Ellen K.," who confided that her memoirs "glossed over even too quickly the sufferings of my heart."[3] For every novel in print there may have been half-a-dozen mute inglorious Brontës.

The impression that there were indeed a great many women entering the literary market during the nineteenth century, and that most of them were aspiring novelists, is fortified by the spate of references to the increase of women novelists in Victorian periodical criticism. In 1853 the *Gentleman's Magazine* marveled at "the great increase in quantity, and general improvement in the quality of NOVELS written by women. . . . Only to enumerate the principal fe-

---

[2] For example, in April 1878 the *Englishwoman's Review* lists new novels by twenty-nine women writers including Emily Hill, Mrs. H. L. Ca, Louise C. Moulton, Mrs. McDowell, Elinor Aitch.

[3] "George Paston" [Emily Symonds], *At John Murray's 1843–1892*, London, 1932, pp. 222–223. "Successive discouragement must not dishearten the first attempt to get a work published," *The English Matron* (London, 1846) told literary aspirants.

male novelists who have been at work for the past twenty or twenty-five years is something startling. In that time we have had at least three or four able novels per annum, not to mention others of respectable promise."[4]

This sense of a female literary invasion in the 1840s is, however, an illusion, an attempt to substitute a quantitative explanation for a qualitative phenomenon. The most extensive study of the sociology of authorhip, by Richard Altick, shows that between 1835 and 1870, women were in fact a slightly *smaller* percentage of the literary professions than in other periods. Although his data come primarily from the first edition of the *Cambridge Bibliography of English Literature*, Altick draws on a sizable sample of the literary population, and his study must be taken into account. He found that the proportion of women writers to men remained steady at about 20 percent from 1800 to 1935, "because of the inadequate educational provisions and the prejudice against careers for females."[5]

Even if women were entering literary professions in unprecedented numbers, they were perpetually a minority. Their presence was remarked upon at just about the time when fiction-writing became a viable male profession, a route to fortune for Thackeray and Dickens, and for men of letters like G. H. Lewes, who complained in 1847 that the literary profession, which should be "a Macedonian phalanx, chosen, compact and irresistible," was being invaded by "women, children and ill-trained troops."[6] Fear of com-

---

[4] "The Lady Novelists of Great Britain," n.s. XL (1853): 18.

[5] "The Sociology of Authorship," *Bulletin of New York Public Library* LXVI (1962): 392. Myron Brightfield in *Victorian England in Its Novels*, 4 vols., Los Angeles, 1968, quotes from 197 women novelists and 247 men novelists. These figures, of course, represent a selection rather than absolute numbers of men and women, but they certainly do not reflect the widely alleged "female dominance" of the 19th-century novel.

[6] "The Condition of Authors in England, Germany and France," *Fraser's* XXXV (1847): 285. For some other nervous jokes about female competition, see "A Gentle Hint to Writing-Women," *Leader* I (1850);

petition made male novelists overestimate the extent of the challenge; Wilkie Collins complained of being told that "out of every twelve novels or poems that are written, nine at least are by ladies. . . . They have carried off the accumulated raw material from under the men's noses."[7] The same complaints had been made since 1771; it is important to realize that "female dominance" was always in the eye of the male beholder. The Victorian illusion of enormous numbers came from the overreaction of male competitors, the exaggerated visibility of the woman writer, the overwhelming success of a few novels in the 1840s, the conjunction of feminist themes in fiction with feminist activism in England, and the availability of biographical information about the novelists, which made them living heroines, rather than sets of cold and inky initials.

The progress toward similar career patterns for male and female novelists was unsteady but distinct over a long period of time. There are three areas in which the career patterns of nineteenth century male and female writers show clear differences: education, means of support, and age at first publication. As we would expect, the differences are most dramatic for the pioneering women writers, who were clearly disadvantaged in comparison to their male contemporaries. The most striking piece of evidence provided by Altick's study also appears in a study by Raymond Williams; it concerns the educational privilege enjoyed by male writers.[8] In Williams' study of 163 major writers from 1780 to 1930, over half the men in each fifty-year period had attended Oxford or Cambridge, and there were substantial

---

J. M. Ludlow, "Ruth," *North British Review* XIX (1853): 90; "Hearts in Mortmain and Cornelian," *Prospective Review* VI (1850): 495.

[7] "A Shy Scheme," *Household Words*, March 20, 1858, p. 315; quoted by Nuel Pharr Davis, *The Life of Wilkie Collins*, Urbana, Illinois, 1956, p. 70.

[8] See Raymond Williams, *The Long Revolution*, London, 1961, for a study like Altick's, but a smaller sample stretched over three centuries. Virginia Woolf makes the same point in "The Leaning Tower," *Collected Essays*, II, London, 1966, p. 168.

figures for other universities. Altick found that during the narrower period he investigated, the percentage of literary men who had attended a university or other post-secondary school rose from 52.5 percent in 1800–1835, to 70.9 percent in 1870–1900, and to 72.3 percent by 1900–1935. Male authors also tended to have had grammar school educations; again, half of those attending grammar schools had gone to one of the famous public schools. The situation for women writers, of course, was very different. Altick reports that much less information of any sort was available on the schooling of the women. About 20 percent of the women writers he studied had been given some formal schooling, as opposed to being taught at home, and this figure remained constant throughout the entire century. After 1870, a few women had gone on to some kind of advanced study. Not until the period 1900–1935 did a university-educated group of women enter the profession, and even then they constituted only 38 percent of the female group. The percentage of women educated at home and school nearly equalled the percentage of men educated at universities.

Women writers were deprived of education because of their sex, not because of their class. For the middle-class Victorian girl, the departure of a brother for school was a painful awakening to her inferior status; the scene echoes in English fiction from George Eliot's *The Mill on the Floss* (1860) to Sarah Grand's *The Beth Book* (1897). One of the outstanding characteristics of the feminine novelists, their envy of classical education, is apparent in Catherine Crowe's *The Story of Lily Dawson* (1852): "It is true, there is little real culture among men; there are few strong thinkers and fewer honest ones; but they have still some advantages. If their education has been bad, it has at least been a trifle better than ours. Six hours a day at Latin and Greek are better than six hours a day at worsted work and embroidery."[9]

[9] *The Story of Lily Dawson*, London, 1852, p. 181.

The classical education was the intellectual dividing line between men and women; intelligent women aspired to study Greek and Latin with a touching faith that such knowledge would open the world of male power and wisdom to them. The feminine novel of the period up to about 1880 reflects women's intense effort to meet the educational standards of the male establishment. It is a commonplace for an ambitious heroine in a feminine novel to make mastery of the classics the initial goal in her search for truth. One recalls Aurora Leigh, being teased by her cousin for writing "ladies' Greek, without the accents"; Maggie Tulliver studying Latin; Ethel May (in *The Daisy Chain*) and Dorothea Casaubon (in *Middlemarch*) struggling with Greek. To Dorothea "these provinces of masculine knowledge seemed . . . a standing-ground from which all truth could be seen more truly."[10]

Women writers, who were almost all self-taught, were expected to meet male standards of scholarship if they ventured to use their knowledge. Nothing was felt to be so shameful and humiliating, or was so gleefully rebuked by critics, as intellectual pretension. In advising Charlotte Yonge John Keble asked "whether when the ladies quote Greek, they had better not say they have heard their fathers and brothers say things."[11] Thus women writers often perpetuated the sterotypes of female ignorance and inaptitude by pretending that their scholarship came from men. And women were just as merciless as men in judging their sisters. In *The Clever Woman of the Family* (1856) Yonge seems to enjoy exposing her heroine's thin acquaintance with the Greek and Hebrew testaments; George Eliot, though less conservative than Yonge, devoted a substantial part of her famous review "Silly Novels by Lady Novelists" to the same deficiencies. Male reviewers in the journals employed an elaborately courteous rhetoric in discussing fe-

[10] Eliot, *Middlemarch*, bk. I, ch. VII, p. 88.
[11] Mare and Percival, *Victorian Best-Seller*, London, 1947, p. 133.

male scholarship; but, while professing to be lenient, they actually pounced on errors with malicious gusto.

Later in the century the doctrine of realism made accuracy of detail essential for any novelist; Kenneth Graham, in *English Criticism of the Novel 1865–1900*, says that during this period "critics are always at their most scathing when they discover a factual error. Detailed verisimilitude is demanded, and any offenses against it are considered fatal to the work: reviews abound with triumphant discoveries of minute inaccuracies."[12] This demand weighed heavily upon women, I believe, long before it became general, and women novelists always suffered more from it. Thus aspiring women writers struggled to educate themselves, often against tremendous financial odds. A recurring theme in the biographies of the first-generation women is intellectual self-discipline. One reason this particular group excelled was that as role innovators they had an extraordinary combination of drive and self-control. We are familiar with the most famous examples: Elizabeth Barrett, invalided at fifteen, spent the next ten years learning German, Spanish, and Hebrew; George Eliot, caring for her widowed father in Nuneaton, studied German, Italian, and Latin, and read theology, history, fiction, poetry, and science. Much later, Eliot showed this same enviable ability to use periods of forced seclusion for study, rather than waste them in nostalgia or self-pity. In the years 1855–1858, "during the long period of social ostracism, when, because of her honest avowal of the union with Lewes, she was not invited to dinner," she read, in Greek, the *Iliad*, the *Odyssey*, the *Ajax*, the *Oedipus* trilogy, the *Electra*, the *Philoctetes*, and the Aeschylus trilogy; and in Latin, Horace, Virgil, Cicero, Persius, Livy, Tacitus, Plautus, Quintilian, and Pliny.[13]

The danger of such strenuous self-cultivation lay in overdoing scholarship and becoming pedantic. George Eliot

[12] *English Criticism of the Novel 1865–1900*, London, 1965, p. 26.
[13] Gordon S. Haight, *George Eliot: A Biography*, Oxford, 1968, p. 195.

recognized this danger, as the figure of Casaubon shows, but she could not help overcompensating in a book like *Romola*; in fact, Romola's dedication to the preservation of her father's library is a paradigm of the feminine novelist's veneration of male culture. Other women novelists, too, felt compelled to bury themselves in research as a defense against accusations of ignorance. Eliza Lynn Linton, for example, never quite recovered from a sense of intellectual deprivation. She never understood why her father, "so well read and even learned in his own person, did not care to give his children the education proper to their birth and his own standing." She tried, with scant success, to teach herself Latin, Greek, and Hebrew; when she finally broke free of home (having persuaded her father to stake her to a trial year in London), she headed straight for the British Museum, insatiably hungry for learning: "I read daily at the British Museum, gathering material for my magnum opus, and making roads into all manner of strange regions."[14]

Linton's first two novels, *Azeth the Egyptian* (1847) and *Amymone* (1848), were based on this intensive research, for which Sara Hennell christened her "Miss Sennacherib." The pedantry of these initial books seems to have satisfied Linton's need to make a public demonstration of her intellectual credentials. It was not until much later that women writers began to understand that the classical curriculum and the conventional schoolroom offered a very limited education, and to appreciate that their own efforts may even have given them an advantage over their brothers. In 1899 Florence Marryat told an interviewer that she had "read everything I could find. . . . I may be said to have educated myself, and probably I got more real learning out of this mode of procedure than if I had gone through the regular routine of the schoolroom."[15] However, the difference between men's and women's education remained a source

[14] G. S. Layard, *Mrs. Lynn Linton: Her Life, Letters and Opinions*, London, 1901, p. 5. Eliza Lynn married William James Linton in 1858.
[15] C. J. Hamilton, *Womanhood* III (1899): 3.

of bitterness into the early twentieth century, as one sees in *A Room of One's Own*.

Having internalized the criteria of the profession, feminine novelists tried not only to raise the level of their own performance, but also to keep less talented and less scrupulous women out of the field altogether. The severity of George Eliot's "Silly Novels" essay is intended to warn incompetent women not to try writing novels, a moral that she hammers home in the last sentence of the piece with a reference to La Fontaine's fable of the ass who thinks he can play the flute.

> Every critic who forms a high estimate of the share women may ultimately take in literature, will, on principle, abstain from any exceptional indulgence towards the productions of literary women. For it must be plain to every one who looks impartially and extensively into feminine literature, that its greatest deficiencies are due hardly more to the want of intellectual power than to the want of those moral qualities that contribute to literary excellence—patient diligence, a sense of the responsibility involved in publication, and an appreciation of the sacredness of the writer's art.[16]

Diligence, responsibility, art—it is not surprising to find these criteria put forth by George Eliot. But writers of far more modest abilities, such as Dinah Mulock Craik, were also insisting that women must take literature seriously, that they must not overestimate their talents or confuse their feminine and their professional roles:

> In any profession there is nothing, short of being absolutely evil, which is so injurious, so fatal, as mediocrity. ... Therefore, let men do as they will—and truly they are often ten times vainer and more ambitious than we—but I would advise every woman to examine herself and

[16] "Silly Novels by Lady Novelists," *Westminster Review* LXVI (1856), in *Essays of George Eliot*, p. 323.

judge herself, morally and intellectually, by the sharpest tests of criticism, before she attempts art or literature, either for abstract fame, or as a means of livelihood.[17]

Such high standards made the first generation severe with their sisters and hard on themselves. The continual pressure to prove themselves, a pressure more internalized than manifest, kept them desperately sensitive to criticism. They nonetheless resorted to positively masochistic metaphors in describing their artistic self-discipline: "Hit again, right sharply," Charlotte Brontë told a critic; George Eliot spoke of her writing as "fasting and scourging oneself."[18] They had little sympathy for the lapses or self-indulgence of others. "Mr. Thackeray," according to Brontë, "is easy and indolent and seldom cares to do his best."[19] As they grew older, women like Mrs. Oliphant, Mrs. Linton, and Anne Mozley, who had always been hard-working journalists, grew increasingly impatient with the laxity and carelessness of liberated youngsters. In their heyday, from about 1845 to 1860, they were not willing to accept what Mrs. Browning labeled in *Aurora Leigh* "the comparative respect which means the absolute scorn," and they expected rigorous and impartial criticism, which they would not lower themselves to avoid by pleading feminine handicaps. Miss Mulock thought that "to exact consideration merely on account of her sex is in any woman the poorest cowardice."[20]

The immense productivity characteristic of nineteenth-century women writers can be traced to their total involvement in the literary professions; they had fewer means of outside support than did male writers. Altick's data shows that, although the percentage of professional—i.e. self-supporting—writers gradually increased throughout the century, most male writers had other professions and sources

[17] *A Woman's Thoughts About Women*, London, 1858, p. 53.
[18] Clement K. Shorter, ed., *The Brontës: Life and Letters*, London, 1908, II, p. 304; and Haight, *George Eliot*, p. 361.
[19] Shorter, *The Brontës*, II, p. 249.
[20] *Woman's Thoughts*, p. 56.

of income. In a number of cases men had been trained for professions that their literary success saved them from having to practice. Middle-class women had very few alternative occupations to writing in the nineteenth century. Other than teaching, their best possibilities were in the business end of publishing; many also worked as publishers' readers and copy-editors. Furthermore, women writers were likely to be dependent on their earnings and contributing to the support of their families, and not, as has been conjectured, indulging themselves at the expense of fathers and husbands.

Unmarried women were increasingly drawn to writing as a means of support. J.M.S. Tompkins, in *The Popular Novel in England 1770–1800*, found that the majority of women writers up to 1780 were married. By 1790 a good many spinsters had appeared in the lists. My research shows that of women writers born between 1800 and 1900, a fairly constant proportion—about half—were unmarried. In a number of cases, women married late in life, after they had established a professional reputation and were able to earn a good market price for their books. Married women writers (such as Margaret Gatty, Emma Marshall, Isabella Banks, and Lucy Clifford) were frequently motivated to publish by their husbands' financial failure, illness, or death, and thus took on double burdens of support. The effects of such financial need can easily be traced in the too-rapid production of competent, not-quite-realized fiction. Mrs. Oliphant, for example, fought a never-ending battle against bankruptcy. The sole support of her own children, and her nephews as well, she lived in perpetual bondage to a string of publishers, selling ideas for books she had not begun to write, and writing books she never cared for, simply to stay ahead. The British Museum has volumes of her letters to publishers, begging for an advance, or referring to a series of travel books, biographies, or textbooks that she was churning out. To Virginia Woolf, these circumstances explain the poverty of her art: "Mrs. Oliphant sold her brain, her very admirable brain, prostituted her culture and enslaved her intellectual liberty in order that she might earn her living and educate her children."[21] The feminine novelists tended to reinvest their income in providing luxuries for their sons, as if in atonement for taking over the role of wage-earner; Mrs. Gatty sent her four sons to Eton, Winchester, Marlborough, and Charterhouse, but spent nothing on clothes for herself or furniture for her home.[22]

But the pot-boilers did keep the pot not only boiling but full. It is significant that Mrs. Gatty and Mrs. Oliphant *could* send their boys to Eton through writing; writing offered unique financial opportunities without sex discrimination. In an article published in 1857, J. M. Kaye put forth literature as the "only profession . . . which does not jealously exclude women from all participation in its honour and its profits. There is no injustice done to women here. The road is open. The race is fair. If woman be the fleeter, she wins."[23] The shift toward acceptability of middle-class women's need to earn money came very slowly, but there is no doubt that from the beginning writing offered the best chances of remuneration. A governess, who held virtually the only other kind of job open to untrained middle-class women, earned only between 20 and 45 pounds a year plus board.

The copyright sale of even a mediocre novel by an unknown author was likely to equal the yearly wage of a governess. The copyright of the average three-decker sold for 100 pounds. Women discovered that it took almost a year to write a novel, but once they had published a book they could get good rates for journalism. Eliza Lynn worked for the *Morning Chronicle* from 1849 to 1851 and was paid a

[21] *Three Guineas*, London, 1977, p. 106.

[22] Gillian Avery, *Mrs. Ewing*, London, 1964, pp. 13–14.

[23] J. M. Kaye, "The Employment of Women," *North British Review* XXVI (1857): 177. "When women's work fails or is underpaid," wrote Mrs. Linton, "it is because it is inferior, and not because the sex is oppressed" (*The Rebel of the Family*, London, 1880, II, p. 56).

guinea a week. In 1851 Mrs. Gaskell checked around and was offered seven shillings a column by the *Critic*. By 1901 the *Times* offered its writers five pounds a column; most papers and magazines were then paying a guinea a column.[24]

Even at its lower levels, fiction offered a better financial return than, say, fancywork, for the time invested. A typical level of earning was exemplified by Adeline Sergeant, who wrote about seventy-five novels, none of which ever became a best seller. Sergeant averaged about one hundred pounds a book and turned out up to five books a year. In 1902, her best year, she made 1,500 pounds.[25] The usual system of publication was the outright sale of copyright for three-volume novels suitable for circulating libraries. Authors received flat sums, the size of which depended upon their reputations and the publishers' estimates of sales. This system had many advantages for women authors, who could earn a steady income by writing a certain number of novels per year. If an author worked with a reputable publisher, direct sale of copyright did not even preclude bonuses on a best seller, and the author of a best seller could command high prices on subsequent books. Royal Gettmann gives several examples of this procedure in his study of the Bentley papers:

> On 26 March 1877 [Jessie Fothergill] sold the copyright of *The First Violin* for forty pounds. Shortly after, someone in the firm recognized the commercial possibilities of the novel, and on 30 May a new agreement was drawn up in which the price was changed to two hundred pounds. The contracts for Miss Fothergill's later books show a regular and considerable increase in the prices paid for her copyrights—two hundred and fifty pounds,

[24] *The Letters of Mrs. Gaskell*, ed. A. Pollard and J.A.V. Chapple, Manchester, 1966, p. 172; and F.M.G., "Journalism," *Womanhood* VI (1901): 23.

[25] Winifred Stephens, *The Life of Adeline Sergeant*, London, 1905, pp. 279–280.

three hundred pounds, five hundred pounds, and six hundred pounds.[26]

It was true, however, that sale of copyright left authors dependent on the goodwill of publishers, and often put women authors in the role of supplicant; the copyright system kept even successful writers at the grindstone of constant production. A certain degree of toughness was required to bargain for one's rights. Dinah Mulock Craik makes a good case study in this respect. She sold the copyrights of her first three novels—*The Ogilvies, Olive*, and *The Head of the Family*—to Chapman & Hall for 150 pounds each. Desperate for money, the then Miss Mulock took what she got gratefully; however, *Head of the Family* went into six editions, and although Edward Chapman promised her better terms for her next book she began to feel herself cheated. In an apologetic letter to Chapman she delicately played on her youth and feminine weakness at the same time that she asked for money:

> Do you think that out of the profits of all that you could spare some addition to the one hundred and fifty pounds you gave me?—I know it is not a right—& yet it seems hardly unfair. . . .
> I have not been able to work this winter—and may not be able to finish my fireside book for months—so that it becomes important to me to gather up all I can—My head is tired out with having worked to [sic] hard when I was young—& now when I could get any amount of pay, I can't write.[27]

By 1856 she had begun to look around for a better deal with another firm. Mrs. Oliphant introduced her to the director of Hurst & Blackett, who decided to publish *John*

[26] Royal A. Gettman, *A Victorian Publisher: A Study of the Bentley Papers*, Cambridge, England, 1960, p. 83.
[27] February 26 AM 19529, in the Morris L. Parrish Collection of Victorian Novelists, Firestone Library, Princeton University.

Halifax, Gentleman. Before Miss Mulock had realized any profits from that book, she approached Macmillan about a regular job:

> After my present book is done I must have a good long rest. My health has rather given way with overwork—If it were possible to get any mechanical literary work— such as being 'publisher's reader'—or the like—which wd give me a settled income without need to write for a year or two—it wd be a great blessing to me.[28]

It is not known whether Macmillan responded, but Hurst & Blackett's generous terms for *John Halifax, Gentleman* gave Mulock the financial respite she needed. Thereafter she had enough security to take a stronger line with publishers. The tone of her correspondence with Chapman became much more forceful and completely lost its earlier ladylike diffidence. In October 1858 she wrote angrily to Chapman, who had used her name in advertising, presumably to cash in on the success of *John Halifax.* Miss Mulock was known to be the author of her novels, but she abhorred publicity and preferred a discreet semi-anonymity: "I see you are advertising my novels as *'Mulock's* Head of the Family etc.' Now this is very objectionable to me, as I have always resented putting my name to any of my books for reasons which I still keep to."[29]

As her work became more successful, Mulock became more assertive in her bargaining and more comfortable with the confrontations and decisions of the trade. According to Mrs. Oliphant, "Henry Blackett turned pale at Miss Mulock's sturdy business-like stand for her money. He used to tell of his encounters with her with affright, very grave, not able to laugh."[30] When Mulock married George Lillie

[28] June 26, 1856, in the Berg Collection, New York Public Library.
[29] October 14, 1858, AM 16888, Morris L. Parrish Collection, Firestone Library, Princeton University.
[30] *Autobiography and Letters of Mrs. M.O.W. Oliphant,* ed. Mrs. Harry Coghill, London, 1899, p. 85. For a detailed study of her career, see

Craik, a partner in the firm of Macmillan's, in 1865, she
found that much of her worry about negotiating contracts
was over. Both the Craiks were known for their business
acumen, and at one point Mrs. Craik was commanding two
thousand pounds for the copyright of a story.

In short, a literary career inevitably developed—or made
use of—women's business skills. If they were not to be taken
advantage of by publishers who, although innocent of sex
discrimination, were out to make money and expected authors to take care of themselves, women had to be able to
demand their rights. In this sense, the Victorian nightmare
of fierce, disputatious, horny-hided professional women had
a source in truth. Geraldine Jewsbury wrestled with the dilemma in a letter to Jane Carlyle in 1850:

> When women get to be energetic, strong characters, with
> literary reputations of their own, and live in the world,
> with business to attend to, they all do get in the habit of
> making use of people, and of taking care of themselves
> in a way that is startling! And yet how are they to help it?
> If they are thrown into the world, they must swim for
> their life.[31]

Troubled by these problems, most feminine novelists
postponed their career decisions until middle age, whereas
men made career commitments early. As Trollope points
out in his *Autobiography*, female aspirants could continue
to strive for publication after many rejections; men had to

Elaine Showalter, "Dinah Mulock Craik and the Tactics of Sentiment: A
Case Study in Victorian Female Authorship," *Feminist Studies* II (1975):
5–23.

[31] *Letters of G. E. Jewsbury to Jane Welsh Carlyle*, ed. Mrs. Alex
Ireland, London, 1892, pp. 367–368. A similar phenomenon occurred in
the United States, where "women were drawn to writing just when it
became a possible business, and they were among the first to sense and
develop its business potential" (Ann Douglas Wood, "The Literature
of Impoverishment: The Women Local Colorists in America, 1865–
1914," *Women's Studies* I [1972]: 7).

make a living somewhere. Thus the rejected young lady might be told to "darn her stockings," but one would say "less tenderly, to the male aspirant: 'You must earn some money, you say. Don't you think that a stool in a counting-house might be better?' "[32] Presumably, men who could not establish themselves early as writers turned to more profit-able occupations. Although there were a few late starters (Trollope was thirty-two, Charles Reade thirty-seven), throughout the century male writers began their careers in their mid-twenties. Prizes offered by the universities, such as the Newdigate Prize, encouraged precocity; from Shelley to Kipling to the Bloomsbury Group, many men were able to achieve publication while still in their teens.

As women's educational opportunities expanded and the question of female vocation became less threatening, the career patterns of women came closer to the male model. The first nineteenth-century generation of women writers tended to begin their careers as novelists late; only 55 per-cent had published by their thirtieth birthday. The third generation—the sensationalists, editors, and children's book writers—had a stronger sense of professional ambition; 73 percent had a book out by the age of thirty. In the third quarter of the century there was a retreat, but by the last generation, the generation of Virginia Woolf and Ivy Compton-Burnett, 58 percent had published by their twenty-fifth birthday, and nearly 75 percent by their thirtieth. This gradual and irregular shift in women's lit-erary career patterns has sometimes been taken to reflect economic crises or anxiety about marriage. But simply find-ing out and making clear to themselves what they should do with their lives was a more difficult and time-consuming process for women than for men. Making up the education-al disability added years to their apprenticeship, as did the subtle battles for independence within the nuclear family. Many women who exhibited precocious talents for litera-

---

[32] Anthony Trollope, *Autobiography*, London, 1950, p. 207.

ture never wrote books. The leap from diaries and letters to three-decker novels was a leap of consciousness that many women never felt strong or independent enough to attempt.

"If self is to be the end of exertions," wrote Mrs. Gaskell to her friend Tottie Fox, "these exertions are unholy, there is no doubt of *that*.—and that is part of the danger in cultivating the individual life, but I do believe we all have some appointed work to do; which no one else can do so well . . . and that first we must find out what we are sent into the world to do, and define it, and make it clear to ourselves (that's the hard part) and then forget ourselves in our work."[33]

Was it selfish to write books? In strict evangelical circles, all imaginative literature was suspect, and children were taught that storytelling could lead to untruth and transgressions. The extraordinary number of women writers who were daughters, sisters, or wives of clergymen suggests that women writers would have been especially sensitive to these arguments. We can gather from biographies that many women never overcame childhood guilt and repression enough to attempt to write. Edmund Gosse describes in *Father and Son* how his mother was forced to give up her fantasy life. Mrs. Gosse recalled that, as a child,

> I used to amuse myself and my brothers with inventing stories, such as I read. Having, as I suppose, naturally a restless mind and busy imagination, this soon became the chief pleasure of my life . . . I had not known there was harm in it until Miss Shore [a Calvinist governess], finding it out, lectured me severely and told me it was wicked. From that time forth I considered that to invent a story of any kind was a sin.[34]

Financial crises sometimes relieved women of this burden of guilt and justified their work, or pushed secret scribblers

[33] Gaskell, *Letters*, p. 106.
[34] Edmund Gosse, *Father and Son*, London, 1973, ch. II, p. 21.

over the brink into print. Some mechanism had to be found to release women's energies: a recommendation from a doctor or a husband (a kind of permission from male authority), a clear didactic purpose or worthy cause, or a situation that required their earning money. Thus the standard chapter in the memoirs—"My First Book"—became a genre in itself; the invalid mother, the bankrupt father, the tubercular husband, and the errant son are wheeled out by demure authoresses in whose downcast eyes we can detect the glint of steely purpose.

Some of the most striking evidence of vocation can be found in the biographies of women who made sincere and heart-rending efforts to overcome their wish to write. Charlotte Brontë is the most famous representative of this group. In 1837 she wrote to the Poet Laureate, Robert Southey, for advice in pursuing her career. Southey was more than discouraging; he advised her to give up any dreams of becoming a poet: "Literature cannot be the business of a woman's life and it ought not to be." These words were like a death sentence to her, but she tried to curb her imagination and conceal her gifts:

> I carefully avoid any appearance of pre-occupation and eccentricity which might lead those I live amongst to suspect the nature of my pursuits. Following my father's advice—who from my childhood has counselled me, just in the wise and friendly tone of your letter—I have endeavoured not only attentively to observe all the duties a woman ought to fulfil, but to feel deeply interested in them. I don't always succeed, for sometimes when I'm teaching or sewing I would rather be reading or writing; but I try to deny myself, and my father's approbation amply rewarded me for the privation.[35]

As long as there were fathers or father surrogates around to dispense approbation in return for submission, women

[35] Quoted in Gaskell, *Life of Charlotte Brontë*, London, 1973, ch. VIII, p. 104.

could gratify at least some needs in self-mortification, as one sees in scores of feminine novels from Maria Edgeworth to George Eliot. One did not have to possess the genius of a Brontë to feel conflicting urges to write and to be loved. Rosa Nouchette Carey, a popular sentimental novelist at the turn of the century, struggled with her guilt as strenuously as did Brontë or Eliot. As a girl she "made a deliberate, and as it afterwards proved, a fruitless attempt to quench the longing to write," and simultaneously "endeavored to be more like other girls." Carey's opportunity came when her brother died, leaving her the sole support of his four children. Such a sanction to write, was not, of course, an unmixed blessing: "The charge tied my hands . . . and prevented the pursuing of my literary labours as fully as I could have otherwise done." But what was important was the lifting of responsibility for her ambition; those four little orphans justified her career. As Rosa Carey saw it, paying self-sacrificial dues to the family not only excused the profession but also transmuted its more egoistic qualities into "real womanly woman's work"[36]—i.e. work for others.

What, though, happened when the male breadwinner refused to die or collapse? Middle-class Victorian male opposition to women wage-earners reflected a good deal of class snobbery and a superstitious fear of women's "losing their bloom"—a euphemism for sexual innocence—in the real world. Inside each individual family, however, the issues were more personal and less theoretical. Some fathers, brothers, and husbands felt threatened by the prospects of female competition within the home. For example, when Charlotte Yonge presented her first novel to her family, her father severely informed her that a lady published for three reasons only: love of praise, love of money, or the wish to do good. It would have been an emotional impossibility for

[36] Helen C. Black, *Notable Women Authors of the Day*, Glasgow, 1893, pp. 149, 151, 156. See also Black's interviews with Mrs. Riddell and Mrs. Lovett Cameron, pp. 19–20, 103.

Charlotte to rebel against her adored father, "a Peninsular and Waterloo soldier, who was the hero of heroes to both my mother and me. His approbation was throughout my life my bliss; his anger my misery."[37] Mr. Yonge was willing to bestow his approbation and withhold his anger if Charlotte was willing to write didactic fiction and to give away the profits. By doing good and taking no pay she was safely confined in a female and subordinate role within the family, and remained dependent upon her father. She gave the money from *The Daisy Chain* to missionaries in Melanesia, never wrote during Lent, prayed for humility with John Keble, and became fixated at an adolescent level in her relations to her parents. Nonetheless, she could not be entirely squelched. She did write the novels and publish them, and she also maintained a surreptitious interest in the less ladylike aspects of her work, secretly reading her reviews, and writing detailed, firm, and extremely businesslike letters to Macmillan about sales and publishing.[38]

Women devised a number of strategies to deal with male hostility, jealousy, and resistance within the family. Studied submission, like Yonge's, accompanied by covert pursuit of self-interest, was one method. Some women seem to have resorted to more straightforward flattery and bribes. The blind novelist Alice King (1839–1894), daughter of the vicar of Cutcombe, Somerset, donated the proceeds of her first novel *Forest Keep* (1862) to the purchase of a stained-glass window for Cutcombe Church. Jean Ingelow spent her first earnings on having her father's portrait painted on ivory. Juliana Ewing bought her husband a piano. If the man in question could not be placated by such tactics, women simply published in secret. The height and the trademark of feminine role-playing was the male pseudonym. Primarily

[37] Ethel Romanes, *Charlotte Mary Yonge: An Appreciation*, London, 1908, p. 16.
[38] See D. B. Green, "Letters to Macmillan," *Notes and Queries*, n.s. x (1963): 450–454.

a way of obtaining serious treatment from critics, the pseudonym also protected women from the righteous indignation of their own relatives.

There is good reason to suppose that a male *persona* was a part of the fantasy life of many of these women from childhood; they could use a masculine name to represent everything in their personalities that transcended the cramping feminine ideal. In the Angrian chronicles the Brontës had a dozen male alter egos; Charlotte used several male aliases as a child, including Charles Thunder, Charles Townsend, and Captain Tree. The pseudonyms of the Brontës and Marian Evans are universally known, but it is not generally known that they inspired dozens of imitators. A partial list would include "Holme Lee" (Harriet Parr, 1828–1900), "Ennis Graham" (Mary Molesworth, 1839–1921), "F. G. Trafford" (Charlotte Riddell, 1832–1906), "Allen Raine" (Anne Puddicombe, 1836–1915), "Lucas Malet" (Mary Kingsley, 1852–1931), "John Strange Winter" (Henrietta Stannard, 1856–1911), "Lanoe Falconer" (Mary E. Hawker, 1848–1908), "George Egerton" (Mary Chavelita Dunne, 1859–1945), "Vernon Lee" (Violet Paget, 1856–1935), "Claude Lake" (Mathilde Blind, 1851–1896), "Ross Neil" (Isabella Harwood, 1840–1888), "John Oliver Hobbes" (Pearl Craigie, 1867–1906), "Martin Ross" (Violet Martin, 1862–1915), "Lawrence Hope" (Adela Nicholson, 1865–1904), and "Michael Fairless" (Margaret Barber, 1869–1901). In these aliases, the novelists were renaming themselves in the same way that they named characters in their novels, frequently replacing the banality of an honest English surname with something more poetic, graceful, and elegant, as well as male. The pseudonyms, on the whole, have an air of semi-aristocracy. Later in the century women expressed their romantic fantasies of self more explicitly in female pseudonyms like "The Duchess," "Ouida," and "Sarah Grand." The practice of using pseudonyms died out with the last Victorian generation, although women writers of that period were fond of using names that could be either male or female, often middle names or initials: Storm Jameson, Radclyffe Hall, G. B. Stern, I. Compton-Burnett, V. Sackville-West. The male pseudonym was much more popular in England than in the United States (American women exploited the feminine stereotype with pastoral pseudonyms like Grace Greenwood, Fanny Forrester, and Fanny Fern), but in the 1880s the Tennessee novelist Mary N. Murfee used the name "Charles Egbert Craddock," and deceived even her publishers for six years.

Geraldine Jewsbury's reasons for using a pseudonym in 1845 show both fear of discrimination and anxiety about causing pain, offending friends, or betraying affection. About her novel *Zoë*, she wrote: "I had rather not have my name stuck to the thing. First, because there are many things said in it that I don't want to walk about amongst some of my reputable friends as being guilty of holding. There are several I am very fond of, and I should be sorry to hurt their feelings; and another reason is, that I myself have a general sort of prejudice against women's novels, with very few exceptions." In the preface to the 1850 edition of her sisters' novels, Charlotte Brontë noted that she and her sisters "had a vague impression that authoresses are liable to be looked on with prejudice." As late as 1880 Henrietta Stannard used the name "John Strange Winter" for her *Cavalry Life* and *Regimental Legends*. "They would stand a better chance," thought her publishers, "as the work of a man."[39]

In journalism unsigned articles had become common in the 1830s because editors felt that intellectual freedom was best served by such a practice. In the 1840s Harriet Martineau, working for the *Edinburgh Review*, disguised her identity with "the mannish way of talking,"[40] as did Elizabeth Rigby in the *Quarterly Review*. Women journalists initially felt that they got better treatment from the public

[39] Jewsbury, *Letters*, pp. 158–159; and Black, *Notable Women Authors*, pp. 49–50.
[40] Haight, *George Eliot*, p. 268.

when they published anonymously and assumed male *personae*. In 1855 George Eliot asked her friend Charles Bray not to tell anyone that she had written the essay on the evangelist Cumming for the *Westminster*: "The article appears to have produced a strong impression, and that impression would be a little counteracted if the author were known to be a *woman*."[41] By the 1860s, a counter-reaction had set in. Frederick Maurice was one of the leaders of a rebellion against journalistic anonymity; he argued, with significant terminology, that he wanted "an honest, manly literature."[42] The *Fortnightly Review*, which made its first appearance in 1865 and was edited by Lewes, pioneered the new style of signed articles; Anthony Trollope wrote its defense. Under the circumstances, Trollope had to allow for *some* exceptions—George Eliot had a piece in the same issue—and he chivalrously excluded women from the stipulation that it was dishonest to conceal one's identity: "One or two female pseudonyms that have preserved themselves in spite of the high literary position which their owners have obtained, of course occur to us in any discussion on this subject. But the nature of a woman is such that we admire her timidity and do not even regret her weakness."[43] The number of women who were still publishing under pseudonyms may be guessed from Bessie R. Parkes' comment in *Essays on Women's Work* (1865): "If editors were ever known to disclose the dread secrets of their dens, they could only give the public an idea of the authoresses whose unsigned names are legion; of their rolls of manuscripts, which are as the sands of the sea."[44]

Yet, like Mrs. Henry Wood, of whom it was said that "no home duty was ever neglected or put aside for literary la-

---

[41] *Essays of George Eliot*, ed., Thomas Pinney, London, 1963, p. 158.

[42] Christopher Kent, "Higher Journalism and the Mid-Victorian Clerisy," *Victorian Studies* XII (1969): 190.

[43] Anthony Trollope, "On Anonymous Literature," *Fortnightly Review*, 1 (1865): 491.

[44] Bessie Parkes, *Essays on Women's Work*, London, 1865, p. 121.

bours," other nineteenth-century women writers did no believe that literary talents took precedence over the normal obligations of womanhood.[45] One of the distinguishing characteristics of the feminine novelists is the seriousness with which they took their domestic roles. It is easy to denigrate these women because they did not have the single-minded dedication to art that supposedly characterizes the romantic male artist, or to pity them for their oppression. But neither condescension nor indignation is warranted. Up until about 1880 feminine novelists felt a sincere wish to integrate and harmonize the responsibilities of their personal and professional lives. Moreover, they believed that such a reconciliation of opposites would enrich their art and deepen their understanding.

A factor that recurs with remarkable frequency in the backgrounds of these women is identification with, and dependence upon, the father; and either loss of, or alienation from, the mother. This may explain, among other things, why early feminine novelists had fewer children than later generations. In the first generation this pattern is particularly striking: the Brontës, George Eliot, Geraldine Jewsbury, Elizabeth Barrett Browning, and Elizabeth Gaskell had all lost their mothers in early childhood. Elizabeth Lynn Linton's mother died when Elizabeth was five years old; Dinah Mulock's mother died when Dinah was in her teens. Even when the mother was present, she was often cold and rejecting. Charlotte Yonge wistfully recalled how her mother had treated her critically from fear of spoiling her: "She was much afraid of my being vain. Once, on venturing to ask if I was pretty, I was answered that all young animals, young pigs and all, were pretty."[46] The scrupulous Elizabeth Sewell tormented herself as a child with the question whether a vow she had made in anger required her to kill her mother. Although few mothers were as austere as

45 Charles W. Wood, *Mrs. Henry Wood: A Memoir*, London, 1895, p. 228.

46 Romanes, *Charlotte Mary Yonge*, p. 19.

Mrs. Yonge, most mothers in middle-class families were more narrow-minded and conventional than the fathers, who had the advantages of education and mobility. The following description of Mary Coleridge's family accurately reflects the typical ambience of these households from the talented daughter's perspective:

> Mamma moved in the background; a centre of rest where Papa was the center of laughter. She arranged the comforts of the celebrated hospitality which Arthur's cordiality inspired. She did not excite or encourage Mary's imagination as her father did. On the contrary, she tried to make her daughter, so indifferent to what she wore or ate, more conventional. But Mary loved her dearly.[47]

The daughter's nonconformity would increase the strains in her relationship with her mother and lead her to make greater demands upon her father for love and attention. Fathers often supervised their daughters' education; they brought interesting friends to the house; they discussed the issues of the day. Quite a few of the women whose names appear in literary histories had fathers or uncles who were professional writers: Caroline Norton, the granddaughter of Sheridan; Sara Coleridge, the poet's daughter; Florence Marryat, daughter of the novelist Frederick Marryat; Adelaide Procter, daughter of the poet "Barry Cornwall"; Christina Rossetti; Mary Kingsley ["Lucas Malet"], the daughter of Charles Kingsley; Annie Ritchie, the daughter of Thackeray; Rhoda Broughton, niece of the sensation novelist Joseph LeFanu; Mrs. Humphry Ward, the niece of Matthew Arnold; Mathilde Blind, stepdaughter of the revolutionary journalist Karl Blind; and so on up to Leslie Stephen's daughter Virginia Woolf. Gifted mothers sometimes had an influence as well, but descent in the female line did not show up until about the end of the century, since the number of women who were professional writers was rela-

47 Theresa Whistler, introduction to *Collected Poems of Mary Coleridge*, London, 1954, p. 29.

tively small. It is not until the generation born between 1860 and 1880 that the daughters of professional women appear in significant numbers, including Marie Belloc Lowndes, daughter of the feminist editor Bessie R. Parkes; Ethel Voynich, daughter of the mathematician George Boole and the feminist philosopher Mary Everett Boole; and Beatrice Harraden, the ward of Mrs. Lynn Linton.

Most modern discussions of the relationship between Victorian women writers and their fathers have emphasized its destructiveness. Mr. Barrett of Wimpole Street is the chief villain of such accounts, and along with the Reverend Brontë has become the archetypal example of the dark devouring love of Victorian patriarchy. Virginia Woolf (who had firsthand knowledge of the type) called this relationship "infantile fixation" and attacked it in the third chapter of *Three Guineas*:

> Since society protected and indeed excused the victims of the infantile fixation [the fathers, she means here] it is not surprising that the disease, though unnamed, was rampant. Whatever biography we open we find almost always the familiar symptoms—the father is opposed to his daughter's marriage, the father is opposed to his daughter's earning her living. Her wish either to marry, or to earn her living, arouses strong emotion in him; and he gives the same excuses for that strong emotion; the lady will debase her ladyhood; the daughter will outrage her womanhood.

It is true that fathers often unconsciously fought their daughters' efforts to become independent, but the exaggeration of Woolf's statement undoubtedly proceeds from her need to combat the lingering shadow of her own father's demands. It is also true that many women did not marry because no man could be found to compete with the paternal charisma; Charles Kingsley's daughter Mary, for example, waited until two years after her glamorous father's death to marry his curate, a man thirteen years her senior. These are, however, extreme cases, and as such they are not indigenous only to the nineteenth century. If some women were prevented by their fathers from attaining full independence, it is also likely that some women, in receiving emotional support from their fathers, found a role model to emulate. Even Elizabeth Barrett Browning, in *Aurora Leigh*, traced Aurora's genius to Mr. Leigh's encouragement.

In a recent comprehensive study Judith Bardwick has linked the emergence of highly developed achievement drives in girls with identification with the father: "If the daughter rejects the maternal role, or if her mother is more rejecting than supportive, or if her relationship with her father is the only source of love and support, she may well identify with his role activities."[48] There are obvious dangers in applying Bardwick's theory, based on the study of twentieth-century American women, to nineteenth-century British women but I think the theory helps us to understand why these women were not, as sympathetic modern critics sometimes imply, the most tragically oppressed artists of their time, struggling against overwhelming odds. The circumstances of their childhood, even when unhappy, may in fact have contributed positively to their vocation as artists.

Furthermore, we should take very seriously the possibility that subordination of self to filial duty gave these women confidence in their own abilities to love, and some authority in depicting the feminine imperative of loving sympathy in their novels. While nursing her dying father, George Eliot wrote, "Strange to say, I feel that these will ever be the happiest days of my life to me. The one deep strong love I have known has now its highest exercise."[49] The exercise of one's emotional potential was a form of experience in which women could, and did, specialize. Thus an opportunity to demonstrate love in difficult circumstances, and in conflict

[48] *Psychology of Women*, London, 1971, p. 138.
[49] Haight, *George Eliot*, p. 67.

with personal wishes, was a genuine, if complex, source of satisfaction, a strength that the feminine subculture afforded.

Combining marriage and motherhood with a career brought other stresses to women's professional patterns. About 50 percent of the women writers born in the nineteenth century married; in the general population, the figure was about 85 percent. Of the married women writers, about 65 percent had children, although they tended to have families well below the Victorian norm of six children. This family limitation suggests a recognition by women novelists of what might reasonably be accomplished in a lifetime. On the other hand, we should not assume that childless married women writers were childless by choice. Olive Schreiner's daughter survived only a few hours; Dorothy Richardson and Katherine Mansfield miscarried illegitimate babies, and were subsequently unable to conceive; Virginia Woolf was persuaded not to have children for medical reasons. Health problems, rather than contraceptive decisions, probably account for some of the small families; Elizabeth Barrett Browning, for example, had four miscarriages before she gave birth to her son.

If we turn to the books of Sarah Stickney Ellis (1810–1872), the daughter of a Quaker farmer who began in 1839 to publish her famous series, *The Women of England, The Wives of England, The Mothers of England,* and so on, we might get the impression that a wife's duties were so detailed and overwhelming as to preclude any other activity. But Mrs. Ellis, who had no children, began to write two years after she married. What most women rejected as unacceptable and unchristian was the use of literary vocation to avoid the responsibilities of home life. Somehow the two had to be balanced. According to Mrs. Gaskell, "no other can take up the quiet regular duties of the daughter, the wife, or the mother, as well as she whom God has appointed to fill that particular place: a woman's principal work in life is hardly left to her own choice; nor can she drop the domestic charges devolving on her as an individual, for the exercise of the most splendid talents that were ever bestowed."[50]

Expression of doubt as to the propriety or efficiency of combining wifehood with authorship came primarily before 1850. In December of that year, Geraldine Jewsbury wrote to Jane Carlyle that Mrs. Gaskell's celebrity had aroused great compassion for her husband in Manchester. "The people here are beginning mildly to be pained for Mr. 'Mary Barton.' And one lady said to me the other day, 'I don't think authoresses ought ever to marry.' "[51] The first generation of single women tended to idealize the matrimonial state and at the same time to feel a sort of obscure resentment toward women who had succeeded in another life style. Jean Ingelow (1820–1897) is a representative figure: "With her shy, nervous, sensitive temperament, her intense solicitude about those she loved, her almost painful anxiety to do her duty at any cost to herself, it was easy to believe her when she affirmed, 'If I had married, I should *not* have written books.' "[52] Caricatures like Dickens' Mrs. Jellyby (in *Bleak House*, 1853) had spread the stereotype of the frowsy career woman. Generally, however, feminine women writers flaunted their domesticity, and genuinely enjoyed it; like Harriet Martineau in her *Autobiography*, they bragged that they could sew shirts or make puddings; like George Eliot, they kept careful records of the asparagus nippers and the second-best blankets; like Dinah Mulock, they insisted that "the best housekeepers, the neatest nee-

---

[50] *Life of Charlotte Brontë*, ch. XVI, p. 238. Jennifer Stern points out that "women writing novels . . . within their own families would not have to face the hostility and loss of status which leaving home nearly always involved" ("Women and the Novel: A Nineteenth-Century Explosion," *Womens Liberation Review* I [1973]: 55).

[51] Jewsbury, *Letters*, p. 383. The *British and Foreign Review* by 1836 notes that the female author need not cease being a good wife, mother, and sister. See Françoise Basch, *Relative Creatures: Victorian Women in Society and the Novel*, London, 1974, p. 107.

[52] *Some Recollections of Jean Ingelow*, London, 1901, p. 126.

dlewomen, the most discreet managers of their own and others' affairs, are ladies whose names the world cons over in library lists and Exhibition catalogues."[53]

Unquestionably, there were conflicts in some of these marriages; Elizabeth Lynn Linton, Florence Marryat, Mrs. Molesworth, Annie Besant, and Frances Hodgson Burnett were among those who separated or divorced. But marriage, in its way, was often liberating for women. "She may read anything now she's married," says Mr. Brooke in *Middlemarch*, and married women could enjoy a wider range of experience outside the home as well as in the library, without fear of scandal. This freedom applied particularly to the wives of army officers and missionaries, who had to follow the regiment (or the mission), but found a wealth of exciting source material when they arrived. Women in these circumstances—Flora Annie Steel, Fanny Penny, Alice Perrin, Mrs. B. M. Croker, Maud Diver, and Ada Cambridge are a few examples—specialized in titillating revelations of exotic native culture and made a sizable contribution to the colonial fiction of their day.[54]

The duties of a mother, however, were universally regarded as preemptive. Here again childless women of the older generation were likely to have an exaggerated notion of the time and effort that motherhood demanded, but in this case they were closer to expressing the majority view. Frances Power Cobbe, a high-powered feminist reformer who never married, insisted that mothers should not try to work outside the domestic sphere until their families were grown: "So *immense* are the claims of a mother, physical

---

[53] *Woman's Thoughts*, p. 56. See also Harriet Martineau's praise of housework in *Deerbrook*, I, London, 1839, p. 296. Even rebellious spirits like Jewsbury prided themselves on their housekeeping. "I should like to see the perfectly *rational proper* Mrs. Ellis of a woman that could have managed as well with me as this poor little authoress of a questionable *Zoë* has done," wrote Jewsbury's houseguest, Jane Carlyle. (*Letters of Jane Carlyle*, ed. Leonard Huxley, London, 1924, p. 280.)

[54] See Benita Parry, *Delusions and Discoveries: Studies of India in the British Imagination 1880–1930*, London, 1973.

claims on her bodily and brainly vigor, and moral claims on her heart and thoughts, that she cannot, I believe, meet them all and find any large margin beyond for other cares and work."[55]

It is not until 1893 that we find a matter-of-fact discussion of the way to juggle a family and a career. In "Journalism as a Profession for Women," Emily Crawford cheerfully advises the prospective journalist to get a good housekeeper and send the children to school.[56] The modern age had arrived. It did not, however, dispel the underlying attitudes in the Victorian treatment of motherhood (it simply changed the terms from "moral" to "psychological").

Any consideration of Victorian criticism would turn up evidence of the view that motherhood and writing are incompatible. George Henry Lewes, for example, reviewing *Shirley*, in 1850, wrote:

The grand function of woman, it must always be recollected, is, and ever must be, *Maternity*: and this we regard not only as her distinctive characteristic, and most endearing charm, but as a high and holy office—the prolific source, not only of the best affections and virtues of which our nature is capable, but also of the wisest thoughtfulness, and most useful habits of observation, by which that nature can be elevated and adorned. But with all this, we think it impossible to deny that it must essentially interfere both with that steady and unbroken application, without which no proud eminence in science can be gained—and with the discharge of all official and professional functions that do not admit of long or frequent postponement. . . . for twenty of the best years of their lives—those very years in which men either rear the grand fabric or lay the solid foundations of their fame

---

[55] *The Duties of Woman*, London, 1881, p. 190. Mary Howitt terrified Mrs. Oliphant by claiming that she had miscarried babies by too much mental work. See Oliphant, *Autobiography and Letters*, p. 36.

[56] *Contemporary Review* LXVII (1893): 370.

and fortune—women are mainly occupied by the cares, the duties, the enjoyments and the sufferings of maternity. During large parts of those years, too, their bodily health is generally so broken and precarious as to incapacitate them for any strenuous exertion; and, health apart, the greater portion of their time, thoughts, interests, and anxieties ought to be, and generally are, centered in the care and training of their children. But how could such occupations consort with the intense and unremitting studies which seared the eyeballs of Milton, and for a time unsettled even the powerful brain of Newton?[57]

Lewes' grandiloquence is misleading; very few men were searing their eyeballs or unsettling their brains by such titanic devotion to scholarship either. It was typical to score debating points in an article like this by comparing the average woman writer to Milton, or more usually, Shakespeare, and then finding her at a disadvantage. Nevertheless, Lewes' argument, representing an enlightened male view, included a good dash of common sense. Childbearing *was* health-destroying, and absorbing. Occasionally one comes across a woman novelist, like Margaret Hungerford (1850–1897) with six children and thirty-one novels, who seems absolutely to have consumed herself in coping with her dual role.

Women did, however, have a different sense of the advantages and disadvantages of maternity than that expressed by Lewes. Whereas he, and other male writers, saw only a conflict of interests, they saw the possibility of a balanced life in which the domestic role enriched the art, and the art kept the domestic role spontaneous and meaningful. Mrs. Gaskell tried to explain her feelings about this to her friend Tottie Fox in 1850:

I am sure it is healthy for them [women] to have the refuge of the hidden world of Art to shelter themselves

---

[57] "Currer Bell's *Shirley*," *Edinburgh Review* XCI (1850): 155.

in when too much pressed upon by daily small Lilliputian arrows of meddling cares; it keeps them from being morbid as you say; and takes them into the land where King Arthur is hidden, and soothes them with its peace. I have felt this in writing, I see others feel it in music, you in painting, so assuredly a blending of the two is desirable. (Home duties and the development of the individual I mean.) . . . I have no doubt that the cultivation of each tends to keep the other in a healthy state.[58]

Twelve years later she suggested to an aspiring authoress that it might be a good idea to postpone writing until her children were older, but she emphasized that maternal experience would enrich any literary talents:

A good writer of fiction must have *lived* an active & sympathetic life if she wishes her books to have strength and vitality in them. When you are forty, and if you have a gift of being an authoress you will write ten times as good a novel as you could do now, just because you will have gone through so much more of the interests of a wife and mother.[59]

Whether this advice was good may be disputed; obviously an aspiring male novelist would not have been told to seek an active and sympathetic life in this way. But Mrs. Gaskell was expressing an idea with which many of her contemporaries concurred. Even though critics said that novel-writing mothers were unlikely to appear, those mothers who did appear got preferential treatment, at least in the short run. It was not exactly that critics revered motherhood and its wisdom, but that they regarded mothers as *normal* women; the unmarried and the childless had already a certain sexual stigma to overcome. In the early part of the century, attacks on the barren spinster novelist were part of the common fund of humor. Harriet Martineau was

[58] *Letters*, p. 106.   [59] *Letters*, pp. 694–695.

an irresistible target for lampoons like Thomas Moore's "Blue Love Song":

> Come wed with me, and we will write
> My Blue of Blues, from morn till night.
> Chased from our classic souls shall be
> All thought of vulgar progeny;
> And thou shalt walk through smiling rows
> Of chubby duodecimos,
> While I, to match thy products nearly,
> Shall lie-in of a quarto yearly.

Mrs. Gaskell became the heroine of a new school of "motherly fiction," and even when she published the controversial *Ruth* (1853), her own unassailable respectability and normality helped win over the readers. J. M. Ludlow, writing in the *North British Review*, used his review of *Ruth* to suggest that only married women with children write novels:

> If the novel addresses itself to the heart, what more natural than that it should then reach it most usefully and perfectly, when coming from the heart of a woman ripe with all the dignity of her sex, full of all wifely and motherly experience? No doubt a young lady—and even an *old* young lady—can write with the fear of God before her eyes, and become a great and good novelist; but somehow, one cannot help suspecting that she would find it much easier to write in the fear of God if she had already to write in the fear of husband and children.

As for the unmarried with great gifts for literature, Ludlow instructed them, "gently and with all reverence," to "endeavor to find your gifts other employment."[60]

"Who the deuce could have written it?" Mrs. Gaskell wrote gleefully to Catherine Winkworth. "It is so truly re-

---

[60] "Ruth," XIX (1853): 90–91.

ligious it makes me swear with delight."[61] Unmarried novelists could hardly have been amused. Many years later, Mary Cholmondeley analyzed for her private journal the sources of her will to write, as compensation for loneliness and suffering:

> I was nothing, a plain silent country girl, an invalid no one cared a straw about . . . but a dull smouldering fire of passion seemed to be kindling in me . . . a slow fire to overcome all these dreadful obstacles of illness and ugliness and incompetence. . . . It is not my talent which has placed me where I am, but the repression of my youth, my unhappy love-affair, the having to confront a hard full life, devoid of anything I cared for intellectually, and being hampered at every turn by constant illness.[62]

In her best novel, *Red Pottage* (1899), Cholmondeley's heroine is a novelist whose masterpiece is burned in manuscript by a zealous clergyman brother, who believes it to be heretical. The will to write inevitably provoked some kind of hostile response, and when women had managed to resolve the conflicts between obedience and resistance, womanhood and vocation, for themselves, they discovered that they faced a critical standard that denied them both femininity and art.

[61] *Letters*, p. 222. This letter is misdated by the editors, since Ludlow's review, to which it clearly refers, appeared in May 1853.

[62] Percy Lubbock, *Mary Cholmondeley: A Sketch from Memory*, London, 1928, pp. 91–92. Invalidism was another acceptable excuse for a woman's choosing a literary career, and often looks like a response to a sexual identity crisis that was literally paralyzing. Some examples are Margaret Barber, Dora Greenwell, Mrs. L. B. Walford and Mrs. Henry Wood.

~~~~~~

CHAPTER III

The Double Critical Standard and the Feminine Novel

To their contemporaries, nineteenth-century women writers were women first, artists second. A woman novelist, unless she disguised herself with a male pseudonym, had to expect critics to focus on her femininity and rank her with the other women writers of her day, no matter how diverse their subjects or styles. The knowledge that their individual achievement would be subsumed under a relatively unfavorable group stereotype acted as a constant irritant to feminine novelists. George Eliot protested against being compared to Dinah Mulock; Charlotte Brontë tried to delay the publication of *Villette* so that it would not be reviewed along with Mrs. Gaskell's *Ruth.* Brontë particularly wanted to prevent the male literary establishment from making women writers into competitors and rivals for the same small space: "It is the nature of writers to be invidious," she wrote to Mrs. Gaskell, but "we shall set them at defiance; they *shall* not make us foes."[1]

We tend to forget how insistently Victorian reviewers made women the targets of *ad feminam* criticism. An error in Gordon Haight's *A Century of George Eliot Criticism* illustrates this common modern oversight; Haight quotes E. S. Dallas as saying of Eliot that no "Englishman" could approach her as a writer of prose. The word Dallas actually used was "English*woman*."[2] To Haight, such a distinction

[1] Clement K. Shorter, *The Brontës: Life and Letters*, London, 1908, II, p. 30.

[2] *A Century of George Eliot Criticism*, London, 1966, p. 37. Dallas's review of *Felix Holt* in the *Times*, June 26, 1866, p. 6, discusses Eliot's place

may seem trivial; to George Eliot, it was not. Gentleman reviewers had patronized lady novelists since the beginning of the nineteenth century; in 1834, for example, the reviewer for *Fraser's* had gloated prematurely over what he believed to be the true authorship of *Castle Rackrent* and *The Absentee*: "Ay: it is just as we expected! Miss Edgeworth *never* wrote *the* Edgeworth novels . . . all that, as we have long had a suspicion, was the work of her father."[3] But the intense concentration on the proper sphere of the woman writer did not appear in criticism until the 1840s. Victorian critics strained their ingenuity for terms that would put delicate emphasis on the specialness of women and avoid the professional neutrality of "woman writer": authoress, female pen, lady novelist, and as late as Hurst & Blackett's 1897 commemorative volume, *Women Novelists of Queen Victoria's Reign*, the elegant "lady fictionists," described by "living mistresses of the craft." Through the 1850s and 1860s there was a great increase in theoretical and specific criticism of women novelists. Hardly a journal failed to publish an essay on women's literature; hardly a critic failed to express himself upon its innate and potential qualities.

This situation, similar to the expanded market for literature by and about women in the late 1960s, suggests that the Victorians were responding to what seemed like a revolutionary, and in many ways a very threatening, phenomenon. As the number of important novels by women increased through the 1850s and 1860s, male journalists were forced to acknowledge that women were excelling in the creation of fiction, not just in England, but also in Europe and America. As it became apparent that Jane Austen and Maria Edgeworth were not aberrations, but the forerunners of female participation in the development of the

---

relative to Jane Austen "among our lady novelists," and concludes, "We don't know any Englishwoman who can be placed near her as a writer of prose."

[3] "A Dozen of Novels," *Fraser's* IX (1834): 483.

novel, jokes about dancing dogs no longer seemed an adequate response.

One form of male resistance, already noted in Chapter II, was to see women novelists as being engaged in a kind of aggressive conspiracy to rob men of their markets, steal their subject matter, and snatch away their young lady readers, to see them as "dominating" because of superior numbers rather than superior abilities. As late as 1851, there were a few hardy souls who continued to deny that women *could* write novels. Coventry Patmore conceded that "there certainly have been cases of women possessed of the properly masculine power of writing books, but these cases are all so truly and obviously exceptional, and must and ought always to remain so, that we may overlook them without the least prejudice to the soundness of our doctrine."[4] Some reviewers found the situation so embarrassing that they had to treat it as an unfortunate accident. In 1853 J. M. Ludlow glumly advised his readers, "We have to notice the fact that at this particular moment of the world's history the very *best* novels in several great countries happen to have been written by women."[5] But by 1855, even before the appearance of George Eliot, the emergence of the woman's novel was so striking that most readers and reviewers would have agreed with Margaret Oliphant in linking it to other symptoms of social progress: "This, which is the age of so many things—of enlightenment, of science, of progress— is quite as distinctly the age of female novelists."[6]

Even those critics who disapproved of changes in the doctrine of the two sexual spheres were far from advocating women's retirement from the literary field. The new questions of women's *place* in literature proved endlessly fascinating, and the Victorians approached them with all the

[4] "The Social Position of Women," *North British Review* XIV (1851): 281.

[5] "Ruth," *North British Review* XIX (1853): 90.

[6] "Modern Novelists—Great and Small," *Blackwoods* LXXVII (1855): 555.

weight of their religious commitments and their interest in the sciences of human nature. Although most periodical criticism, especially between 1847 and 1875, employed a double standard for men's and women's writing and seemed shocked or chagrined by individual women's failures to conform to the stereotypes, a few critics, notably G. H. Lewes, George Eliot, and R. H. Hutton, were beginning to consider what women as a group might contribute to the art of the novel.

Most of the negative criticism tried to justify the assumption that novels by women would be recognizably inferior to those by men. When the Victorians thought of the woman writer, they immediately thought of the female body and its presumed afflictions and liabilities. They did so, first, because the biological creativity of childbirth seemed to them directly to rival the aesthetic creativity of writing. The metaphors of childbirth familiarly invoked to describe the act of writing directed attention toward the possibility of real conflict between these analogous experiences. In an 1862 review of Mrs. Browning, Gerald Massey wrote: "It is very doubtful if the highest and richest nature of woman can ever be unfolded in its home life and wedded relationships, and yet at the same time blossom and bear fruit in art or literature with a similar fulness. What we mean is, that there is so great a draft made upon women by other creative works, so as to make the chance very small that the general energy shall culminate in the greatest musician, for example. The nature of woman demands *that* to perfect it in life which must half-lame it for art. A mother's heart, at its richest, is not likely to get adequate expression in notes and bars, if it were only for the fact that she must be absorbed in other music."[7]

Second, there was a strong belief that the female body was in itself an inferior instrument, small, weak, and, in Geraldine Jewsbury's words, "liable to collapses, eclipses,

[7] "Last Poems and Other Works of Mrs. Browning," *North British Review* XXXVI (1862): 271.

failures of power . . . unfitting her for the steady stream of ever-recurring work."[8] Victorian physicians and anthropologists supported these ancient prejudices by arguing that women's inferiority could be demonstrated in almost every analysis of the brain and its functions. They maintained that, like the "lower races," women had smaller and less efficient brains, less complex nerve development, and more susceptibility to certain diseases, than did men. Any expenditure of mental energy by women would divert the supply of blood and phosphates from the reproductive system to the brain, leading to dysmenorrhea, "ovarian neuralgia," physical degeneracy, and sterility. Physicians estimated that "maternal functions diverted nearly 20 percent of women's vital energies from potential brain activity."[9]

Female intellectual distinction thus suggested not only a self-destructive imitation of a male skill but also a masculine physical development. Elizabeth Barrett referred in a general way to this widespread association when she apostrophized her heroine, George Sand, as "thou large-brained woman and large-hearted man," but it was often used more snidely in allusions to George Eliot's "large hand" and "large eye"—metaphors of artistic mastery that invariably suggested to the Victorians large noses and large feet.[10] This physical imagery was further popularized by Victorian phrenologists like George Combe, who believed creative traits to be revealed by the shape of the skull. The bizarre theories of the phrenologists and the quacks were reinforced by the expertise of scientists like James Macgrigor Allan, who stated dogmatically to his fellow anthropologists in 1869 that "in intellectual labour, man has surpassed, does

[8] Introduction to *The Half-Sisters*, London, 3 vols., 1848.

[9] John S. Haller and Robin M. Haller, *The Physician and Sexuality in Victorian America*, Urbana, 1974, pp. 65–66.

[10] Browning's sonnet, "To George Sand: A Desire" (1844), was frequently cited by critics of women novelists. Gerald Massey writes that Eliot "lay hold of life with a large hand, looked at it with a large eye, and felt it with a large heart" ("Last Poems and Other Works of Mrs. Browning," 271).

now and always will surpass woman, for the obvious reason that nature does not periodically interrupt his thought and application."[11] Advanced thinkers were influenced by these ideas even if they rejected them. George Eliot wondered whether women's lack of originality might be attributable to her brain structure: "The voltaic-pile is not strong enough to produce crystallization."[12] Mill, refuting the brain-weight argument in *The Subjection of Women*, thought it necessary to mention that the heaviest brain on record belonged to a woman.[13]

Although women writers often believed that they did labor under innate handicaps of mind and body, they nonetheless felt pressured to prove both their reliability and their physical endurance. What women must demonstrate, Eliot wrote, is the capability for "accurate thought, severe study, and continuous self-command."[14] As they met deadlines, edited magazines, and coped with the strenuous burdens of part-publication and serialization, women writers expressed more openly their irritation with those sisters who exploited the old stereotypes of weakness and sickliness. In reviewing Harriet Martineau's *Autobiography* in 1877, for example, Mrs. Oliphant could not conceal her annoyance at Martineau's woeful claim that overwork had destroyed her health and would send her to an early grave. Oliphant commented that "many a hard literary worker will smile at these tremendous prognostications."[15] Similarly,

[11] "On the Real Differences in the Minds of Men and Women," *Journal of the Anthropological Society of London* VII (1869): LXIX. For a discussion of Allan's ideas, see Katharine M. Rogers, *The Troublesome Helpmate: A History of Misogyny in Literature*, London, 1966, pp. 219–221.

[12] "Woman in France," in *Essays of George Eliot*, ed. Thomas Pinney, London, 1963, p. 56.

[13] "The Subjection of Women," in John Stuart Mill and Harriet Taylor Mill, *Essays on Sex Equality*, ed. Alice S. Rossi, Chicago, 1970, ch. 3, p. 199.

[14] "Three Novels," in *Essays of George Eliot*, p. 334.

[15] "Harriet Martineau," *Blackwood's* CXXI (1877): 487.

women physicians like Alice Putnam Jacobi made a point of debating male doctors on the question of female health and of correcting some of their more peculiar assumptions. Even so, arguments from physiology retained sufficient force in 1929 to lead Virginia Woolf to ignore a century of three-deckers and suggest that women's physical weakness meant that they should write shorter books than men.[16]

Another explanation given in criticism for the inferiority of female literature was women's limited experience. Vast preserves of masculine life—schools, universities, clubs, sports, businesses, government, and the army—were closed to women. Research and industry could not make up for these exclusions, and, as indicated in *Fraser's*, women writers were at a disadvantage: "A man's novel is generally a more finished production than a woman's; his education and experience give him a wider range of thought and a larger choice of character, and he usually groups his personages and incidents more artistically, and writes better English than his rivals."[17] As a form of social realism and a medium for moral and ethical thought, the novel obviously required maturity and mobility in its creators. Further, it required a complete set of emotions. Since the Victorians had defined women as angelic beings who could not feel passion, anger, ambition, or honor, they did not believe that women could express more than half of life. E. S. Dallas proclaimed it "evident that from that inexperience of life, which no amount of imagination, no force of sympathy, can ever compensate, women labour under serious disadvantages in attempting the novel."[18]

Denied participation in public life, women were forced to cultivate their feelings and to overvalue romance. In the novels, emotion rushed in to fill the vacuum of experience, and critics found this intensity, this obsession with personal

[16] *A Room of One's Own*, London, 1945, p. 134.

[17] "Novels of the Day," LXII (1860): 205.

[18] "Currer Bell," *Blackwood's* LXXXII (1857): 79. See also "The Lady Novelists of Great Britain," *Gentleman's Magazine*, n.s. XL (1853): 18–25.

relationships, unrealistic and even oppressive. The chief fault of Julia Kavanagh's *Daisy Burns*, according to the *Westminster*, was the fatiguingly sustained high pitch of emotion that it shared with other novels by women: "Human nature is not so constituted as to be able to keep a never-failing fountain of tears always at work; deep passion and wild sorrow pass over us—whom do they spare?—but they are not the grand occupation of our lives, still less the chief object of them."[19] The question of *whose* lives were so occupied is neglected here; the reviewer writes from the masculine perspective. Harriet Martineau, George Eliot, Mrs. Oliphant, and Florence Nightingale also criticized the overemphasis on love and passion in feminine fiction, but they understood that lack of education, isolation, and boredom had distorted women's values and channeled creative energy into romantic fantasy and emotional self-dramatization.

The simplistic psychology and naive religious optimism characteristic of some feminine writing reflected a female subculture in which confirmation in the church was often the most dramatic external event between the schoolroom and marriage; church-organized charity work, the only activity outside the home; and piety, the speciality of women and children. Reviewers deplored the immaturity of the fiction but could not bring themselves to do away with or expand the role. Charles Dickens and Wilkie Collins parodied the Puseyite fanaticism of Charlotte Yonge's *Heir of Redclyffe* in *Household Words*; even Guy's death scene they found "marred or made obscured, either by the writer's want of experience of human nature, or utter uncompatability of abstraction from one narrow circle of ideas."[20] W. R. Greg, although he abhorred the "false morality of

[19] "The Progress of Fiction as an Art," *Westminster Review*, LX (1853): 372.

[20] "Doctor Dulcamara, M.P.," in *The Uncollected Writings of Charles Dickens: Household Words, 1850–1859*, II, ed. Harry Stone, London, 1969.

THE DOUBLE CRITICAL STANDARD

lady novelists," their faith in the expedience of self-sacrifice and in the workings of providence, could not see how women's ethical horizons could be much expanded: "If the writer be a young lady, whole spheres of observation, whole branches of character and conduct, are almost inevitably closed to her."[21]

While it was theoretically possible for women novelists to write about female physical experience, including childbirth and maternal psychology, they faced many obstacles to self-expression in their own sphere. Victorian women were taught to keep these experiences to themselves, to record them in very private diaries (such as Mrs. Gaskell's diary about her first child, Marianne), or to share them in intimate friendships with one or two other women. There were strong taboos against sharing them with men. As one historian explains: "From early childhood, girls . . . were taught self-effacement and modesty, were encouraged to feel shame about their bodies, and were advised to try to 'hide' the natural conditions of menstruation and pregnancy. The single woman of the middle-class was forced to deceit if she was to taste any of the freedom of knowledge given her brothers. The married woman of the class was constantly told not to trouble her husband with her own petty problems, to bear the pain of illness in silence, and to prevent knowledge of all indelicate matters from reaching 'innocent' ears."[22] Women educated to perceive themselves, in the popular horticultural imagery of the period, as lilies-of-the-valley or violets seeking the shade were understandably ambivalent about the self-revelation necessary in fiction.[23] The conflict between art and self-exposure, rather

[21] "The False Morality of Lady Novelists," *National Review* VII (1859): 148.

[22] Mary S. Hartman, introduction to *Victorian Murderesses: A True History of Thirteen Respectable French and English Women Accused of Unspeakable Crimes*, New York, 1976. I am indebted to Mary Hartman for allowing me to read her book in manuscript.

[23] See, for example, Miss M. A. Stodart, quoted in Inga-Stina Ewbank, *Their Proper Sphere: A Study of the Brontë Sisters as Early-Vic-*

than any physical weakness, probably accounts for the stress symptoms of sickness and headache suffered by novelists like Geraldine Jewsbury, who fell ill each time she completed a book and finally gave up writing fiction on her doctor's orders.

Victorian critics agreed that if women were going to write at all they should write novels. Yet this assessment, too, denigrated and resisted feminine achievement. Theories of female aptitude for the novel tended to be patronizing, if not downright insulting. The least difficult, least demanding response to the superior woman novelist was to see the novel as an instrument that transformed feminine weaknesses into narrative strengths. Women were obsessed by sentiment and romance; well, these were the staples of fiction. Women had a natural taste for the trivial; they were sharp-eyed observers of the social scene; they enjoyed getting involved in other people's affairs. All these alleged female traits, it was supposed, would find a happy outlet in the novel. "Women," wrote E. S. Dallas, "have a talent for personal discourse and familiar narrative, which, when properly controlled, is a great gift, although too frequently it degenerates into a social nuisance."[24] Such an approach was particularly attractive because it implied that women's writing was as artless and effortless as birdsong, and therefore not in competition with the more rational male eloquence.

To critics who sentimentalized and trivialized women's interest in psychological motivation, the novel was the inevitable crystallization of femininity. The spectacle of J. M. Ludlow, straining to explain away Mrs. Gaskell and her sis-

---

torian Female Novelists, London, 1966, p. 39: "Publicity can, to woman, never be a native element; she may be forced into it by circumstances, but the secret sigh of every truly feminine heart will be for the retirement of private life. The lily of the valley which shields itself under the huge high leaf, the violet which seeks the covert of the shady hedge, may both be forced from under their retreat, and be compelled to stand in the broad open sunshine, but will not their withered and blighted petals tell us that they are pining for the congenial shade?"

[24] "Currer Bell," *Blackwood's* LXXXII (1857): 77.

ter writers without appearing ungentlemanly or making any concessions about female intelligence, is an instructive illustration:

> Now, if we consider the novel to be the picture of human life in a pathetic, or as some might prefer the expression, in a sympathetic form, that is to say, addressed to human feeling, rather than to human taste, judgment, or reason, there seem nothing paradoxical in the view, that women are called to the mastery of this peculiar field of literature. We know, all of us, that if man is the head of humanity, woman is its heart; and as soon as education has rendered her ordinarily capable of expressing feeling in written words, why should we be surprised to find that her words come more home to us than those of men, where feeling is chiefly concerned?[25]

By eliminating from his definition of the novel all the qualities he could not bring himself to see in women, Ludlow could accept even his own response to women's novels without having to modify any of his stereotypes. So intent was he on showing the perfect compatability of the stereotype and the product that he could dismiss the question of "expressing feeling in written words" as the merest trick of the literate. Rather than protesting against such criticism, women writers, as we have seen, reinforced it by playing down the effort behind their writing, and trying to make their work appear as the spontaneous overflow of their womanly emotions. This strategy was partly a way of minimizing the professional and intellectual aspects of the work, and partly a way of describing the powerful drives for self-expression that, especially for feminine novelists like Mrs. Oliphant, made the act of writing initially a possession by the muse: "I have written because it gave me pleasure, because it came natural to me."[26]

25 "Ruth," *North British Review*, XIX (1853): 90.
26 Robert Colby and Vineta Colby, *The Equivocal Virtue: Mrs. Oliphant and the Victorian Literary Marketplace*, Hamden, Connecticut, 1966, p. 5.

The feminine subcultural ideology did, however, have strengths as well as weaknesses. Men like Ludlow and Dallas, and even Hutton, may have regarded fiction as a form of repressive desublimation for women, a safe and suitable channel for energies that might otherwise have been turned to business, politics, religion, and revolutionary action. But feminine novelists, as Lorna Sage brilliantly suggests, came to take their role as the educators of the heart very seriously, so that "while deferring to male knowledge and power, they subtly revise and undermine the world from which they are excluded." Sage describes how Margaret Hale in Mrs. Gaskell's *North and South*, for example, quietly introduces the industrialist Mr. Thornton to the feminine values of domestic duty, familial loyalty, and personal affection, so that gradually his discussions of political economy, collective action, and violent strikes recede into the background. Gaskell transposes the political into "local, individual terms, much as she tames Mr. Thornton and redirects his savage energies into private life."[27] I would add to Sage's observations the fact that the women's victories are economic as well as emotional. Like Jane Eyre and Shirley Helstone, Margaret not only tames Thornton but also, in a final humiliation, endows him with her legacy so that he can pay off his debts and keep his mill. To get a great deal of money and to give it to a man for his work was the feminine heroine's apotheosis, the ultimate in the power of self-sacrifice.

One of the most persistent denigrations of women novelists was the theory that only unhappy and frustrated women wrote books. G. H. Lewes, writing in 1852, was one of the earliest to analyze the "compensatory" nature of female literature:

If the accidents of her position make her solitary and inactive, or if her thwarted affections shut her somewhat from that sweet domestic and maternal sphere to which her whole being spontaneously moves, she turns to litera-

[27] "The Case of the Active Victim," *Times Literary Supplement* (July 26, 1974): 803–804.

ture as to another sphere. . . . The happy wife and busy mother are only forced into literature by some hereditary organic tendency, stronger even than the domestic.[28]

In 1862, Gerald Massey repeated Lewes' point: "Women who are happy in all home-ties and who amply fill the sphere of their love and life, must, in the nature of things, very seldom become writers."[29] And the same idea, in almost the same words, was still cropping up as late as 1892; Catherine J. Hamilton's introduction to *Women Writers: Their Works and Ways* concurs: "Happy women, whose hearts are satisfied and full, have little need of utterance. Their lives are rounded and complete, they require nothing but the calm recurrence of those peaceful home duties in which domestic women rightly feel that their true vocation lies."

Feminine novelists responded to these innuendos of inferiority, as to others, not by protest but by vigorous demonstration of their domestic felicity. They worked hard to present their writing as an extension of their feminine role, an activity that did not detract from their womanhood, but in some sense augmented it. This generation would not have wanted an office or even "a room of one's own"; it was essential that the writing be carried out in the home, and that it be only one among the numerous and interruptible household tasks of the true woman. Mrs. Gaskell wrote in her dining-room with its four doors opening out to all parts of the house; Mrs. Oliphant half-complained and half-boasted that she had never had a study, but had worked in "the little 2nd drawing room where all the (feminine) life of the house goes on."[30] When interviewers came to visit, Mrs. Linton would display her embroidered cushions, fire-

---

[28] "The Lady Novelists," *Westminster Review*, n.s. II (1852): 133–134.
[29] "Last Poems of Mrs. Browning," 271.
[30] *Autobiography*, pp. 23–24. In her interviews with Victorian women novelists, Helen Black frequently notes that all evidence of the woman's profession is absent from the home: "Where are the manuscripts, the 'copy,' the 'proofs' . . .? There is no indication of her work on the old oak knee-hole writing table" ("Rhoda Broughton," *Notable Women Authors of the Day*, Glasgow, 1893, p. 40).

screens, and chair-seats; Mrs. Walford would pour tea; Mrs. Oliphant would pose in black silk and lace. Mrs. Craik modestly described the position of the feminine novelists: "We may . . . write shelvesful of books—the errant children of our brain may be familiar half over the known world, and yet we ourselves sit as quiet by our chimney-corner, live a life as simple and peaceful, as any happy common woman of them all."[31]

This grass-roots approach, this domestication of the profession, was also a trap. Women novelists might have banded together and insisted on their vocation as something that made them superior to the ordinary woman, and perhaps even happier. Instead they adopted defensive positions and committed themselves to conventional roles. If womanliness was defined as something that had to be proved, it had to be proved again and again. The feminine writers' self-abasement backfired and caused the kind of patronizing trivialization of their works found in George Smith's obituary of Mrs. Gaskell: "She was much prouder of ruling her household well . . . than of all she did in those writings."[32]

Even a sophisticated critic like Lewes, who believed that a full knowledge of life was dependent upon the depiction of feminine as well as masculine experience, had difficulties in separating a theory of female literature from his own sexual stereotypes. In his significantly titled pre–George Eliot essay, "The Lady Novelists," Lewes begins with the "abstract heights" of female "nature," rather than with the empirical evidence of female achievement:

The domestic experience which forms the bulk of woman's knowledge finds an appropriate form in novels; while the very nature of fiction calls for that predominance of Sentiment which we have already attributed to the feminine mind. Love is the staple of fiction, for it "forms the

[31] *A Woman's Thoughts About Women*, London, 1858, p. 58.

[32] "Mrs. Gaskell and Her Novels," *Cornhill Magazine* xxix (1874): 192.

story of a woman's life." The joys and sorrows of affection, the incidents of domestic life, assume typical forms in the novel. Hence we may be prepared to find women succeeding better in *finesse* of detail, in pathos and sentiment, while men generally succeed better in the construction of plots and the delineation of character.[33]

Obviously, being "prepared" to find such a polarization of narrative skills would affect critical judgments. When Lewes turns, in a rather whimsical way, to specific writers, he can only discern the combinations of Sentiment and Observation that he has already decided are feminine traits: the signs of gentility, domesticity, and breeding that the title of his article implies. For Lewes, as for other Victorian critics, women of genius did not require a modification in sexual theory; the apparent exception was readily seen to be charmingly and ineffectually disguising her true womanhood. Thus, Jane Austen's books are first and foremost "novels written by a woman, an Englishwoman, a gentlewoman"; George Sand has vainly "chosen the mask of a man; the features of a woman are everywhere visible"; and Sand's philosophy is "only a reflex of some man whose ideas she has adopted."[34] When he gets to Charlotte Brontë, Lewes has a moment's trouble with his categories, but he reminds the reader that if one is not "blinded" by the masculine force of *Jane Eyre*, one can perceive the "rare powers of observation" that stamp it as feminine.[35]

A much more successful effort to define a theory of female literature was Richard Holt Hutton's "Novels by the Authoress of 'John Halifax,' " which appeared in the *North British Review* in 1858. Hutton, who later became a percipient and responsible critic of George Eliot, used his review of Dinah Mulock to analyze "the main characteristics on which feminine fictions, as distinguished from those of men, are strong or defective." Hutton began his article with

[33] "The Lady Novelists," 133.
[34] Ibid., 135, 136.   [35] Ibid., 139.

practical criticism and moved outward toward the theoretical; although he would obviously have come out with different views with Austen or Brontë, rather than Mulock, as his chief example, his inductive method was a good one, and he was careful to keep his generalizations narrow. Hutton recognized the problems of choosing a representative female author, and explained that Mulock had been selected chiefly because she was not a genius, but a competent writer who might better represent "the kind of faculty which is potential or actual in most clever women."[36]

Hutton agreed with Lewes that "feminine ability has found for itself a far more suitable sphere in novel-writing than in any other branch of literature,"[37] but he attributed the predilection of women's deficiencies in intellectual training and discipline, rather than to any positive correlation between female psychology and narrative realism. For the philosophical modes that he valued most highly, he thought, women substituted documentation, a copious circumstantial descriptiveness. Observation thus could be seen not as an innate feminine gift but as a developed compensatory skill. Hutton theorized that differences in masculine and feminine education and intellectual processes had led to two poles of narrative structure. In men's novels some kind of philosophy, some general idea, dictated the artistic composition of the narrative. The characters were placed in this broad intellectual framework, like Waverley in Scott's contrasts of past and present, or Becky in Thackeray's satire. Women's novels, on the other hand, concentrated on the characters themselves. Reader identification with the characters gave those novels a special intensity, but one that was transitory since it was intellectually limited. By these standards, Hutton defined Dickens as a "feminine" writer, one of the many indications in his article that he was not insisting on rigid biologically sexual terms.

[36] "Novels by the Authoress of *John Halifax*," *North British Review* XXIX (1858): 254, 255.
[37] Ibid., 254.

Yet "feminine" is always a pejorative term for Hutton. He found that even in delineating character, their speciality, women were at a serious disadvantage, partly because of changing fashions in the novel:

> In many ways, the natural limitations of feminine power are admirably adapted to the standard of fiction held up as the true model of a feminine novelist in the last century. It was then thought sufficient to present finished sketches of character, just as it appeared under the ordinary restraints of society; while the deeper passions and spiritual impulses, which are the springs of all the higher drama of real life, were, at most, only allowed so far to suffuse the narrative as to tinge it with the excitement necessary for a novel.[38]

In other words, when readers began to look to fiction for a more ambitious realism, for psychological analysis, and for intellectual subtlety, women were handicapped by the social pressures of feminine gentility. Women were expert at rendering the surface, but art now required an exploration of the springs of life.

Like Lewes and Mill, Hutton felt that lack of imagination was the "main deficiency of feminine genius": "It can observe, it can recombine, it can delineate, but it cannot trust itself farther: it cannot leave the world of characteristic traits and expressive manner, so as to imagine and paint successfully the distinguishable, but not easily distinguished, world out of which those characteristics grew."[39] Because they were unable to speculate about motivations, to project themselves into the unseen interiors of their characters, particularly their male characters, women writers, Hutton thought, were increasingly being forced into use of the autobiographical form to give their books superficial unity and a center of imaginative authenticity. Although a vivid central character based on personal experience seemed to

[38] Ibid., 257.   [39] Ibid., 258.

89

be within their abilities, women's concentration on such a character could wreck the novel's aesthetic balance.

Hutton traced this deficiency in imagination to cultural circumstance rather than to nature. Women were at a disadvantage, first, because their direct experience was so limited; and second, because they were poorly educated, especially in the masculine fields of science, economics, and philosophy, which developed the ability to generalize and theorize: "The same mind that has been trained to go apart with laws of matter, and laws of wealth, and laws of intellect, and to elaborate them as if no outer world for the time existed at all, also enables men to go apart with conceptions of character."[40] On the other hand, Hutton thought, "the patient and pliant genius" of women enabled them to deal with the evolution and gradual growth of character; because of this ability to portray growth, writers such as Mulock or Charlotte Yonge could deal with moral and spiritual problems without becoming didactic.

Hutton had to modify some of these views when George Eliot appeared on the scene, and he might have modified them sooner if he had understood *Jane Eyre*, *Villette*, or *Wuthering Heights*. But literary stereotypes adapted very slowly to any real evidence of feminine achievement. If we break down the categories that are the staple of Victorian periodical reviewing, we find that women writers were acknowledged to possess sentiment, refinement, tact, observation, domestic expertise, high moral tone, and knowledge of female character; and thought to lack originality, intellectual training, abstract intelligence, humor, self-control, and knowledge of male character. Male writers had most of the desirable qualities: power, breadth, distinctness, clarity, learning, abstract intelligence, shrewdness, experience, humor, knowledge of everyone's character, and open-mindedness.

This double standard was so widely accepted through

40 Ibid., 260.

about 1875 that critics and readers automatically employe it in the game of literary detection. Approaching an anonymous or pseudonymous novel, reviewers would break it down into its elements, label these masculine or feminine, and add up the total. The predominance of masculine or feminine elements determined the sex of the author. As a critical instrument this practice was not very reliable; considering the odds based on chance alone, the percentage of correct guesses is not impressive. Male writers were occasionally misidentified as women. R. D. Blackmore's first novel, *Clara Vaughan* (1864), had a female narrator; and the *Saturday Review*, convinced they had detected an authoress, used the opportunity for an attack on maidenly ignorance: "Another decided feature by which our lady novelists are wont to betray the secret of their authorship is the characteristic mode in which they unconsciously make sport of the simplest principles of physics, and of the most elementary rules or usages of the law."[41] Blackmore had practiced law in London for five years. But even embarrassing errors such as this could not persuade reviewers that the sexual double standard needed revision.

Jane Eyre was published in 1847; and *Adam Bede*, in 1859. Both novels appeared under pseudonyms, and on both occasions critics were baffled by qualities in the novels that could not be simplistically defined as masculine or feminine. When the authors behind the pseudonyms were revealed to be women, critics were dismayed. The main difference between the two episodes was that Charlotte Brontë had been shocked, dismayed, and hurt to discover that her realism struck others as improper; George Eliot had seen what had happened to Charlotte Brontë, and was prepared.

Early critics of *Jane Eyre* were obsessed with discovering the sex of Currer Bell. "The whole reading-world of

[41] Quoted by Waldo Dunn in *R. D. Blackmore*, London, 1956, p. 112. See also Kenneth Budd, *The Last Victorian: R. D. Blackmore and His Novels*, London, 1960, p. 33.

England was in a ferment to discover the unknown author. . . . Every little incident mentioned in the book was turned this way and that to answer, if possible, the much-vexed question of sex."[42] Incidents included clothes, domestic details, and conversations. Harriet Martineau, for example, determined on the basis of chapter 16, in which Grace Poole sews curtain rings on Rochester's bed drapings, that the book "could have been written only by a woman or an upholsterer."[43] Circumstantial evidence aside, the presentation of female sexuality and human passion disturbed and amazed readers. If Currer Bell was a woman, they could not imagine what sort of woman she might be. Even while critics acknowledged the presence of genius, they felt stunned by its unconventionality. The *Christian Remembrancer* declared that it would be hard to find "a book more unfeminine, both in its excellencies and its defects . . . in the annals of female authorship." According to Lewes, "a more masculine book in the sense of vigour was never written."[44] Others, like the American E. P. Whipple, were "gallant enough to detect the hand of a gentleman" in composing the "profanity, brutality, and slang."[45] The relationship between Rochester and Jane, and Jane's admission of passion for her married employer, could not be accepted. Thus one sees over and over in the reviews words like "sensual," "gross," and "animal." Tom Winnifrith, who has written a comprehensive study of the reception of *Jane Eyre*, has the impression that the most hostile reviews were written by women.[46]

The appearance of Mrs. Gaskell's *Life of Charlotte Brontë* while the novelist's fame was at its posthumous

---

[42] Elizabeth Gaskell, *The Life of Charlotte Brontë*, London, 1973, pp. 230–231.

[43] Harriet Martineau, *Autobiography*, II, London, 1877, p. 324.

[44] "Jane Eyre," *Christian Remembrancer* XV (1848); "Currer Bell's Shirley," *Edinburgh Review* XCI (1850): 158.

[45] "Novels of the Season," *North American Review* LXVII (1848): 357.

[46] *The Brontës and Their Background: Romance and Reality*, London, 1973, p. 125. Mrs. Gaskell noted that "*women* infinitely more than men" disapproved of *Ruth* as well (*Letters*, p. 226).

height convinced critics that Brontë could not have been guilty of immorality, and also provided them with some explanations for her knowledge of passion. The *Saturday Review* was happy to exonerate Charlotte and to blame her education in Brussels for the unfeminine sophistication of the novels:

> Women regarded her novels with that sort of fluttering alarm which is always awakened in unpolluted breasts by the signs of a knowledge greater than their own. Men recognized the truthful touches which these novels contained, but wondered how they came to be there, for the general purity of their tone refuted the notion that they were the symptoms of depravity. . . . We cannot doubt that Miss Brontë derived an instruction which to a less noble, unstained and devotional mind might have been perilous, from her residence in a foreign school, her observation of foreign manners, and her analysis of the thoughts of foreigners.[47]

The *Quarterly Review* looked closer to home, at the influence of Branwell, "thoroughly depraved himself, and tainting the thoughts of all within his sphere."[48] Many readers, including Charlotte Yonge, felt that Branwell's influence on his sisters had been dastardly, but they found it comfortably in accordance with their notions of male and female temperament.

George Eliot, as the editor of the *Westminister Review* and the translator of Strauss and Feuerbach, had already offended conservative factions. As the mistress of Lewes, she had put herself outside the boundaries of Victorian respectability. Thus she risked more critical hostility by revealing herself than Charlotte Brontë did, as she, Lewes, and the publisher Blackwood were well aware. It was the example of *Jane Eyre*, however, that Lewes cited in explaining the pseudonym to Blackwood: "When *Jane Eyre* was

[47] "The Professor," III (1857): 550.
[48] James Craigie Robertson, "Eliot's Novels," CVIII (1860): 470.

finally known to be a woman's book, the tone [of criticism] noticeably changed."[49] Furor about the sex of the author characterized the publication of *Adam Bede*, as it had the publication of Eliot's first, less successful book, *Scenes from Clerical Life*. With a few distinguished exceptions, reviewers believed George Eliot to be a clerical gentleman. The *Saturday Review* later confessed, "to speak the simple truth, without affectation or politeness, it [*Adam Bede*] was thought to be too good for a woman's story."[50]

Barbara Bodichon and Anne Mozley were among those who guessed the truth. Bodichon, a radical feminist, rejoiced in the authorship as a triumph for womanhood: "1. That a woman should write a wise and *humorous* book which should take a place by Thackeray. 2. That YOU *that you* whom they spit at should do it!"[51] Anne Mozley, the reviewer for *Bentley's Quarterly Review*, was certain that the book was a woman's in spite of its felicity, force, and freedom of expression because it was written by an outsider, an observer: "The knowledge of female nature is feminine, not only in its details, which might be borrowed from other eyes, but in its whole tone of feeling . . . the position of the writer towards every point in discussion is a woman's position, that is, from a stand of observation rather than more active participation." Her review went on to cite other evidence of female culture as proof that a woman had written the book: "the knowledge of female nature . . . the full close scrutiny of observation . . . acquaintance with form life in its minute particulars . . . the secure ground . . . in matters of domestic housewifery." Finally, Mozley triumphantly cited, "women are known dearly to love a 'well-directed moral.' "[52] Mozley's analysis was shrewd and per-

---

[49] Gordon S. Haight, *George Eliot: A Biography*, London, 1968, p. 268.

[50] "The Mill on the Floss," IX (1860): 470.

[51] Letter of April 26, 1859, in *The George Eliot Letters*, III, ed. Gordon S. Haight, London, 1954, p. 56.

[52] "Adam Bede and Recent Novels," I (1859): 436–437.

ceptive. The brilliant conjectures of the *Westminster Review*, however, were not; the editor, John Chapman, had learned the secret from Herbert Spencer. He nevertheless congratulated himself on his prescience when the pseudonym was revealed to the public in 1860.[53]

Lewes hoped that the pseudonym had won the book a fair reading; to Barbara Bodichon he wrote: "They can't now unsay their admiration." But he was wrong. At least one journal went back for a second look. William Hepworth Dixon, the editor of the *Athenaeum* (who sometimes reviewed his own books under a pseudonym), wrote a vicious notice for the gossip column: "It is time to end this pother about the authorship of 'Adam Bede.' The writer is in no sense a great unknown; the tale, if bright in parts, and such as a clever woman with an observant eye and unschooled moral nature might have written, has no great quality of any kind."[54] With the appearance of *The Mill on the Floss*, criticism of George Eliot noticeably changed and cheapened; it placed her among the "modern female novelists" and judged her by the collective standards. The *Saturday Review* was "not sure that it is quite consistent with feminine delicacy to lay so much stress on the bodily feelings of the other sex."[55] The *Quarterly* went back to its sneers at female ignorance: "There are traces of knowledge which is not usual among women (although some of the classical quotations might at least have been more correctly printed)."[56]

[53] See "The Mill on the Floss," *Westminster Review* LXXIV (1860): 24–33.

[54] Haight, *George Eliot*, pp. 290–291. For an account of Dixon, see Leslie Marchand, *The Athenaeum: A Mirror of Victorian Culture*, Chapel Hill, 1941, p. 80.

[55] "The Mill on the Floss," 471.

[56] James Craigie Robertson, "George Eliot's Novels," CVIII (1860): 471. "The parenthetical hint that the 'classical quotations' in my books might be 'more correctly printed' is an amusing example of the genuineness that belongs to review-writing in general, since there happens to be only *one* classical quotation in them all," Eliot wrote John Blackwood (February 20, 1860; *Letters*, III, pp. 356–357).

The Brontës, in their radical innocence, confronted all sexually biased criticism head-on. Charlotte constantly had to be restrained by her publishers from attacking critics in the prefaces to her books, and she frequently wrote directly to reviewers and journals in protest. She admonished the critic of the *Economist*: "To you I am neither man nor woman. I come before you as an author only. It is the sole standard by which you have a right to judge me—the sole ground on which I accept your judgment."[57] Anne Brontë prefaced the second edition of *Wildfell Hall* with a defiant declaration of equal literary rights: "I am satisfied that if the book is a good one, it is so whatever the sex of the author may be." George Eliot stopped reading reviews of her books when criticism became personal; all were vetted by Lewes. However, one sees signs of self-censorship both in her shift after 1860 to less autobiographical fiction, and in her careful elimination of possible double entendres in proof.

George Eliot was virtually alone among feminine novelists in speculating about the psychological and moral impact of women's experience on the structure and content of the novel. She found most of the feminine literature of her day inept and derivative, and wondered "how women have the courage to write and publishers the spirit to buy at a high price the false and feeble representations of life and characters that most feminine novels give."[58] She considered some of the literature inauthentic, "an absurd exaggeration of the masculine style, like the swaggering gait of a bad actress in male attire."[59] In "Silly Novels by Lady Novelists," Eliot denounced the covert victories of feminine values, the fantasies of instant intellectual mastery and intuitive spiritual authority. She understood that the habits of the professional were at variance with the indoctrination

[57] Shorter, *The Brontës*, II, pp. 63–64.
[58] Quoted in Ewbank, *Their Proper Sphere*, p. 12.
[59] "Woman in France," *Essays of George Eliot*, p. 53.

of women, but, in literature, as in other activities, she wished women to substitute "the hard drudgery of real practice" for feminine fantasy and self-indulgence.[60] Eliot also believed, however, that women writers had a "precious speciality, lying quite apart from masculine aptitudes and experience," a speciality that was grounded in the maternal emotions.[61] Somehow, she thought, the maternal affections would lead to "distinctive forms and combinations" in the novel.[62]

The feminine novelists did share the cultural values of Victorian middle-class women, and they clung to the traditional notion of femininity. They were not, however, simply ordinary women who happened to write books; they were different from the start. Lewes and Massey were partly correct that "happy wives and busy mothers" did not become writers, but they failed to understand that women with strong imaginative drives and achievement needs could not be content with domesticity. Even those women writers who began to work because they needed to earn money soon found themselves changed by the disciplines and rewards of the profession. They were not like "any happy common woman"; they were more organized, more businesslike, more assertive, more adventurous, more flexible, and more in control of their lives.

Being Victorian women, they were concerned about these changes in themselves. Geraldine Jewsbury worried about the psychological transformations of female professionalism both in her letters to Jane Carlyle and in her novels. In the latter, she put her own doubts, ludicrously exaggerated, into the mouths of libertines and rogues: "The intrinsic value of a woman's work out of her own sphere is nothing, and what are the qualities developed to make up for it? . . . The bloom and charm of her innocence is gone;

[60] "Three Novels," *Essays of George Eliot*, p. 334.
[61] "Silly Novels by Lady Novelists," *Essays of George Eliot*, p. 324.
[62] "Woman in France," p. 53.

97

she has gained a dogmatic, harsh, self-sufficing vanity, which she calls principle; she strides and stalks through life, neither one thing nor another."[63]

Critics, too, wondered if the women novelists had removed themselves so far from the sphere of the common woman that they had lost the power to describe it. Richard Simpson pointed out some of the obvious problems in a review of George Eliot:

> Though she ought to be able to draw women in herself, for the simple reason that she is a woman, yet she may be too far separated from the ordinary life of her sex to be a good judge of its relations. The direct power and the celebrity of authorship may obscure and replace the indirect influence and calm happiness of domestic feminine life. For admiration and affection do not easily combine. Celebrity isolates the authoress, and closes her heart; it places her where experience of the ordinary relations of the sex is impossible, and where she is tempted to supply by theory what is lacking in experience. She gives us her view of woman's vocation, and paints things as they ought to be, not as they are. Women work more by influence than by force, by example than reasoning, by silence than speech; the authoress grasps at direct power through reasoning and speech. Having thus taken up the male position, the male ideal becomes hers,—the ideal of power,— which expressed by her feminine heart and intellect, means the supremacy of passion in the affairs of the world.[64]

---

[63] *The Half-Sisters*, ii, p. 23.

[64] "George Eliot's Novels," *Home and Foreign Review*, iii (1863), in David Carroll, ed., *George Eliot: The Critical Heritage*, London, 1971, p. 241. See also Coventry Patmore, "The Social Position of Women," *North British Review* xiv (1851): 279: "Books are written by literary men and women, a class whose peculiar temperament very often unfits them for the performance of duties, and the enjoyments of the quiet pleasures of domestic life; and this unfitness too frequently betrays itself in erroneous notions concerning the average condition of the family life."

On the contrary, women novelists had authority to describe the lives of ordinary women, those powerless lives of influence, example, and silence, precisely because they had outgrown them. As critics like Simpson uneasily sensed, they were writing not only to develop direct personal power, but also to change the perceptions and aspirations of their female readers. The strong utilitarian thrust of feminine criticism—what good will this book do us?—was partly the spirit of the age, but it was also a part of the search for new heroines, new role-models, and new lives.

CHAPTER IV

Feminine Heroines: Charlotte Brontë
and George Eliot

WOMEN beginning their literary careers in the 1840s were
seeking heroines—both professional role-models and fictional ideals—who could combine strength and intelligence
with feminine tenderness, tact, and domestic expertise. At
the same time, they perceived themselves and their fictional
heroines as innovators who would provide role-models for
future generations. As Geraldine Jewsbury explained to
Jane Carlyle:

> We are indications of a development of womanhood
> which is not yet recognized. It has, so far, no ready-made
> channels to run in. But still we have looked and tried, and
> found that the present rules for women will not hold us,
> —that something better and stronger is needed. . . .
> There are women to come after us, who will approach
> nearer the fullness of the measure of the stature of a
> woman's nature. I regard myself as a mere faint indica-
> tion, a rudiment of the idea, of certain higher qualities
> and possibilities that are in women.[1]

The feminine novelists needed intimacy with other wom-
en both for inspiration and for sympathetic friendship, but
they were much less likely than male novelists to have personal contact with other professional writers. They took
advantage of such opportunities as came their way: they
corresponded with each other, sought each other out, and
occasionally, like Dinah Craik and Elizabeth Lynn Linton,

[1] Quoted by Virginia Woolf in "Geraldine and Jane", *The Common
Reader*, Second Series, London 1932, pp. 199–200.

100

encouraged younger female disciples. Jewsbury had a si:
who wrote poetry, and found more sisterly support in h
passionate friendship with Jane Carlyle; the Brontë sisters
supported each other. Most women of this generation, however, depended upon literature and the circulating library
to provide the sense of connectedness; fictional heroines
had to take the place of sisters and friends. Ellen Moers
sees this purposeful reading as one of the special professional characteristics of literary women:

> Male writers could study their craft in university or cof-
> fee house, group themselves into movements or coteries,
> search out predecessors for guidance or patronage, col-
> laborate or fight with their contemporaries. But women
> through most of the 19th century were barred from the
> universities, isolated in their own homes, chaperoned in
> travel, painfully restricted in friendship. The normal lit-
> erary life was closed to them. Without it, they studied
> with a special closeness the works written by their own
> sex, and relied on a sense of easy, almost rude familiarity
> with the women who wrote them.[2]

That the feminine novelists learned to make use of the
past and draw confidence from the example of their predecessors does not mean that they simply became adoring
disciples. Women novelists of an older generation, such as
Hannah More, Maria Edgeworth, and even Jane Austen,
were too didactic for a younger group of aspiring professionals. Feminine novelists often believed the popular stereotypes of the old-maid authoress. Elizabeth Barrett, for
example, had been warned by Mary Russell Mitford that
all "literary ladies were ugly. 'I have never met one in my
life,' she wrote, 'that might not have served for a scarecrow
to keep the birds from the cherries.' " Thus, meeting Lady
Dacre in 1838, Barrett expected "a *woman of the masculine
gender*, with her genius very prominent in eccentricity of

[2] Ellen Moers, "Women's Lit: Profession and Tradition," *Columbia
Forum*, 1 (Fall 1972): 28.

manner and sentiments," and was astounded to find instead someone with "as much gentleness and womanliness as if she would be content with being loved."[3]

Jane Austen was an early favorite of male critics, recommended, like a priggish elder sister, to unruly siblings and apprentices. G. H. Lewes recommended Austen to Charlotte Brontë in 1848, but Brontë rejected her as being elegant and confined, "a carefully fenced, highly cultivated garden, with neat borders and delicate flowers."[4] Brontë herself did not wish to submit to pruning and miniaturization. By 1853 Austen's name had become a byword for female literary restraint, as is demonstrated by the protest of a critic for the *Christian Remembrancer*: " 'A writer of the school of Miss Austen' is a much-abused phrase, applied now-a-days by critics who, it is charitable to suppose, have never read Miss Austen's works, to any female writer who composes dull stories without incident, full of level conversation, and concerned with characters of middle life."[5]

Works of female rebels were more inspiring than those of the docile Jane Austen. George Sand's novels of passion were eagerly read (twelve were translated into English in the 1840s). Sand, with her trousers and her lovers, became the counter-culture heroine of many feminine writers. It was Sand whose life suggested how women writers might develop. In an awkward and desperately sincere sonnet, published in 1844 and quoted often throughout the century, Elizabeth Barrett addressed Sand as a tremulous amalgam of genius and true womanhood:

> True genius, but true woman! dost deny
> Thy woman's nature with a manly scorn,
> And break away the gauds and armlets worn

[3] *Elizabeth Barrett to Miss Mitford*, ed. Betty Miller, London, 1954, pp. vii, 29–30.

[4] Quoted in Gaskell, *Life of Charlotte Brontë*, London, 1973, ch. XVI, p. 240.

[5] Quoted in Kathleen Tillotson, *Novels of the Eighteen-Forties*, London, 1954, p. 144.

By weaker women in captivity?
Ah, vain denial! That revolted cry
Is sobbed in by a woman's voice forlorn!—
Thy woman's hair, my sister, all unshorn,
Floats back dishevelled strength in agony,
Disproving thy man's name! and while before
The world thou burnest in a poet-fire,
We see thy woman-heart beat evermore
Through the large flame. Beat purer, heart, and higher,
Till God unsex thee on the heavenly shore,
Where unincarnate spirits purely aspire.

Sand became a heroine, not because she had transcended femininity, but because she was involved in the turbulence of womanly suffering. The sonnet's title, "To George Sand: A Recognition," emphasized the feminine writer's need to respond to the "woman-heart" revealing itself in the "poet-fire." The "weaker women in captivity" could recognize the sister behind the man's name.

The feminine writers were thus looking for two kinds of heroines. They wanted inspiring professional role-models; but they also wanted romantic heroines, a sisterhood of shared passion and suffering, women who sobbed and struggled and rebelled. It was very difficult for the Victorians to believe that both qualities could be embodied in the same woman. The simplest resolution would have been find the role-model in life, the heroine in literature, but it did not work out that easily. The tendency of critics, instead, was to polarize the female literary tradition into what we can call the Austen and the Sand lines, and to see subsequent women writers as daughters of Jane or daughters of George.

In rejecting Austen and deciding instead to write about "what throbs fast and full, though hidden, what the blood rushes through, what is the unseen seat of life,"[6] Charlotte

---

[6] Letter of 1850, quoted in Q. D. Leavis, introduction to *Jane Eyre*, Penguin edition, Harmondsworth, 1966, pp. 10–11.

Brontë had chosen a volcanic literature of the body as well as of the heart, a sexual and often supernatural world. She was thus seen as the romantic, the spontaneous artist who "pours forth her feelings . . . without premeditation."[7] George Eliot was seen as the opposite: a writer and a woman in the Austen tradition, studied, intellectual, cultivated. In her reviews of the silly lady novelists, Eliot defined her own professional ideal, the "really cultured woman," who

> is all the simpler and the less obtrusive for her knowledge . . . she does not make it a pedestal from which she flatters herself that she commands a complete view of men and things, but makes it a point of observation from which to form a right estimate of herself. She neither spouts poetry nor quotes Cicero on slight provocation. . . . She does not write books to confound philosophers, perhaps because she is able to write books that delight them. In conversation she is the least formidable of women, because she understands you, without wanting to make you understand that you *can't* understand her.[8]

As Eliot's disparagement (in her *Letters*) of Dinah Mulock, Margaret Oliphant, and Mary Braddon shows, the cultivated woman, while never engaged in overt competition with men, was very much in competition with other women.

By 1860 the Austen-Sand lines had incorporated Brontë and Eliot, so that any woman who published a book could expect to find herself compared to one or the other extreme. Brontë and Eliot themselves were invariably matched with Sand and Austen, with some variation from book to book. It was not until the end of the century that critics pointed out the steady intellectual development in Eliot, and it is only very recently that attention has been paid to the pre-

---

[7] "The Mill on the Floss," *Westminster Review* LXXIV (1860), in *George Eliot: The Critical Heritage*, ed. David Carroll, London, 1971, p. 139.

[8] "Silly Novels by Lady Novelists," in *Essays of George Eliot*, ed. Thomas Pinney, London, 1963, p. 317.

meditated structure and controlled imagery in Brontë's novels. The complacent manner in which the *Saturday Review* tried to reduce George Eliot's originality to an Austen-Brontë hybrid was typical of the Victorian effort to put a woman novelist in her place, in all senses:

> We may think ourselves very fortunate to have a third female novelist not inferior to Miss Austen and Miss Brontë; and it so happens that there is much in the works of this new author that reminds us of these two well-known novelists without anything like copying. George Eliot has a minuteness of painting and a certain archness of style that are quite after the manner of Miss Austen, while the wide scope of her remarks, and her delight in depicting strong and wayward feelings show that she belongs to the generation of Currer Bell.[9]

As Charlotte Brontë and George Eliot increasingly came to dominate their period and to represent the models against which other women novelists were measured, they too became the objects of both feminine adulation and resentment. Feminine novelists could not evade rivalry with Brontë and Eliot, as male novelists could, by restricting them to the women's league. In a letter to Blackwood's pleading the case of her new novel, Mrs. Linton inevitably compared it to *Jane Eyre* and *Adam Bede*; she insisted that it was "not a weaker book than any of these." (It was rejected.)[10] For twenty years, Mrs. Oliphant, who was also published by Blackwood's, had to negotiate subjects in terms of what Eliot was writing (for example, to drop a biography of Savonarola lest it follow too closely on *Romola*) and to hear annoying comparisons of *Salem Chapel* and *Adam Bede*.[11] Oliphant was, however, one of the first to

9 *Saturday Review* IX (April 14, 1860): 470.

10 See Vineta Colby, *The Singular Anomaly: Women Novelists of the Nineteenth Century*, New York, 1970, p. 29.

11 See *Autobiography and Letters of Mrs. M.O.W. Oliphant*, ed. Mrs. Harry Coghill, London, 1899, pp. 185–186, 187–188, 190.

note that *Jane Eyre* had changed the direction of the female tradition: "Perhaps no other writer of her time has impressed her mark so clearly on contemporary literature, or drawn so many followers onto her own peculiar path."[12] Oliphant saw herself as less passionate than Brontë, but also (a source of self-congratulation) as less feminine: "I have had far more experience and, I think, a fuller conception of life. I have learned to take perhaps more a man's view of mortal affairs."[13] Nonetheless, self-esteem was precariously maintained in the shadow of these colossal figures, and those less successful often wondered whether they must forever be content to follow haltingly on Brontë's peculiar path, or build a cottage on the Eliot estate.

Even before the Gaskell biography, contemporaries such as Jane Carlyle and Harriet Martineau had been intrigued by Brontë. In *The Life of Charlotte Brontë*, Gaskell helped create the myth of the novelist as tragic heroine, a myth for which readers had been prepared by *Jane Eyre*. The Brontë legend rapidly took on the psychic properties of a cult, complete with pilgrimages to Haworth and relics of the three sisters. Women novelists like Elizabeth Sewell found the biography a personal document, "intensely, painfully interesting."[14] In America, too, the *Life* became the treasured book of thousands of women.[15] A kind of spiritual identification with the Brontës went so far that in 1872 Harriet Beecher Stowe claimed to have managed a two-hour conversation with Charlotte in a gossipy seance, a "weird & Brontëish" chat, she proudly confided to George Eliot, in which Charlotte had given "a most striking analysis" of Emily.[16] As late as the 1890s, the society novelist Mrs. L. B.

12 "Modern Novelists—Great and Small," *Blackwood's* LXXVII (1855): 568.

13 Oliphant, *Autobiography*, p. 67.

14 *The Autobiography of Elizabeth M. Sewell*, ed. Eleanor C. Sewell, London, 1908, p. 159.

15 See Barbara Bodichon, *An American Diary 1857–58*, ed. Joseph W. Reed, Jr., London, 1972.

16 *The George Eliot Letters*, v, ed. Gordon S. Haight, London, 1955, pp. 280–281. Eliot was skeptical.

Walford liked to show visiting journalists the tea set she had purchased from the Brontë parsonage, and today the London department store Harrods carries an excellent line of Brontë cake and an unlikely Brontë liqueur.

George Eliot was a much more formidable figure. Feminine novelists were compulsively drawn to compare themselves to both Brontë and Eliot, but Brontë exemplified in every sense the bonds of sisterly affection. Eliot was reserved, inaccessible, and opaque. In her maturity she violated the values of sisterly communion in the female subculture by avoiding close friendships with other women writers. She had even violated the essential rule of respectability, and not only gotten away with it but also made a sanctuary of exile. She made a great deal of money and worked under the best of circumstances, with Lewes as her business manager, with an attentive and generous publisher, and eventually with an adoring young husband. Her female contemporaries never faltered in their praise of her books, but they felt excluded from, and envious of, her world. Her very superiority depressed them.

But criticism of the Eliot legend was one of the ways in which feminine novelists were attempting to define themselves. Mrs. Oliphant's *Autobiography* was an unusual experiment in introspection occasioned by the Cross biography of Eliot: "I have been tempted to begin writing by George Eliot's life. . . . I wonder if I am a little envious of her? I always avoid considering formally what my own mind is worth. I have never had any theory on the subject."[17] In *My Literary Life*, Eliza Lynn Linton acidly recalled her early meeting *chez* John Chapman with Marian Evans, who "held her hands and arms kangaroo fashion; was badly dressed; had an unwashed, unbrushed, unkempt look altogether; and . . . assumed a tone of superiority over me which I was not then aware was warranted by her undoubted leadership. From first to last she put up my mental bristles." Linton thought of herself as forthright and spontaneous, the sort of woman who is loved for her faults. She

[17] Oliphant, *Autobiography*, p. 4.

107

was made to feel uncomfortably inadequate by the novelist: "She was so consciously 'George Eliot'—so interpenetrated head and heel, inside and out, with the sense of her importance as the great novelist and profound thinker of her generation, as to make her society a little overwhelming, leaving us baser creatures the impression of having been rolled very flat indeed."[18] Eliot also attracted worshipful disciples, but though Mary Cholmondeley, sitting down to her chapter in Shropshire in the 1890s, "raised her eyes in humility and fidelity to George Eliot,"[19] most nineteenth-century women novelists seem to have found her a troubling and demoralizing competitor, one who had created an image of the woman artist they could never equal, one who had been "kept in a mental greenhouse and taken care of," while they staggered "alone and unaided, through cloud and darkness."[20] Their sense of professional inferiority frequently exploded into hostility; Alice James asserted: "She makes upon me the impression . . . of mildew, or some morbid growth."[21]

George Mandeville's Husband, a forgotten novel written in 1894, throws some light on the jealousies, animosities, and ambitions that underlay women novelists' response to George Eliot. The author, Elizabeth Robins, was an American actress living in England, a feminist who wrote several successful novels, acted in Ibsen's first London productions, and later became a chief propagandist for the militant suffragettes of the W.S.P.U. Yet George Mandeville's Husband, which she published under a pseudonym, is a denunciation of pseudointellectual women novelists and a satire on George Eliot. "George Mandeville" resembles George Eliot

[18] My Literary Life, London, 1899, pp. 86–87.

[19] Percy Lubbock, Mary Cholmondeley: A Sketch from Memory, London, 1928, p. 49.

[20] Oliphant, Autobiography, p. 5; Dinah Craik, "The Mill on the Floss," MacMillan's III (1861), in George Eliot: The Critical Heritage, p. 157.

[21] The Diary of Alice James, ed. Leon Edel, London, 1965, p. 41.

in name only; she is a pretentious second-rater who sacrifices her husband and daughter for the adulation of a bunch of cranks and hacks. Her husband avenges himself by turning the daughter into a Victorian Angel. He maintains that he would rather his daughter "scrubbed floors than wrote books," but as he describes the busy little nest he envisions for her he realizes "with a sudden and unusual emotion . . . that the dozen womanly things he vouchsafed to her did not altogether satisfy the imagination even of this woman-child." Such moments of doubt, however, are rare; throughout the book Wilbraham denounces professional women—most viciously, George Eliot.

When his daughter mentions George Eliot in evidence of women's abilities, Wilbraham responds with an abusive monolog:

> Yes, yes, all women say George Eliot, and think the argument unanswerable. As if to instance one woman (who, by the way, was three parts man) did more than expose the poverty of their position. . . . She was abnormal. . . . Read her letters and diaries. When you grow up, study her life—not as it was commonly reported, but as it *was*: She was a poor burdened creature, fitter to be pitied than blazoned abroad as example and excuse.

His daughter caves in immediately and concedes, "George Eliot *looks* awful. Her picture frightens me!"

It would be interesting to know how the novel was received in 1894. Robins seems to empathize with George Mandeville's ambitions, and she hints that Wilbraham's suffocating love, rather than the mother's neglect, destroys the daughter. Yet the attack on George Eliot is full of passionate conviction. In one authorial interruption, Robins generalizes about the experience of a woman writer in her day:

> Who shall not say there was no element of courage and of steadfast strength in the woman who, year in, year out,

sat chained to her writing-table, ceaselessly commemorat-
ing the futile and inept, leaving behind her day by day
upon that sacrificial altar some fragment of youth and
health, some shred of hope, some dead illusion. To sit
down daily to the task of being George Eliot, and to rise
up "the average lady-novelist" to the end, must, even if
only dimly comprehended, be a soul-tragedy of no mean
proportion.[22]

Eliot's example was as inescapable as it was inimitable.
Robins' own prose in this passage is an unconscious imitation of Eliot's style, as George Bernard Shaw warned her.[23]
The Eliot mystique of majestic, cerebral, and ultimately
sibylline detachment influenced both the prose and the professional styles of the next generation. Mrs. Humphry
Ward, Mary Cholmondeley, and "John Oliver Hobbes"
(Pearl Craigie) continued to act the Eliot role long after it
had become an anachronism. The seriousness that seemed
regal in Eliot looked pretentious and foolish in Mrs. Craigie
and Mrs. Ward; and an irreverent group of critics (including Max Beerbohm) caricatured the solemnity that won
Ward the nickname "Ma-Hump."

Feminine novelists had been persuaded that Eliot represented their highest evolutionary stage, but in the early
twentieth century a new female aestheticism saw possibilities that liberated them from her legend. Dorothy Richardson discarded Eliot's example simply because she thought
that Eliot wrote "like a man."[24] Most of the feminist novelists, however, detected a more complicated personality behind the literature than had the Victorians. Craigie, who
wrote an essay on Eliot for the Encyclopedia Britannica,
saw in the famous intellectual restraint a heroic struggle
rather than a stony indifference. For her, Eliot's moral

[22] "C. E. Raimond," *George Mandeville's Husband*, London, 1894, pp.
42, 61, 57–58, 62–63.

[23] Letter of February 13, 1899, in G. B. Shaw, *Collected Letters 1898–1910*,
ed. Dan H. Laurence, London, 1965, p. 77.

[24] *Dawn's Left Hand*, in *Pilgrimage*, IV, London, 1979, p. 240.

greatness came from "her infinite capacity for mental suffering and her need of human support," so disciplined and elevated that the novels were "wholly without morbidity in any disguise."[25]

Appropriately, an essay written by Virginia Woolf in 1919 helped restore Eliot to her rightful position after a period of Victorian and Edwardian backlash. In this extremely sympathetic piece, Woolf concedes all the flaws in the novels, but finds in the heroines Eliot's hard-won triumph over her own self-mistrust, and her fidelity to female experience:

> The ancient consciousness of woman, charged with suffering and sensibility, and for so many ages dumb, seems in them [Eliot's heroines] to have brimmed and overflowed and uttered a demand for something—they scarcely knew what—for something that is perhaps incompatible with the facts of human existence. . . . For her too the burden and the complexity of womanhood were not enough; she must reach beyond the sanctuary and pluck for herself the strange bright fruits of art and knowledge. Clasping them as few women have ever clasped them, she would not renounce her own inheritance—the difference of view, the difference of standard —nor accept an inappropriate reward.[26]

In this essay a woman critic was able for the first time to reconcile the two sides of the George Eliot legend, to bring suffering and sensibility into relation with art and knowledge. Victorian women writers, when they contemplated George Eliot, had felt somehow betrayed. They thought she had rejected them because she had avoided intimacy; they thought she had despised them because she had held them to a rigorous standard. They could not equal her, and they could see no way around her. It was not until the genera-

[25] Quoted in Colby, *Singular Anomaly*, p. 222.
[26] "George Eliot," *The Common Reader*, 2nd edition, London, 1925, p. 217.

111

tion of the 1890s had dramatically—even sensationally—redefined the role of the woman writer that Virginia Woolf could look back and see in George Eliot, not a rival, but a heroine.

The legends attached to Brontë and Eliot in their lives were reversed in the heroines of their novels. Brontë's Jane Eyre is the heroine of fulfillment; Eliot's Maggie Tulliver is the heroine of renunciation. Together *Jane Eyre* and *The Mill on the Floss* are full and powerful descriptions of growing up as a female in Victorian England. Both contain a few explicit feminist passages, but they are classic feminine novels. They realistically describe an extraordinary range of women's physical and social experiences, but also suggest experiences through the accumulation of images and symbols. Of the two novels, *Jane Eyre*, published thirteen years earlier, is by far the more experimental and original; the significance of Brontë's use of structure, language, and female symbolism has been misread and underrated by male-oriented twentieth-century criticism, and is only now beginning to be fully understood and appreciated. Although both novels deal with the same subject, defined by Q. D. Leavis as "the moral and emotional growth of a passionate, badly managed child into a woman,"[27] the heroine Jane Eyre achieves as full and healthy a womanhood as the feminine novelists could have imagined; the gifted and lovable Maggie Tulliver represses her anger and creativity, and develops a neurotic, self-destructive personality. The formal differences in the two novels, between Brontë's freewheeling, almost surrealistic expression of her heroine's inner life, and Eliot's much more conventional, naturalistic, and self-conscious narrative, suggest in themselves the differences in the novelists' approaches to feminine fictions of release and control.

In *Jane Eyre*, Brontë attempts to depict a complete female identity, and she expresses her heroine's consciousness through an extraordinary range of narrative devices. Psy-

[27] Introduction to *Jane Eyre*, p. 28.

chological development and the dramas of the inner life are represented in dreams, hallucinations, visions, surrealistic paintings, and masquerades; the sexual experiences of the female body are expressed spatially through elaborate and rhythmically recurring images of rooms and houses. Jane's growth is further structured through a pattern of literary, biblical, and mythological allusion. Brontë's most profound innovation, however, is the division of the Victorian female psyche into its extreme components of mind and body, which she externalizes as two characters, Helen Burns and Bertha Mason. Both Helen and Bertha function at realistic levels in the narrative and present implied and explicit connections to Victorian sexual ideology, but they also operate in an archetypal dimension of the story. Brontë gives us not one but three faces of Jane, and she resolves her heroine's psychic dilemma by literally and metaphorically destroying the two polar personalities to make way for the full strength and development of the central consciousness, for the integration of the spirit and the body. Thus *Jane Eyre* anticipates and indeed formulates the deadly combat between the Angel in the House and the devil in the flesh that is evident in the fiction of Virginia Woolf, Doris Lessing, Muriel Spark, and other twentieth-century British women novelists.

The novel opens at Gateshead, with Jane's transition from the passivity and genderlessness of childhood into a turbulent puberty. This emotional menarche is clearly suggested, despite the fact that Jane is only ten years old, by the accumulation of incident and detail on the psychic level. "I can never get away from Gateshead till I am a woman," she tells Mr. Lloyd;[28] and, having passed through the gate, she has evidently entered upon womanhood by the end of chapter 4. Her adolescence is marked first by her sudden and unprecedented revolt against the Reeds, a self-assertiveness that incurs severe punishment and ostracism, but also wins

[28] Ch. 3, p. 56. Page references are to the Penguin edition, Harmondsworth, 1966; I have also indicated chapters.

113

her freedom from the family. It is also colored by her pervasive awareness of the "animal" aspects of her being—her body, with its unfeminine needs and appetites, and her passions, especially rage. From the undifferentiated awareness of her "physical inferiority" to the Reed children, Jane becomes minutely conscious both of the "disgusting and ugly"[29] physical sadism of John Reed, and of her own warm blood and glittering eyes. The famous scene of violence with which the novel begins, John Reed's assault on Jane and her passionate counterattack, associates the moment of rebellion and autonomy with bloodletting and incarceration in the densely symbolic red-room.

It is thus as if the mysterious crime for which the Reeds were punishing Jane were the crime of growing up. The red-room to which Jane is sentenced by Mrs. Reed for her display of anger and passion is a paradigm of female inner space:

> The red-room was a spare chamber, very seldom slept in.
> . . . A bed supported on massive pillars of mahogany hung
> with curtains of deep red damask, stood out like a taber-
> nacle in the centre, the two large windows, with their
> blinds almost drawn down, were half shrouded in fes-
> toons and falls of similar drapery; the carpet was red; the
> table at the foot of the bed was covered with a crimson
> cloth. . . . This room was chill, because it seldom had a
> fire; it was silent, because remote from the nursery and
> kitchens; solemn, because it was known to be so seldom
> entered. The housemaid alone came here on Saturdays,
> to wipe from the mirrors and the furniture a week's quiet
> dust; and Mrs. Reed herself, at far intervals, visited it to
> review the contents of a certain secret drawer in the
> wardrobe, where were stored divers parchments, her
> jewel-casket, and a miniature of her deceased husband.[30]

With its deadly and bloody connotations, its Freudian wealth of secret compartments, wardrobes, drawers, and

[29] Ch. 1, p. 42.   [30] Ch. 2, p. 45.

jewel chest, the red-room has strong associations with the adult female body; Mrs. Reed, of course, is a widow in her prime. Jane's ritual imprisonment here, and the subsequent episodes of ostracism at Gateshead, where she is forbidden to eat, play, or socialize with other members of the family, is an adolescent rite of passage that has curious anthropological affinities to the menarchal ceremonies of Eskimo or South Sea Island tribes. The passage into womanhood stresses the lethal and fleshly aspects of adult female sexuality. The "mad cat," the "bad animal" (as John Reed calls Jane),[31] who is shut up and punished will reappear later in the novel as the totally animalistic, maddened, and brutalized Bertha Mason; *her* secret chamber is simply another red-room at the top of another house.

The obsession with the "animal" appetites and manifestations of the body, and the extreme revulsion from female sexuality are also articulated through one of the submerged literary allusions in the text to *Gulliver's Travels*. This book has been one of Jane's favorites, but after her experience in the red-room it becomes an ominous and portentous fable; Gulliver seems no longer a canny adventurer, but "a most desolate wanderer in most dread and dangerous regions,"[32] a pilgrim in the adult world like herself. Like Gulliver, Jane moves from the nursery world of Lilliput to an encounter with the threatening and Brobdingnagian Reverend Brocklehurst ("What a face he had, now that is was almost on a level with mine! what a great nose! and what a mouth! and what large, prominent teeth!"),[33] and an increasing Calvinist awareness of the "vile body" that leads to the climatic encounter with Bertha, the female Yahoo in her foul den.

A strain of intense female sexual fantasy and eroticism runs through the first four chapters of the novel and contributes to their extraordinary and thrilling immediacy. The scene in the red-room unmistakably echoes the flagellation ceremonies of Victorian pornography. As in whipping

[31] Ch. 1, p. 41; ch. 2, p. 44.   [32] Ch. 3, p. 53.
[33] Ch. 4, p. 64.

scenes in *The Pearl* and other underground Victorian erotica, the *mise-en-scène* is a remote chamber with a voluptuous decor, and the struggling victim is carried by female servants. Jane is threatened with a bondage made more titillating because the bonds are to be a maid's garters: " 'If you don't sit still, you must be tied down,' said Bessie. 'Miss Abbot, lend me your garters; she would break mine directly.' Miss Abbot turned to divest a stout leg of the necessary ligature. This preparation for bonds, and the additional ignominy it inferred, took a little of the excitement out of me." This threatened chastisement of the flesh, although not actually carried out in the red-room scene, is a motif that links Jane with Helen Burns, who submissively accepts a flogging at Lowood School from a teacher named Miss Scatcherd. Jane herself, we learn later, has been flogged on the "neck" in Mrs. Reed's bedroom.[34]

Whipping girls to subdue the unruly flesh and the rebellious spirit was a routine punishment for the Victorians, as well as a potent sexual fantasy; as late as the 1870s the *Englishwoman's Domestic Magazine* conducted an enthusiastic correspondence column on the correct way to carry out the procedure. It is interesting here to note that sexual discipline is administered to women by other women, as agents for men. Bessie (Jane's favorite servant) and Miss Abbot, acting on behalf of Mrs. Reed, who in turn is avenging her son, lock Jane up; at Lowood the kindly Miss Temple starves the girls because "she has to answer to Mr. Brockle-

---

[34] Ch. 2, p. 44. For a discussion of Victorian flagellation literature see Steven Marcus, "A Child is Being Beaten," in *The Other Victorians*, London, 1966. Marcus is dealing with male sexual fantasies, however. In their edition of *Jane Eyre*, Jane Jack and Margaret Smith note that the word "neck" "used sometimes to be used with a wider significance than now, for a woman's breast or (as here) shoulders. There is an element of the Victorian euphemism about it." *Jane Eyre*, London, 1969, p. 586, n. 61. For a recent discussion of Victorian corporal punishment of girls, see Mary S. Hartman, "Child-Abuse and Self-Abuse: Two Victorian Cases," *History of Childhood Quarterly* (Fall 1974): 240–241.

hurst for all she does";[35] at Thornfield Grace Poole is hired by Rochester as Bertha's jailor. Thus the feminine heroine grows up in a world without female solidarity, where women in fact police each other on behalf of patriarchal tyranny. There is sporadic sisterhood and kindness between the women in this world, and Jane finds it ultimately at Marsh End with Diana and Mary Rivers; but on the whole these women are helpless to aid each other, even if they want to.

Lowood School, where Jane is sent by her aunt, is the penitentiary for which the red-room was the tribunal. Like Lowick, Casaubon's home in *Middlemarch*, Lowood represents sexual diminishment and repression. In this pseudo-convent, Jane undergoes a prolonged sensual discipline. Here the girls are systematically "starved" (in Yorkshire dialect the word means "frozen" as well as "hungry"), and deprived of all sensory gratification. Clad in stiff brown dresses, "which gave an air of oddity even to the prettiest," and shorn of their hair, the last sign of their femininity, the girls of Lowood are instructed in the chastity they will need for their future lives as poor teachers and governesses. Brocklehurst proclaims that his mission "is to mortify in these girls the lusts of the flesh."[36]

As an institution, Lowood disciplines its inmates by attempting to destroy their individuality at the same time that it punishes and starves their sexuality. Distinctions between the little girls and the "great girls," the pre-adolescents and the young women, are obliterated by the uniform all are forced to wear. The purpose of Brocklehurst in starving the "vile bodies" is to create the intensely spiritualized creature the Victorians idealized as the Angel in the House. Virtually sexless, this creature, as Alexander Welsh provocatively suggests in *The City of Dickens*, is in fact the Angel of Death, who has mystical powers of intercession in the supernatural order, and whose separation from the body is

[35] Ch. 5, p. 82.   [36] Ch. 5, p. 79; ch. 7, p. 96.

the projection of the Victorian terror of the physical reminders of birth and mortality.[37]

The Angel of Lowood is Helen Burns, the perfect victim and the representation of the feminine spirit in its most disembodied form. Helen is a tribute to the Lowood system: pious, intellectual, indifferent to her material surroundings, resigned to the abuse of her body, and, inevitably, consumptive. She is one extreme aspect of Jane's personality, for Jane too is tempted by the world of the spirit and the intellect, and has a strong streak of masochism. Helen is the woman who would make a perfect bride for St. John Rivers; she is his female counterpart. But although Helen, "with the aspect of an angel," inspires Jane to transcend the body and its passions, Jane, rebellious on her "pedestal of infamy" in the classroom, resists the force of spiritual institutionalization, as she will later resist the physical institutionalization of marriage with Rochester.[38] Ultimately, it is Helen's death that provides the climax of the Lowood experience. She dies in Jane's arms, and Jane achieves a kind of victory: the harsh regime of Lowood is modified, its torments palliated. Like Bertha Mason, Helen is sacrificed to make way for Jane's fuller freedom.

The "animal" aspects of womanhood, which have been severely repressed during Jane's sojourn at Lowood, reassert themselves when, at eighteen, she goes as governess to Thornfield Hall. Bertha Mason, who is confined to, and who *is*, the "third story" of Thornfield, is the incarnation of the flesh, of female sexuality in its most irredeemably bestial and terrifying form. Brontë's treatment of the myth of the Mad

[37] *The City of Dickens*, London, 1971, pp. 155–160, 222–225. Welsh suggests that Jane herself has Angelic qualities; but the novel emphasizes her unwillingness to accept the role; when Brocklehurst tells her about the child who emulates the angels by learning psalms, Jane replies, "Psalms are not interesting" (ch. 4, p. 65). As a young woman, she tells Rochester emphatically, "I am not an angel . . . and I will not be one till I die: I will be myself" (ch. 24, p. 288).

[38] Ch. 7, p. 99.

Wife is brilliantly comprehensive and reverberative, and rich with historical, medical, and sociological implications, as well as with psychological force.

Bertha's origins in folk history and literature are interesting in themselves. There are numerous literary precedents in the Gothic novel, particularly Mrs. Radcliffe's *Sicilian Romance*, for mysterious captives; the situation, in fact, is repeated to the point of appearing archetypal. Other explanations for Bertha depend upon real case histories that Brontë had encountered. Mrs. Gaskell mentions one in her *Life of Charlotte Brontë*; Q. D. Leavis refers to another, a Yorkshire legend about North Lees Hall Farm, where a mad wife had allegedly been incarcerated. Indeed, there were several Yorkshire houses with legends of imprisoned madwomen: Wycollar Hall, near Colne, and Norton Conyers, which had a chamber called "the madwoman's room."[39] The legends themselves express a cultural attitude toward female passion as a potentially dangerous force that must be punished and confined. In the novel, Bertha is described as "the foul German spectre—the vampyre," "a demon," "a hag," "an Indian Messalina," and "a witch." Each of these is a traditional figure of female deviance with its own history in folklore. The vampire, who sucked men's blood (as Bertha does when she stabs her brother), and the witch, who visited men by night and rode them to exhaustion, were the products of elemental fears of women. H. R. Hays suggests that in England the "basic charge against the witch as a night demon and seducer springs clearly from the experiences of a repressed and celibate male clergy," that is, from erotic dreams accompanied by nocturnal emissions.[40]

Brontë herself, alluding to the latest developments in Victorian psychiatric theory, attributed Bertha's behavior to

[39] Introduction to *Jane Eyre*, p. 9. H. F. Chorley, reviewing *Jane Eyre* in the *Athenaeum* in 1847, also knew of a possible source. See Miriam Allott, *The Brontës: The Critical Heritage*, London, 1974, p. 72.

[40] *The Dangerous Sex: The Myth of Feminine Evil*, New York, 1965, p. 42.

"moral madness."[41] Opposed to the eighteenth-century belief that insanity meant deranged reason, the concept of "moral insanity," introduced by James Cowles Pritchard in 1835, held madness to be "a morbid perversion of the natural feelings, affections, inclinations, temper, habits, moral dispositions, and natural impulses, without any remarkable disorder or defect of the intellect, or knowing and reasoning faculties, and particularly without any insane illusion or hallucination."[42] Women were thought to be more susceptible than men to such disorders and could even inherit them. Sexual appetite was considered one of the chief symptoms of moral insanity in women; it was subject to severe sanctions and was regarded as abnormal or pathological. Dr. William Acton, author of the standard textbook on *The Functions and Disorders of the Reproductive Organs* (1857) admitted that he had occasionally seen cases in the divorce courts of "women who have sexual desires so strong that they surpass those of men." Acton also acknowledged "the existence of sexual excitement terminating even in nymphomania, a form of insanity which those accustomed to visit lunatic asylums must be fully conversant with; but, with these sad exceptions, there can be no doubt that sexual feeling in the female is in the majority of cases in abeyance."[43]

The periodicity of Bertha's attacks suggests a connection to the menstrual cycle, which many Victorian physicians understood as a system for the control of female sexuality. Bertha has "lucid intervals of days—sometimes weeks," and her attack on Jane comes when the moon is "blood-red and half-overcast."[44] "In God's infinite wisdom," a London physician wrote in 1844, "might not this monthly discharge be

[41] Letter to W. S. Smith, January 4, 1848, in Shorter, *The Brontës: Life and Letters*, I, London, 1908, p. 383.

[42] Eric T. Carlson and Norman Dain, "The Meaning of Moral Insanity," *Bulletin of the History of Medicine* XXXVI (1962): 131. See also "Moral Insanity," in Vieda Skultans, *Madness and Morals: Ideas on Insanity in the Nineteenth Century*, London, 1975, pp. 180–200.

[43] Quoted in Marcus, *The Other Victorians*, p. 31.

[44] Ch. 27, p. 336; ch. 25, p. 304.

ordained for the purpose of controlling woman's violent sexual passions . . . by unloading the uterine vessels . . . so as to prevent the promiscuous intercourse which would prove destructive to the purest . . . interests of civil life?"[45] As Carroll Smith-Rosenberg points out, the image of the "maniacal and destructive woman" closely parallels that of the sexually powerful woman: "Menstruation, 19th century physicians worried, could drive some women temporarily insane; menstruating women might go berserk, destroying furniture, attacking family and strangers alike. . . . Those 'unfortunate women' subject to such excessive menstrual influence," one doctor suggested, "should for their own good and that of society be incarcerated for the length of their menstrual years."[46]

In precise contrast to the angelic Helen, Bertha is big, as big as Rochester, corpulent, florid, and violent. When Jane sees her in the chamber on the third story, she is almost subhuman:

> In the deep shade, at the farther end of the room, a figure ran backwards and forwards. What it was, whether beast or human being, one could not, at first sight tell; it grovelled, seemingly on all fours; it snatched and growled like some strange wild animal; but it was covered with clothing, and a quantity of dark, grizzled hair, wild as a mane, hid its head and face.[47]

Like Gulliver observing the Yahoos, Jane is pushed almost to the brink of breakdown by her recognition of aspects of herself in this "clothed hyena." Much of Bertha's dehumanization, Rochester's account makes clear, is the result of her

[45] George Robert Rowe, *On Some of the Most Important Disorders of Women*, London, 1844, pp. 27–28, quoted in Carroll Smith-Rosenberg, "Puberty to Menopause: The Cycle of Femininity in Nineteenth-Century America," *Feminist Studies* 1 (1973): 25.

[46] Edward Tilt, *The Change of Life*, New York, 1882, p. 13, quoted in Smith-Rosenberg "Puberty to Menopause," 25. See also Skultans, *Madness and Morals*, pp. 223–240.

[47] Ch. 26, p. 321.

confinement, not its cause. After ten years of imprisonment, Bertha has become a caged beast. Given the lunacy laws in England, incidentally, Rochester has kept the dowry for which he married her, but cannot file for divorce even in the ecclesiastical courts. Rochester's complicity in the destruction of his wife's spirit is indicated in Jane's recognition of the third story's resemblance to a corridor in "Bluebeard's castle," in Rochester's accounts of his sexual exploitation of Bertha, Céline, Giacinta, and Clara, and in Jane's uneasy awareness that his smile "was such as a sultan might bestow on a slave."[48]

Madness is explicitly associated with female sexual passion, with the body, with the fiery emotions Jane admits to feeling for Rochester. In trying to persuade her to become his mistress, Rochester argues that Jane is a special case: "If you were mad," he asks, "do you think I should hate you?" "I do indeed, sir," Jane replies; and she is surely correct.[49] Thus it becomes inevitable that Bertha's death, the purging of the lusts of the flesh, must precede any successful union between Rochester and Jane. When they finally marry, they have become equals, not only because Rochester, in losing his hand and his sight, has learned how it feels to be helpless and how to accept help, but also because Jane, in destroying the dark passion of her own psyche, has become truly her "own mistress."[50]

The influence of *Jane Eyre* on Victorian heroines was felt to have been revolutionary. The post-Jane heroine, according to the periodicals, was plain, rebellious, and passionate; she was likely to be a governess, and she usually was the narrator of her own story. Jane, Maggie Tulliver, Mrs. Gaskell's Mary Barton and Margaret Hale (in *North and South*), Mrs. Oliphant's *Miss Marjoribanks*, and even Miss Yonge's Ethel May (in *The Daisy Chain* and its sequels) were more intellectual and more self-defining than the sweet and submissive heroines favored by Bulwer-Lytton, Thackeray,

48 Ch. 11, p. 138; ch. 24, p. 297.   49 Ch. 27, pp. 328–329.
50 Ch. 37, p. 459.

and Dickens. Some reviewers applauded the change; *Bentley's Quarterly Review*, for example, found Bulwer-Lytton's "conception of female excellence" rather old-fashioned by 1859, since the "august band of female novelists has . . . set up counter ideals . . . women who can stand alone, reason, lead, instruct, command; female characters wrought out with such power that they take hold on men's minds."[51]

There were many others who were alarmed by the drive to self-fulfillment Jane exhibited; *The Spectator* in April 1860 deplored the "pale, clever, and sharp-spoken young woman" who had become the fashion; the *Saturday Review* pretended resignation to the dominance of "glorified governesses in fiction," who, like the poor, would be always with them, since literature had "grown to be a woman's occupation."[52] Even the *Westminster Review* wished for an end to the reign of "the daughters direct of Miss Jane Eyre. . . . Of these heroine governesses one can only wish that England may have more of them and the circulating libraries less."[53] On a more personal note, Walter Bagehot objected that women novelists, out of jealousy for their heroines, made them unattractive: "Possibly none of the frauds which are now so much the topic of common remark are so irritating, as that to which the purchaser of a novel is a victim on finding that he has only to peruse a narrative of the conduct and sentiments of an ugly lady."[54]

Twentieth-century women novelists have frequently rewritten the story of Jane Eyre with endings Brontë could not have projected. In Jean Rhys' *Wide Sargasso Sea*, Bron-

[51] "Novels by Sir Edward Bulwer-Lytton," 1 (1859): 91–92. See also Margaret Oliphant, "Charles Dickens," *Blackwood's* LXXVII (1855): 465; "Mr. Thackeray and His Novels," *Blackwood's* LXXVII (1855), 95; and comments by Dinah Craik on a novel she read for Macmillan's in 1860: "When Mr. C. has to do with boys & men he does them capital—but his women are *not* women exactly—airy ideals—not flesh & blood." Berg Collection, New York Public Library.

[52] "Women's Heroines," *Saturday Review* XXIII (1867): 261.

[53] *Westminster Review*, n.s. XIII (1858): 297–298.

[54] "The Waverley Novels," *Literary Studies*, II, London, 1879, p. 167.

të's novel is sympathetically retold from the perspective of an oppressed and betrayed Bertha Mason. Rhys emphasizes the racial aspect of Bertha's Creole background; Bertha comes to represent the native, the heart of darkness, the Other. In Doris Lessing's *The Four-Gated City* (1969), the heroine is housekeeper to a seductive man, whom she falls in love with; he too, it turns out, has a mad wife, who lives in the basement. The distance between the Brontë attic, which rationalizes lust in the mind, and the Lessing basement, which accepts the dark mystery of the body, is one measure of the development of the female tradition. More profoundly, at the end of the novel Lessing's heroine liberates the mad wife, and together they leave and take an apartment. Can we imagine an ending to *Jane Eyre* in which Jane and Bertha leave Rochester and go off together? Obviously such a conclusion would be unthinkable. Such possibilities and such solutions are beyond the boundaries of the feminine novel. Jane's marriage to Rochester is essentially a union of equals, but in feminine fiction men and women become equals by submitting to mutual limitation, not by allowing each other mutual growth.

George Eliot admired *Jane Eyre*, although she protested against Jane's refusal to become Rochester's mistress: "All self-sacrifice is good, but one would like it to be in a somewhat nobler cause than a diabolical law which chains a man body and soul to a putrefying carcase."[55] What Eliot was unable to understand in Brontë's fiction was the difference between self-sacrifice and self-assertion. Jane Eyre suffers in running away from Rochester, but she acts out of the instinct of self-preservation: "*I* care for myself. The more solitary, the more friendless, the more unsustained I am, the more I will respect myself."[56] For Jane Eyre, action is a step toward independence; even if it begins as escape, it is ultimately directed toward a new goal. For George Eliot, be-

[55] Gordon S. Haight, *George Eliot: A Biography*, London, 1968, p. 65.
[56] *Jane Eyre*, ch. 27, p. 344.

lieving that "all self-sacrifice is good," renunciation becomes a virtue in itself. *The Mill on the Floss* (1860) sympathetically analyzes the unfulfilled longings of an intelligent young woman in a narrow and oppressive society, but nonetheless elevates suffering into a female career.

There are many similarities between *Jane Eyre* and *The Mill on the Floss* that reflect the themes and techniques of the feminine novelists. Ellen Moers has pointed out that the Red Deeps, where Maggie meets Philip Wakem, are "a real geography of sexual indulgence—a woman's private terrain";[57] this terrain is Eliot's equivalent of the red-room, an adolescent female space in which sexual longing and dread are mingled. Like Brontë, Eliot uses folklore to provide metaphors for the deviant woman. As a little girl, Maggie is fascinated by the stories of witchcraft in Defoe's *History of the Devil*: "That old woman in the water's a witch; they've put her in to find out whether she's a witch or no, and if she swims she's a witch, and if she's drowned—and killed, you know—she's innocent, and not a witch, but only a poor silly old woman. But what good would it do her then, you know, when she was drowned?"[58] Like Jane, Maggie has the option of angelic innocence, which leads to death, or "witchlike" self-preservation, which leads to social rejection. Another important metaphor for Maggie is the gypsy queen, a fantasy that Eliot realistically and humorously undercuts. The myth of the gypsy camp, which Eliot along with Brontë and other Victorian novelists adapted from romantic poetry and painting, stands for an escape from the zero-sum game of Victorian social codes, at the price of such amenities of civilization as tea, books, and groceries. Maggie's contact with this world, briefer, more disillusioning, and more humiliating than Jane's experiments with rebellion, is instructive. The Bertha in Maggie, the alter ego, the semi-criminal double, who is violent and

[57] "Women's Lit," 34.
[58] *The Mill on the Floss*, London, 1973, bk. I, ch. 3, p. 12.

sexual, has no real part to play in the novel. She is clearly a childish fantasy of Maggie's, fleeting, silly, and quickly repressed.

Brontë locates the conflict between passion and repression within Jane, and represents it as Helen vs. Bertha (as well as St. John vs. Rochester); Eliot represents the conflict primarily as a sexual difference, as Maggie vs. Tom. Eliot's original title for the novel (she was calling it "Sister Maggie" until January 1860) and the title of the first book ("Boy and Girl") highlight the relationship of Maggie and Tom, and the conceptualization of feminine passion and masculine repression that are the extremes of sex-role conditioning. One Victorian critic, Richard Simpson, observed about Eliot that "the antithesis of passion and duty figures itself to her mind as a kind of sexual distinction; so that if woman could be defecated [sic] from all male fibres, she would be all passion, as man, purged of all feminine qualities, would be all hard duty." Tom Tulliver is an instance of a male nearly pure; the purest form of woman is "a being with black hair and large dark eyes . . . a mass of yearnings, passions, and feelings,"[59] in short, Maggie.

Eliot goes to some pains to show how the differences in expectations, education, and daily treatment by the family form Maggie and Tom. Tom's life is not easy, any more than Maggie's is, but the disciplines to which he is called are lighter for him to assume because they are basically in accordance with his personality. The qualities that denote Tom's mind—will, self-control, self-righteousness, narrowness of imagination, and a disposition to dominate and to blame others, all the traits of the authoritarian personality —Eliot sees as masculine, and the correlatives of status and self-esteem. Tom is never so "susceptible," never so much "like a girl," as when he is made to feel stupid at school.[60]

[59] "George Eliot's Novels," *Home and Foreign Review* III (1863), in *George Eliot: The Critical Heritage*, p. 239.

[60] *Mill on the Floss*, II, ch. 1, p. 131. Blackwood wrote her that "Tom's life at Stelling's is perfect. It is perfectly wonderful how you have been

If there is any single aspect of sexual differentiation that Eliot points to as significant, it is this difference in self-esteem that depends upon the approbation of the family and social circle. Tom learns when very young not to doubt himself, while Maggie, to the end of her life, is self-doubting and unassertive. Maggie's self-esteem is pitifully dependent on Tom's love, and she will sacrifice any legitimate claim of her own personality to avoid rejection by him.[61]

Unlike Tom Tulliver, Stephen Guest, and Lucy Deane, Maggie Tulliver and Philip Wakem are insecure in their sexual identity, and this insecurity is one of the shared emotions that brings them together. Because he is a cripple, Philip has led a girl's life; he has been barred from sports and swordplay and ultimately forced to be "perfectly quiescent," as immobilized as Maggie herself. It is a commonplace in feminine fiction for the sensitive man to be represented as maimed; Linton Heathcliff in *Wuthering Heights*, Phineas Fletcher in Dinah Craik's *John Halifax, Gentleman*, Charlie Edmondstone in Charlotte Yonge's *The Heir of Redclyffe*, and even such late versions as Colin Cravan in Frances Hodgson Burnett's *The Secret Garden* all suggest that men condemned to lifelong feminine roles display the personality traits of frustrated women. Philip, for example, has enough empathy to penetrate Maggie's mournful resignation, but he also has a "peevish susceptibility," compounded of "nervous irritation" and the "heart-bitterness produced by the sense of his deformity."[62]

Because he shares many of Maggie's dilemmas, Philip is uniquely qualified to analyze them for her and for the reader. Maggie is unable to channel her passionate energy into productive work, to yoke her pride, ambition, and intelli-

---

able to realise the boy's feelings. Men will read it like reminiscences of what they themselves felt—suffered" (*George Eliot Letters*, p. 263).

[61] For an extremely interesting Horneyan analysis of Maggie's defensive strategies, see Bernard J. Paris, "The Inner Conflicts of Maggie Tulliver," *A Psychological Approach to Fiction*, Bloomington, 1974.

[62] *Mill on the Floss*, II, ch. 4, p. 156.

gence into a single effective force, as Tom does, and she therefore must find some strategy for subduing her own nature and securing Tom's approval. Her tactics, as Philip perceives, are escapist and renunciatory. In most conflicts Maggie cannot face the truth about her own feelings and has to persuade herself that other people are making her do things. In her clandestine meetings with Philip in the Red Deeps, she is vaguely aware that he is sexually unattractive, and that she is becoming entrapped in an exploitative and oppressive relationship; but rather than admitting these feelings and accepting the responsibility of acting upon them, she allows the meetings to be discovered and passively accompanies Tom to a showdown with Philip. It is clear that Tom, although he is brutal and even sadistic, speaks truthfully to Philip, and that in accusing Philip of taking advantage of his sister's loneliness he is acting out some of Maggie's anger and aggression. At the end of the scene Maggie is "conscious of a certain dim background of relief in the forced separation from Philip,"[63] but she deceives herself into believing that she is simply relieved to be free of concealment. When Maggie *does* feel sexually attracted to a man, she has no vocabulary for her emotions and must define her physical excitement as "love"; she must pretend that Stephen Guest has kidnapped her and that she is helplessly drifting away, when it is obvious that they are colluding in the elopement. Even after her awakening in the boat, when she makes the decision to resist Stephen, Maggie cannot move toward a purposeful construction of her life.

Whereas Jane Eyre, in a roughly similar impasse, runs away to start an independent life, Maggie is perversely drawn to destroy all her opportunities for renewal: to refuse the job in another town, to plead compulsively for Tom's forgiveness, to remain in the oppressive network of the family and the community, waiting hopelessly for them to validate her existence. Pain and self-abnegation become

[63] Ibid., v, ch. 5, p. 329.

the all-absorbing experiences of her life: "life stretched before her as one act of penitence, and all she craved, as she dwelt on her future lot, was something to guarantee her from more falling."[64]

"You are not resigned," Philip warns Maggie. "You are only trying to stupefy yourself."[65] Jane Eyre lets the torrent of pain pour over her; " 'I came into deep waters,' " she quotes from Scripture; " 'the floods overflowed me.' "[66] Maggie never penetrates to the depths of her own pain; she diverts all her energy into escape and self-stupefaction. The ultimate flood is lethal, it seems, because the heart's need has been dammed up for so long.

Eliot's metaphor for Maggie's evasion of responsibility is opium. Her personal credo, expressed in a letter to Barbara Bodichon, was "to *do without opium*, and live through all our pain with conscious, clear-eyed endurance"—not, one notes, resistance.[67] Maggie, however, struggles to "dull her sensibilities," to subdue her longing, to transcend the volcanic Brontëan anger and hatred that could "flow out over her affections and conscience like a lava stream."[68] Philip serenades her appropriately with an aria from *La Somnambula*.

The submerged image of the opiate in *The Mill on the Floss*, one that Eliot uses more explicitly in some other novels, reflects the world of Victorian feminine turmoil. Physicians reported that many women were driven to real opium and opium derivatives by the hopeless monotony and restriction of their lives. Headache remedies, patent medicines and sleeping-draughts, nostrums to which many women were addicted, contained high percentages of alcohol and opium. In 1857 one physician wrote: "Many women would pass the most indifferent night. . . . The chagrins of life would prey too severely; regrets and disappointments and

---

[64] Ibid., VII, ch. 2, p. 467.
[65] Ibid., V, ch. 3, p. 309. [66] *Jane Eyre*, ch. 26, p. 324.
[67] Letter of December 26, 1860, *George Eliot Letters*, III, p. 366.
[68] *Mill on the Floss*, IV, ch. 3, p. 268.

129

painful reminiscence would visit them too acutely did they not deaden the poignancy of suffering, actual or remembered, by the 'drowsy syrups.' "[69] In 1871 another doctor related the causes of female drug addiction to the female role in a passage that might easily describe Maggie in St. Oggs: "Doomed, often, to a life of disappointment, and it may be, of physical and mental inaction, and in the smaller and more remote towns, not unfrequently, to utter seclusion, deprived of all social diversion, it is not strange that nervous depression with all its concomitant evils, should follow—opium being discreetly selected as the safest and most agreeable remedy."[70]

Florence Nightingale, a member of Eliot's generation, diagnosed the narcissism, depression, addictiveness, and inertia of Victorian women as suppressed anger and lack of real work in the world: "If ever women come into contact with sickness, with poverty, and crime in masses, how the practical reality of life revives them! They are exhausted, like those who live on opium or on novels, all their lives—exhausted with feelings which lead to no action."[71] Maggie's fictional heroines, too, are losers, dark sufferers like Scott's Minna and Rebecca, for whom all endings are unhappy.

The Victorians were bothered by Maggie Tulliver's lack of moral balance rather than by her passivity; they wondered what sort of example she might be to "the hundreds of clever girls, born of uncongenial parents."[72] But the problems of Eliot's passive, self-destructive heroine seem

[69] Dr. Robert Dick, *The Connexion of Health and Beauty*, London, 1857, quoted in Patricia Branca, *The Silent Sisterhood*, London, 1975, p. 149. See also Barbara Hardy, "The Image of the Opiate in George Eliot's Novels," *Notes and Queries* (November 1957): 487–490.

[70] Dr. F. E. Oliver, "The Use and Abuse of Opium," quoted by John S. Haller and Robin M. Haller, *The Physician and Sexuality in Victorian America*, Urbana, 1974, p. 279.

[71] "Cassandra," in Ray Strachey, *The Cause*, London, 1978, p. 407.

[72] Dinah Craik, "The Mill on the Floss," *Macmillan's* III (1861), in *George Eliot: The Critical Heritage*, p. 157.

much more persistent in women"s literature than those of Brontë's rebel. Maggie is the progenitor of a heroine who identifies passivity and renunciation with womanhood, who finds it easier, more natural, and in a mystical way more satisfying, to destroy herself than to live in a world without opium or fantasy, where she must fight to survive. This heroine, like Maggie, has moments of illumination, awakenings to an unendurable reality; but she quickly finds a way to go back to sleep; even death is preferable to the pain of growth. Kate Chopin's *The Awakening* (1899) and Edith Wharton's *The House of Mirth* (1905) both deal with the futile struggle for consciousness. Chopin's Edna Pontellier thinks "it is better to wake up after all, even to suffer, rather than to remain a dupe to illusions all one's life"; but when her lover abandons her she drowns herself.[73] Wharton's Lily Bart wakes courageously to the "winter light" in a narrow room, but she too is unable to adjust to a life of worʰ and adult responsibility. Emotions and ideas that she has never been educated to understand rush in on her, and in the end she takes a lethal overdose of chloral, enjoying "the gradual cessation of the inner throb."[74]

In Margaret Drabble's *The Waterfall* (1972), the twentieth-century heroine, despite all the new sciences of introspection, is as much a victim of her emotions, as little in control of her life, as is Maggie Tulliver. Drabble's novel, with its Victorian images of floods and cascades, ironically comments on the continuity of the female tradition:

> These fictional heroines, how they haunt me. Maggie Tulliver had a cousin called Lucy, as I have, and like me she fell in love with her cousin's man. She drifted off down the river with him, abandoning herself to the water, but in the end she lost him. She let him go. Nobly she regained her ruined honor, and, ah, we admire her for it, all

[73] *The Awakening*, London, 1978, p. 189.
[74] *The House of Mirth*, London, 1966, II, ch. 13, p. 359.

that superego gathered together in a last effort to prove that she loved the brother more than the man.

She should have . . . well, what should she not have done? Since Freud we guess dimly at our own passions, stripped of hope, abandoned forever to that relentless current. It gets us in the end; sticks, twigs, dry leaves, paper cartons, cigarette ends, orange peels, flower petals, silver fishes. Maggie Tulliver never slept with her man. She did all the damage there was to be done to Lucy, to herself, to the two men who loved her, and then, like a woman of another age, she refrained. In this age what is to be done? We drown in the first chapter.[75]

[75] *The Waterfall*, Harmondsworth, 1971, p. 154.

CHAPTER V

Feminine Heroes: The Woman's Man

THE heroines were only half the story. Charlotte Brontë lamented to her friend James Taylor: "In delineating male character, I labour under disadvantages; intuition and theory will not adequately supply the place of observation and experience. When I write about women, I am sure of my ground—in the other case I am not so sure."[1] As Brontë explained, women had to build their heroes from imagination, since so many areas of masculine experience were impenetrable. Male critics found these portraits, which were in large part projections of aspects of the women themselves, laughably deficient as representations of men. The *Dublin University Magazine* claimed that it "could have made some strictures upon the character of Mr. Rochester . . . bearing us out in an idea we have long entertained, that a female pen is inadequate to portray the character and the passions of a man."[2] By the 1850s the "woman's man," impossibly pious and desexed, or impossibly idle and oversexed, had become as familiar a figure in the feminine novel as the governess. Usually the term was used simply as critical shorthand for an inept, feeble, or bombastic hero, whose presence assured reviewers that they had detected a female pen. And often they were right. The *Westminster Review*, for example, nabbed Millicent Grogan behind the pseudonym "Erick Mackenzie" when she published *The Roua Pass* in 1857: "In opposition to the title page we must express our belief that the authorship is feminine. The predominant male characters are undoubtedly women's men;

---

[1] Letter to James Taylor, March 1, 1849, in Clement Shorter, *The Brontës: Life and Letters*, II, London, 1908, p. 30.

[2] "An Evening's Gossip on New Novels," XXXI (1848): 614.

that is, they are a woman's idea of what men are, mixed up with certain salient manly characteristics which have been conceived from observation and are possible to us."[3]

Feminine novelists were eager to make public confessions of their deficiencies in male portraiture. Mrs. Linton thought it "impossible for a woman to understand the loftier side of a man's nature," since "she knows nothing, subjectively, of the political aims, the love for abstract truth, the desire for human progress, which take him out of the narrow domestic sphere, and make him comparatively indifferent to the life of sense and emotion." Therefore women's men were all absurd, contemptible and unrealistic; all were either angels or devils: "They are goody men of such exalted morality that Sir Galahad himself might take a lesson from them. Or they are brutes with the well-worn square jaw and beetling brow, who translate into the milder action of modern life the savage's method of wooing a woman by first knocking her senseless and then carrying her off."[4]

This dual hero represented two strains in the tradition of the novel; women writers modified the tradition by bringing to it their own moral, aesthetic, and psychological problems. There are many terms we could apply to the tradition of these heroes: light and dark, conservative and radical, classical and romantic. Model heroes, of course, were neither an essential ingredient of women's novels nor an exclusively feminine property. They look back to the passive hero of Sir Walter Scott's fiction, the hero who mirrors the conservative ideal of Burke, as gentleman, landowner, and citizen.[5] Victorian writers frequently projected the character of "nature's gentleman" into a religious context, using

[3] "Belles Lettres," LXVIII (1857): 305.
[4] "Women's Men," *The Girl of the Period*, II, London, 1883, pp. 246–247.
[5] See Alexander Welsh, *The Hero of the Waverley Novels*, New Haven, 1963, for an account of this hero.

134

their novels to show how Christian self-discipline and faith could lead to prosperity and success.

Yet the portrayal of men obviously raised special problems for women novelists. As early as 1840 critics had pointed out that Jane Austen had wisely refrained from presenting men in groups. Feminine novelists were not about to follow Jane Austen's example; Charlotte Brontë, for example, defiantly began *Shirley* with an all-male gathering. Still, her chapter describes a curate's tea-party, not a barracks-room brawl. The limitations that critics took for ignorance, however, were frequently the result of prudence or self-censorship. Like her sisters Anne and Emily, Charlotte might have shown men drunken and violent. But it did not pay, she had learned from *Wuthering Heights* and *The Tenant of Wildfell Hall*, for ladies to show how much they knew about men's lives.

Margaret Oliphant admitted to her friend Isabella Blackwood: "The men of a woman's writing are always shadowy individuals, and it is only members of our own sex that we can fully bring out, bad and good. Even George Eliot is feeble in her men, and I recognize the disadvantage under which we all work in this respect. Sometimes we don't know sufficiently to make the outline sharp and clear; sometimes we know well enough, but dare not betray our knowledge one way or other: the result is that the men in a woman's book are always washed in, in secondary colours. The same want of anatomical knowledge and precision must, I imagine, preclude a woman from ever being a great painter; and if one does make the necessary study, one loses more than one gains."[6] Charlotte Yonge was also pragmatically shrewd about the balance of literary and personal reputation women risked if they tried to depict realistic men: "It is true," she counseled an aspiring novelist in 1892, "that women's good heroes are apt to be called prigs. But be content to

[6] *Autobiography and Letters of Mrs. M.O.W. Oliphant*, ed. Mrs. Harry Coghill, London, 1899, p. 178.

have them so. If you sacrifice your womanly nature in the attempt at the world's notion of manly dash, you only sacrifice yourself and mar the performance, unless it is only a very slight sketch from the outside."[7]

The model hero was even less the product of adulation than of ignorance. To a considerable degree, he was the projection of women's fantasies about how they would act and feel if they were men, and, more didactically, of their views on how men *should* act and feel. It is customary for critics of the Victorian novel to see women's heroes as fantasy lovers, daydreams of romantic suitors. Critics have been rather slow to perceive that much of the wish-fulfillment in the feminine novel comes from women wishing they were men, with the greater freedom and range masculinity confers. Their heroes are not so much their ideal lovers as their projected egos.

The model heroes are the product of female fantasies that are much more concerned with power and authority than with romance. Many of these heroes are extremely aggressive in bourgeois economic terms. They are successful; they live out the fairy tale of Victorian upward mobility with the single-minded energy that characterized their female creators. John Halifax, for example, the hero of Dinah Craik's 1856 bestseller, *John Halifax, Gentleman*, begins as a beggar, but works hard, subdues fires, riots, and floods (Mrs. Craik's awestricken metaphors for male sexual temptation, which she imagined as titanic) marries an heiress, and buys property. Near the end of his life he has a family estate, a family firm, and a chance to run for Parliament. He might just as well have been called John Bull or Dick Whittington. Such respectability, security, and performance—the fruits of patriarchy—eluded women writers, who practiced just as radical a form of sublimation, but with much more limited rewards.

Yet women writers internalized the values of their so-

[7] "Authorship," in *A Chaplet for Charlotte Yonge*, ed. Georgiana Battiscombe and Marghanita Laski, London, 1965, p. 192.

ciety, and inevitably these affected their ambitions. Even in Charlotte Brontë's *The Professor* (1857), the hero Crimsworth is obsessed during his exile in Belgium with the need to rejoin the Tory squirarchy that had rejected and victimized him. Crimsworth does not delude himself with expatriate romanticizations, nor pretend to scorn the system he has temporarily escaped. He and his wife work and scrimp for ten years to go back to England, buy property, and retire; Crimsworth also decides to send his son to Eton, where he himself had spent a miserable adolescence. Young Victor Crimsworth will learn self-mastery in an all-male world. When women wrote, they identified with the power and privilege of the male world, and their heroes enabled them to think out their own unrealized ambitions. Even the good grey Charlotte Yonge has a fiercer side, which astounds her biographers; it is not simply a quirk in her character that she loved the military and preferred above all to talk about military strategy in the Peninsular War.

Mid-Victorian doctrines of manliness popularized by Thomas Hughes, among others, show up in almost identical form in the women's novels. The love of sport and animals, the ability to withstand pain, the sublimation of sexuality into religious devotion, and the channeling of sexuality into mighty action are traits the model heroes share. In Hughes' novels, however, manliness is achieved through separation from women; in the women's novels, mothers, sisters, and wives are the sources of instruction on the manly character.[8] Obviously there was a circumstantial need for a woman novelist to introduce her hero into a woman's world, as Guy Morville in *The Heir of Redclyffe* (1853) is "adopted" by Mrs. Edmund Stone, and as the crippled Lord Cairnforth in Mrs. Craik's *A Noble Life* (1866) is "adopted" by the motherly Helen. Male authors had easy access to the

[8] See Henry R. Harrington, "Childhood and the Victorian Ideal of Manliness in *Tom Brown's Schooldays*," *Victorian Newsletter* (Fall 1973): 13–17. In addition to the novels, Hughes wrote *Notes for Boys on Morals, Mind and Manners* (1855) and *The Manliness of Christ* (1879).

world of school and university; women needed the narrative interaction of the hero and the family. Probably women made their model heroes orphans to allow for some movement and suspense in these inevitable family adoptions, in which a degree of semi-incestuous love could also be described.

The unavoidable conflict between female fantasy and the actual situation of the women novelists also produced some curious convolutions in the fiction. Model heroes, while frequently ridiculous, are rarely boring. They are more devious than male versions of the manly ideal. In women's novels, model heroes are barred from the direct exercise of violence and power. They do not avenge themselves on their malefactors by administering a good punch on the jaw or by winning elections; instead they win indirect and devastating victories with the tactics of guilt, another sign that they find their source in the female situation. Guy Morville is the grand master of guilt. When a vigorous course of humility, self-control, and cheek-turning leaves Guy's enemy Philip still disposed to hit, Guy nurses Philip through an infectious fever, catches it, and dies. Philip, we are assured, can look forward to a life that is totally blighted and haunted by guilty memory. No contemporary reader of this influential novel commented on the perfect stupidity and recklessness that Guy exhibits in this *dénouement* (he drags his pregnant wife to the village where the fever is raging and insists on nursing Philip day and night by himself, although he is rich enough to hire any number of professionals). Yet the power motive in such willful self-sacrifice is clear enough and probably accounts for much of Guy's appeal. It is the motive of the child who daydreams about running away and making everybody sorry, and of the Victorian woman who was encouraged to seek influence through martyrdom. Such self-sacrifice is the ultimate source of emotional power because there is no defense against it. The plots of several popular novels written on this theme by women combine the elements of the romance of success with the skillful manipulation of guilt, thus giving expression to two aspects of the woman writer's position.

In Mrs. Isabelle Bank's *The Manchester Man* (1875), the virtuous hero, Jabez Clegg, finally triumphs over the unrepentant villain by opposing to the irresistible force of sadism an immovable object of masochism. The message is that the meek will inherit the earth if they can hold out long enough. Although the rewards are masculine—property, status, and power—the tactics are feminine. It is tempting to make fun of this formula, to see in it both worldly hypocrisy and feminine slyness. But such a conclusion would be most unjust. There is nothing cynical in the authors' devout conviction that virtue would be rewarded; and, as women struggling to make a living with their pens, they were not about to pretend to despise rewards that came in the form of money. The emotional strategies were in keeping with the essentially conservative and unquestioning nature of these novels. As G. M. Young points out, "the evangelical faith in duty and renunciation was a woman's ethic," and the feminine novelists were "reared in an atmosphere which made them instinctively Custodians of the Standard."[9]

The second group of "women's men," the brutes, were collateral descendants of Scott's dark heroes and of Byron's Corsair, but direct descendants of Edward Fairfax Rochester. Certainly Victorian critics credited Rochester with the paternity; in 1851 the *North British Review* spoke confidently of Mrs. Craik's heroes (in *Olive* and *The Ogilvies*) as being of "the Mr. Rochester stamp"; in 1854 and 1857 the *Westminster* talked about the "fashion" and the "rage" of novels patterned after *Jane Eyre*; by 1857 the *Athenaeum* actually referred to "the school of Currer Bell." The influence of *Jane Eyre* was international; within a year of its publication, an American critic wrote with mock terror about the "Jane Eyre fever" reaching epidemic proportions

[9] *Victorian England: Portrait of an Age*, London, 1960, pp. 3-4.

—young men caught it and began to swagger and swear in the Rochester style.[10]

Women writers as well as men recognized the source of this heroic style. Caroline Norton gave a hostile description of the brute hero in *Lost and Saved* (1863): "Ever since Jane Eyre loved Mr. Rochester, a race of novel-heroes have sprung up. . . . Brutal and selfish in their ways, and rather repulsive in person, they are, nevertheless, represented as perfectly adorable, and carrying all before them, like George Sand's galley-slave." These heroes do have a decided family resemblance. They are not conventionally handsome, and often are downright ugly; they have piercing eyes; they are brusque and cynical in speech, impetuous in action. Thrilling the heroine with their rebellion and power, they simultaneously appeal to her reforming energies. As Mrs. Grogan put it in *The Roua Pass*, they are "sardonic, sarcastic, satanic, and seraphic." Unlike the model heroes, they are not dedicated to their careers.

When *Jane Eyre* first appeared, Rochester aroused a variety of negative critical emotions, ranging from bafflement to horror. The consensus seems to have been that, although Rochester might perhaps be accepted as real, no decent girl could possibly love him. Yet in the novel he is loved by a presumably decent girl. Thus the book must be by a woman; no man would so abuse womanhood. This opinion, essentially another reference to the feminine ideal, persisted throughout the next fifteen years. The problem with the brute hero, the reason that he was considered so much a feminine property, was not that he was an unconvincing man, but that to the conservative male Victorian mind he was unlovable. Critical prejudice comes out strongly in attacks on Rochester's attractions like this one from the High

10 I. Gregory Smith, "Recent Works of Fiction," *North British Review* xv (1851): 226; "Belles Lettres," *Westminster Review* LXI (1854): 622; "Contemporary Literature," *Westminster Review* LXVI (1856): 335; "Our Library Table," *Athenaeum* VI (1857): 881; and E. P. Whipple, "Novels of the Season," *North American Review* LXVII (1848): 355–356.

Church *Christian Remembrancer*: "When loved he is past middle-age, and when wedded he is blind and fire-scarred ... [in Rochester] you have an Acis such as no male writer would have given his Galatea, and yet what commends itself as a true embodiment of the visions of the female imagination."[11]

Among other wicked heroes appearing in women's novels of the 1840s was Heathcliff; if Rochester shocked critics, Heathcliff simply outraged them. "A deformed monster," was the American critic E. P. Whipple's open-minded view. But *Wuthering Heights* was not widely read until much later in the century, and thus it exerted little influence. Geraldine Jewsbury's first novel, *Zoë*, appeared in 1845, only shortly before the publication of *Jane Eyre*. Its sadistic hero, Count Mirabeau, is based on the charismatic womanizing hero of the French Revolution. Miss Jewsbury herself was everything the Victorian imagination pictured Currer Bell to be: truly unconventional, daring, self-possessed, giddy, and passionate. Her hero is original and glamorous, if not intellectually and psychologically profound. Like Rochester, he is impulsive and mysterious; he completely enthralls Zoë, who is willing to overlook his rakish past; and he even gives Zoë an account of how he cast off his mistress for her sake. But Miss Jewsbury carried her hero much further into wickedness than Charlotte Brontë did hers; Mirabeau demands that Zoë abandon her children so that he can have all her love. She adores him and is tempted for a moment, but of course refuses, and he leaves her.

William C. Roscoe's article on the Brontës, written in 1857, is candidly bitter about the success of Charlotte's heroes, particularly Crimsworth, Rochester, and Louis Moore:

> Miss Brontë was a great upholder of the privileges of her sex, yet no writer in the world has ever so uniformly rep-

[11] *Christian Remembrancer* xv (1848); quoted in Miriam Allott, *The Brontës: The Critical Heritage*, London, 1974, p. 90.

resented women at so great a disadvantage. They invariably fall victims to the man of strong intellect, and generally muscular frame, who lures them on with affected indifference and simulated harshness; by various ingenious trials assures himself they are worthy of him, and when his own time has fully come, raises them with a bashaw-like air from their prostrate condition, presses them triumphantly to his heart, or seats them on his knees, as the case may be, and indulges in a condescending burst of passionate emotion. All these men are in their attachments utterly and undisguisedly selfish, and we must say we grudge them their easily won victories over the inexperienced placid little girls they lay siege to. It is not thus that generous men make their advances, or that women worthy of the name are won.[12]

George Eliot's closest approach to the rough lover was Felix Holt, and the critical response to him was quite in line with the attitudes displayed toward the Brontës' heroes. One critic complained in 1866: "If the nature of women is truly delineated by writers of their own sex, an overbearing spirit and a kind of masculine roughness are the qualities which above all others ensure success in love. In ordinary practice reproof and contradiction will be sparingly employed by the judicious suitor; but in novels the incivility of the hero rarely fails of its desired effect."[13] Another reviewer objected that Esther would not have loved Felix: "Her taste must have revolted from him. . . . he is not the man a woman would readily fall in love with."[14]

Men, it appears, saw these heroes as tyrants who took advantage of helpless heroines, but nothing could have

[12] "The Miss Brontës," *Poems and Essays,* II, London, 1860, p. 350.

[13] G. S. Venables, "Felix Holt the Radical," *Edinburgh Review* LXXIV (1866): 226.

[14] H. H. Lancaster, "George Eliot's Novels," *North British Review* XLV (1866): 117. See also "George Eliot," *British Quarterly Review* XLV (1867): 176, on the love of Jermyn and Mrs. Transome in *Felix Holt.*

been further from their authors' intentions. At least one woman critic recognized the appeal of the rough lover. Mrs. Oliphant, who personally tended to portray the safer, blander, clerical hero, shrewdly observed that the brute flattered the heroine's spirit by treating her as an equal rather than as a sensitive, fragile fool who must be sheltered and protected. Rochester's treatment of Jane and Mirabeau's treatment of Zoë were signs of the new generation declaring its independence—"a wild declaration of the 'Rights of Woman' in a new aspect."[15] Like the dark heroes in Scott's novels, the descendants of Rochester represent the passionate and angry qualities in their creators. Since the conventions of the novel and of womanhood made it all but impossible for the heroines to exhibit sexuality and power, feminine novelists projected these aspects of themselves onto their heroes.

An equally rebellious and adventurous version of the women's hero was the clergyman, or, to adopt George Eliot's term, the "clerical sex." Many reviewers besides George Eliot (who pilloried the species of the oracular and the white–neck-cloth novel in her review of the silly lady novelists), noticed the sudden proliferation of parsons in women's literature and attempted to account for them in their usual jocular manner. As the *Saturday Review* observed in 1859, "the English Clergyman is a person who can be easily worked up into a hero or an ideal. He is a gentleman, he is going to Heaven, he may make love. He has the attractions of both worlds."[16] The clergyman, it was said, was an intermediate sex, not so virile, hairy, and aggressive as the ordinary man, and thus much more accessible to the soft female imagination. The appropriateness of such a hero for women was delicately implied by the *Westminster Review* in 1860: "Clergymen are debarred from the expression at least of many passions that laymen are allowed to exhibit

15 "Modern Novelists—Great and Small," *Blackwood's* LXXVII (1855): 557.
16 "Parsons and Novels," *Saturday Review* VII (1859): 708–709.

without the same amounts of blame; these are chiefly the rougher and coarser feelings of our nature and their outward signs; the consequence is, that the proceedings of the clergy are less direct; and because less direct, more refined, and ultimately partake more of the character of female management than of the somewhat coarse energy of masculine methods."[17]

Most of the religious novels by male authors during the middle of the century were in fact by clergymen, who saw the potential of the genre for religious propaganda and moral suasion. According to Margaret M. Maison, the Oxford Movement was the chief catalyst for the explosion of religious novels in the 1840s. In the case of women authors, too, there is much more involved in the choice of the parson as hero than expedience or evasion of more stringent artistic demands. The religious novel was the essential instrument of female participation in the male monopoly on theological debate.[18]

Charlotte Yonge, Felicia Skene, and Elizabeth Sewell were among the many women who wanted to be clergymen, and who instead channeled their immense energies into the portrayal of imaginary clerics through whom they could preach. Dinah Craik used clerical rhetoric when she justified her recourse to the pen, and she even called one book *Sermons Outside the Church*. She thought of authorship as the fulfillment of a divine calling, a "talent" in the biblical sense: "Authors who feel the solemnity of their calling cannot suppress the truth that is within them. . . . they must go straight on, as the inward voice impels, and He who seeth their hearts will guide them aright."[19]

The Anglican novelist Elizabeth Missing Sewell, author

[17] "The Mill on the Floss," *Westminster Review* LXXIV (1860): 24.

[18] For a fine analysis of the rebellion against patriarchal religion by an American woman novelist, see Christine Stansell's "Elizabeth Stuart Phelps: A Study in Female Rebellion," *Massachusetts Review* XIII (1972): 239–256.

[19] Quoted in Robert A. Colby, *Novels with a Purpose*, Bloomington, 1967, p. 10.

of *Amy Herbert* (1844) had begun in the nursery to compose sermons and to find comfort in prayers and hymns. Yet from her earliest childhood her brothers—themselves destined to become clergymen—discouraged her from pursuing theological studies. Their nickname for her was Blighted Betty. Teased, ridiculed and scolded, she "always felt myself rather a black sheep in the family, though I am sure I had longings for something better, and vague dreams of distinction, kept under from the sense of being a girl."[20] In adolescence she taught Sunday school, did parish work, and daydreamed about a college for girls, while her brothers went to Winchester and Oxford, took holy orders, and became involved in the Tractarian movement.

Sewell's brothers squelched all her efforts at independent thought, but at the same time William (the oldest and her favorite) gave his name as "editor" of her anonymous books, getting her such sums as five pounds for them. Inevitably, her feelings toward authorship were composed of pleasure and shame. Her own ambivalence about women writers was reinforced by her brothers' "protective" attitudes. Nonetheless, enough indignation comes through in her autobiography to suggest that she was aware of their scornful tampering with her life. We can scarcely believe that Sewell gives us the following without irony: "As my brother (the Warden of New College) once said of me to a lady who made some inquiries about me, 'My sister Elizabeth is not remarkable in any way,' and I heartily endorsed the opinion."[21]

It took a family crisis to prod Sewell into print; accus-

[20] *The Autobiography of Elizabeth M. Sewell*, ed. Eleanor C. Sewell, London, 1908, pp. 15–16. See also the discussion of Sewell in Vineta Colby, *Yesterday's Woman: Domestic Realism in the English Novel*, Princeton, 1974, pp. 178–184.

[21] *Autobiography*, p. 21. Kathleen Tillotson notes that William Sewell's anti-Catholic novel *Hawkstone* (1845) portrayed an evangelical who "is allowed to repent after many sufferings, but the atheist falls into melted lead and the Jesuit is eaten by rats" (*Novels of the Eighteen-Forties*, p. 118, n. 2).

tomed to making fun of women writers, she somewhat shamefacedly became one to support her family after her father's death. The excessive diffidence that marked her relationship with her brothers vanished when she sat down to write. Her autobiography shows that she was an extremely conscientious and deliberate novelist with a sophisticated understanding of plot, character, and narrative technique; but she used her books to dramatize her own views on theological and educational questions. Afficionados of the Victorian religious novel usually give Miss Sewell high marks for morbid scrupulosity and obedience; they give the impression that her female characters, helpless and humble, spend most of their time on their knees. It is true that Sewell regarded self-control and dutifulness as good disciplines for women who could not expect much support if they rebelled; she felt that there was no point in their uselessly dispelling their energies. But she saw no reason for them to abandon their intellectual independence. Her theory of education was intended to produce freedom, originality, and reasoning ability.

In her novels, Sewell consistently undercuts notions of a male monopoly on truth and wisdom, particularly when it claims to interpret the will of God. Her heroines are frequently spinsters or widows—intentionally so, because she wished to de-emphasize the importance of marriage. Her women are as thoughtful, devout, and responsible as any clergyman could be, but they are also more realistic. They oppose to the remoteness and frigidity of Anglican ritual a much cheerier and folksier view of religion, the view of practical women concerned with the daily needs of the people around them. A curate who advocated "the idea of people standing during the Church service" was denounced by Sewell in her journal: "I should like to have him turned into a woman not in very strong health (and this is the rule, not the exception), and then see how he would like the custom."[22] In Sewell's novel, *Journal of Home Life* (1867), Mrs.

[22] *Autobiography*, p. 130.

Bradshaw laughs at a rector's earnest and depressing views on the afterlife, and proclaims her own version of a snug, cozy, and heated Heaven: "a place where we shall be quite comfortable and never need hot-water bottles," rather than a drafty church where we listen to incomprehensible sermons for eternity.

Sewell had little patience with the cant of the authoress who pretended to be awed by the masculine, and particularly the clerical, soul. She had seen her brothers and their friends, and she knew better. She was "not fascinated," therefore, by *Chollerton*, an inept clerical tale in which the authoress shied away from descriptions of her hero's feelings, professing herself unable to intrude "into that sacred edifice which formerly a woman's foot was forbidden to profane." "Really," Sewell sniffed, "my humility cannot reach that depth. I think I *can* imagine something of what a clergyman might feel, and I should never consider it an intrusion to go wherever men go, taking them as men. Of course the altar is different; but there the distinction is not between men and women, but between God and man."[23]

Felicia Skene, another unmarried Anglican novelist, did her early work under the influence of a charismatic clergyman, whom she reproduced in her books. She eventually rebelled, however, and warned other women not to submit to the manipulative authority of the parson but to find their own way and their own words. She herself turned to nursing and social work; she visited prisons, helped prostitutes, and wrote books about those problems, such as *Hidden Depths* (1866). Through the clerical heroes of such popular works as Mrs. Oliphant's *Salem Chapel* (1863) and Mrs. Linton's *Under Which Lord?* (1869), women found ways to state their own views and to become their own authorities.

We might expect that women writers would have been credited with a special ability to depict *feminine* character, and that this would outweigh the liability of their limited experience. But such was not the case. E. P. Whipple ob-

[23] Ibid., pp. 131–132.

served casually in 1848 that of course the best and noblest women characters had been created by men; he added kindly that women could occasionally fill in some authentic details; and the *British Quarterly Review* appealed to the "testimony of all the greatest *men* in literature" to redeem the image of women.[24]

The assumption that the most charming heroines and the most profound insights into female psychology came from men was a natural corollary to the Victorian belief that women were partial and defective versions of the full humanity represented by men. Men could comprehend the emotions of the less-developed creature, but women could never stretch their understanding upward. In 1850 the *Prospective Review*, analyzing some novels suspected to be by women, was perfectly forthright about the difference:

> For the sympathies and powers of the man embrace those of the woman, and though many of his sentiments and feelings are less delicate and intense, they are of the same nature,—and besides, those of a woman are habitually laid bare to him in life, even in their most secluded manifestations. But there is much in a man, consisting less in particular feelings than in their modes of operation, that a woman through her sympathies can never touch, and to depict which she is driven to the results of an experience for which her habits and opportunities little fit her. If in a book the complete and faithful portrait of a woman is drawn, and a vital character unfolded through all its profound mysteries and evanescent manifestations, the work may still be that of a man; but if a man's character be so drawn, it is all but conclusive against its having a woman for its author.[25]

In portraying heroes, women had to assume that men were human beings like themselves. Toward the end of the

[24] "George Eliot," *British Quarterly Review* XLV (1867): 176.
[25] "Hearts in Mortmain and Cornelian," *Prospective Review* VI (1850): 496–497.

century, feminist novelists began to feel that the two sexes were indeed very different. They reversed the Victorian critical dictum; the most extreme group came to believe that men lacked an inner life, or at least one as rich and fruitful as their own. Turning the old biological stereotypes around, they began to see the culture and psychology of patriarchy as harsh and sterile and to seek the promise of spiritual and social evolution in the profound sympathies of the female psyche.

This view, I think, was latent in feminine fiction long before the feminists made it explicit and political. George Eliot's portrait of Tom Tulliver's emotional petrifaction is an outstanding example. As early as 1863, Richard Simpson protested that in Eliot's world, women have "almost the monopoly of the emotional nature—of the passions, which are the elements of life; a bubbling and fermenting source of power, whose impulses seem like the acts of external force, instinctive, indefinite, vague, involuntary, but rich and mighty, like a divine energy within us. Perhaps she does not think that women possess it more really than men, but that in the woman it is not overlaid with all the unreasonable products of manly reason; with overlogical feats, and over honeycombed brain."[26] When Victorian critics accused feminine novelists of misrepresenting masculine emotions, they often seem to have meant that men did not have emotions, but only reason, logic, and will. The claim to female emotional superiority that Simpson objected to in Eliot was the inevitable outcome of the sexual specialization of Victorian society. Women forced to make a career of their emotions naturally placed a high value on intuition and the inner life, and felt a kind of contemptuous pity for the ordered public world of what the feminist "Ellis Ethelmer" called "maledom cold and sere."[27]

[26] "George Eliot's Novels," in *George Eliot: The Critical Heritage*, ed. David Carroll, London, 1971, p. 245.
[27] Ellis Ethelmer, "Woman the Messiah," quoted in *Shafts*, April 1895, p. 41.

The recurring motif in feminine fiction that does seem to show outright hostility, if not castration wishes, toward men, is the blinding, maiming, or blighting motif. Rochester is blinded in the fire at Thornfield and also loses the use of his hand. Another fire blinds Romney, the hero of Elizabeth Barrett Browning's *Aurora Leigh*. In Brontë's *Shirley*, Robert Moore, seriously ill, is tended by an Amazon nurse who reduces him to a childlike state of helpless dependency. In *The Mill on the Floss*, Tom Tulliver nearly cripples himself while playing with a sword. In Olive Schreiner's best seller, *Story of an African Farm* (1883), the handsome and arrogant Gregory ultimately disguises himself in his mother's old bonnet and shawl and goes to wait on his beloved as a day nurse.

J.M.S. Tompkins confesses in her Fawcett Lecture on *Aurora Leigh* to feeling "some embarrassment when a woman-writer blinds her hero, as a prelude to the acknowledgment that the woman has been right all along";[28] and few women can help sharing her feelings. It seems to be a bald and vengeful sort of symbol, and one would prefer female aggression to be less directly conveyed. But these humiliations of the hero are not merely punitive. Although feminine novelists, as I have shown in Chapter IV, presented the permanently handicapped man as feminine in the pejorative sense, they believed that a limited experience of dependency, frustration, and powerlessness—in short, of womanhood—was a healthy and instructive one for a hero.

An interesting novel that appeared in 1869 contains one of the clearest expositions of this process of emotional education through symbolic role-reversal. In Florence Wilford's *Nigel Bartram's Ideal*, the heroine, Marian Hilliard, is a novelist obviously modeled on Charlotte Brontë and George Eliot. She has written an anonymous best seller called *Mark's Dream*, a book that no one can believe is from a woman's pen. People discuss it in her presence: "Yes, you

[28] November 28, 1961, London; privately printed by the Fawcett Society.

are right, there is a severe painful consistency in the whole of that last scene. A lady writer could never have resisted the temptation of making a comfortable religious finale, and the author, whoever he is, has been too true to his art for that." Marian, who is restoring a church with her profits from the book, is a quiet, retiring person whom no one suspects even of intelligence, much less genius. She carries Eliot's ideal of unpretentious female culture to its extremes of self-abnegation.

Ironically, it is Marian's very timidity and lack of self-assertion that makes Nigel Bartram fall in love with her. Like Lewes, he is a journalist and critic. His ideal woman is a gentle being just clever enough to appreciate him; as for women novelists, he abominates them all. On the basis of hints from Marian, he begins to surmise that the writer of *Mark's Dream* may be a woman; and he excoriates the putative authoress in a review as "one who had a strange and sad acquaintance with the darker side of life, who understood but too well the black secrets of the human hearts; who had herself sinned and suffered, and had written out of the depths of her own miserable experience."[29] These accusations, similar to the ones hurled at Currer Bell, both alarm and wound Marian, but she decides that her best course is to repress her gifts as she conceals her identity and to marry Bartram without telling him the truth.

Of course, the truth comes out after the wedding, and Bartram forbids his wife to publish ever again. She pines away, and he half-kills himself with overwork and jealousy until he breaks down completely. In his illness comes a most interesting reversal of the plot. Being helpless himself teaches Bartram what it feels like to have to depend on others and forego one's proper work. He also learns that, just as it is no shame for a man to be weak, it is no disgrace for a woman to be strong. Marian keeps the household go-

---

[29] *Nigel Bartram's Ideal*, London, 1869, pp. 14, 36. There is a stimulating discussion of this novel in Patricia Thomson, *The Victorian Heroine: A Changing Ideal*, London, 1956, pp. 107–108.

ing until he recovers, and then they become literary partners. He provides ideas and research for essays; she does the actual writing. Their mutual dependency and mutual respect is not quite up to the level of Beatrice and Sidney Webb, for instance, but it is one of the few visions of an emancipated egalitarian marriage in the Victorian novel.

This last example provides, I think, the clue to the others. Women writers did not agree that their feelings were simply a "delicate" version of the noble male passions, and thus contained within the masculine soul like carved cups. They believed that female emotions were the complement, and the salvation, of masculine reserve. When they imagined heroines who were extensions of themselves, heroines for whom they felt protective affection, they had genuine difficulty imagining suitable men for them. It was not enough that the men who loved Jane and Caroline and Aurora and Lyndall should be clever, idealistic, and devoted. Above all, they had to be whole people. Thus Rochester's blindness, Tulliver's wound, Moore's sickness, and Gregory's transvestism are symbolic immersions of the hero in feminine experience. Men, these novels are saying, must learn how it feels to be helpless and to be forced unwillingly into dependency. Only then can they understand that women need love but hate to be weak. If he is to be redeemed and to rediscover his humanity, the "woman's man" must find out how it feels to be a woman.

CHAPTER VI

Subverting the Feminine Novel
Sensationalism and Feminine Protest

> No *man* would have dared to write and publish such books as
> some of these are: no *man could* have written such delineations
> of female passion. . . . No! They are women, who by their writ-
> ings have been doing the work of the enemy of souls, glossing
> over vice, making profligacy attractive, detailing with licentious
> minuteness the workings of unbridled passions, encouraging
> vanity, extravagance, wilfulness, selfishness in their worst forms.
> . . . Women have done this,—have thus abused their power and
> prostituted their gifts,—who might have been bright and shin-
> ing lights in their generation.—FRANCIS E. PAGET, *Lucretia; or,
> The Heroine of the Nineteenth Century* (1868)

WITH the coming of sensation fiction and the spectacular
best sellers of the 1860s, the Golden Age of the Brontës,
Mrs. Gaskell, and George Eliot seemed to pass abruptly
into the Age of Brass. By 1869 one critic had noted "a sensible decline in the powers of women's novels, an indication
that the feminine genius of this generation has touched its
high-water mark, and the ebb has begun."[1] Such a sentiment was partly nostalgia, a yearning for a sunnier by-gone
world that also affected the reception of Dickens' dark novels of the 1860s, and partly an acknowledgment of the passing of a generation. Charlotte, the last of the Brontës, died
in 1855, and Mrs. Gaskell in 1865. George Eliot was still
alive and productive, but many readers felt after *The Mill
on the Floss* she had passed her peak and would never
again equal the pastoral magnificence of her earlier works.

[1] "Works by Mrs. Oliphant," *British Quarterly Review* LXIX (1869):
300–301.

More significant than the passing of this older generation was what had taken its place. During the sixties, the literary market for women expanded enormously, and the business potential of the literary profession was fully exploited by women editors, publishers, and printers. All the commercial, competitive, self-promoting aspects of the literary life that had been played down or ignored by the first two generations of nineteenth-century women writers were conspicuous in the careers of the third generation. Writers like the sensation novelists Mary E. Braddon, "Ouida," Charlotte Riddell, Amelia B. Edwards, Florence Marryat, Helen Reeves, and Rhoda Broughton, and the children's book writers Mary Molesworth, Juliana Ewing, and Frances Hodgson Burnett entered the profession earlier than women had previously; they stayed in it with fewer interruptions, and they were more likely to be married and to have large families. Their ambitions were fulfilled in business as well as art; they enjoyed the management end of publishing and delighted in exerting professional power. In their writing, the sensationalists especially valued passion and assertive action; they saw themselves as daughters of Charlotte Brontë rather than George Eliot. After rereading *Shirley*, Braddon described Brontë as "the only *genius* the weaker sex can point to in literature. Great as George Eliot may be, in her somewhat passionless style, her work appears to me to be rather the outcome of a fine mind, cultured to the highest point, than . . . the fiery force of the genius which . . . 'does what it must.' "[2]

In the 1860s women made an effort to break down the male monopoly of publishing. There had been many ladies' magazines in England during the nineteenth century, but they had been conservative and domestic in tone, antagonistic to the women's rights movement, and usually edited and

[2] Robert Lee Wolff, "Devoted Disciple: The Letters of Mary Elizabeth Braddon to Sir Edward Bulwer-Lytton, 1862–1873," *Harvard Library Bulletin* XII (April 1974): 150.

owned by men.[3] The new women's press, however, was edited and controlled by women and was both feminist and activist in its principles. In March 1860 Emily Faithfull founded the Victoria Printing Press, which trained and employed women for the printing trades; it was this press that published many of the women's journals and magazines. Miss Faithfull's own journal, *The Victoria Magazine* (1863–1880), and its offshoot, *Women and Work* (1874), specialized in problems of female employment. The *Englishwoman's Review*, founded in 1857 by Barbara Bodichon and Bessie R. Parkes, took on a new mission in 1866 when it was subtitled "A Journal of Women's Work." Lydia Becker's *Women's Suffrage Journal* and Josephine Butler's crusading magazine *The Shield* both began publication in 1870. As Bessie Parkes observed in *Essays on Women's Work* in 1865, journalism gave women effective opportunities to change public opinion: "With the growth of the press has grown the direct influence of educated women on the world's affairs. Mute in the Senate and in the church, their opinions have found a voice in sheets of ten thousand readers."[4]

The business skills and the unflagging energy of this generation made them formidable competitors, and their popularity, as well as their aggressiveness, antagonized many of their male contemporaries. Confronted with a choice be-

[3] For an account of women's magazines, see Alison Adburgham, *Women in Print*, London, 1972; and Cynthia L. White, *Women's Magazines 1893–1968*, London, 1972.

[4] Pp. 120–121. Publishing was still, of course, controlled by men; as late as the 1890s even fashion magazines like *Queen, The Ladies, Lady's Pictorial, Lady*, and *Women's Gazette* were edited by men, a fact Evelyn March Phillips noted as "deplorable": "One would think women should know best what will please women, but as editors we are told they are deficient in the capacity which grasps a business situation. . . . Many are sub-editors, and manage special departments, and on every paper, I think I may say, the bulk of the work is done by women" ("Women's Newspapers," *Fortnightly Review* LXII [1894]: 665).

tween the novels of Dinah Craik and Mary Braddon, Henry James opted for the "dull, pious, and very sentimental" mediocrities of the former, preferring Craik's self-effacing feminine style to Braddon's confidence. Admitting that Braddon's novels were "brilliant, lively, ingenious and destitute of a ray of sentiment," James nonetheless found these qualities disagreeable in a woman: "the masculine cleverness, the social omniscience . . . become an almost revolting spectacle."[5] As soon as they began to make money, the sensationalists invested it in their own careers, publishing and editing magazines and retaining book copyrights. Mrs. Wood edited the *Argosy*, Braddon edited *Belgravia*, Charlotte Riddell edited *St. James Magazine*, and Florence Marryat edited *London Society*. These editorial positions, like the ones Dickens and Thackeray occupied at *Household Words* and the *Cornhill*, provided innumerable opportunities for the exercise of influence and power.

In his study of the Bentley Papers, Royal Gettmann speculates that the sudden emergence of the sensationalists' best-selling novels reflected a change in the novel-reading population:

> In the 1860s the three-deckers of Mrs. Henry Wood and others reflected a shift in the interests—and possibly the make-up—of library patronage: for example, masculine life in clubs, ships and camps was replaced by domestic life, and humour gave way to sentiment. It is perhaps significant that during the following decades there was a marked increase in the number of women writers. In the 'thirties and 'forties approximately 20 per cent of the books published by the House of Bentley were by women whereas in the 'seventies and 'eighties the proportion was more than doubled.[6]

Certainly the publisher proceeded as if there had been a shift from male to female values, hiring women readers,

[5] *Notes and Reviews*, Cambridge, Mass., 1921, pp. 171–172.
[6] *A Victorian Publisher*, Cambridge, England, 1960, p. 248.

most of them novelists in their own right, to judge the manuscripts coming in; Geraldine Jewsbury, Adeline Sergeant, Minna Featherstonehaugh, Gertrude Mayer, Lady Dorchester, and Mrs. G. W. Godfrey were among those who read for Bentley's. In the 1840s the success of women novelists had been perceived as a female invasion; in the 1860s women writers' advances were often perceived as a female monopoly. Charles Reade complained of difficulties in distributing his books, because the small circulating libraries were against him: "They will only take in ladies' novels. Mrs. Henry Wood, 'Ouida,' Miss Braddon—these are their gods."[7]

In the 1860s, popular new magazines serialized novels and made them available to a vast audience. Sensation fiction in particular was a business; Braddon explained to Bulwer-Lytton that she had learned "to look at everything in a mercantile sense" and to write for "the Circulating Library and the young lady readers who are its chief supporters."[8] The market allowed little time for revision or careful writing. Braddon wrote the last volume-and-a-half of *Lady Audley* in two weeks to meet her deadline. Critics identifying themselves with high culture, like Henry Mansel, were shocked at the commerciality of sensation fiction; in 1863 Mansel wrote that "no divine influence can be imagined as presiding over the birth of this work beyond the market-law of demand and supply."[9]

But while Mansel frowned and novelists like Reade and George Gissing strained to meet the rigid requirements of the three-decker, women writers seemed positively refreshed by the challenges. The sensationalists seem to have found tension and pressure a stimulus to production, and the act of writing a welcome escape from their personal problems. Florence Marryat wrote her first novel, *Love's*

[7] Quoted by Alan Walbank, *Queens of the Circulating Library*, London, 1950, p. 154.

[8] Wolff, "Devoted Disciple" (April 1974): 132.

[9] "Sensation Novels," *Quarterly Review* CXIII (1863): 490–491.

Conflict (1865), "in the intervals of nursing" her eight children, all stricken with scarlet fever.[10] Even the relatively sedate Mrs. Wood, an invalid who wrote propped up on her sofa, had an implacable, almost mechanical drive to fill up pages that must have chilled the hearts of all but her most secure rivals. Her son admired her because "she never knew what it was not to be in the humour for writing. It was not only that she could always write, but she ever felt a desire to do so—a power urging her, whether she would or no."[11] Gissing was basically sympathetic to independent women, but he seems nonetheless to have felt an instinctive fear of the aggressive professionalism of the women writers. Mary Braddon and her husband John Maxwell appear in *New Grub Street* (1891) as Mr. and Mrs. Jedwood, the corrupt publisher and the best-selling novelist who supports him; another character in the novel, the editor Mrs. Boston Wright, has "lost" one husband in a shipwreck and another in a mysterious fire.

The success of the women novelists and the ease with which they wrote resulted from the happy correspondence between the messages they wished to communicate and the extreme stylization of the sensation novel, a genre in which everything that was not forbidden was compulsory. As Kathleen Tillotson po nts out,[4] the purest type of sensation novel is the novel-with-a-secret,"[12] For the Victorian woman, secrecy was simply a way of life. The sensationalists made crime and violence domestic, modern, and suburban; but their secrets were not simply solutions to mysteries and crimes; they were the secrets of women's dislike of their roles as daughters, wives, and mothers. These women

[10] C. J. Hamilton, "Interview with Florence Marryat," *Womanhood* III (1899-1900): 3. Like other sensationalists, Marryat wrote easily and rarely revised; see Helen C. Black, *Notable Women Authors of the Day*, Glasgow, 1893, p. 88.

[11] Charles W. Wood, *Mrs. Henry Wood: A Memoir*, London, 1895, pp. 217-218.

[12] Kathleen Tillotson, "The Lighter Reading of the Eighteen-Sixties," introduction to *The Woman in White*, Boston, 1969, p. xv.

novelists made a powerful appeal to the female audience by subverting the traditions of feminine fiction to suit their own imaginative impulses, by expressing a wide range of suppressed female emotions, and by tapping and satisfying fantasies of protest and escape. Leslie Fiedler has suggested that the technology of the novel and its potential for mass distribution make the best seller an art form that embodies the communal unconscious; "the machine-produced commodity novel is, therefore, dream-literature, mythic literature, as surely as any tale told over the tribal fire. Its success, too, depends on the degree to which it responds to the shared dreams, the myths which move its intended audience."[13] The enormous popularity of the women sensationalists reflects the skill with which they articulated the fantasies of their readers, fantasies that they themselves fervently shared.

Like the domestic novelists of the previous generation, the sensationalists encouraged a special relationship, a kind of covert solidarity, between themselves and their readers. The audience for the sensation novel was, or was widely assumed to be, female, middle-class, and leisured. Bentley's novels during the 1860s were "primarily intended for the private entertainment of women with daylong leisure," rather than for the struggling housewife to whom Eliza Warren's 1863 best seller, *How I Managed My Household on £200 a Year*, was addressed.[14] Victorian women living in enforced idleness needed some outlet for the frustrations that they could not channel into work. In 1874 Charlotte Jackson reported for Bentley's on *Mildred's Folly*: "It is an improbable story, but many people, from having led, I suppose, very uneventful lives, like impossible stories, and have the excitements they wish for in the unrealities of fiction."[15]

[13] "The Death and Rebirth of the Novel," in John Halperin, ed., *The Theory of the Novel*, New York, 1974, p. 191.

[14] Jeanne Rosenmayer Fahnestock, "Geraldine Jewsbury: The Power of the Publisher's Reader," *Nineteenth-Century Fiction* XXVIII (1973): 263.

[15] Add. MS 46661, Bentley Papers, British Museum.

159

The sensationalists supplied some of these excitements by inverting the stereotypes of the domestic novel and parodying the conventions of their male contemporaries. Sensation novels expressed female anger, frustration, and sexual energy more directly than had been done previously. Readers were introduced to a new kind of heroine, one who could put her hostility toward men into violent action. Their heroines, a shocked Mrs. Oliphant recorded, are women "who marry their grooms in fits of sensual passion, women who pray their lovers to carry them off from husbands and homes they hate; women, at the very least of it, who give and receive burning kisses and frantic embraces, and live in a voluptuous dream."[16] In many sensation novels, the death of a husband comes as a welcome release, and women escape from their families through illness, madness, divorce, flight, and ultimately murder.

Many Victorian readers saw female sensation fiction as sexually provocative. From *Punch*, which parodied "Lady Disorderly's Secret", to the *Christian Remembrancer*, which brooded on the "utter unrestraint" of passion in the heroines, journalists denounced the corrupting tendencies of sensationalism. Dr. George Black warned in 1888 that incautious perusal of such novels had a "tendency to accelerate the occurrence of menstruation."[17] In a parody of Braddon and Wood called *Lucretia; or, The Heroine of the Nineteenth Century* (1868), the Tractarian Francis Paget explained his opposition to sensation novels, using a rhetoric positively apoplectic in its vehemence, a series of little orthographic explosions:

> And the writers of these books, ay, of the very foulest of them,—authors who have put forth confessions of the darkest profligacy that an utter reprobate could make,

---

[16] "Novels," *Blackwood's* III (1867): 259.

[17] *Young Wife's Advice Book*, London 1888, p. 5. For some attacks on sensationalism, see Tillotson, "The Lighter Reading"; and Richard Stang, *The Theory of the Novel in England 1850–1870*, London, 1959, pp. 58–59.

and who have degraded woman's love into an animal propensity so rabid and so exacting, as to profess an opinion that its gratification will be cheaply purchased at the cost *of an eternity in hell*,—these writers are, some by their own admission, some by internal evidence (where the publication is anonymous) *women*; and the worst of them, UNMARRIED WOMEN![18]

The sensationalists and their women readers were less preoccupied with sexuality than with self-assertion and independence from the tedium and injustice of the feminine role in marriage and the family. They shared a conviction that men could not understand the nuances of women's experience; as one novelist put it in 1866: "I wondered secretly whether the dimmest glimmerings of the inside of most women's souls . . . ever penetrates into the brains of men, doubly shuttered and blinded by the happy conviction that they do understand our little minds from attic to cellar."[19] Braddon protested indignantly against charges that her books were full of "the lurking poison of sensuality," and invoked the testimony of her phrenologist that in fact she lacked "animal power."[20] Braddon's novels had so little overt sexuality in them that they were permitted in the Victorian schoolroom when *Ruth* and *The Mill on the Floss* were excluded.[21] The messages schoolgirls and their mothers were picking up had relatively little to do with adultery and bigamy, but much to do with an implied criticism of monogamy, the marriage-market, and the obstacles placed in the paths of intelligent women. They could sympathize with the plight of Braddon's characters, for example, with the "bright ambitious young creature, with the soul of a

[18] *Lucretia; or, The Heroine of the Nineteenth Century*, London, 1868, p. 297.

[19] Rose Piddington, *The Gain of a Loss* (1866), quoted in Myron Brightfield, *Victorian England in its Novels*, Los Angeles, 1968, IV, p. 275.

[20] Wolff, "Devoted Disciple" (April 1974): 143.

[21] See Amy Cruse, *The Victorians and Their Books*, London, 1935, p. 326.

Pitt," who "sits at home and works sham roses in Berlin wool, while her booby brother is thrust out into the world to fight the mighty battle."[22]

Braddon's criticism of the feminine heroine's world is obvious. The sensationalists were still feminine novelists, thwarted in a full exploration of their imaginative worlds by Victorian convention and stereotypes; but they did move well beyond the code of renunciation and submission that informed earlier fiction. In their own novels, they deliberately revised and rewrote the feminine tradition, challenging the myth of the happy, December-May marriage in Mrs. Marsh and Charlotte Yonge, and the pattern of self-sacrificing masochism in George Eliot.

Female sensationalists also revised and challenged the conventions of male sensationalism. Wilkie Collins is generally credited with the mastery of the genre, but the four novels he wrote in the 1860s, *The Woman in White* (1860), *No Name* (1862), *Armadale* (1866), and *The Moonstone* (1868) are relatively conventional in terms of their social and sexual attitudes. The first sentence of *The Woman in White* announced Collins' endorsement of Victorian sex-roles: "This is the story of what a Woman's patience can endure, and what a Man's resolution can achieve." In this novel, the Gothic situation of the beautiful helpless heroine victimized by cruel men provides the excitement. Laura Fairlie is a sweet blue-eyed blonde, incarcerated under a false name in a lunatic asylum by a husband who wants to destroy her sanity and her identity. Collins also creates an active, intelligent female character in Laura's stepsister, Marian Halcombe, but he takes care to make her unfeminine and ugly—she is the only Victorian heroine of my acquaintance with a mustache. With her "large firm masculine mouth and jaw" and her "masculine form," Marian Halcombe, as her first name suggests, is an anomalous figure somewhat similar to George Eliot (Collins did not like wom-

[22] Mary E. Braddon, *The Doctor's Wife* (1864), quoted in Brightfield, *Victorian England*, IV, p. 287.

en novelists). Furthermore, Marian falls ill at the crucial moment and must rely on the tougher man to solve the mystery. Like Dickens, Collins inevitably ends his novels with sentimental happy marriages of patient woman and resolute man, marriages whose success is validated by the prompt appearance of male offspring.

The female pattern is quite different. Mary E. Braddon's *Lady Audley's Secret* (1862) presents us with a carefully controlled female fantasy, which Braddon understands and manipulates with minute exactitude. Braddon's bigamous heroine deserts her child, pushes husband number one down a well, thinks about poisoning husband number two, and sets fire to a hotel in which her other male acquaintances are residing. It is strange that sympathetic critics of Braddon's work, like Michael Sadleir, have felt that her talents atrophied in the grip of convention, and that she "schooled herself to write a thwarted sensationalism which did not at bottom make sense."[23] Braddon's sensationalism makes excellent, although rather frightening, sense; and she pursued it with clear-headed consistency, insisting on "the right of the imaginative writer to choose his subjects from that field whence all the great writers of the past derived their fables—that is to say, the tragic, criminal, & exceptional situations of life."[24]

Braddon's own life was full of exceptional situations. Her father's inability to keep a job and his sexual philandering caused her mother to leave the husband she had never loved when Mary Elizabeth was four. Money was always short in the family, and in 1857 Braddon became an actress to support herself and her mother. In 1860, when she left the stage and began to write, she met John Maxwell, a publisher of periodicals. Maxwell's wife was in an Irish mental hospital; until her death in 1874 enabled them to marry, Braddon lived with Maxwell, acting as stepmother to his

[23] Michael Sadleir, *Things Past*, London, 1944, p. 79.
[24] Wolff, "Devoted Disciple" (April 1974): 144.

five children, bearing him six children of their own, and even paying off his business debts by her writing.[25]

Unlike George Eliot, who was forced into an extremely conservative public stance by her radical life style, Braddon refused to support ideals in which she did not believe. In particular, she satirized the sentimental codes of feminine weakness and affection and the romantic belief in tragic passion. Heroes and heroines of the past often tended to irritate her; she found "that unhappy Camilla [in Fanny Burney's novel] who is always getting into some new scrape"[26] especially annoying. In her letters to Collins and to Bulwer-Lytton, Braddon tactfully evaded their suggestions of how she might "improve" and "deepen" her writing:

> I *will* try & write a better book upon the principle suggested in your beautiful letter—but I am such weary miles away from you in the wide realms of thought, that I feel as if *rapprochement* was impossible. . . . I have begun to question the expediency of very deep emotion, & I think when one does that one must have pretty well passed beyond the power of feeling it. It is this feeling, or rather this incapacity for any strong feeling, that, I believe, causes the flippancy of tone which jars upon your sense of the dignity of art. I can't help looking down upon my heroes when they suffer because I always have in my mind the memory of wasted suffering of my own.[27]

Lady Audley's Secret, though it is often brash and hasty, has been much underrated. It is not only a virtual manifesto of female sensationalism, but also a witty inversion of Victorian sentimental and domestic conventions, certainly equal to the work of Wilkie Collins and Charles Reade. In Braddon's novels generally, women take over the properties

[25] See Wolff's comments in "Devoted Disciple," *Harvard Library Bulletin*, XII (January 1974): 5–9; and Norman Donaldson, Introduction to *Lady Audley's Secret*, New York, 1974.

[26] "Devoted Disciple" (April 1974): 150.

[27] "Devoted Disciple" (January 1974): 15–16.

of the Byronic hero. The bigamist is no longer Rochester, but the demure little governess. Readers responded by making the novel one of the greatest successes in publishing history; there were eight editions the first year alone, and it was never out of print during Braddon's lifetime.

The brilliance of *Lady Audley's Secret* is that Braddon makes her would-be murderess the fragile blond angel of domestic realism: not Bertha Mason, but Rosamond Oliver; not Maggie Tulliver, but Lucy Deane; not Marion Halcombe, but Laura Fairlie.[28] The dangerous woman is not the rebel or the bluestocking, but the "pretty little girl" whose indoctrination in the female role has taught her secrecy and deceitfulness, almost as secondary sex characteristics. She is particularly dangerous because she looks so innocent. As a governess Lucy Graham (one of Lady Audley's aliases) is everyone's ideal:

> Wherever she went she seemed to take joy and brightness with her. In the cottages of the poor her fair face shone like a sunbeam. . . . Everyone loved, admired, and praised her. The boy who opened the five-barred gate that stood in her pathway ran home to tell his mother of her pretty looks, and the sweet voice in which she thanked him for the little service. The verger at the church, who ushered her into the servants pew; the vicar who saw the soft blue eyes uplifted to his face as he preached his simple sermon; the porter from the railway station, who brought her sometimes a letter or a parcel, and who never looked for reward from her; her employer; his visitors; her pupils; the servants; everybody, high and low, united in declaring that Lucy Graham was the sweetest girl that ever lived.[29]

[28] Mrs. Oliphant credited Braddon with setting a new fashion: "She is the inventor of the fair-haired demon of modern fiction. Wicked women used to be brunettes long ago, now they are the daintiest, softest, prettiest of blonde creatures; and this change has been wrought by Lady Audley and her influence on contemporary novels" ("Novels," *Blackwood's*, III (1867), p. 263.

[29] *Lady Audley's Secret*, London, n.d., ch. 1, p. 9.

Braddon's villain is Wilkie Collins' victim, and Braddon's satire of the conventions of *The Woman in White* extends to many other details. Throughout her novel, Braddon shows that a determined woman can liberate herself by actively applying the methods through which Collins' passive heroine is nearly destroyed.[30] Braddon's heroine, while fair, is far from helpless. Deserted by her upper-class husband, who has gone to seek his fortune in the Australian goldfields, she leaves her child with her aged father, fakes her own death by switching identities with a consumptive girl, and becomes a governess under an assumed name. When old Sir Michael Audley proposes to her, she accepts him readily, hoping that she will have to endure "no more dependence, no more drudgery, no more humiliations." When the first husband returns and confronts her, she impulsively pushes him into a well. Lady Audley's other crimes involve efforts to cover up the murder, but in the end it turns out that the husband has survived, and she is not really guilty of shedding blood. She confesses that she is the victim of insanity hereditary in the female line, and she ends her days in a private lunatic asylum on the Continent.[31]

What *is* Lady Audley's secret? Here, I think, is the most subversive aspect of the book. A series of secrets are revealed in succession: first, that she has a double identity; second, that she is a bigamist; third, that she has attempted murder; fourth, that she has not succeeded; and finally, that she is mad. But *is* she mad? The doctor who is consulted by the family at first refuses to give the desired diagnosis:

[30] According to Norman Donaldson, Braddon "owed the idea of the book" to *The Woman in White*, and "many instructive comparisons can be drawn between the two works, especially in the contrasted means used to tell the stories." Introduction to the Dover Edition, New York, 1974, p. vii.

[31] The Victorians believed that women were more susceptible to insanity, and twice as likely as fathers to transmit it to their children, especially to their daughters. See Andrew Wynter, "Inheritance of Insanity in the Female Line," in Vieda Skultans, ed., *Madness and Morals: Ideas on Insanity in the Nineteenth Century*, London, 1975, p. 235.

There is no evidence of madness in anything she has done. She ran away from her home, because her home was not a pleasant one, and she left in the hope of finding a better. There is no madness in that. She committed the crime of bigamy because by that crime she obtained fortune and position. There is no madness there. When she found herself in a desperate position, she did not grow desperate. She employed intelligent means and she carried out a conspiracy which required coolness and deliberation in its execution. There is no madness in that.[32]

Madness, as Phyllis Chesler has recently documented, can be used as a way of labeling deviance from the feminine role; and, as we have seen apropos of *Jane Eyre*, the Victorians evolved a theory of insanity that held women to be particularly vulnerable.[33] Lady Audley's unfeminine assertiveness, so different from the plastic passivity of a Laura Fairlie, must ultimately be described as madness, not only to spare Braddon the unpleasant necessity of having to execute an attractive heroine with whom she in many ways identifies, but also to spare the woman reader the guilt of identifying with a cold-blooded killer. Braddon teases the reader with the explanation that Lady Audley's insanity is latent and intermittent, coming on her only in moments of stress: the aftermath of childbirth, the desertion of her husband, and his return to haul her out of happiness and prosperity. As every woman reader must have sensed, Lady Audley's real secret is that she is *sane* and, moreover, representative.

Braddon provides persuasive evidence for such an interpretation in a lengthy monologue spoken by Robert Audley, the detective in the story. Ostensibly denouncing the immemorial wickedness of women, the monologue is really a thinly veiled feminist threat that women confined

---

[32] *Lady Audley's Secret*, ch. XXXIV, p. 290.
[33] See Phyllis Chesler, *Women and Madness*, London, 1974; and Skultans, *Madness and Morals*, pp. 223–236.

to the home and denied legitimate occupations will turn their frustrations against the family itself:

> They are Semiramides, and Cleopatras, and Joans of Arc, Queen Elizabeths, and Catherines the Second and they riot in battle, and murder, and clamor, and desperation. If they can't agitate the universe and play at ball with hemispheres, they'll make mountains of warfare and vexation out of domestic molehills; and social storms in household teacups. . . . To call them the weaker sex is to utter a hideous mockery. They are the stronger sex, the noisier, the more persevering, the most self-assertive sex. They want freedom of opinion, variety of occupation, do they? Let them have it. Let them be lawyers, doctors, preachers, teachers, soldiers, legislators—anything they like—but let them be quiet—if they can.[34]

The threat of domestic murder in *Lady Audley's Secret* was not an isolated one. One complaint critics gave against sensation novels was that they "made murder easy to the meanest capacity" by providing the "most approved recipes for poisoning" to the interested student of toxicology.[35] In his memoir *As I Remember*, E. E. Kellet recalls that domestic murder was suspected to be much more common than could be proved:

> What people showed was not always what they felt, and the family home could be a prison-house from which there was a sinister way of escape. . . . A doctor once told me that he did not believe there was a single medical practitioner in London, of twenty years standing, who had not serious reason to believe that wives in his practice had poisoned their husbands, and husbands their wives; but in the vast majority of cases the doctors could not utter their suspicions.[36]

[34] *Lady Audley's Secret*, ch. XXV, p. 160.
[35] Paget, *Lucretia*, quoted in Richard Altick, *Victorian Studies in Scarlet*, New York, 1970, p. 81.
[36] *As I Remember*, London, 1936, pp. 232–233.

Middle-class women's fascination with violent crime had long been accepted as an inexplicable, but charming, feminine paradox. The minor novelist Eliza Stephenson noted in 1864 "that women of family and position, women who have been brought up in refined society, women who pride themselves upon the delicacy of their sensibilities, who would faint at the sight of a cut finger and go into hysterics if the drowning of a litter of kittens were mentioned in their hearing—such women can sit for hours listening to the details of a cold-blooded murder."[37]

In Juliana Ewing's classic account of Victorian girlhood, *Six to Sixteen*, there is a comic scene in which respectable Yorkshire ladies and gentlemen speculate about the potential cruelty of their amiable teen-age daughters, a cruelty that had been proclaimed by the *Milliner and Mantuamaker* (a parody of the *Englishwomen's Domestic Magazine*):

> There was a most extraordinary correspondence, too, after that shoemaker's daughter in Lambeth was tried for poisoning her little brother. . . . The letters were all about all the dreadful things done by girls in their teens. . . . But the most awful letter was from 'A Student of Human Nature,' and it ended up that every girl of fifteen was a murderess at heart.[38]

The Constance Kent case in the 1860s, in which a sixteen-year-old girl from a respectable Wiltshire family was accused of, and ultimately confessed to, cutting the throat of her three-year-old half-brother, was one source of this kind of speculation. Doctors and journalists, as well as "students of human nature," suggested that the crime was notably feminine: "It was a wanton murder, not done by the hand of a man, for there is a *finesse* of cruelty about it that no men, we believe, however depraved, could have been guilty

37 Altick, *Victorian Studies*, p. 42.
38 *Six to Sixteen*, Boston, n.d., p. 126.

of; but it is the revengeful act of a woman—morbid, cruel, cunning."[39]

The trials of middle-class murderesses attracted enthusiastic and sympathetic female followers. Court reporters at the Madeleine Smith trial (held in Edinburgh in 1857) were shocked by the zest of the women observers who lined up outside the courtroom every day to hear all the gory and erotic details. Mary S. Hartman describes the consistent pattern of "supportive identification" between middle-class women and murderesses of their own class:

> The contemporary press constantly complained of the "unseemly" interest of "proper" females in the cases; but the explanation of that interest appears to lie less in the morbid thrills produced by exotic behavior than in the opportunities for vicarious fulfillment of unarticulated desires. In the earlier period, the reports on the women's responses are limited to accounts of their behavior as spectators at the trials, and include expressions of sympathy in courtrooms, attempts to visit the accused with gifts and flowers, and displays of popular enthusiasm for the women's defense counsels. Later, however, expressions of sympathy and identification become more vocal. Women write letters to the judges, and to newspapers, sign petitions, form defense organizations and openly attack courts and society on such issues as the double standard. The accused murderesses, it would appear, had acted out what many of these women, in their most secret thoughts, had hardly dared to imagine. For many of the "respectable" women absorbed in the trials, the experience seems to have been less of attending a freak show than of looking into a distorting mirror.[40]

[39] Quoted in Mary S. Hartman, "Child-Abuse and Self-Abuse: Two Victorian Cases," *History of Childhood Quarterly* II (Fall 1974): 244.

[40] Mary S. Hartman, introduction to *Victorian Murderesses: A True History of Thirteen Respectable French and English Women Accused of Unspeakable Crimes*, New York, 1976. See also Hartman, "Murder for Respectability: The Case of Madeleine Smith," *Victorian Studies*

Braddon sustained her appeal to thwarted female energy through a long and successful career, shuffling and recombining the same elements of feminine ambition that were channeled first into marriage and then into criminal deception. *Taken at the Flood*, for example, echoes the plot of *Lady Audley*; Sylvia, ambitious and self-educated, marries a rich old man to escape from her exploitative father, and then discovers that marriage is simply another form of bondage and servitude. Like Lady Audley, Sylvia tries to kill her husband. Braddon's descriptions of feminine discontent influenced many other novelists of the day, including George Eliot. Madame Laure in *Middlemarch*, the actress who kills her husband because he is too possessive, is a character right out of sensation fiction. In Eliot's *Daniel Deronda*, Gwendolen comes very close to murdering Grandcourt.

Mrs. Henry Wood came from an older generation than most of the sensationalists; her novels are more sentimental than Braddon's, but equally adroit in tapping female frustrations. She herself was married to an unsympathetic businessman. Her son recorded that his father "had not a spark of imagination. . . . It was an effort to him to read a novel." Mrs. Wood began to write fiction in the aftermath of a prolonged, apparently psychosomatic, illness. Writing was a form of release that enabled her to recover from her illness and cope cheerfully with the stresses of her life. Like Braddon, she knew exactly what she wanted to say: "Once thought out, plot and incident were never changed; the story, in being written, did not develop fresh views and possibilities. It was not permitted to do so; the author had her matter well in hand—a fixed purpose."[41]

Wood's *East Lynne* (1862) was another best seller; like

---

xvi (June 1973): 399. George Eliot and George Lewes were among those following the case; see *The George Eliot Letters*, ii, ed. Gordon S. Haight, London, 1954, pp. 360, 362, 363, and 366.

41 *Mrs. Henry Wood: A Memoir*, p. 218.

Lady Audley, it became a popular stage melodrama in England and the United States. The heroine, Lady Isabel Carlyle, is forced by her male relatives to marry a man she does not love. Her husband, like Sir Michael Audley and Henry Wood, is prosperous, kind, indulgent, and congenial; but, as Mrs. Wood hints, where passion is absent, mere goodness cannot suffice. Lady Isabel pines away, reads novels from the West Lynne Library, painfully bears two children, and becomes an invalid. Wood adopts a moral and prudential tone, but she clearly sympathizes with the feelings of the wife who is neither deceived nor mistreated, but sexually frustrated and simply bored to death:

> Young lady, when he, who is soon to be your lord and master, protests to you that he shall always be as ardent a lover as he is now, believe him if you like, but don't reproach him when disappointment comes. . . . it is in the constitution of man to change, the very essence of his nature. . . . his manner must settle down into a calmness, which to you, if you are of an exacting temperament, may look like indifference or coldness, but you will do well to put up with it, for it will never now be otherwise.[42]

Motivated by sexual passion that seems perverse because Mrs. Wood is so reticent in explaining it, Lady Isabel deserts her husband and children and runs away with a base seducer. For this surrender to impulsive passion, Mrs. Wood provides a terrible punishment. Lady Isabel is abandoned by her lover, she loses her illegitimate child in a train wreck, and, in the same wreck, she is disfigured beyond all recognition. She returns to her home in disguise and becomes a governess to her own children. Her husband has obtained a divorce and married her worst enemy. She must even weep at the deathbed of her son without revealing her identity. Yet the magnitude of her disciplines seems necessary as a deterrent, so tempting is her flight. Mrs. Wood even intervenes to issue an explicit warning:

[42] *East Lynne*, London, 1895, p. 148. ("Going From Home").

Lady-wife-mother! Should you ever be tempted to abandon your home, so will you awaken! Whatever trials may be the lot of your married life, though they may magnify themselves to your crushed spirit as beyond the endurance of woman to bear, *resolve* to bear them; fall down on your knees and pray to be enabled to bear them.[43]

The urgency of Mrs. Wood's message suggests that she felt herself to be speaking to a large and desperate audience. When women found it nearly impossible to obtain a divorce and had no means of support outside marriage, fantasies of pure escape had a great deal of appeal; and thus in sensation novels, as Guinevere Griest tells us in her study of Mudie's Library, "fleeing, not always strictly necessary to the plot, was very popular."[44]

The heroine of Rhoda Broughton's *Cometh Up as a Flower* (1867) reads *East Lynne* and decides not to run away from her husband. Instead she dies of a respectable consumption, thanking God that "the great smith who strikes off all fetters, is knocking off mine."[45] Broughton's sensationalism, like that of her predecessors, is thwarted by the need to conform to moral formulas, but she gives a more complete picture of family stress than they had ventured. Male competitors like Mortimer Collins grumbled that the new favorite heroine was the "silly girl . . . who cometh up as a flower or throweth her husband down a well,"[46] but Broughton's Nell Le Strange is witty, exuberant, and cheerfully frank.[47] Nell is one of those Victorian hero-

[43] *East Lynne*, p. 212 ("Charming Results").

[44] *Mudie's Circulating Library and the Victorian Novel*, Bloomington, 1970, p. 130.

[45] *Cometh Up as a Flower: An Autobiography*, London, 1899, p. 411.

[46] Quoted in Amy Cruse, *Victorians and Their Books*, p. 332.

[47] Braddon, who did not like many of her disciples, considered Broughton a worthy competitor, and they eventually became close friends. Even before they met, Braddon wrote to Bulwer-Lytton that there was "a certain order of genius" in her rival's books (quoted in Wolff, "Devoted Disciple" [April 1974]: 152). Michael Sadleir thinks that Broughton was disadvantaged by the exigencies of the three-deckers;

ines left as the head of a motherless household, but unlike Ethel May or Esther Summerson, she makes no bones about her possessive delight in her father's love and attention, and her bitter jealousy of her sister Dolly. She sometimes catches herself "wondering whether, in the event of Dolly's death, I should be enabled to cry a little and wear a decent semblance of grief."[48] Nell is also outspokenly passionate; when she meets a handsome guardsman in the woods, her happiness is "limitless, frenzied, drunken."[49] But he is married already, and Nell, to repair the family fortunes, must agree to a marriage of convenience with the rich, old, and ugly Sir Hugh. Her account of the arranged marriage, with its degrading daily and nightly confrontations of the buyer and the bought, suggests a genuinely radical analysis of women's position in the family, anticipating Mill's essay on *The Subjection of Women*, which appeared two years later:

> His arm is around my waist, and he is brushing my eyes and cheeks and brow with his somewhat bristly mustache as often as he feels inclined—for am I not his property? Has he not every right to kiss my face off if he chooses, to clasp me and hold me and drag me about in whatever manner he wills, for has he not bought me? For a pair of first class blue eyes warranted fast colour, for ditto super-fine red lips, for so many pounds of prime white flesh, he has paid a handsome price on the nail, without any haggling, and now if he may not test the worth of his purchases, poor man, he *is* hardly used![50]

Nell struggles heroically with her revulsion and her self-contempt, but she wishes wistfully that her husband would transfer his attentions to the cook. In contrast to the ser-

---

she had to add ten chapters to *Cometh Up* to fit the requirements. Her best books are "admirable specimens of feminine novel-writing—at once astringent, deeply sympathetic to the sufferings of women, subtly observed and deftly humorous" (*Things Past*, p. 85).

48 *Cometh Up*, p. 22.   49 Ibid., p. 110.
50 Ibid., p. 326.

vants, her lot seems even more hopeless, for "all Sir Hugh's other servants, if they disliked their situations, or got tired of them, might give warning and leave; but I, however wearied I might get of mine, could never give warning, could never leave. I was a fixture for life." Furthermore, her girlish hopes, nurtured by sentimental fiction and religion, that the marriage ceremony would magically keep her from being attracted to other men prove false, and she must view herself as "a very bad, wicked woman."[51]

Mrs. Oliphant, in an indignant review of Broughton's novels, proclaimed her feeling that "it is a shame to women so to write; and it is a shame to the women who read and accept as a true representation of themselves and their ways the equivocal talk and fleshly inclinations herein attributed to them."[52] But the flood of popular books by women sensationalists in the 1860s and 1870s shows that readers recognized themselves in the outspoken heroines. The exuberant frankness of the fiction wears better than we might suppose; many of these books still startle and amuse.

Helen Mather's 1875 best seller, *Comin' Thro' the Rye* is an interesting example. The first volume, "Seed Time," is based on the author's own childhood with a sadistic father whom all the children, but particularly the daughters— "his white slaves"—hated and feared. Written in secret and published anonymously, the novel gives an uninhibited view of the Victorian papa's relentless exploitation of his daughters: "If he had his way he would keep all his daughters withering forever on their virgin stalks, and when they were miserable, peaky old maids turn round upon them, and twit them with their incapacity to get a man to marry either of them."[53]

Although Helen Mathers believed that the only escape from father was marriage, she hints forcefully through a series of unmistakable innuendos that male sexuality is totally destructive. Her heroine, Nell, is one of twelve chil-

[51] Ibid., p. 358.   [52] "Novels," 275.
[53] *Comin' Thro' the Rye*, I, London, 1875, p. 150.

dren (like Mathers herself); in the background of this huge family is a sweet and exhausted mother, obvious victim of the paternal lust. Father is portrayed as choleric and explosively virile: "We all look upon the governor as a kind of bombshell, or volcano, or loaded gun, that may blow up at any movement and will infallibly destroy whatever is nearest to him."[54] Other men are equally repellent, if less powerful. The courting servants whom the children spy upon are red, clumsy and gross; the oily clergyman, "folding his fat hands and simmering gently in the hot sun like a seal," is both a hypocrite and a fool.[55] Even twelve-year-old Nell feels superior when he tells her that babies weep for original sin; she has seen a great many babies, and she knows better. Growing up in the country, surrounded by an abundance of animal and human fertility, Nell finds sex comic and absurd. She cannot understand "how people can like being married," nor "what fathers were invented for."[56] Naturally, enough, Nell's ambition is to be part of her brother's world, and the high point of her life is being sent to a progressive boarding-school where she is taught to play cricket in knickerbockers. Discarding her detested petticoats, Nell feels for the first time that she is in the world on an equal footing with men, both in terms of agility gained and modesty lost: "How my gowns, petticoats, crinolines, ribbons, ties, cloaks, hats, bonnets, gloves, tapes, hooks, eyes, buttons, and the hundred and one et ceteras that make up a girl's costume, chafe and irritate me!"[57]

Unfortunately, Mathers was unable to sustain this confident tone through three volumes. Nell falls in love with a mysterious stranger, who dies. Having used her own experience to create Nell as a girl, Mathers could neither abandon

---

[54] Ibid., p. 14.   [55] Ibid., p. 40.   [56] Ibid., p. 79.

[57] Ibid., p. 45. Of her own writing, Mathers told an interviewer: "Often, just as I have settled down to do a good morning's work . . . my boy Phil rushes up and lays his air gun or his banjo on the table, or my husband brings in some little commission or a heap of notes to be answered for him" (Black, *Notable Women Authors*, p. 72).

the sentimental conventions of the three-decker, nor believe in them. Her solution to this dilemma was perhaps the only one possible for a novelist in her circumstances; she concocted a romance for her heroine, but ended it unhappily. Nell is left in limbo; we have no right to predict that she will do anything with her life, but at least she is not confined to a marriage.

Women novelists of an older generation who survived into the 1860s reacted to the sensationalists with genuine shock, but also with a degree of envy. Having learned to conceal and repress their own protest, in their writing at least, they bitterly resented the ease with which younger women were speaking their minds. Feminine novelists had internalized the codes of genteel womanhood, and as they grew older they held even more tenaciously to the outworn ideals. Even Geraldine Jewsbury, who had been so daring in the days of *Zoë*, turned guardian of the hearth. As a reader for Bentley's from 1858 until 1880, she passed stern judgment on the new fiction. "If I were a *man* reading this MS," she wrote of Mrs. Godfrey's *Dolly* in 1872, "I shd enquire 'are the young women of England trying to qualify themselves for courtezans?'—the breaking down of all sense of shame & modesty opens the way to that bottomless pit."[58] Jewsbury's battle with Rhoda Broughton was particularly fierce. She tried to persuade Bentley to reject Broughton's books, and she reviewed them acidly in the *Athenaeum* when they appeared. Broughton satirized her in *A Beginner* (1894) as Miss Grimston, reviewing for *The Porch* "with a tomahawk," but was characteristically untroubled by Jewsbury's attacks. "I am surprised at the mildness of Athenaeum's abuse," she wrote a friend in 1870. "I am sure I don't recognize old Jewsbury's pen dipped in vinegar and gall."[59]

Mrs. Lynn Linton lambasted the sensationalists and their heroines in her *Saturday Review* series, "The Girl of the Period" (1869). In her later novels, like *The Rebel of the*

[58] Fahnestock, "Geraldine Jewsbury," p. 262.
[59] Sadleir, *Things Past*, p. 104.

177

Family (1880), she caricatured rebelling women as man-haters and lesbians. Bell Blount, the Lady President of the West Hill Society for Women's Rights, lives with another woman, her "little wife," and proclaims that "the world will never be regenerated until women have the upper hand and men are relegated to their proper place as our slaves and the mere workers of the world."[60] Linton's heroine resists the rhetoric of women's rights and marries: "Love seemed so much better than all this hard antagonism!—womanly submission so much sweeter than all this egotistical independence!"[61]

Some other women novelists, while publicly protesting against the sensuality and egoism of the younger generation, tried to break through some of the restraints they had always observed and to portray female emotions more honestly. In two late novels, *The Ladies Lindore* (1883) and *Lady Car* (1889), Margaret Oliphant told the story of Lady Caroline Lindore, whose ambitious father forces her into marriage with a rich but boorish landowner, Pat Torrance.

Miserable though she is, Lady Car is a perfect lump of female passivity, and she makes no resistance to her fate. Mrs. Oliphant dramatized her heroine's wretchedness, and even her sense of sexual violation and repugnance, but did not endow her with the will to change. In an unusually explicit passage, Lady Car confesses to her mother that her husband's death (in a drunken fall) has made her ecstatically happy for the first time in years:

> I am like a mad woman . . . mad—with joy. . . . To think that I shall never be subject to all *that* any more—that he can never come in here again—that I am free—that I can be alone. . . . Never to be alone: never to have a corner in the world where—some one else has not a right to come, a better right than yourself, I don't know how I have borne it.[62]

[60] *The Rebel of the Family*, I, London, 1880, p. 67.
[61] Ibid., p. 301.
[62] *The Ladies Lindore*, II, Leipzig, 1884, p. 232.

178

As in Rhoda Broughton's novels, the death of the husband is not tragedy but liberation. Mrs. Oliphant was also using the metaphor of the room to represent the sexual integrity of the female body and the intellectual integrity of spirit. But what does Lady Car do with her freedom and solitude? Educate herself, plan to remain independent, teach her children not to make the same mistakes? Nothing whatever. In fact, she finds freedom as intolerable a lot as slavery. In the sequel we find her remarried, this time for "love," and just as unhappy. The sexual contact of the husband she loves also disgusts her; and her children, by Torrance, do not conform to her expectations.

Mrs. Oliphant's identification with her heroine makes the novel uncomfortable for the reader, who feels pressed to participate in her orgy of self-pity. She makes much, for example, of Lady Car's alienation from the children of the first marriage, who seem like creatures of a coarser race. The last drops of sympathy are ruthlessly extracted for the mother's loneliness and disillusion. It never occurs to Mrs. Oliphant that anything but fate and genetics is to blame. She implicitly accepts the idea that the bliss of motherhood is a right that Lady Car has been cheated of, and she does not consider whether Lady Car has been mistaken in her expectations that motherhood will compensate for the weakness of her personality. Lady Car is so feeble a creature, so tepid and self-obsessed, that her rejection of the children seems nasty evidence of the way weak people try to manipulate others through guilt.

Mrs. Oliphant never faced the dangers of a social myth that places the whole weight of feminine fulfillment on husband and children. She herself made impossible demands on her sons and suffered perpetually because of their "failures." In the novel, at least, there are alternatives to passive suffering that involve planning and effort on the part of the sufferer, and absolve the tormentors of their guilt. Old-fashioned Victorian moralists might have recommended a good dose of duty; twentieth-century feminists would insist on divorce. But a third possibility, present in both centuries, is that the heroine stop searching for her happiness in others, and begin trying to generate it through her own accomplishments. Lady Car is, in fact, a parasite, and if she sucks sorrow rather than joy she has only herself to blame.

The way to get rid of folly, as George Eliot said, is to rid oneself of false expectations. But even as they recorded their disillusion, their frustration, their anger, indeed, their murderous feelings, the sensationalists could not bring themselves to undertake a radical inquiry into the role of women. The novels of the 1860s, and 1870s, pregnant with their inchoate rage, generally miscarry. Anger is internalized or projected, never confronted, understood, and acted upon. Again and again the heroines reach the brink of self-discovery only to fall back. Even the female thrillers were limited explorations of women's consciousness; they evaded analysis of the hostilities and longings they hinted of. Both Lady Audley and Lady Isabel desert their children as well as their husbands, but Braddon and Wood were careful not to attack the cult of motherhood outright. Lady Isabel is a precursor of Ibsen's Nora, but she is a Nora without ideology, one who simply moves from one doll's house to another; Lady Audley moves out of the doll's house and into the madhouse.

Michael Sadleir places the blame for the deficiencies of the three-deckers on the rigid demands of the market. But whatever the external pressures, this generation of women writers deeply internalized their feminine conflicts. Through the structure of the three-decker, they repeatedly acted out their inability to confront their own feelings and to accept the force of their own needs. Typically, the first volume of a woman's sensation novel is a gripping and sardonic analysis of a woman in conflict with male authority. By the second volume guilt has set in. In the third volume we see the heroine punished, repentant, and drained of all energy. The fear of being morbid, unnatural, and unfeminine kept women writers from working out the implications of their plots.

The very tradition of the domestic novel opposed the heroine's development. It was so widely accepted that marriage would conclude the representation of the fictional heroine, that "my third volume" became a coy euphemism for this period of women's lives.[63]

The death of George Eliot in 1880 left women novelists leaderless, in a sense, although her example and her legend continued to weigh heavily upon them for many years. But with her death the feminine aesthetic had exhausted itself. Women novelists needed an ethic that went beyond self-sacrifice, and a programme that went beyond escape and revenge. The decline of the three-decker after 1880 helped them break some of the shackles of form, and the feminist ideology of the 1880s gave them an important role to play, as well as some new ideas about self-preservation that went beyond fantasies of domestic murder to political organization. "I see that the world is not a bit better for centuries of self-sacrifice on the woman's part," wrote Sarah Grand, matriarch of the feminist novelists, ". . . and therefore I think it is time we had a more effectual plan."[64]

With the closing of the Feminine phase and the death of one of its great figures, a kind of richness was lost; a sense of intimacy and shared understanding between novelists and readers disappeared. Feminist ideology temporarily diverted attention from female experience to a cultist celebration of womanhood and motherhood. It was inevitable and necessary that women novelists confront male society and culture, and that they rebel against the feminine tradition. But it was unfortunate that the rebellion took place just as the literature of the sensationalists was opening up genuinely radical and experimental possibilities in feminine domestic realism. The high spirits and comic exuberance of the sensationalists were soon submerged in the portentous anthems of the feminists.

[63] See Thackeray, *The Newcomes*, bk. I, ch. XXIII.
[64] Sarah Grand, *The Heavenly Twins*, London, 1894, p. 80.

██

CHAPTER VII

The Feminist Novelists

Saw the infants doomed to suffering,
Saw the maidens slaves to lust,
Saw the starving mothers barter
Souls and bodies for a crust.
Then she rose—with inward vision,
Nerving all her powers for good;
Feeling one with suffering sisters
In perfected womanhood.
—"*The New Woman*," 1895

IN the 1880s and 1890s, women writers played a central role
in the formulation and popularization of feminist ideology.
Unlike their male contemporaries, such as Hardy and Gissing, who believed that the artist was inevitably doomed by
the cheap commercialism of the new age, women were ex-
hilarated by the prospect of a new age in which female
ability would have more scope. The abrupt disappearance
of the three-decker novel in the 1890s helped women writers who had never been comfortable with this format to
experiment with short fiction: "dreams," "allegories," "fantasias," and "keynotes."

Whereas the feminine novelists had expressed female cultural values obliquely and proclaimed antifeminism publicly, the feminist novelists had a highly developed sense of
belonging to a sisterhood of women writers, a kinship that
conveyed obligations as well as privileges. Mary Haweis
neatly connected the claims of feminism and business in her
1894 address to the Women Writers Dinner: "Our first duty
as women writers is to help the cause of other women,
whilst keeping up the value of the daily and monthly jour-

nals."[1] More sentimentally, Olive Schreiner planned her novel *From Man to Man* as a gesture of tender support for suffering sisters: "I feel that if only one lonely and struggling woman read it and found strength and comfort from it one would not feel one had lived quite in vain."[2] For the first time in the century, women writers were the anointed priestesses of their sex, and their creed was Influence. Their mission was made to seem cosmically grandiose and at the same time, the merest extension of their innate female propensities and skills. As Mrs. Haweis put it: "In women's hands—in women writers' hands—lies the regeneration of the world. Let us go on with our tongues of fire, consecrated to an entirely holy work, cleansing, repairing, beautifying as we go, the page of the world's history which lies before us now."[3] Such domestic imagery came naturally to Mrs. Haweis, whose most successful book was a treatise on *The Art of Housekeeping*. Women would begin to apply their art on a grand scale, tidying, mending, and scrubbing society; at the same time they would be what Mrs. Haweis called "Recording Angels," exposing society's vice with careful and loving concern. In the hands of the feminists, the conscientious tradition of Mrs. Craik and George Eliot took on a messianic fervor; as Katherine Bradley (half the writing team of "Michael Field") confided in her journal in 1884, "We hold ourselves bound in life and in literature to reveal—as far as may be—the beauty of the high feminine standard of *the ought to be*."[4]

The chivalrous vision of the sacred influence of women

[1] *Words to Women: Addresses and Essays*, ed. Reverend H. R. Haweis, London, 1900, p. 70. In 1895 the feminist journal *Shafts* appealed for sisterly support: "Is the helping of a woman's paper a less worthy object than the purchase of knick-knacks, superfluous dress, and jewelry?"

[2] "Note on the Genesis of the Book," *From Man to Man*, London, 1982.

[3] *Words to Women*, p. 71.

[4] *Works and Days*, ed. T. and D. C. Sturge Moore, London, 1933, p. 8.

had been a central concept of the Victorian feminine ideal. This vision, most completely articulated in Ruskin's essay "Of Queen's Gardens" (in *Sesame and Lilies*, 1864) projected the hope of national redemption onto the spiritual virginity of women who were unravaged by the power drives of a rapacious commercial society. Ruskin outlined a theory of the compensations of the female sex-role that was both flattering and narcotic. In particular, he emphasized the physical and psychological boundaries of "woman's true place," the Home. While men laboring in the outside world are "wounded" and "hardened," to use his sexually loaded rhetoric, women intact in the home—"the place of Peace; the shelter, not only from injury, but from all terror, doubt, and division"—are secure in themselves and havens of safety for the threatened male. Ruskin makes it clear that the Home is not a concrete place, with walls and a roof, but a mystical projection of the female psyche, something a woman generates through her femaleness alone: "Wherever a true wife comes, this home is always around her. The stars only may be over her head; the glowworm in the night-cold grass may be the only fire at her foot, but home is yet wherever she is."

One might have predicted that by the 1880s this theory of female influence would have been discarded. However, the feminists merely transposed it into an activist key, making the ideal of true womanhood the basis of the politics of the female subculture. This time around, women rejected the passivity and the noncompetitive separation of spheres basic to the feminine ideal. To the old theory of female influence, they added what they had learned about campaign organization, legal strategy, publicity, self-assertive careerism, charisma, and political confrontation. While their male contemporaries, such as Gissing, Moore, and Hardy, imagined a New Woman who fulfilled their own fantasies of sexual freedom (a heroine made notorious to feminists' disgust, by Grant Allen's 1895 best seller *The Woman Who Did*), feminist writers of the 1880s and 1890s demanded self-control for men, rather than license for themselves.[5] They took the idea of female influence seriously, and they intended to make it a genuine source of power. Their version of New Womanhood, though not as sensational as Allen's, was more pragmatic, and probably more threatening. One can understand why it seemed to many of their contemporaries (including Freud) that in seeking to enforce the empty promises of the feminine ideal, the feminists were putting teeth in the vagina.

Social Darwinism offered a model for the enforcement of

[5] Grant Allen gives a thorough account of his ideas about women in "Plain Words on the Woman Question," *Fortnightly Review* LII (1889): 448–458, arguing for motherhood before self-fulfillment. Women were indignant at Allen's treatment of free love as a feminist concept in *The Woman Who Did*. It was well known that in private he espoused antifeminist views. In 1891, at a house-party hosted by Edith Nesbit and Hubert Bland, Allen "held forth to a largely feminine audience on the inferiority of women" (Doris Langley Moore, *E. Nesbit: A Biography*, London, 1951, p. 109). In the *Contemporary Review*, Millicent Garrett Fawcett wrote: "It is satisfactory to remember that Mr. Grant Allen has never given help by tongue or pen to any practical effort to improve the legal or social status of women. He is not a friend, but an enemy, and it is as an enemy that he endeavors to link together the claim of women to citizenship and social and industrial independence with attacks upon marriage and the family" ("The Woman Who Did," LXVII [1895]: 630.) As for Gissing, even the conservative *Saturday Review* objected to his female stereotypes: "Our women folk are not all angels, but . . . they are not invariably fools, wantons, sneaks, and nagging sluts. Mr. Gissing's sustained snarl at the sex at large grows a shade wearisome, not to say vexatious" (LXXXIII [April 10, 1897]: 363; quoted by Lloyd Fernando, "Gissing's Studies in Vulgarism: Aspects of His Anti-Feminism," *Southern Review* IV [1970]: 49). Like Gissing, Hardy favored women's suffrage because he hoped it would bring about sexual reforms. In a letter to Mrs. Fawcett in 1906, Hardy explained that he thought "the tendency of the women's vote will be to break up the present pernicious conventions in respect of manners, customs, religion, illegitimacy, the stereotyped household (that it must be the unit of society), the father of a woman's child (that it is anybody's business but the woman's own except in cases of disease or insanity)" (Fawcett Library, London). Women could not afford such radicalism, so long as their economic independence was made difficult.

female influence, and evolutionary theory attracted many feminists. Mathilde Blind (George Eliot's first biographer) wrote a poetic epic on Darwinism, *The Ascent of Man*, in 1888. At the same time, Olive Schreiner was telling Havelock Ellis about her "attempt to apply the theory of evolution to elucidate sex problems."[6] "Ascent" is the key word in women's theory of social evolution. In a feminist rhetoric characteristic of the times, Amy Bulley summed up the moderate position in 1890:

> As a social factor, as an engine of evolution, of human development, the entry of women into full life is a change so vast and so pregnant, that to those who take in its significance the idea is overwhelming. Its final outcome cannot be foreseen; it is only clear that with the development of society is bound up henceforward the more complete and perfect evolution of women.[7]

Women began to believe that they had a moral right to assume leadership, since they were in the spiritual avantgarde. England seemed to be crying out for the kind of moral leadership women wished to provide. To sheltered

[6] *Letters of Olive Schreiner*, ed. S. C. Cronwright-Schreiner, London, 1924, p. 112. Leo J. Henkin, in *Darwinism in the English Novel 1860–1910*, New York, 1940, does not distinguish between male and female versions of social Darwinism, but many references in the fiction show contemporary awareness of the issues. For example, in Edward Jenkins' *Lord Bantam* (1872), there is the "Society for Developing the Mental and Moral Stamina of Women"; and, in Rhoda Broughton's *A Beginner* (1894), the "World Women's Federation for the Regeneration of Men." Many writers besides Olive Schreiner attempted to use Darwin to elucidate sex problems; a sample of these texts includes Jane Hume Clapperton, *Scientific Meliorism* (1885); J. B. Haycraft, *Darwinism and Race Progress* (1895); Eliza Burt Gamble, *The Evolution of Woman: An Inquiry into the Dogma of Her Inferiority to Man* (1894); and Frances Swiney, *The Cosmic Procession, or the Feminine Principle in Evolution* (1906). Miss Swiney argued that "man, on a lower plane, is undeveloped woman" (p. 221).

[7] "The Political Evolution of Women," *Westminster Review* LXXXIV (1890): 8.

186

and sexually naive ladies, the revelations of the Contagious Diseases Acts campaigns (1864–1884) came with traumatic force.[8] The campaign reached its full strength at just about the time that *The Subjection of Women* appeared. On December 31, 1869, the *Daily News* published a manifesto demanding the abolition of the Acts that was signed by 124 prominent women, including Florence Nightingale and Harriet Martineau. From then on, respectable women were confronted with an ever-escalating series of shocking stories of male brutality, profligacy, and vice. It was not just that brutish soldiers benefitted from government supervision of brothels. The policeman and the doctor became agents of the state in their forcible examinations of women accused of prostitution. In an age when many women preferred death to pelvic examination, the Lock Hospital in which prostitutes were confined for examination and treatment, with its horrific stories of violation, touched the darkest female fantasies. The suicide of an innocent suspect, Mrs. Percy, in 1875, consolidated the view of a male alliance dedicated to the persecution of women.

The female crusaders against male vice were often fanatical in their insistence that the male sex drive was causing cosmic degeneracy and devolution. They opposed to the gross and "hoggish habits" of men the idealization of a female sex drive sublimated into maternity, and thus stripped of all its less acceptable associations. All this is easily ridiculed, but we must recall how the world looked to them at the time. They were frightened by more than the Contagious Diseases campaign. "The Maiden Tribute of Modern Babylon," W. T. Stead's sensational series on child prostitution

[8] The Contagious Diseases Acts, instituted during the Crimean War, attempted to control syphilis by enforced examination, detection, and treatment of prostitutes in garrison towns. Women objected because men were neither examined nor punished for their part in the transactions. Glen Petrie's *A Singular Iniquity: The Campaigns of Josephine Butler*, London, 1971, is a good recent study. See also E. M. Sigsworth and T. J. Wyke, "A Study of Victorian Prostitution and Venereal Disease," in *Suffer and Be Still*, London, 1980, pp. 77–99.

in London in the *Pall Mall Gazette*, presented women with new information on male tastes for virgins, whips, and rape. Even the unsolved murder orgies of Jack the Ripper in 1885 nourished female paranoia. It was frequently suggested that the Ripper, who dissected the sex organs of the whores he killed and laid them out for the police (he once claimed to have eaten them), was a doctor or a syphilitic, or both, taking revenge on women because they carried disease.

Most important, we must understand that the fear of venereal disease was a 'powerful factor in sexual attitudes.[9] The crucial factor for women was not the hideous and loathsome disfigurement of syphilis, graphically portrayed in the medical books of the day, but the fact that the worst form of the disease was hereditary. Syphilitic fathers (as London saw in Ibsen's *Ghosts* in 1891) carried a dreadful and inescapable taint. Medical experts confirmed that syphilis (incurable at the time) was almost invariably transmitted to innocent wives and children. Thus it was with the sense that future generations were endangered that women took up the righteous battle to change and elevate the sexual morality of men. They were going to administer maternal love unto the world, and the maternal instinct, epitomized for Ruskin by the sheltering home or garden, became for them a mighty fortress.

Although some feminist writers, like Mona Caird, hoped that men and women would liberate themselves together, extremists interpreted the female embodiment of altruistic goodness as a monopoly and saw no benefits to be derived

[9] For some comments on how this fear affected men, see Brian Harrison, "Underneath the Victorians," *Victorian Studies* x (1967): 256. Women's anxieties were stimulated by popular medical manuals like Henry Arthur Allbutt's *Disease and Marriage* (1891). "Many a woman," Allbutt wrote, "has said, 'Doctor, what am I suffering from? I was a strong healthy girl before I was married, and now look at me. I am but a wreck.' How many a babe, anxiously and lovingly expected, has, instead of being a source of pleasure, been a thing of loathsomeness?" Between 1880 and 1900, about fifteen hundred infants died annually of hereditary venereal infections.

from trading with men. "In short, dear Mr. C——," said Vernon Lee to an acquaintance, "woman's love is so essentially *maternal* that it were tedious to enumerate possible deviations from this basic character; while man's love, as obviously and invariably, is triune, that is, acquisitive, possessive and BESTIAL!"[10] Like Florence Nightingale a generation before, Beatrice Webb saw motherhood as a biological trap that drained women's political and intellectual energies. In 1887 she wrote in her diary that "it will be needful for women with strong natures to remain celibate; so that the special force of womanhood—motherly feeling—may be forced into public work."[11]

Much of feminist literature represented a reaction to a male sexual force that struck even the most passionate women as alien—indiscriminate, incessant, and injurious. We must recall that the Victorians believed that the wife could not refuse her husband's advances; his conjugal rights were absolute. In an interesting comment on Victorian virility, George Egerton wrote that "marriage becomes for many women a legal prostitution, a nightly degradation, a hateful yoke under which they age, mere bearers of children conceived in a sense of duty, not love."[12] "Nightly" is the key word here. The regularity and frequency of men's sexual urge seemed brutish in comparison to women's cyclic spasms. It turned what should have been exquisite communion into routine drudgery. The sexual frustration that the writers expressed led to other kinds of feminist theory as well: to Marie Stopes' explanations of the "fundamental pulse" of "the periodicity of recurrence of desire in women," which she identified as a fortnightly phenomenon;[13]

[10] Peter Gunn, *Vernon Lee: Violet Paget 1856–1935*, London, 1964, p. 134.

[11] *My Apprenticeship*, London, 1971, p. 223. On Nightingale, see George Pickering, *Creative Malady*, London, 1974, p. 131.

[12] "Virgin Soil," *Discords*, London, 1895, p. 155.

[13] *Married Love* (1918), Dr. Stopes' first book, advocated mutual adjustment to the female sexual cycle: "Our code . . . has blindly sacrificed not only the woman, but with her the happiness of the majority

and to the more fantastic theosophical prescriptions of Frances Swiney, who thought intercourse once every few years sufficient.[14]

Fearing neither divine nor Freudian judgment, the feminists wrote openly about their sexual attitudes, making explicit the sexual protest hinted at by their predecessors, the sensationalists. Their candor is often startling. Flora Annie Steel, on the first page of her aptly named autobiography, *The Garden of Fidelity* (1929), attributed her lifelong frigidity to paternal influence: "There was nearly three years between my birth and that of my elder brother. . . . I have often wondered if this voluntary cessation of marital relations on my father's part had anything to do with my inborn dislike to the sensual side of life." Strange, indeed, to blame heredity (she was the second of eleven children), but her statement is a reminder that a dislike for the sensual side of life was a cherished quality of the Victorian Angel, which even feminists and rebels confessed with a certain pride. *The Yellow Aster* (1894), a "problem novel" by Kathleen Caffyn ("Iota"), dealt explicitly with the frigid wife but saw her salvation in maternity.

Obviously, late Victorian feminism was full of contradictions and conflicts. These were women who made the maternal instinct the basis of their ideology. Yet many of them were disgusted by sex and terrified by childbirth. Mrs. Haweis confessed to her journal that, upon the birth of her first child, she had not felt the surge of maternal ecstasy that she had anticipated: "Even—I believe it—if the poor little squealer died, I do not think I should grieve much after a day or two."[15] Of course, as Linda Gordon points out

---

of men, who, in total ignorance of its meaning and results, have grown up thinking that women should submit to regularly frequent, or even nightly, intercourse. For the sake of a few moments of physical pleasure, they lose realms of everexpanding joy and tenderness" (p. 56).

[14] See Samuel Hynes, *The Edwardian Turn of Mind*, London, 1968, p. 204. Miss Swiney also "believed that sperm was a virulent poison,"

[15] Bea Howe, *Arbiter of Elegance*, London, 1967, p. 116.

in her study of feminist birth control ideas in the United States, feminists' hostility and fear of sex "came from the fact that they were women, not that they were feminists."[16] Victorian ladies were supposed to dislike sex. Male ignorance, the dangers in pregnancy, venereal disease and childbearing, and the lack of any way to express their own sexual needs made abstinence the only rational response to the sexual dilemma many feminists perceived. Annie Besant's contraceptive handbook, *The Law of Population*, reflects a more practical approach to the same problems.

The veneration of motherhood and maternal love, combined with repugnance for the actual process of intercourse and childbirth, led to some very peculiar fantasies. Some feminist writers, like Lady Florence Dixie and "Ellis Ethelmer" in England, and Charlotte Perkins Gilman in the United States, imagined worlds ruled by women, feminist revolutions, and virgin births. In Dixie's *Gloriana; or the Revolution of 1900* (1890), Gloriana disguises herself as a boy, and as Hector L'Estrange, "splendid batsman, bowler, oarsman . . . undefeatable at books," goes from Eton to Oxford to Parliament, where she unmasks herself and begins to pass equal rights legislation.[17] Ethelmer's *Woman Free* (1893), a long poem in heroic couplets, celebrates the coming end of the menstrual cycle. Arguing that menstruation had its Lamarckian origins in prehistoric rapes, Ethelmer believed that *Woman Free* would shake off "this noisome habit" and

> Her body, saved from enervating drain,
> Shall lend a newer vigour to the brain;
> Wide shall she roam in realms of untold thought,
> Which ages still her shackled intellect sought.[18]

[16] Linda Gordon, "Voluntary Motherhood: The Beginnings of Feminist Birth Control Ideas in the United States," *Feminist Studies* 1 (Winter–Spring 1973): 12.

[17] *Gloriana; or the Revolution of 1900*, London, 1890, p. 7.

[18] *Woman Free*, London, 1893, p. 17.

Gilman, in *Herland* and *Moving the Mountain*, imagined Amazon utopias in which women would reproduce spontaneously in a maternal meritocracy.

In demanding that women be liberated from the menstrual cycle, Ethelmer was anticipating Germaine Greer; yet Ethelmer's fantasies were politically and technologically naive and thus ultimately depressing. As Sheila Rowbotham writes, "The dominated can tell stories, they can fantasize, they can create Utopia, but they cannot devise the means of getting there. They cannot make use of maps, plan out the route, and calculate the odds."[19] The Amazons of Mary Coleridge's poem, "The White Women" (1900), who "never bowed their necks beneath the yoke," are creatures of an imagined golden age of the past, not models for the future.

The feminists' urge to break away from the yoke of biological femininity also expressed itself as the wish to be male. According to Mary Coleridge's biographer, "no one so feminine can ever have longed more to be a man. In her fantasies again and again she takes this part, and in her novels it is always the portraits of young men which are attempted from within, and the very few women are merely sketched from a man's point of view."[20] One of Olive Schreiner's heroines muses about "how nice it would be to be a man." A series of swashbucklers and mysteries played with the idea of the split personality—not the split between good and evil that fascinated Stevenson and Wilde, but the split between male purpose and female passivity that reflected feminist conflict. In Ethel Voynich's *The Gadfly* (1896) and the Baroness Orczy's *The Scarlet Pimpernel* (1905), the Sydney Carton figure—drawling fop by day, dashing revolutionary by night—was revived. The revolutionary energies of the women novelists are entirely projected onto male fig-

[19] "Women's Liberation and the New Politics," in *The Body Politic: Writings from the Women's Liberation Movement in Britain 1969–1972*, ed. Michelene Wandor, London, 1972, p. 9.

[20] Theresa Whistler, introduction to *The Collected Poems of Mary Coleridge*, London, 1954, p. 50.

ures, who are androgynous in the sense that their disguise is to appear effeminate. Like their creators, these heroes survive by concealing their real strength and purposes, and "passing" as limp and ineffectual.

Their sense of physical oppression and sexual exploitation led feminists to identify with the prostitute, a figure who had always aroused the sympathies, however covert, of women novelists. Mrs. Gaskell and Dinah Craik had defended her; through the Contagious Diseases campaign, women argued and petitioned for her. One important effect of the Contagious Diseases campaign was that it gave women an excuse to use some of the sexual vocabulary previously reserved for men. How could a lady refuse to call a spade a spade when that utensil was digging the grave of her sisters? Mrs. Butler wrote to an M. P. who had questioned the propriety of women's attendance at debates on the Acts: "At the very base of the Acts lies the false and poisonous idea that women (i.e., ladies) have 'nothing to do with this question,' and ought not to hear of it, much less meddle with it. . . . I cannot forget the misery, the injustice and the outrage which have fallen upon women simply because we stood aside, when men felt our presence to be painful."[21]

The feminists, however, were fervent associationists, and they dissipated their energies in many causes. In 1895 one feminist journal, *Shafts*, advertised meetings of the Women's Vegetarian Union, the Anti-Vivisection League, the Anti-Spitting Association, the Psychic Society, the Anti-Tobacco Society, the Anti-Narcotic League, and the Anti-Caged-Birds Society. They knew very clearly what they were *against*, but only vaguely what they were *for*. The feminist writers were engaged in the kind of quarrel that, according to Yeats, leads to rhetoric but not poetry. Thus the writers of this period—Olive Schreiner, Sarah Grand,

---

[21] E. Moberley Bell, *Josephine Butler*, London, 1962, pp. 140–141. Mrs. Butler's insistence on speaking about prostitution outraged many; it represented "the height of indecency," to one physician. See Sigsworth and Wyke, in *Suffer and Be Still*, pp. 97–98.

Mrs. Craigie ("John Oliver Hobbes"), Beatrice Harraden, Ethel Voynich, Mary Coleridge, Ménie Muriel Dowie, and George Egerton—have not fared well with posterity.

There are many signs that feminist writers were troubled by the new tensions in their role. Their lives show an increase in psychosomatic illnesses and stress diseases, afflictions that contributed to the decline in their literary productivity.[22] Whereas the invalidism of the feminine novelists was often a strategic evasion of the feminine role or a power tactic (as George Eliot recognized when she had Rosamond Vincy threaten her father, "You would not like me to go into a consumption, as Arabella Hawley did"), feminist invalidism seems to have been an evasion of work. Even freed from the pressures of the three-decker, many women writers of this period found it difficult to finish their books or to write more than one. In this generation female suicide became conspicuous for the first time; the suicides included Eleanor Marx, Charlotte Mew, Adela Nicolson, and Amy Levy.

The confused aspirations and dreams and the claustro-

---

[22] In a letter to Havelock Ellis, Schreiner compared her symptoms to those of her women friends: "The pain in my stomach that I used to get when I had to eat before people was really asthma in the stomach, caused by the terrible excitement of my heart from nervousness and misery. I have an interesting letter from that Miss A. P.—I told you of who suffered even more than I did. She has described *all* I suffered. A.—, you know, also suffered in the same way, and Eleanor Marx, I know, did. . . . But now here comes an interesting fact. A—P—'s sister is the most terrible sufferer from asthma that I ever saw in Europe, and Eleanor's sister, Jenny, suffered from her earliest childhood till the day of her death from asthma. I think I have often told you of the curious relation I have found between that convulsive feeling in the stomach and the asthma. I will send you all the letters I get from women about it" (*Letters*, pp. 198–199).

Lloyd Fernando, who quotes this passage, comments: "The 'New Woman' . . . faced rather more insidious defeat within her own psyche, in the form of numerous and persisting ailments which she did not fully understand" ("The Radical Ideology of the 'New Woman,'" *Southern Review* II [1967]: 215).

phobic femaleness of the feminist aesthetic are most suggestively embodied in the life and works of Olive Schreiner. A freethinker marked to the marrow of her bones with the Calvinism of her missionary parents; a disciple of Darwin, Mill, and Spencer who floated in seas of sentimentality; a dedicated writer who could never finish a book; a feminist who hated being a woman; a maternal spirit who never became a mother—everything about her life is a paradox. In her ambivalence, her self-deception, her psychosomatic illnesses, we can read the distress signals of a transitional generation. Claustrophobia—the sense of confinement in a space too small for comfort and growth—is a central image for Schreiner. Her womanhood, with its compelling inner space, was a haven to which she made cyclic withdrawals and from which she made sporadic efforts to escape.

Sheila Rowbotham convincingly describes Schreiner's feminism as "a mystical connection to other women with whom she could communicate only through the common experience of pain."[23] Such a connection was best sustained when the other women were far away. For all her commitment, Schreiner did not enjoy the company of women. Intense relationships quickly cloyed or proved too demanding. Despite her genuine compassion for Kaffir women, for London prostitutes and millgirls, and for the suffragettes, she could not tolerate the pressure of daily exposure to their problems. Sometimes she felt suffocated by female flesh, including her own, as we see in a hysterical letter to Havelock Ellis in 1888: "Oh, it is awful to be a woman. These women are killing me. . . . Please see that they bury me in a place where there are no women. I've not been a woman really, though I've seemed like one."[24] Yet in all of her books Schreiner employed a potent female symbolism. Lyndall in *Story of an African Farm* (1883) wears a ring,

---

[23] *Women, Resistance and Revolution*, London, 1974, p. 94. See also Vineta Colby's chapter on Schreiner in *Singular Anomaly*, New York, 1970.

[24] Olive Schreiner, *Letters*, p. 142.

which she will give to the first man who tells her he would like to be a woman. We need not depend on Freud to elucidate this for us; in *Woman and Labour* Schreiner explains it herself: "As the *os cervix* of woman, through which the head of a human infant passes at birth, forms a ring, determining for ever the size at birth of the human head, a size which could only increase if in the course of ages the *os cervix* of woman should itself slowly expand . . . so exactly the intellectual capacity, the physical vigour, the emotional depth of woman, forms also an untranscendable circle, circumscribing with each successive generation the limits of the expression of the human race."[25] No man will volunteer to wear the ring of womanhood: to bear the children and to know the pain.

In Schreiner's novels, the quintessential female role is frequently associated with a grotesque obesity, like pregnancy or dropsy. In *Story of an African Farm*, Em, the passive domestic farm girl is "grown into a premature little old woman of sixteen, ridiculously fat."[26] Tante Sannie, the Boer woman, weighs 250 pounds and is too fat to kneel; she dreams of sheeps-trotters and snorts in her sleep. A gross parody of womanhood, a sort of Hottentot Venus, she devours three husbands, the last being her nineteen-year-old albino nephew: "Didn't I tell you this morning that I dreamed of a great beast like a sheep, with red eyes and I killed it?" she asks her maid triumphantly. "Wasn't the white wool his hair, and the red eyes his weak eyes, and my killing him meant marriage?"[27] Reduced to their sexual functions, women in Schreiner's novels seem monstrous, swollen, and destructive. They are the parasites described in *Woman and Labour*, whose better nature has atrophied through disuse. In *From Man to Man* (1926), the innocent Baby Bertie, seduced and betrayed, ends up as the prisoner

[25] *Woman and Labour*, London, 1978. ch. III, pp. 129–130.
[26] *Story of an African Farm*, London, 1971, p. 155.
[27] Ibid., p. 201.

of a rich Jew who keeps her in overheated rooms where she grows fatter and fatter, although she scarcely eats. At last, her body too heavy for her tiny feet, she is practically immobile. In an effort to alleviate her despair, the Jew buys her three kittens, and she acts out a fantastic motherhood, embroidering tiny garments for them and putting them to bed in little cradles. Schreiner's fictional world is obsessed with a femaleness grown monstrous in confinement—a world full of Bertha Masons.

In place of the impressively sustained productivity of the sensationalists, Schreiner put a neurotic compulsiveness. Always frantically at work, she was not a productive or self-disciplined writer. Her manuscripts disappeared mysteriously or were discarded; they waxed and waned over the years, pieced together out of fragments, endless revision, loving reconsiderations, accretions, and patches. After the great success of *African Farm*, many publishers were eager for her work; but unlike Mrs. Humphry Ward, who was stimulated by public demand to the point of paralysis from writer's cramp, Schreiner developed writer's block. Ernest Rhys asked her to undertake the introduction to a new edition of Mary Wollstonecraft's *Vindication of the Rights of Woman*, but even this congenial assignment proved impossible. For years Schreiner published only "dreams," sentimental allegories in the most nauseating *fin-de-siècle* style (Oscar Wilde, who had written some himself, published several of Schreiner's in the magazine he was editing). Anything longer than half-a-dozen pages triggered her anxieties.

The sensationalists thought about what would please and what would sell, and wrote their books in a businesslike way, putting (Mrs. Ward averred) their knees under the desk so many hours a day; Schreiner stressed the wild, impetuous seizure by the Muse. Writing, as she described it, was an semi-ecstatic trance state in which the unconscious revealed itself. Every word she wrote was saturated with ardent emotion, adolescent to the point of solipsism in its privacy. The labors of construction and plotting were be-yond her; her greatest joy came in the recording of an intui-tive flash, or a polemical harangue.

In Schreiner's letters the artist's natural reluctance to face criticism is transmuted into a morbid female fear of self-exposure and rejection: "The thought that hundreds and thousands will read my work does affect and kindle me, not because I wish to teach them but because, terrible as it is to show my work to them at all, the thought of throwing it to them to be trodden under foot is double desecration of it. . . . The best stories and dreams I have had nothing would induce me to write at all because I couldn't bear any person to read them."[28] If her best work is that which was unwritten, then the next-best, one deduces, is that which was incomprehensible. With Schreiner we see a perverse will to fail that rationalizes itself as the artist's superiority and need for self-protection.

Yet Schreiner made an important contribution to the fe-male tradition. Her use of female symbolism, her commit-ment to feminist theory, and her harshly physical allegories, which the suffragettes read to each other in Holloway Pris-on, were part of her effort to articulate the tense, indirect perceptions of a new womanhood. Even her insistent and sometimes nagging narrative voice takes us to the reality of female experience. That voice, soft, heavy, continuous, is a genuine accent of womanhood, one of the chorus of secret voices speaking out of our bones, dreadful and irritating but instantly recognizable. Other women whom she influ-enced—Virginia Woolf, Dorothy Richardson, and Doris Lessing—were to make much better use of it, but Schreiner hit upon it first. It is the fitful, fretful rhythm of women's daily lives, a Beckett monolog without a beginning or an end.

Schreiner's male contemporaries failed to understand this quality in her books, although George Meredith was the reader who recommended that Chapman and Hall publish

[28] Quoted in Colby, *Singular Anomaly*, p. 88.

Story of an African Farm. Other male novelists very naturally tended to see Schreiner's work as deficient in the qualities they themselves possessed. H. Rider Haggard and Andrew Lang wondered why she had chosen to write silliness about "people always tackling religious problems, or falling in love in new and heterodox lines, instead of shooting deer, and finding diamonds, or hunting up the archeological remains of the Transvaal."[29] George Moore found more than he wanted to know about sandhills, ostriches, and women, "but of art nothing; that is to say, art as I understand it—rhythmical sequence of events described with rhythmical sequence of phrase."[30]

In adopting the pseudonym "Ralph Iron" and in calling two main characters Waldo and Em, Schreiner was paying homage to her favorite philosopher, Ralph Waldo Emerson, and indicating that her tone would be ironic. She intended *African Farm* to represent her vision of life; at one point she had considered titling it *Mirage: A Series of Abortions.* The book is about man's moral redemption in a meaningless universe, through identification with female suffering. Its plot is diffuse, but the central situation of the persecuted orphan, Waldo, who falls in love with his childhood ally, Lyndall, has reminded many readers of *Wuthering Heights.*

Schreiner's Lyndall is the first wholly serious feminist heroine in the English novel, and she remains one of the few who is not patronized by her author. Through Lyndall's monologs, Schreiner analyzes the connections between sex-role conditioning, narcissism, parasitism, and frustration. The tragedies of Victorian heroines like Maggie Tulliver and Dorothea Casaubon become the sources of Schreiner's powerful analysis:

We are cursed, Waldo, born cursed from the time our mothers bring us into the world till the shrouds are put

[29] Quoted by Donald Stone, *Novelists in a Changing World*, Cambridge, Mass., 1972, p. 52.

[30] *Confessions of a Young Man*, ch. x, quoted in Colby, *Singular Anomaly*, p. 106.

on us. . . . They begin to shape us to our cursed end . . . when we are tiny things in shoes and socks. We sit with our little feet drawn up under us in the window, and look out at the boys in their happy play. We want to go. Then a loving hand is laid on us: "Little one, you cannot go," they say; "your little face will burn and your nice white dress be spoiled." We feel it must be for our good, it is so lovingly said; but we cannot understand; and we kneel still with one little cheek wistfully pressed against the pane. Afterwards we go and string blue beads, and make a string for our neck; and we go and stand before the glass. We see the complexion we were not to spoil, and the white frock, and we begin to look into our own great eyes. Then the curse begins to act on us. It finishes its work when we are grown women, who no more look out wistfully at a more healthy life; we are contented. We fit our sphere as a Chinese woman's foot fits her shoe, exactly, as though God had made both—and yet he knows nothing of either. In some of us the shaping to our end has been quite completed. The parts we are not to use have been quite atrophied, and have even dropped off; but in others, and we are not less to be pitied, they have been weakened and left. We wear the bandages, but our limbs have not grown to them; we know that we are compressed, and chafe against them.

But what does it help? A little bitterness, a little longing when we are young, a little futile searching for work, a little passionate striving for room for the exercise of our powers,—and then we go with the drove. A woman must march with her regiment. In the end she must be trodden down or go with it; and if she is wise, she goes.[31]

Lyndall's brief rebellion does not succeed. She leaves the farm and tries to make an independent life without her lover, but her illegitimate child lives only two hours, and she follows it stoically into the grave. Like *The Mill on the*

[31] *Story of an African Farm*, p. 189.

Floss, the novel ends with the meditations of Lyndall's two lovers, in effect, over her grave. Gregory, chastened by his experience as Lyndall's deathbed nurse, marries her cousin Em (as Stephen Guest marries Lucy Deane). Waldo, like Philip Wakem, becomes an intellectual, and finds peace in transcendentalism. In the world Schreiner describes, men are redeemed by female suffering, while women perish in teaching the lesson.

From 1875 until her death, Schreiner wrote and rewrote a long novel, which was posthumously published in 1926 as *From Man to Man*. "It will be quite different from any other book that ever was written," she wrote Havelock Ellis in 1887, "whether good or bad I can't say. I never *think*; the story leads me, not I it, and I guess it's more likely to make an end of me than I am ever to make an end of it."[32] Although the book is indeed very odd, and extremely melodramatic in its plot and emotions, it has some remarkable passages, and it evokes with outstanding power the female psychology of a generation. *From Man to Man*, despite its title, is about sisterhood and motherhood; Schreiner dedicated it to "My Little Sister Ellie, who died, aged eighteen months, when I was nine years old. Also to My only Daughter, Born on the 30th April, and died the 1st May. She never lived to know she was a Woman."

Two sisters, Rebekah and Baby Bertie, are the central characters of the book. Bertie is seduced by her tutor and subsequently forced by gossip and malice to leave South Africa and go to England, where she helplessly sinks into a life of sin. Rebekah marries and has children, but becomes increasingly dependent and frustrated. Ultimately she discovers that her husband is unfaithful and separates from him, raising his illegitimate mulatto child with her own. In the outline for the book Rebekah finally finds her sister in a Capetown brothel and tenderly nurses her on her syphilitic deathbed. Both these characters represent aspects of

[32] *Letters*, p. 125.

Olive Schreiner's own personality, but Rebekah is a particularly convincing portrait of the woman who is not so much trapped as self-imprisoned. In Rebekah's cultivation of her female sensibility and ideology, and in her frustrated retreat from experience, we can see the crisis of the woman artist at the turn of the century. Schreiner has many affinities with Virginia Woolf, and *From Man to Man* anticipates the language, as well as the symbolism, of *A Room of One's Own*, published two years later.[33]

The private room is the novel's most potent and disturbing symbol. Rebekah makes a little place for herself in a corner of the children's room:

> The room was a small one, made by cutting off the end of the children's bedroom with a partition. She had had it before as a study for herself where she could always hear the children call if they needed her at night. It was hardly larger than a closet, but there was a window in it and a small outer door, and both looked out on to the rockery and the plumbingo hedge but on nothing else, and there was a small door close beside the window, which she had put in that at any time she might run out and work a little in the garden.[34]

Here she keeps her fossil collection, her science books (including Darwin), and a picture of the Madonna; here she retires at night to sew and to meditate and to write snatches in a journal. The room is all too clearly and pathetically the embodiment of her femaleness; it is connected to the children and Nature, and linked to the evolutionary past, literally a womb with a view. As she feverishly scribbles what no one will read, Rebekah is like a prisoner in a cell: "On the brown carpet on the floor was a mark like a footpath where the nap had been worn off, running right around the desk. This was where she walked round and round, because

[33] Virginia Woolf reviewed the *Letters of Olive Schreiner* for the *New Republic*, March 18, 1925, 103.

[34] *From Man to Man*, p. 171.

the room was not large enough to allow of walking up and down."[35] One recalls Mrs. Gaskell's account of the Brontës' circling the drawing-room table at Haworth Parsonage, and also Charlotte Perkins Gilman's *The Yellow Wallpaper* (1891), a horror story of a woman going mad during a rest cure. These confined women adopt the compulsive behaviors of caged animals.

Rebekah has to make do with her room; she makes it as attractive as she can and forbids her husband to enter it. But she does not deceive herself about it; the room is exclusive because it has to be a refuge, not because it contains anything of value. In her fantasies, she imagines "what it must be like to be one of a company of men and women in a room together, all sharing somewhat the same outlook on life."[36] And although she works out a feminist philosophy that derives "life, growth, and evolution" from mother-love, she cannot help wishing to be a man:

How nice it would be to be a man. She fancied she was one till she felt her very body grow strong and hard and shaped like man's. She felt the great freedom opened to her, no place shut off from her, the long chain broken, all work possible for her, no law to say this and this is for woman. You are woman. . . . Oh how beautiful to be a man and be able to take care of and defend all the creatures weaker and smaller than you are.[37]

For someone so keenly aware of female oppression, Schreiner is sadly underambitious. When all is said and done, the novels are depressing and claustrophobic. The heroines are granted only the narrowest of possibilities; the treatment of them is disconcertingly unadventurous, even timid. Lyndall dies after childbirth; Bertie meets a fate worse than death; Rebekah retreats, daydreams, and desultorily cultivates a fragmented and undisciplined art. Like Schreiner, they give up too easily and too soon. In his

[35] Ibid., p. 175.   [36] Ibid., p. 174.   [37] Ibid., p. 226.

introduction to *African Farm*, the South African novelist Dan Jacobson writes regretfully about the "almost overwhelming sense of talents wasted and frustrated in what appears to be a perversely deliberate way."[38]

And yet, as Jacobson fully recognizes, there is "something almost heroic" in Schreiner's effort to make art out of "a society that has never been given any kind of a voice of its own."[39] Schreiner's first book, *Undine*, was set in a fantasized England, copied from the novels of Jane Austen. *African Farm* confronted the drab reality of kopjes and cactus. The real problem of the colonial writer, Jacobson suggests, is not just the "hitherto undescribed, uncelebrated wordless quality"[40] of the life around him, but its inferiority in contrast to the apparent richness and color of the parent literature. As a South African and as a woman, Schreiner was writing out of a double colonialism. The uncelebrated landscapes she was trying to record were both the barren Karoo and the claustrophobic, inner landscape of the new woman. The authenticity of her struggle—its rawness, its personality—touched readers, especially women readers, and awakened their deepest selves; these qualities made Schreiner important for other women writers. Doris Lessing remembered *African Farm* as the first book she had read that reflected what she herself "knew and could see," and also, ultimately, "an endeavor, a kind of hunger, that passionate desire for growth and understanding, which is the deepest pulse of human beings."[41]

Like Olive Schreiner, Sarah Grand came from a silent culture and made herself a novelist through sheer force of will.[42] About 1890 she left an unhappy marriage to a much

---

[38] Introduction to *Story of an African Farm*, London. 1971, p. 15.

[39] Ibid., p. 18.

[40] Ibid., p. 18.

[41] "Afterword to *The Story of an African Farm*," *A Small Personal Voice*, ed. Paul Schleuter, New York, 1974, pp. 99–100.

[42] Grand is mentioned in Amy Cruse, *After the Victorians*, London, 1938; and in G. B. Needham and R. P. Utter, *Pamela's Daughters*, London, 1937. A picture of her is included with a brief biographical

older man, and the memory of a deprived childhood in Ireland and Northern England, and created a new persona for herself in London. Frances Clarke McFall was left behind, and "Sarah Grand," the matriarch, the beautiful female prophet, was born. Her self-image, the role she chose to play, was very different from the image suggested by a Currer Bell or a George Eliot. Grand saw herself as a great teacher and as a woman of genius.

Grand's most successful novel was *The Heavenly Twins* (1893), which sold 20,000 copies the first week.[43] Stylish, assured, and strikingly original, *The Heavenly Twins* is a strongly feminist novel that deals with sex-role conditioning, venereal disease, and women's right to independence. The twins of the title are irrepressible children called Angelica and Diavolo, who are identical in intellect, will, and daring. Contemporary readers saw the twins as mischievous "madcaps" or "pickles," like the naughty children then in literary vogue, but Grand meant to show through them the false division of sex roles into "angelic" female and

note in *Twentieth Century Authors* (Kunitz), p. 563. Mark Twain was only one of her distinguished contemporary admirers; his much-annotated copy of *The Heavenly Twins* is in the Berg Collection of the New York Public Library. George Bernard Shaw linked her with Whistler, Ibsen, and Wagner as a misunderstood genius. See his letter to R. Golding Bright, May 18, 1894, in *Collected Letters 1874–1897*, ed. Dan H. Laurence, London, 1965, p. 461.

[43] A. V. Cunningham, "The 'New Woman Fiction' of the 1890s," *Victorian Studies* (December 1973): 179. One woman novelist claimed that *The Heavenly Twins* created "one of the greatest sensations in literature. It was reviewed, talked of, discussed wherever one went" ("Rita," *Reflections of a Literary Life*, London, 1936, p. 174). The accolade came, as usual, in attacks from other, older, women novelists. Mrs. Lynn Linton warned a young friend to maintain the "sweet womanly virtues which make woman half divine, and the true antiseptic of society. You don't find these qualities in The Heavenly Twins, Yellow Asters, and all the new women who set themselves to blaspheme nature and God and good" (*Mrs. Lynn Linton: Her Life, Letters, and Opinions*, ed. G. S. Layard, London, 1901, p. 292).

"devilish" male.[44] The novel takes them from the age of five through adolescence, and carefully describes the gradual divergence of their lives. As children they are essentially androgynous, but age brings socially conditioned differences. Although Angelica is "the elder, taller, stronger, and wickeder of the two, the organizer and commander of every expedition,"[45] it is Diavolo who gets the opportunities for education and self-development, and who finally goes off to Sandhurst leaving his sister behind. After a bizarre interlude in which she goes about disguised as her brother, Angelica subsides into early domesticity, with the advantage of a fatherly, indulgent husband and with a vague hope of doing good in the world, somehow, someday.

The second half of the novel follows the fortunes of two young brides in the same town, Edith and Evadne, who represent the Old and the New Woman. Edith is steeped in religion and the feminine mystique; Evadne has educated herself in science, medicine, and the works of John Stuart Mill.

It is Edith's fate to be courted by an officer from H.M.S. *Abomination*, the debauched and syphilitic Sir Mosley Menteith. Menteith is an evolutionary throwback whose eyes "were small, peery, and too close together," and whose head "shelved backwards like an ape's."[46] Edith, of course, is too naive and spiritual to understand the signs of venereal disease, even when she has a dream that a man comes to her with the face "like the Dear Lord's" and hands her a deformed child covered with sores.[47] Against Evadne's warning, she marries Menteith, and soon the truth is inescapably at hand in the form of her own diseased child and her own inexorable mental deterioration. Her days are

---

[44] For an interesting discussion of opposite-sex twins in literature, see Carolyn G. Heilbrun, *Towards a Recognition of Androgyny*, London, 1973, pp. 34–45.

[45] *The Heavenly Twins*, London, 1894, p. 7.

[46] Ibid., p. 178. [47] Ibid., p. 156.

darkened by "the shadow of an awful form of insanity,"[48] and she eventually dies in agony.

Evadne, on the other hand, has studied anatomy, physiology, pathology, prophylactics, and therapeutics. When Diavolo stabs himself in the thigh with a penknife, she quietly applies a tourniquet. When she discovers that her husband, Major George Colquhoun, is unchaste and has had a mistress, she refuses to consummate her marriage. Grand subverts the conventions of the novel about female chastity and male sexuality by taking them seriously. In a scene that rewrites the feminine conventions of *Jane Eyre* and *Daniel Deronda*, Evadne explains to her husband that her virginal standards are too high to allow her to accept him: "You see, my taste is cultivated to so fine an extent, I require something extremely well-flavored for the dish which is to be the pièce-de-resistance of my life-feast. My appetite is delicate, it requires to be tempted, and a husband of that kind, a moral leper—."[49]

The speech cuts two ways: first, as an obvious feminist condemnation of male vice; second, as a hint that the emphasis on "Angelic" womanhood has created a race of frigid virgins. Evadne's story is realistically unheroic; she agrees to live platonically with her husband to avoid scandal. He quickly finds other outlets while she sickens from sexual frustration and blocked maternal drives. In choosing a sexless marriage, she is at least partly acting out her own terror of passion (she also chooses to promise her husband that she will not become active in the women's movement). Eventually repression and avoidance lead to a breakdown. Evadne is a clear example of the women Florence Nightingale had described in "Cassandra," women who tried to drug themselves rather than act on their pain. Evadne herself is "saved" by the death of her husband, but she uses her freedom to marry again.

In a later novel, *The Beth Book* (1898), Grand drew on

[48] Ibid., p. 280.   [49] Ibid., p. 79.

207

her own life to describe the creative psychology of the woman artist. The early chapters describe Beth's childhood in Ireland, in an atmosphere saturated with sexuality and violence. Her father, an alcoholic Navy captain, is alternately affectionate and abusive; her mother is chronically depressed by his infidelities; the Irish nurses come from squalid communities rife with incest and illegitimacy. Beth's childhood memories are associated with death and decay: poisoned meat, maggoty cheese, hanged men, drowned men, an exhumed corpse. Grand suggests that the sexual ambiguity and the physical corruption of the world Beth witnesses as a child both fascinates and repels her.

As an adult, Beth contracts a disastrous marriage to a doctor who treats prostitutes in a Lock Hospital, a man who practices vivisection, spends her money, and brings his mistress to live in the house. She seems almost to have chosen to repeat the nightmare world of her childhood. Beth goes beyond Evadne, ultimately freeing herself completely from the ideology of marriage, but liberation itself is accomplished through a feminist fantasy. Desperately searching her house for a private space, Beth discovers a secret room, which she must enter on her hands and knees; it looks just like the room of the aunt who, alone in the family, had loved her. In this secret space, Beth improbably learns to discipline herself as a writer:

Her mind, which had run riot, fancy-fed with languorous dreams in the days when it was unoccupied and undisciplined, came steadily more and more under control and grew gradually stronger as she exercised it. She ceased to rage and worry about her domestic difficulties, ceased to expect her husband to add to her happiness in any way, ceased to sorrow for the slights and neglects that had so wounded and perplexed her during the first year of her life in Slane; and learned by degrees to possess her soul in dignified silence, so long as silence was best, feeling in herself *that* something which should bring her up out of all this and set her apart eventually in another sphere, among the elect—feeling this through her future faculty to her comfort, although unable as yet to give it any sort of definite expression.[50]

We are shown the reasons for Beth's need of solitude and secrecy; she is at a disadvantage in education and in economic position, and her husband ridicules her efforts to write. Nonetheless the secret chamber is a claustrophobic image, and patently related to Sarah Grand's conception of her literary purpose. In the secret room, secure from male intrusion, Beth plans to write "for women, not for men. I don't care about amusing men. Let them see to their own amusements, they think of nothing else. Men entertain each other with intellectual ingenuities and Art and Style, while women are busy with the great problems of life, and are striving with might and main to make it beautiful."[51] This housewife's daydream goes even further. Beth scores her greatest triumph in literature by publishing her novel anonymously and having it well-reviewed by an influential journal called the *Patriarch*. Even the male establishment, frittering its time away on frivolities, has to acknowledge her mastery.

Grand's own star set as rapidly as it rose. Always a staunch suffragist, she became active in the suffrage campaign after her husband's death in 1898. Her name appears regularly in the accounts of the movement, first as a member of the Women Writers Suffrage League, and later as the president of the Tunbridge Wells branch of the National Union of Women's Suffrage Societies. On a lecture tour of the United States, she claimed to have been interviewed twenty-four times in as many hours. But the end of the suffrage campaign meant the end of her own era as novelist and *cause célèbre*. In 1920 she moved to Bath, and her last years were flat, stale, and unprofitable, despite her position

[50] *The Beth Book*, London, 1980, p. 370.
[51] Ibid., p. 376.

as mayoress (honorary hostess), and the adoration of a younger woman, Gladys Singers-Bigger, who literally gave up her life to the commemoration of Sarah Grand.[52] Her only son, Archibald, was alienated from her; literary projects failed dismally. The ceremonies of civic life in Bath, to which she paid scrupulous attention, were nonetheless inflated and provincial, as one sees in a sad bit of doggerel composed by the faithful Gladys to commemorate a holiday distribution of cakes:

> Thronged by the Poor the Mayoress moves,
> Granting to each small guest
> The bag of cakes her smile improves,—
> Paper bags at her breast.[53]

It was not to be a provincial Lady Bountiful, opening the Crysanthemum Show and attending the banquet for German subway officials, that Grand had embarked upon her career.

Many of the same qualities of wish-fulfillment and incoherent rebellion can be found in the life and works of "George Egerton" (Mary Chavelita Dunne). Less celebrated than Olive Schreiner, but better known today than Sarah Grand, she was another "advanced" woman writer of the nineties who never developed sufficiently as an artist to sustain her first celebrity. She considered her art "of less importance" than her "life as a woman," and consequently she

---

[52] Miss Singers-Bigger, in her mid-thirties when she met Sarah Grand, kept detailed journals about her idol, calling her "My Little Mother" and "Mother of My Spirit". (See *Darling Madame: A Portrait of Sarah Grand* by Gillian Kersley, Virago, 1983.) Her complete journals and records of Sarah Grand's life are in the Public Reference Library, Bath, England. Among these materials is the *Sarah Grand Miscellany*, "a collection of favorite passages from her Works contributed voluntarily by readers all over the world, known and unknown personally to the author." Despite the efforts of Singers-Bigger and Charles Whitby, a Bath clergyman, it was never published. I am indebted to the late Professor W. K. Wimsatt, who allowed me to see a manuscript memoir by Sarah Grand in his possession.

[53] Ms 2352, "Lilies of the Hill," Public Reference Library, Bath.

put less energy into it.[54] Her greatest successes were two volumes of short stories, *Keynotes* (1894) and *Discords* (1894), which dealt with intensely observed fragments of female experience and disillusion. Both volumes were published by John Lane, whose penchant for women, both as lover and publisher, had earned him the sobriquet "Petticoat Lane"; *Keynotes* inaugurated and gave a name to the popular series, with its Beardsley-designed motif, that Lane issued in the nineties. *Keynotes* was scandalous enough to achieve parody at the hands of *Punch*; "She-notes" by "Borgia Smudgiton" appeared in 1894. "She-Notes," in fact, were precisely what George Egerton had intended to write. As she described the genesis of her first book:

I realised that in literature, everything had been better done by man than woman could hope to emulate. There was only one small plot left to tell: the *terra incognita* of herself, as she knew herself to be, not as man liked to imagine her—in a word, to give herself away, as man had given himself away in his writings. . . . Unless one is androgynous, one is bound to look at life through the eyes of one's sex, to toe the limitations imposed on one by its individual physiological functions. I came too soon. If I did not know the technical jargon current to-day of Freud and the psycho-analysts, I did know something of complexes and inhibitions, repressions and the subconscious impulses that determine actions and reactions. I used them in my stories. I recognised that in the main, woman was the ever-untamed, unchanging, adapting herself as far as it suited her ends to male expectations; even if repression was altering her subtly. I would use situations or conflicts as I saw them with a total disregard of man's opinions, I would unlock a closed door with a key of my own fashioning.[55]

[54] "A Keynote to *Keynotes*," in *Ten Contemporaries*, ed. John Gawsworth, London, 1932, p. 60.
[55] Ibid., p. 58.

211

This description was written in 1932, and we may suppose that Egerton benefited from hindsight. The stories do, however, show her feminist rebellion, as well as the influence of the Scandinavian realists with whom she is generally bracketed. Ironically, the first set of stories, which she submitted to T. P. Gill, a columnist for the *Weekly Sun*, was automatically assumed to have come from a man; the pseudonym was not questioned. Gill wrote to "George Egerton," suggesting that the stories might be a shade too stimulating and that they could lead to whoring or, what was worse, masturbation:

> For example, take the effect on a young fellow in his student period (such readers are as numerous as the old women in the clientele of Zola) of a particularly warm description of rounded limbs and all the rest. It puts him in such a state that he either goes off and has a woman or it is bad for his health (and possibly worse for his morals) if he doesn't.[56]

Egerton had no coherent feminist politics to argue, but she was aware of a repressed sex-antagonism in human relationships, which women had to project into a variety of destructive behaviors because they were afraid to confront its true source. This view is touched upon in some of the relatively sunny stories in *Keynotes*; Egerton puts her most violent expressions of antagonism in the mouths of minor characters on the fringes of the narrative. In "The Spell of the White Elf," the heroine's housekeeper wishes to "have a child, ma'am, without a husband or the disgrace; ugh, the disgusting men!" The heroine does not share this feeling, but she comments with careful vagueness about its prevalence: "Do you know, I think that is not an uncommon feeling amongst a certain number of women. . . . It seems congenital with some women to have deeply rooted in their innermost nature, a smoldering enmity, ay, sometimes a

56 Terence de Vere White, *A Leaf from the Yellow Book*, London, 1958, pp. 23–24.

physical disgust to men, it is a kind of kin-feeling to the race-dislike of white men to black."[57]

\ In *Discords*, these feelings are much more central to the stories. Egerton is interested in exploring the effects of women's suppressed anger, disgust, and rage in situation where their emotional and economic dependence on men makes it impossible for them to confront their real enemies; in each story the woman projects her grievance onto a more manageable opponent. Taken together, these stories provide a thorough study of the psychology of oppression; their titles—short and sardonic—show real skill and control. In "Gone Under," a harrowing story of a woman whose lover arranges to have their illegitimate child murdered by the midwife, the heroine internalizes her despair and hatred, and commits suicide; the title suggests not only death and surrender but also the process of repression. "Wedlock" is a sensational tale of a woman who murders her three step-children because her jealous husband has separated her from her own child. Again, the woman protagonist avoids an attack on the man and takes revenge indirectly on the weak. Even in less violent stories, the heroines make other women the objects of their hatred and refuse to confront men. "Virgin Soil," which Wendell Harris rightly describes as a thinly disguised tract against the absence of sex-education for women, is an encounter between a mother and daughter. The daughter has come home to accuse her mother of destroying her life. The chosen husband is a philanderer and a lecher; the daughter, like Rhoda Broughton's Nell L'Estrange, is safe from his demands only when he is pursuing the cook, (episodes that she regards as "lovely oases in the desert of matrimony").[58] To say that they are sexually incompatible is grossly to underestimate the situation: "I

[57] "The Spell of The White Elf," *Keynotes* in *Keynotes & Discords*, London, 1983, p. 80.

[58] "Virgin Soil," *Discords* in *Keynotes & Discords*, London, 1983, p. 153; and Wendell V. Harris, "Egerton: Forgotten Realist," *Victorian Newsletter* (Spring 1968): 34.

loathe him, shiver at the touch of his lips, his breath, his hands; . . . my whole body revolts at his touch."[59] Yet it is the mother whom she comes to revile. The graphic emotion of this story comes through clearly enough; yet the rhetoric cannot disguise the falseness of the situation. Why not an encounter between husband and wife? What was the mother to have done?. It seems that we are to believe that, having known the facts of life, the daughter would not have associated herself with a man physically unattractive to her. The real complaint, however, is not the girl's ignorance but the man's boorishness, his transformation of marriage into "a legal prostitution, a nightly degradation, a hateful yoke."[60]

This passage makes clear that the struggle is not between mothers and daughters, but between husbands and wives. Ultimately, Egerton's avoidance of these central confrontations depresses the reader. One feels repeatedly an atmosphere of wasted talent, a capacity never really stretched. Although Egerton was aware of her preferences as a writer, she did not perceive them as problems; whether from arrogance or self-protective obtuseness, she rejected all outside criticism. As with Olive Schreiner, her lack of growth seems perversely deliberate. Six of the stories, she later revealed, were written in ten days; as long as the stories "came in droves and said themselves,"[61] she was content to obey the dictates of her muse. From the very beginning she had been warned by T. P. Gill that art went beyond the rendering of personal experience: "Olive Schreiner has never written a book worth reading since her *African Farm*. She put all her heart, all her experience, into that. The rest is bosh. Most people have *one* story to tell. The creative artist does not merely utter his own heart cry."[62] But she ignored him; perhaps she could not help herself. The tone of her 1932 memoir is irritatingly complacent: "I could not take myself seriously. I was intransigent, a bad seller of myself . . . the long

59 "Virgin Soil," p. 160. 60 "Virgin Soil," p. 155.
61 "A Keynote to *Keynotes*," p. 59.
62 White, p. 30.

214

book was not my pigeon. I made too the mistake of letting the publisher know that to me he was a tradesman, the middleman between the author and his public."[63] However, her nephew tells us that in reality she was humble and eager to please her publishers, her critics, and her readers. In the end she could not please anyone.

In retrospect, it looks as if all the feminists had but one story to tell, and exhausted themselves in its narration. They represent a turning-point in the female tradition, and they turn inward. Beginning with a sense of unity and a sense of mission, a real concern for the future of womanhood, an interest in the "precious speciality" of the female novelist, they ended, like Sarah Grand, with the dream that by withdrawing from the world they would find a higher female truth. Given the freedom to explore their experience, they rejected it, or at least tried to deny it. The private rooms that symbolize their professionalism and autonomy are fantastic sanctuaries, closely linked to their own defensive womanhood.

In *Lolita*, Nabokov tells a story of a monkey at the Jardin de Plantes that was given an easel and paints; the creature's first painting showed the bars of its cage. It is a pity that the feminists, showing the limits of their world in their writing, also elevated their restricted view into a sacred vision.

[63] "A Keynote to *Keynotes*," p. 59.

◇◇◇

CHAPTER VIII

Women Writers and the Suffrage Movement

THE lyrical and diffuse feminist protest literature of the 1890s became political in the hands of the suffragettes. Most Victorian women novelists had dissociated themselves from the women's suffrage movement, which had its theoretical origins as far back as Mary Wollstonecraft's *Vindication of the Rights of Woman* (1792) and its formal English organization in Manchester in 1865. The strategy of public antifeminism came partly from women writers' reluctance to take on the extra burden of this huge battle and partly from their own sense of being superior and exceptional. In an early article on "The Enfranchisement of Women" (1851), Harriet Taylor had attacked women novelists for being "anxious to earn pardon and toleration" from men by pretending to be content with their lot: "The literary class of women, especially in England, are ostentatious in disdaining the desire for equality or citizenship, and proclaiming their complete satisfaction with the place which society assigns to them."[1] Charlotte Brontë, who thought it sensible not to brood on evils beyond repair, and Mrs. Gaskell, who believed that women should fight for others but not for themselves, were offended by Taylor's innuendoes. George Eliot and Elizabeth Barrett Browning approved of feminism in theory, but did not think that Victorian women were ready to assume the responsibilities of political equality. Browning believed that, "considering men and women in the mass, there *is* an *inequality* of intellect."[2] Charlotte Yonge, Elizabeth Linton, Dinah Craik, Christina Rossetti, and Margaret Oliphant, among the feminine writers, were

[1] *Westminster Review* LV: 310.
[2] Aletha Hayter, *Mrs. Browning*, London, 1962, p. 183.

vehemently opposed to what Oliphant called "the mad notion of the franchise for women."[3]

There were women writers who supported the suffrage idea from the first. In 1866 a petition requesting the franchise was signed by 1,500 women; John Stuart Mill presented it in their behalf to the House of Commons. Barbara Bodichon, Jessie Boucherett, Rosamond Hill, and Elizabeth Garrett were the authors of the petition, and the women writers who signed it included Amelia Edwards, Matilda Betham-Edwards, Harriet Martineau, Annie Keary, and Anna Swanwick. The names of the greatest women of the day—George Eliot and Florence Nightingale—were conspicuously absent. Both had refused to participate, Eliot on the grounds that woman's harder lot should be "the basis for a sublimer resignation in woman and a more regenerating tenderness in men,"[4] Nightingale on the grounds that "there are evils which press more hardly on women than the want of the suffrage."[5]

In 1889 a number of prominent women and wives of prominent men, alarmed at the radicalism of the feminists, signed "An Appeal Against Female Suffrage," which was published in the *Nineteenth Century*. Mrs. Leslie Stephen, Mrs. Walter Bagehot, Mrs. Matthew Arnold, Mrs. Humphry Ward, Christina Rossetti, Elizabeth Linton, and Beatrice Potter joined in asserting that the limits of the emancipation process had been reached. Later Beatrice Potter—who had become Mrs. Webb—recanted; her explanation of her earlier motives probably speaks for other women as well: "At the root of my anti-feminism lay the fact that I had never myself suffered the disabilities assumed to arise from my sex."[6]

[3] *Autobiography and Letters of Mrs. M.O.W. Oliphant*, ed. Mrs. Harry Coghill, London, 1899, p. 211.

[4] Gordon S. Haight, *George Eliot: A Biography*, London, 1968, p. 396.

[5] Cecil Woodham-Smith, *Florence Nightingale*, London, 1950, ch. XX, p. 487.

[6] *My Apprenticeship*, London, 1971, p. 354.

From about 1905 to 1914 a new militancy in the suffrage movement created a climate in which excuses of the sublimity of suffering, the existence of other problems, or the class privileges of a female elite no longer sufficed. Women writers could not continue to ignore the issues or to remain neutral. Under the charismatic leadership of the Pankhursts, the suffrage campaign became an integral part of the female consciousness. On both sides of the issue, women produced an enormous quantity of writing, from political pamphlets to novels. Relatively little of this work is distinguished as fiction, but it is of immense interest historically; it provided the link between the ambivalent altruism of the feminists and the self-contained theories of the postwar female aesthetic.

Elizabeth Robins became the president of the Women Writers Suffrage League in 1908. In Robins the suffragettes had one of their most versatile and vigorous crusaders. Like Olive Schreiner and Sarah Grand, she had a dazzling personality that attracted disciples, men as well as women.[7] Under the pseudonym of "C. E. Raimond" she had written several novels, including *George Mandeville's Husband* (1894); one novel, *The Magnetic North* (1894), became a best seller. Robins' play, *Votes for Women* (1907), which she later made into a novel, was the most influential piece of literary propaganda to come out of the suffrage movement.

The Women Writers Suffrage League was the brainchild of two young journalists, Cecily Hamilton and Bessie Hatton; they founded it in 1908 as an auxiliary of the National Union of Women's Suffrage Societies, with the object of obtaining "the Parliamentary Franchise for women on the same terms as it is, or may be, granted to men." In this endeavor the talents of writers were of particular use. Other auxiliaries committed their specific skills to the goals of the campaign; the actresses' league, for example, came to make

[7] For an account of her charm in her old age, see "Profile of Leon Edel," *New Yorker* (March 13, 1971): 54.

218

up and disguise the W.S.P.U. leadership in their hideouts from the police.[8] The W.W.S.L. prospectus stated that:

> Its methods are the methods proper to writers—the use of the pen. The qualification for membership is the publication or production of a book, article, story, poem, or play, for which the author has received payment, and a subscription of 2s6d to be paid annually. . . . Women writers are urged to join the League. A body of writers working for a common cause cannot fail to influence public opinion.[9]

League members were expected to send frequent letters to newspapers, to contribute to suffrage periodicals, and to write essays, stories, and plays dramatizing the demand for the vote. On the whole they did not engage in militant confrontations, but Elizabeth Robins and Beatrice Harraden, close advisors of the Pankhursts, frequently attended planning and fund-raising meetings. Another enthusiastic member, Violet Hunt, recalled selling tracts on Kensington High Street with May Sinclair and futilely attempting to get Henry James to sign a suffrage petition. Like most of the women writers, Violet Hunt was less than eager to participate in the large protest marches that led to jail terms, hunger strikes, and the horrors of forcible feeding. She was excused by the Pankhursts on the grounds that she had to support an invalid mother, that staple furniture of the woman writer's home: "So my nose remains its own shape, not squashed against the flank of a horse—voted by Miss Evelyn Sharp as the safest place of all when the mounted police were turned out to disperse us."[10]

---

[8] See Antonia Raeburn, *The Militant Suffragettes*, London, 1973, for an account of the W.S.P.U. auxiliaries, and Andrew Rosen, *Rise Up, Women!* London, 1974, for a general history of the W.S.P.U.

[9] Elizabeth Robins, *Way Stations*, London, 1913, p. 107.

[10] *The Flurried Years*, London, 1926, p. 7. When she asked James to sign a petition in 1909, he replied, "No, I confess, I am not eager for the

Nonetheless, the women writers were a conspicuous part of the campaign. In the great demonstration of June 1910, over a hundred women writers marched behind the "scrivener's banner" with Olive Schreiner, Sarah Grand, Gertrude Warden, Alice Meynell, May Sinclair, Flora Annie Steel, Mrs. Israel Zangwill, Mrs. Havelock Ellis, and Evelyn Sharp. For several years they, and their counterparts in the Men's Suffrage League and the Fabian Society, kept up a steady stream of commentary on the question of the vote and the subjection of women. There were fervent novels, like G. Colmore's *Suffragette Sally* (c. 1911) and Charlotte Despard's and Mabel Collins's *Outlawed: A Novel on the Woman Suffrage Question* (1908); short stories, like Evelyn Sharp's "Rebel Women" (c. 1912); and collections of poems, like Elizabeth Gibson's *From the Wilderness* (1910). Plays with a suffrage theme became popular, not only at regional and London meetings of the societies, but also in the West End. Cicely Hamilton wrote several such plays; her comedy about a women's general strike, *How the Vote Was Won*, had its debut April 13, 1909, at the Royalty Theatre; *A Pageant of Great Women*, a capsule history of artists, rulers, saints, and warriors that starred Ellen Terry, opened at the Scala Theatre in November 1909. Beatrice Harraden's skit *Lady Geraldine's Speech* and Bessie Hatton's more emotional *Before Sunrise*, on the familiar feminist theme of the girl forced to marry a syphilitic roué, were other well-known W.W.S.L. productions.

Of all the suffrage plays, Elizabeth Robins' *Votes for Women* (re-titled *The Convert* as a novel) excited the most comment. Its plot, which was the same in the play and the novel, was melodramatic but enthralling. Against a detailed and realistic background of suffragette activism, Robins presented the struggle between a militant woman, Vida Levering, and her former lover, Geoffrey Stoner, now an

---

avenement of a multitudinous and overwhelming female electorate—and don't see how any man in his senses *can* be!" (p. 52).

M. P. In the past the heroine had been forced to have an abortion because her lover dared not face marrying her. When he falls in love with a more aristocratic young girl, his magnetic and persuasive ex-mistress blackmails him into backing the suffrage bill with the threat of seducing his eager fiancée into the woman's movement. These motives and tactics were not those of the W.S.P.U., but in representing the struggle for the vote as a sexual combat between two individuals Robins was expressing the underlying anxieties and emotions of many of her contemporaries. Samuel Hynes, one of the few scholars to write about Elizabeth Robins, says that the tone of *Votes for Women*, "is not that of a debate but of a bitter, deep-felt, intimate quarrel, like a husband and wife on the brink of divorce. When the standard cases of suffering women are brought up—the ruined maids, the Piccadilly whores, the tramp women, the starving working mothers—they are involved in order that their sufferings may be laid to one cause, the sexual viciousness of men. The sex war has begun, and the play is a dispatch from the front, fiercely partisan and militant."[11]

The play and the novel also give a very clear and reliable account of what it felt like to be a suffragette. Involved in the campaigns almost from the start, Robins made a special effort with her documentation for this work. In November 1906, she accompanied Christabel Pankhurst and Mary Gawthorpe to Huddersfield for the by-election, "to get the atmosphere," as she told Hannah Mitchell, a socialist suffragette.[12] Mrs. Mitchell later recognized bits of her own interviews with Robins in the novel. At this point Robins had completed a draft of the play, which she wrote "at white heat" in the fall of 1906; but, as she wrote to Millicent Fawcett, it seemed too controversial and partisan to be produced: "Instead of wearying out my soul by battering at their doors, I shall set to and turn the thing into a book as

[11] *The Edwardian Turn of Mind*, Princeton, 1968, p. 202.

[12] Hannah Mitchell, *The Hard Way Up*, ed. Geoffrey Mitchell, London, 1977, p. 163.

fast as ever I can. No trouble to get *that* accepted, however much a firebrand!"[13]

As it turned out, theater managers were more willing to risk controversy of this sort than she had suspected, and the play was produced at the Court Theatre in April 1907 with C. Aubrey Smith and Edmund Gwenn. Critics particularly admired the Trafalgar Square suffrage meeting that took up most of the second act. The *Morning Post* called it "a marvel of realism. It may advance the cause of female suffrage more than any number of meetings in Trafalgar Square could do."[14] The novel was published in October 1907. It was the first thing that Robins had written "under the pressure of a strong moral conviction,"[15] and it displayed a histrionic intensity not wholly artistic. *The Convert*, however, is a worthy contribution to the literature of the suffrage movement, particularly in its willingness to face the spectre of sex-antagonism, and it should be read in conjunction with H. G. Wells' *Ann Veronica*. Robins repeatedly suggests that the handling of the suffragettes had brutally sexual significance, a fact that should have been obvious but was repressed in contemporary historical accounts. In the later years of the suffrage campaign, forcible feeding by tubes inserted through the nostrils or down the throat became the standard procedure for treating hunger-striking suffragettes in the prisons; like the Lock Hospital examinations of the Contagious Diseases Act, the whole struggle took on the quality of a rape.

Mary Leigh described her ordeal to her solicitor in 1909: "The sensation is most painful. . . . I have to lie on the bed, pinned down by wardresses; one doctor stands up on a chair holding the funnel end at arms' length, so as to have the funnel end above the level, and then the other doctor,

[13] Letter of November 1, 1906, in the Fawcett Library, London.
[14] April 8, 1907. For other reviews see Scrapbook 10A of Newspaper Clippings 1907 at the Fawcett Library.
[15] Letter to Millicent Garrett Fawcett, November 1,, 1906.

who is behind, forces the other end up the nostrils."[16] Although this practice disgusted most citizens, it also appealed to sadistic fantasies; one account of the suffrage campaign mentions that a rumor in the pubs was that the imprisoned suffragettes were being forcibly fed through the rectum.[17]

Without being in the least explicit, Robins' novel manages to create an atmosphere of sexual tension and anxiety. There are veiled allusions to the sexual humiliation of the suffragettes by the police: "They punish us by underhand maltreatment—of the kind most intolerable to a decent woman."[18] Among themselves, the women decide who should volunteer to endure such abuse: "The older women saw they ought to save the younger ones from having to face that sort of thing. That was how we got some of the wives and mothers."[19] Robins herself used the term "sex-antagonism"; she saw the suffrage campaign as reflecting a deep hostility between men and women that finds its characteristic expression in sexual intercourse. Because they are able to acknowledge the existence of sex-antagonism, the suffragettes are free to act; other women deplete their energy in efforts to deny their own hostilities and revulsions. When a dowager protests that she deplores the sex-antagonism of the campaign, a suffragette replies, "You're so conscious it's here you're afraid to have it mentioned."[20]

[16] Statement of Mary Leigh, September 22, 1909, quoted in *Shoulder to Shoulder*, ed. Midge Mackenzie, London, 1975, pp. 128–129. See also statements by Sylvia Pankhurst (Acc. 57.70/13) and Janie Terrero ("Prison Experiences," 1912, Acc. 58.87.62) in the Museum of London.

[17] Sir Harry Johnston, *Mrs. Warren's Daughter: A Story of the Woman's Movement*, London, 1920, p. 246. Janet Arthur, a Scottish suffragette, "was subjected to the final indignity of rectal feeding" (George Dangerfield, *The Strange Death of Liberal England*, New York, 1961, p. 387). In large demonstrations suffragettes were "indecently assaulted" by plainclothes police (Raeburn, *Militant Suffragettes*, pp. 154–155).

[18] Elizabeth Robins, *The Convert*, London, 1980, p. 158.

[19] Ibid., p. 163.   [20] Ibid., p. 238.

Although her main purpose was political, Robins was also interested in a new direction for women's literature. Like George Egerton, she wanted to explore the *terra incognita* of the female psyche, both for its own sake and for the sake of confounding male complacency about human nature. She referred to male complacency in a speech to the W.W.S.L. in 1907: "If I were a man, and cared to know the world I lived in, I almost think it would make me a shade uneasy—the weight of that long silence of one-half the world."[21]

Robins further understood that the suffrage campaign needed a new literature of female psychology to raise the middle-class woman's consciousness about her life. Why had such a phenomenon failed to occur previously? In *Woman's Secret* Robins linked the woman writer with other members of a dependent working class that must turn out the products demanded by the market:

> Let us remember it is only yesterday that women in any number began to write for the public prints. But in taking up the pen, what did this new recruit conceive to be her task? To proclaim her own or other women's actual thoughts and feelings? Far from it. Her task, as she naturally and even inevitably conceived it, was to imitate as nearly as possible the method, but above all the point of view, of men.
>
> The realization that she had access to a rich and as yet unrifled storehouse may have crossed her mind, but there were cogent reasons for concealing her knowledge. With that wariness of ages, which has come to be instinct, she contented herself with echoing the old fables, presenting to a man-governed world puppets as nearly as possible like those that had from the beginning found such favour in men's sight.
>
> Contrary to the popular impression, to say in print what she thinks is the last thing the woman-novelist or

21 Elizabeth Robins, *Woman's Secret*, W.S.P.U. pamphlet in the collection of the Museum of London, p. 6.

journalist is so rash as to attempt. Here even more than elsewhere (unless she is reckless) she must wear the aspect that shall have the best chance of pleasing her brothers. Her publishers are not women.[22]

Cicely Hamilton suggested in a fascinating feminist polemic called *Marriage as a Trade* that women's psychological conditioning and experience were so specialized that, while superficially imitative, they were actually rebelling against their training by writing at all: "Any woman who has attained to even a small measure of success in literature or art has done so by discarding, consciously or unconsciously, the traditions in which she was reared, by turning her back upon the conventional ideas of dependence that were held up for her admiration in her youth." Hamilton also explored the theory that women writers viewed "romance" from an economic perspective, so that their love stories were not frivolous fantasies, but accounts of female survival: "To a woman, a woman in love is not only a woman swayed by emotion, but a human being engaged in carving for herself a career or securing for herself a means of livelihood. Her interest in a love story is, therefore, much more complex than a man's interest therein, and the appreciation which she brings to it is of a very different quality."[23] Hamilton's ideas were on the brink of a feminist criticism, but she bogged down in her efforts to connect women's literature to the specific goal of the vote.

Meanwhile the members of the Anti-Suffrage League, called Antis, were busily proclaiming their view of the world; they also had writers on their side. It was true, as Janet Courtney ruefully admitted afterward, that the Antis inevitably attracted "all the ultra-feminine and the ladylike incompetents,"[24] so that their propaganda was not as efficiently circulated, or as persuasively written, as that

---

[22] Ibid., pp. 8–9.
[23] *Marriage as a Trade*, London, 1981, pp. 110, 117.
[24] Janet Courtney, *The Women of My Time*, London, 1934, p. 174.

of the suffragettes. Some women writers, like "John Oliver Hobbes" (Mrs. Craigie), emulated George Eliot's majestic reserve and continued to see themselves as exceptions to the general inferiority of women: "I have no confidence in the honour of the average woman or her brains. The really distinguished women have been trained and influenced by men, and a man-hater I distrust and detest—she has the worst qualities of both sexes invariably. The great women Saints, the great Queens . . . the women writers,—Eliot, Sand, Brontë, Mrs. Browning, Christina Rossetti,—were all trained by men: they all liked men and preferred them infinitely before women."[25] Marie Corelli, who had made a career of portraying *femmes fatales*, saw in grace and beauty, and wiles and seduction, a truer and more lasting source of power than the vote. In her 1906 pamphlet for the Antis, "Woman, or—Suffragette?" she described her own macabre version of female activism: "The clever woman sits at home, and like a meadow spider spreads a pretty web of rose and gold, spangled with diamond dew. Flies—or men —fumble in by scores,—and she holds them all prisoners at her pleasure with a silken strand fine as a hair." The decorative imagery of gold, diamonds, and silk does little to conceal the very unpleasant central metaphor of the female spider. In fact, Marie Corelli had a profound New Womanish faith in female dominance, and saw the proper relation of the sexes as that of goddess and worshiper. In 1905 she declared that "Woman must learn the chief lesson of successful progress, which is not to copy Man, but to carefully preserve her beautiful Unlikeness to him in every possible way so that, while asserting and gaining intellectual equality with him, she shall gradually arrive at such ascendancy as to prove herself ever the finer and the nobler Creature."[26]

It can reasonably be argued that the Antis cherished a

[25] John Morgan Richards, *The Life of John Oliver Hobbes*, London, 1911, p. 326.

[26] Marie Corelli, "The Advance of Women," *Free Opinions*, London, 1905, p. 184.

more romantic fantasy of the evolutionary advantages of femininity than did the suffragettes, and, despite their political differences, shared the intellectual tradition of the feminists. One has to wonder how genuinely Mrs. Craigie despised man-haters, when she felt it "impossible not to notice the inferiority of the English males in nearly every class. I am struck by it as I watch the Bank Holiday crowds. Pretty-looking, refined girls with common, sickly, feeble men. If the men were strong, one could stand their roughness. But they are inane."[27]

Mrs. Humphry Ward, who had worked for women's higher education and for social reform, was appalled by what seemed the selfish individualism of the new campaign, and she became the first president of the Anti-Suffrage League in 1908. In the tradition of Mrs. Gaskell, "she felt it to be the duty of all educated women to work themselves to the bone for the uplifting of women and children less fortunate than themselves, and so to repay their debt to the community; but clamour for their own rights was a different thing; ugly in itself, and likely to lead, in her opinion, to a sex-war of very dubious outcome."[28] Ward's self-sacrificing "feminine" position, which was appropriate in women novelists of Gaskell's generation, was awkwardly outdated in the twentieth century. Ward was sixteen years older than Elizabeth Robins, and as her insistence on writing under her married name suggests, her strongest identification came from her role as wife and mother. She was appalled by the demands of the suffragettes for the personal freedom that the vote symbolized:

So women everywhere—many women at any rate—were turning undiscriminately against the old bonds, the old yokes, affections, servitudes, demanding "self-realization," freedom for the individuality and personal will;

27 Richards, *Life of John Oliver Hobbes*, p. 325.
28 Janet Penrose Trevelyan, *The Life of Mrs. Humphry Ward*, London, 1923, p. 225.

rebelling against motherhood and lifelong marriage; clamouring for easy divorce and denouncing their own fathers, brothers, and husbands as either tyrants or fools; casting away the old props and veils; determined, apparently, to know everything, however ugly, and to say everything, however outrageous.[29]

Ward herself was a regal woman who "played the public personage to perfection; it came quite naturally to her."[30] Other women writers reacted vehemently against her pretensions and her arrogance. In 1887, the Irish novelist May Hartley wrote angrily to Macmillan to complain about Mrs. Ward's having reviewed one of her books: "She condescends to allow jealousy and spite *according to my informants* to bias her judgments of other *women* writers." The same informants had told Mrs. Hartley that Mrs. Ward's consistent unfairness to women writers had caused her name to be struck from the reviewers list of the *Times*.[31] Whether or not this rumor was true, Mrs. Ward was a difficult and intimidating person, whose own warmth and feminine sympathy were held in careful check.

Yet Ward had absorbed many of the attitudes and prejudices of the feminists. Even in her anti-suffrage novel *Delia Blanchflower* (1914), her concern for women makes itself felt. One of her male observers meditates on his "profound pity" for women's "sorrows and burdens," for "their physical weakness, for their passive role in life." Ward did not favor passivity; herself an indefatigable public servant, she shared with women of an older generation, like Florence Nightingale and Dinah Craik, a desire to see women's maternal energies directed outward, and she believed in the beneficent effects of altruistic sisterhood. Painfully and personally aware of the deficiencies of women's education,

[29] *Delia Blanchflower*, quoted in Vineta Colby, *The Singular Anomaly: Women Novelists of the Nineteenth Century*, New York, 1970, p. 158.
[30] Courtney, *Women of My Time*, p. 20.
[31] Add. Mss. 54970, Macmillan Papers, British Museum.

she devoted the early years of her marriage to raising funds for a women's college at Oxford. These were the acceptable "feminist" activities of a "feminine" woman writer.

More significantly, the relationships between women in her books, "the tender and adoring friendship of women for women," reflect the intense bonds of the female subculture. Vineta Colby insists that these intimate friendships, which "modern readers would immediately designate as lesbian," are intended by Ward as "decorous outlets for her characters' passions . . . not only proper, but even poetic and elevating."[32] It is foolish to see the female friendships as perverted or unnatural, but they are also more than decorative. Ward's most powerful feelings are expressed in them. Bonds of loyalty, empathy, charity, and love between women are her answer to female oppression. Ward was also capable of a fierce response to any overtly sexual slurs. In 1913, when Dr. Almroth Wright published a notorious letter in the *Times* pronouncing suffrage militance a disease related to menopause and digressing on the ever-present danger of female "physiological emergencies," Ward (who was sixty-two) was as outraged as any suffragette. In her reply, she repudiated "for myself, and, I have no doubt whatever, for thousands of men and women who feel with me on the suffrage controversy, all connection with the bitter and unseemly violence which that letter displays."[33]

Ward shared with the suffragettes, and particularly with Mrs. Pankhurst, a sense that women were united by the terrible and holy suffering of childbirth. This shared experience obliterated class distinctions and brought all women down to the lowest common denominator of the body. Mrs. Pankhurst had been radicalized by her early experiences as Registrar of Births and Deaths in Manchester; Ward was profoundly stirred and disturbed by the pain of her own three pregnancies and deliveries. Clara Duff, after her first child was born, confessed to Ward: "I was so terribly upset

[32] Colby, *Singular Anomaly*, p. 122.
[33] See Roger Fulford, *Votes for Women*, London, 1968, pp. 229–230.

by the horrors I had gone through I never could bear to see a woman in the street who was going to have a baby. I used to go home and cry! Mrs. Humphry Ward's eyes filled with tears and she took hold of my hand and said, 'Oh, my dear, did you feel like that? I did too, and I thought it was morbid and no one else would ever understand.' "[34]

Rather than confronting the sources and the causes of women's suffering in the political and sexual systems, as the feminists did, Ward chose to channel her feelings into the feminine networks of charitable agencies and settlement houses. Impelled by acute sympathy for women in their maternal role, she published a pamphlet on infant-feeding to distribute in the Oxford slums. In her novels, moments of feminist illumination are inevitably connected to the physical pain of childbirth or disease, and the rebellious energy that such moments inspire is rapidly reinvested in feminine altruism. Ward and her privileged heroines found in social work both an outlet for, and a sublimation of, their own inner conflicts about womanhood.

In her most famous novel, *Robert Elsmere* (1888), Ward gave a cautious but sensitive account of a postpartum depression. Catherine Elsmere confides to her husband that childbirth has been so cruelly traumatic, has brought her so abruptly to a confrontation with mortality, that she has begun to question the fundamental institutions of her life. The pain of labor

> seems to take the joy even out of our love—and the child. I feel ashamed almost that mere physical pain should have laid such hold on me—and yet I can't get away from it. It's not for myself. . . . Comparatively I had so little to bear! But I know now for the first time what physical pain may mean—and I never knew before! I lie thinking, Robert, about all creatures in pain—workmen crushed by machinery, or soldiers, or poor things in hospitals—

[34] Anne Fremantle, *Three-Cornered Hat*, London, 1971, p. 67.

above all of women! Oh, when I get well, how I will take care of the women here! What women must suffer even here in out-of-the way cottages—no doctor, no kind nursing, all that agony and struggle![35]

The pain of workmen and soldiers might be blamed on bosses and generals; women's "agony and struggle" too might be attributed to an oppressive system: to inadequate medical care, to religious resistance to anaesthesia, to the lack of contraception, to the sexual demands of husbands, and ultimately to God's curse on Eve. But Ward's heroine quickly modulates the enunciation of her suffering; she denies it as a personal problem and rededicates her life to good works. Her outburst is nonetheless a brief moment of authenticity in an intellectual novel of abstruse theological argument.

However hostile they may be to the methods and the theories of the suffragettes, Ward's heroines are helplessly susceptible to the poverty and the pain of other women. In *The Testing of Diana Mallory* (1908), the aristocratic Diana can resist the suffragette debates of her socialist friend Marion, but not the spectacle of Marion's fatal illness, the squalor of the slums, or the sound of "the wailing of babes":

One day, after a discussion on votes for women which had taken place beside Marion's sofa, Diana, when the talkers were gone, had thrown herself on her friend.

"Dear, you can't wish it!—you can't believe it! To brutalize—unsex us!"

Marion raised herself on her elbow, and looked down the narrow cross street beneath the windows of her lodging. It was a stifling evening. The street was strewn with refuse, the odors from it filled the room. Ragged children with smeared faces were sitting or playing listlessly in the gutters. The public-house at the corner was full of anima-

---

[35] *Robert Elsmere*, London, n.d., bk. III, ch. XIX, p. 259.

tion, and women were passing in and out. Through the roar of traffic from the main street beyond a nearer sound persisted: a note of wailing—the wailing of babes.

"There are the unsexed!" said Marion panting. "Is their brutalization the price we pay for our refinement?" Then as she sank back: "Try anything—everything—to change that."[36]

While the Antis opposed militance from the right, another group of women opposed it from the left. These were the anarchistic socialists, friends of the Fabian Society, contributors to the *New Age* magazine in London and to *Liberty* in New York. The chief organ of this group was a periodical that went through three phases: the *Freewoman,* the *New Freewoman,* and the *Egoist.* All of these papers were financed by Harriet Shaw Weaver and edited by Dora Marsden, a graduate of Manchester University who had gone to jail with the W.S.P.U. in 1910. As Storm Jameson described her, Dora Marsden was "a small delicately-boned woman . . . with a subtle and powerful mind and a passion for philosophy, I believe, her only passion."[37] She was working on a book ("apparently endless," wrote Robert McAlmon) of feminist metaphysics, and her essays on Bergson, Hegel, and Nietzsche helped break the provincialism of English literary philosophy. According to McAlmon, Harriet Weaver began publishing a paper in order to circulate Miss Marsden's work.[38]

In its initial format, the *Freewoman* (1911–1913) attacked the suffragists' obsession with the vote as the means to emancipate women, and developed its own philosophy of free love and individualism. Dora Marsden wrote lengthy and increasingly theoretical editorials defining a humanist

[36] *The Testing of Diana Mallory,* London, 1908, p. 381.

[37] *Journey From the North,* I, London, 1969, p. 77.

[38] See Robert McAlmon and Kay Boyle, *Being Geniuses Together,* London, 1970, p. 82. McAlmon writes of Harriet Weaver: "When she was nineteen she was caught reading George Eliot's *Mill on the Floss* and was publicly reprimanded from the pulpit by the village minister."

philosophy and an aesthetic credo equally applicable to men and women; from the beginning male writers were involved in the paper.

The second incarnation, the *New Freewoman*, was born on June 15, 1913, with a minimized allegiance to feminism and a more general concern for other new ideas. In her first editorial, Marsden dissociated the periodical from the suffrage campaign: "For fear of being guilty of supporting the power of another 'empty concept' we hasten to add that the term 'Woman Movement' is one which deserves to go the way of all such—freedom, liberty, and the rest—to destruction."[39] As subsequent issues made clear, the *New Freewoman* was "not for the advancement of Woman, but for the empowering of individuals, men and women."[40] As the year wore on, the writers of the *New Freewoman* indicated more and more disgust with the fanaticism of the suffragettes.

An immediate source of irritation and alienation was the publication of Christabel Pankhurst's notorious *The Great Scourge and How to End It* (1913). The great scourge was venereal disease. Pankhurst estimated that 75 to 80 percent of all men were infected by gonorrhea; but, more basically, she argued that male lust lay at the root of female oppression:

> One of the chief objects of the book is to enlighten women as to the true reason where there is opposition to giving them the vote. That reason is sexual vice.
>
> The opponents of votes for women know that women, when they are politically free, and economically strong, will not be purchasable for the base uses of vice.[41]

[39] *New Freewoman* (June 15, 1913): 5.

[40] July 1, 1913, p. 25. For an account of the history of the periodical, hostile to its feminist phase, see Louis K. MacKendrick, "The *New Freewoman:* A Short Story of Literary Journalism," *English Literature in Transition* (1972): 180–188.

[41] *The Great Scourge*, London, 1913, IX.

In *The Great Scourge*, Pankhurst was simply restating feminist ideas that had been popularized in the 1890s by Sarah Grand and George Egerton. Her estimates of the extent of male vice were grotesquely exaggerated, but popular health manuals and medical texts at the turn of the century were equally frightening.[42] The timing of her pamphlet, however, was wrong. Coming in 1913, it seemed maidenly and hysterical to a generation that had seen the postimpressionists and read *The Way of All Flesh*.

Rebecca West, then a daring young journalist at the beginning of her career, responded with indignation at Pankhurst's prudery, seeing it as a step backward: "There was a long and desperate struggle before it became possible for women to write candidly on subjects such as these. That this power should be used to express views that would be old-fashioned . . . in the pastor of a Little Bethel is a matter for scalding tears."[43] Most suffragettes, however, could not imagine that sexual revolution would take the form of female license rather than male chastity. In this the *New Freewoman* was exceptional. In its single year of existence, it published some of the frankest material on sexuality to appear for several decades. In specific response to the prudery of the militant suffragists, Dora Marsden ran a series of articles suggesting a prostitutes' guild, like a labor union; she also published an extraordinary piece on female frigidity, which she believed to be an acquired characteristic of repression and economic dependence.

If women are not under-sexed, their sexual apathy is beautifully simulated. It is conceivable that this simulation may exist up to the point of yielding to man, but can

[42] In their work in Manchester the Pankhursts had seen the effects of venereal disease on women. In 1914 Mrs. Pankhurst said, "The main motive behind the suffragette campaign had been her horror at the prevalence of filthy sexual disease and moral squalor" (quoted in David Mitchell, *The Fighting Pankhursts*, New York, p. 141).

[43] Roger Fulford, *Votes for Women*, p. 256. Christabel Pankhurst, born in 1880, was twelve years older than Rebecca West.

it exist through the sexual act? Proof must, necessarily, be largely in regard of personal experiences, and such a record might not, in good taste, be produced; but what else can be inferred when widely experienced male sexual varietists almost unanimously concur in the statement that only a small proportion of the women with whom they have been associated (not prostitutes) experience a normal sexual orgasm, and that the sphincter of the vagina is rarely active?[44]

Obviously Dora Marsden was not undersexed, and, although she offered space in the periodical for the discussion of such trendy subjects as free love, Neo-Malthusianism, vegetarianism, and spiritualism, she continued to consider these questions primarily from a feminist viewpoint, albeit a very radical one. For example, Edward Carpenter, as typical a progressive cult figure as could be found, wrote an article on "The Status of Women in Early Greek Times" (August 1) in which he argued that homosexuals, or Uranians, as he called them, were more egalitarian to women than heterosexual men. The next month Marsden coolly refuted him: "There is an undeniable tendency in many homosexuals to look upon woman as an inferior. . . . It is hardly to be presumed . . . that the men who entertain this instinctive aversion to women are absolutely uninfluenced by it when summoned by women to support their demand for independence."[45]

Over the year, however, impatience with the suffragettes, and pressure from such male contributors as Ezra Pound and John Gould Fletcher to print imagist poetry and translations from French and Japanese writers, took the *New Freewoman* farther and farther away from feminist questions. In the issue of December 15, Marsden announced that henceforth the paper would be called the *Egoist*. A letter from five men suggesting that the old title led to confusion with "organs devoted solely to the advocacy of an unimpor-

[44] September 15, 1913: 174.   [45] September 1, 1915: 115.

tant reform in an obsolete political institution," and Marsden's own feeling that the time for rhetoric was past, forced the decision. "The time has arrived," she wrote "when mentally-honest women feel that they have no use for the springing-board of large promises of powers redeemable in a distant future. . . . They know that their works can give evidence now of whatever quality they are capable of giving them."

Egoism and feminism, however, were strange bedfellows. In the *Egoist*'s five years of publication (1914–1919), male writers, including Pound, Eliot, and Ford Madox Ford, dominated its pages. In June 1914 Dora Marsden resigned her editorship to Harriet Weaver, who made the journal famous by publishing *Portrait of the Artist as a Young Man* and extracts from *Ulysses*. While the literary value of the *Egoist* appreciated over the years, its feminist potential declined. Leonard and Virginia Woolf both recorded their shock upon making the acquaintance of Miss Weaver, "a very mild blue-eyed advanced spinster," not at all what the "editress of the Egoist ought to be. . . . Her neat mauve suit fitted both body and soul; her grey gloves laid straight by her plate symbolised domestic rectitude; her table manners were those of a well-bred hen."[46]

On balance, the suffrage movement was not a happy stimulus to women writers. If they participated in its militant phase, they did get some sense of effective solidarity, but not as writers. Despite Elizabeth Robins' remarks, no real manifesto of female literature was produced; the Women Writers Suffrage League remained a political and, in many ways, a social organization. Alice Meynell, who opposed militance, nonetheless enjoyed her Women Writers dinners and the bustle of the marches. Several of the most committed activists felt frightened by the demanding fanaticism of the Pankhursts and by the dimension of the sacrifices

[46] Quoted from diaries of April 14, 1918, in Leonard Woolf, *Beginning Again*, London, 1964, p. 246. The "spinster" is Leonard's, the "editress," Virginia's.

they were asked to make for the Cause. Evelyn Sharp meant to pay the suffragettes a compliment when she had a male character in one of her short stories describe them as soldiers: " 'This is the kind of thing you get on a bigger scale in war,' he said, in a half-jesting tone, as if afraid of seeming serious. 'Same mud and slush, same grit, same cowardice, same stupidity and beastliness all around. . . . The women here are fighting for something big; that's the only difference.' "[47] Sharp does not make clear who is being stupid and beastly, but the warlike qualities of the W.S.P.U. were morally ambiguous. The Pankhursts maintained an internal military discipline, as well as a battle with the government; they awarded medals for valor and demanded unquestioning obedience.

Women writers respected the militants for their courage, but at the same time they expressed a combination of guilt and hostility toward the Pankhursts, simultaneously confessing their own lack of commitment and attacking the Pankhursts as being bullies and neurotics. Beatrice Harraden confided to Elizabeth Robins that she was glad when Mrs. Pankhurst thought kindly of her: "I always feel I've failed her by not giving up absolutely everything for the cause."[48] Stella Benson, herself a suffragette, caricatured movement despotism as

The Chief Militant Suffragette, who believed that she held feminism in the hollow of her hand. . . . She was familiar with the knack of wringing sacrifices from other people. She was a little lady in a minor key, pale and plaintive, with short hair like spun sand. She dressed as nearly as possible like a man, and affected an eyeglass. She probably thought that in doing this she had sacrificed enough for the cause of women. She had safely

[47] "The Women at the Gate," in *Rebel Women*, London, c. 1912, p. 13.
[48] Letter of September 14, 1912, in the Fales Collection, New York University Library.

found a husband before she cut her hair. I suppose she had sent more women to prison than any one magistrate in London, but she had never been in prison herself.[49]

Virginia Woolf, who once addressed some envelopes for the Adult Suffrage League, always depicted suffragists as incomplete and marginal people, seeking in the process and violence of the movement a passion that was lacking in their own lives. She described such a personality least sympathetically in Miss Kilman, the repressed governess in *Mrs. Dalloway*, and most sympathetically in Mary Datchet, the feminist in *Night and Day* who fully comprehends the compensatory nature of her life's work:

> She had entered in the army, and was a volunteer no longer. She had renounced something, and was now— how could she express it?—not quite "in the running" for life. She had always known that Mr. Clacton and Miss Seal were not in the running, and across the gulf that separated them she had seen them in the guise of shadow people, flitting in and out of the ranks of the living— eccentrics, undeveloped human beings, from whose substance some essential part had been cut away.[50]

There was also a strong class-element in the response of women writers to the suffrage movement, as Virginia Woolf's writing makes salient. Besides having other unfortunate qualities, Miss Kilman perspires and wears unsuitable clothing and obtrudes her poverty. In joining the movement, women writers had to abandon class distinctions, the privileges of being ladies. In Mrs. Humphry Ward's description of a suffrage society called "The Daughters of Revolt," a dressmaker and a farmer's daughter are included; the prospective companionship of the vulgar and the uncouth could frighten women back to their drawing-rooms.

[49] R. Ellis Roberts, *A Portrait of Stella Benson*, London, 1939, p. 40.
[50] *Night and Day*, London, 1969, ch. 20, p. 246.

In short, women writers found themselves confronted through the suffrage movement by a number of challenges and threats: by the spectre of violence, by the ruthlessness of female authoritarianism, by the elimination of class boundaries, by a politics of action rather than influence, by collectivism, and by the loss of the secure privacy in which they had been cultivating their "special moral qualities." The shift was too abrupt to be liberating, and in a reaction against it many women writers of this generation seem to have retreated from social involvement into a leisurely examination of the sensibility, into the cultivation of a beautiful womanly Unlikeness.

In *The Tree of Heaven* (1917), May Sinclair takes her heroine from a suffrage demonstration, to Holloway Gaol, and finally to a welcoming banquet for released prisoners, at which the Women's Marseillaise is sung: "The singing had threatened her when it began; so that she felt again her old terror of the collective soul. Its massed emotion threatened her. She longed for her white-washed prison cell, for its hardness, its nakedness, its quiet, its visionary peace."[51] Inside that cell, women could preserve the illusion of specialness, of being different. Outside it, they encountered the complexity of being merely human. It is no wonder that they sometimes yearned to go back.

[51] *The Tree of Heaven*, London, 1917, p. 225.

CHAPTER IX

::

The Female Aesthetic

THE last generation of Victorian women novelists began to publish during the suffrage campaigns and the First World War. Suffragette writers had taken up John Stuart Mill's challenge to transmute the moral issues of Victorian feminism into an aesthetic philosophy. After the war, women novelists, half-inspired by the promise of a purely female art, half-frightened by the spectacle of how closely feminist militance resembled its masculine form, began to develop a fiction that celebrated a new consciousness. The female aesthetic applied feminist ideology to language as well as to literature, to words and sentences as well as to perceptions and values. Perhaps the war, coming at the height of suffrage militance, inflicted a sense of collective guilt upon activist women; certainly members of the W.S.P.U. transferred their energies from the vote to the war with suspicious alacrity. Women writers responded to the war by turning within; yet they renounced the demands of the individual narrative self. The world seemed dominated by the violence of ego; women writers wanted no part of it. Thus the fiction of this generation seems oddly impersonal and renunciatory at the same time that it is openly and insistently female. The female aesthetic was to become another form of self-annihilation for women writers, rather than a way of self-realization. One detects in this generation clear and disturbing signs of retreat: retreat from the ego, retreat from the physical experience of women, retreat from the material world, retreat into separate rooms and separate cities. Under the banner of the female aesthetic marched the army of the secession.

At the time, however, female aestheticism looked like a step forward. Some women novelists and critics felt that, as Mill had predicted, the literature of women had finally emancipated itself from its cultural subjection to a male tradition, and that its historical moment had arrived. It is true that James Joyce and Dorothy Richardson were pursuing some of the same experiments, and that Virginia Woolf and D. H. Lawrence had similar visions of sexual polarity. Yet no reader would mistake one for the other, mainly because their verbal territories scarcely overlap, but also, as women writers liked to repeat, because women were holding to their own experience, values, and grievances. Virginia Woolf felt altogether pleased with what she saw of women's fiction in 1929: "It is courageous; it is sincere, it keeps closely to what women feel. It is not bitter. It does not insist upon its femininity. But at the same time, a woman's book is not written as a man would write it."[1]

In 1920 a critical study called *Some Contemporary Novelists (Women)* by R. Brimley Johnson attempted to define the collective nature of women's fiction and to explain what was meant by the female version of realism: "The new woman, the female novelist of the twentieth century, has abandoned the old realism. She does not accept *observed* revelation. She is seeking, with passionate determination, for that Reality which is behind the material, the things that matter, spiritual things, ultimate Truth. And here she finds man an outsider, wilfully blind, purposely indifferent."[2] Johnson romanticized this quest in relating it to the war, which he thought had brought "a new spirituality" to a disillusioned generation. But he also thought it stemmed from feminist ideology.

In terms of subject matter and approach, the novels that Johnson discussed have a number of common traits that

---

[1] "Women and Fiction," *Women and Writing*, ed. Michèle Barrett, London, 1979, p. 241.

[2] *Some Contemporary Novelists (Women)*, London, 1920, pp. xiv–xv.

come from their feminism. They reverse the orthodox argument that women have limited experience by defining reality as subjective. In *The Creators* (1910) May Sinclair wrote that experience "spoils you. It ties you hand and foot. It perverts you, twists you, blinds you to everything but yourself. I know women—artists—who have never got over their experience, women who'll never do anything because of it." When she read Dorothy Richardson's novels, Sinclair was charmed by the total obliteration of structured experience: "Nothing happens. It just goes on and on."[3] Several of the novels were attacks on the Victorian nuclear family; Eleanor Mordaunt's *The Family* (1915) and Rose Macaulay's *Potterism* (1920) were especially biting; Ivy Compton-Burnett's austere sensationalism was based on an exposure of the murderous psychic combat of parents and children.

Early twentieth-century novels were also anti-male, both in the sense that they attacked "male" technology, law, and politics, and that they belittled masculine morality. We can hear the muted clash of swords in the 1909 correspondence between Clive Bell and Virginia Woolf over the first drafts of *The Voyage Out*. Bell began diplomatically but quickly became less tactful: "Our views about men & women are doubtless quite different, and the difference doesn't matter much; but to draw such sharp & marked contrasts between the subtle, sensitive, tactful, gracious, delicately perceptive, & perspicacious women, & the obtuse, vulgar, blind, florid, rude, tactless, emphatic, indelicate, vain, tyrannical, stupid men, is not only rather absurd, but rather bad art, I think." Woolf responded with even more devastating courtesy, depersonalizing the disagreement, but putting Bell in his place: "Possibly, for psychological reasons which seem to me very interesting, a man, in the present state of the

[3] May Sinclair, *The Creators*, quoted in Johnson, *Some Contemporary Novelists*, p. 37; and "The Novels of Dorothy Richardson," *Little Review*, IV (April 1918), quoted in Johnson, *Some Contemporary Novelists*, p. 135.

world, is not a very good judge of his sex; and a 'creation' may seem to him 'didactic.' "[4]

It is by "their tiresome restlessness," wrote Amber Reeves, "their curiosity, their disregard for security, for seemliness, even for life itself, that men have mastered the world, and filled it with the wealth of civilization . . . that they have armed the race with science, dignified it with art."[5] Civilization and the illusion of progress was a by-product of the masculine way of being, which women writers now came to see as sterile, egocentric, and self-deluding. Coming to terms with the paradox of male culture required an ironic inversion of some of the most cherished Victorian notions of male and female codes of living. Women were claiming that men's allegiance to external "objective" standards of knowledge and behavior cut them off from the "real reality" of subjective understanding. Just as the Victorians had maintained that women were too emotionally involved and anarchic to judge personality, let alone history, women now sweetly hinted that men were too caught up in the preservation of a system to comprehend its meaning.

Yet for all their new awareness, the heroines of this fiction remain victims; indeed they are victimized by their awareness. Whereas the heroines of Victorian fiction often did not perceive that they had choices, and in fact had only a selection of bad options, these heroines are confronted with choices and lack the nerve to seize their time. F. M. Mayor's *The Rector's Daughter* (1924) describes the plight of Mary Jocelyn, who deliberately abandons all hope of fulfillment or self-expression out of devotion to her father. Similarly Radclyffe Hall, in *The Unlit Lamp* (1924), makes her heroine Joan a self-destructive martyr to duty. In the end Joan's lover cries, "How long is it to go on, . . . this incredibly wicked thing that tradition sanctifies? You were so

[4] Quentin Bell, *Virginia Woolf: A Biography*, i, London, 1972, pp. 209, 211.

[5] Quoted in Johnson, *Some Contemporary Novelists*, p. xiv.

splendid. How fine you were! You had everything in you
that was needed to have put life within your grasp, and you
had a right to life, to a life of your own; everyone has. You
might have been a brilliant woman, a woman that counted
for a great deal, and yet what are you now?"[6] Men resisted
the tyranny of the family and broke away into silence, exile,
and cunning; women succumbed. The female *Künstler-
roman* of this period is a saga of defeat. Women novelists
punish and blame their heroines for their weakness, their
laziness, and their lack of purpose, for the manuscript yel-
lowing in the desk, for the risk abjured. There is indeed a
new interest in the creative psychology of women, but it is
full of self-recrimination.

Part of the problem was tension between the novelists'
lives as women and their commitment to literature. Members of a generation of women in rebellion against the traditional feminine domestic roles, they tried free love, only to
find themselves exploited; if they then chose marriage, they
often felt trapped. Storm Jameson, who admitted that her
ideas about childbearing had come primarily from *Anna
Karenina*, found herself near madness from the monotonous
drudgery of her marriage: "I cannot explain my pathological hatred of domestic life and my frantic need to be free."[7]
D. H. Lawrence could maintain that the secret of artistic
stability was to love a wife.[8] Women, however, found themselves pulled apart by the conflicting claims of love and art.
Those who fared best were emotional tycoons like Katherine Mansfield and Vita Sackville-West, who made their
own terms with men and also retained title to the adoration
and the services of less-demanding women friends. Other
women—Stella Benson was one—insisted vehemently "on

[6] Radclyffe Hall, *The Unlit Lamp*, London, 1981, p. 300. See also May
Sinclair, *Mary Olivier: A Life*, London, 1980, for an elaborate study of
female role-conflict and renunciation.

[7] *Journey from the North*, I, London, 1969, p. 88.

[8] D. H. Lawrence to Thomas Dacre Dunlap, 7 July 1914, D. H.
Lawrence, *Collected Letters* Vol. 1, London, 1962, pp. 284–286.

being a writer first and a wife second; a man would insist and I insist. A hundred years hence it will seem absurd that a woman should have to say this, just as it would seem absurd now if we should hear that Mr. William Blake's wife wanted him to take up breeding pigs to help her and he obstinately preferred writing poetry."[9] But it came to nothing in the end. When the crises came, women went bitterly with their husbands, as they had always done.

Self-sacrifice generates bitterness and makes, as Yeats said, a stone of the heart. But beyond the outspoken contempt for male selfishness in this fiction is a much more intense self-hatred. Women gave in and despised themselves for giving in. Insofar as it is recorded in the novels, the concept of female autonomy is frighteningly undercut by theories of post-Darwinian determinism and retributive systems of almost theological rigidity. In Rebecca West's powerful novel *The Judge* (1922), for example, male egoism is portrayed in Richard Haverland, a twentieth-century Rochester whose romantic action is shown to be empty and escapist. Two women, Haverland's mother, Marion, and his lover, Ellen Melville, have to pay the price for his impulsiveness, his emotionalism, and his immaturity. Marion, who had sacrificed the potential of her own life to protect her son—she had agreed to a sexless marriage with a man she despised in order to make Richard legitimate—learns that one sacrifice leads inevitably to others. Her husband rapes her and she must bear a despised legitimate son. Richard kills his brother and flees with Ellen, who is pregnant with his illegimate child. At the end, only Marion's suicide seems adequate to the situation. The story of Ellen Melville, a socialist and a suffragette, is equally futile; her dream of female equality is seen to have been a snare and a delusion. West's epigraph for the novel reflects on the political hierarchies that lead to diminishing returns of affection and hope: "Every mother is a judge who sentences the children for the sins of the fathers."

[9] R. Ellis Roberts, *Portrait of Stella Benson*, London, 1939, p. 215.

Men are the sinners, but women are both the judges and the convicts. One feels overwhelmingly that the women are punished in this novel, punished for their innocence, for their self-betrayal, for their willingness to become victims. The collapse of the long love affair between West and H. G. Wells, which took place about this time, probably accounts for some of the bitterness of the book. As "their relationship deteriorated rapidly, with Rebecca increasingly anxious to break free and Wells increasingly determined not to let her go,"[10] the tensions between West and Wells as artists became more pronounced. Ellen Melville, the suffragette who seems fated to relive an earlier generation's pattern of womanly suffering and self-sacrifice, is clearly related to West's disillusionment with the compromises she had made with Wells. He disliked *The Judge* very much and told her so; he called it "an ill conceived sprawl of a book with a faked climax, an aimless waste of your powers."[11] The book is flawed, but it is not aimless. Many of West's subsequent books, both fiction and reportage, dealt with the same questions of betrayal and judgment.

In the short stories of Katherine Mansfield, the moment of self-awareness is also the moment of self-betrayal. Typically, a woman in her fiction who steps across the threshold into a new understanding of womanhood is humiliated, or destroyed. Mansfield's fiction is cautionary and punitive; women are lured out onto the limbs of consciousness, which are then lopped off by the author. In "Bliss," for example, Bertha's recognition that the feeling she calls "bliss," the "fire in her bosom," is sexual ardor, is quickly followed by her discovery of her husband's adultery.

Virginia Woolf was disgusted with "Bliss," which she read in the *English Review* in 1918. Woolf confided to her diary: "She is content with superficial smartness; and the

[10] Gordon N. Ray, *H. G. Wells and Rebecca West*, London, 1974, p. xv.
[11] Ray, p. 123. See also Norman and Jeanne Mackenzie, *The Time Traveller*, London, 1973, p. 339.

whole conception is poor, cheap, not the vision, however imperfect, of an interesting mind. She writes badly too. And the effect was, as I say, to give mc an impression of her callousness and hardness as a human being. I shall read it again, but I don't suppose I shall change."[12] Yet in Mansfield's brutality, Woolf recognized herself, her own hardness and her own vulnerability. Mansfield insisted that Woolf recognize the bond: "We have got the same job, Virginia," she wrote after their first meeting, "and it is really very curious and thrilling that we should both . . . be after so nearly the same thing. We are, you know. There's no denying it."[13] A 1924 short story by Woolf, "The New Dress," echoes the theme and even the language of "Bliss." *Mrs. Dalloway* is closest of all to Mansfield's style and subject matter; Woolf merely substitutes revery for epiphany. Both Woolf and Mansfield see women as artists whose creative energy has gone chiefly into the maintenance of myths about themselves and about those they love. To become aware of the creation of a myth is to lose faith in it. Mansfield's characters are seen repeatedly at this moment of realization and collapse, but Mrs. Dalloway manages to escape by projecting her anxieties onto someone else. There is something instructive and chilling in the survival tactics of this fiction. Writing about one of Mansfield's most famous stories, "Miss Brill" (in which a lonely woman's marginally sustaining fantasy of self is wrecked when she overhears two lovers making fun of her irí a park), Margaret Drabble recalled that she had been horrified by its cruelty: "I couldn't get it out of my mind: I think it changed something in me forever . . . one would not like to have written it oneself, however fine the achievement."[14] As Septimus Smith becomes the scapegoat for Mrs. Dalloway's failures, so the

[12] *A Writer's Diary*, ed. Leonard Woolf, London 1965, p. 14.
[13] *The Letters of Katherine Mansfield*, I, ed. J. Middleton Murry, London, 1928, p. 71.
[14] "Katherine Mansfield: Fifty Years On," *Harpers & Queen* (July 1973): 107.

heroines of Katherine Mansfield's stories become the scapegoats for hers.

The most consistent representative of female aestheticism was Dorothy M. Richardson, who might have been the Gertrude Stein of the English novel if she had been more self-promoting and more affluent. Edward Garnett, accepting the first volume of *Pilgrimage* for the firm of Duckworth in 1915, christened Richardson's work "feminine impressionism" and saw its connections with the work of other women novelists (Garnett had recommended Olive Schreiner's *Women and Labour* to Fisher Unwin, and he had also accepted Woolf's *The Voyage Out*). Richardson's later admirers linked her with Proust and Joyce; but her real tradition was female, and her subject was female consciousness. In considering her career and her art, we can see how her narrative techniques and her aesthetic theories grew out of a struggle to depersonalize and control a female identity that was potent with the promise of self-destruction.

Richardson had the professional life of a Mary Wollstonecraft or a George Eliot: she began as a teacher, then worked as a translator and journalist; she had affairs with selfish and unscrupulous men, and made contact with both the solid center and the louche fringes of London intellectual society. She was nearly forty years old when she began to write *Pointed Roofs*, the first volume of her twelve-volume, thirty-year study of "Miriam Henderson," a heroine whose life paralleled her own up to the point of authorship. In its diffuse way, *Pilgrimage* is a portrait of the young woman on the way to becoming an artist, and it is in this convolution—the novel ends when the heroine is ready to write it—that Richardson most resembles Proust and Joyce.

Like Olive Schreiner, Sarah Grand, and many other women writers, Dorothy Richardson was the child of a forceful but unreliable father and a passive, depressed mother. In a family of girls, she became the surrogate son, a role that her sister-in-law later attributed to her "wilful and at times unmanageable nature."[15] In times of financial difficulty—unhappily frequent in the Richardson home—Dorothy was spared the domestic routines that her sisters had to take on. On the other hand, she was expected to be her father's companion at meetings of the British Association for the Advancement of Science, an organization he devotedly supported. Her father's scientific rationalism and the "deadness" of the association oppressed her, and later she came to identify "the dark veil under which I grew up"[16] as the shadow of male scientific philosophy. Her own pseudo-maleness within the family became a source of uneasiness, particularly when she found herself identifying with her mother. Unlike her resilient, socially ambitious father, Dorothy felt threatened by the precariousness of their financial position and deeply humiliated in times of hardship. When Charles Richardson was finally declared bankrupt in 1893, his wife's invalidism was complicated by deep depression. Dorothy, herself feeling "trapped and helpless,"[17] had to respond to, and care for, her mother; in November 1895 they went on a desperate holiday together to Hastings. But Mrs. Richardson was by then too despondent and alienated to be helped, and Dorothy returned one afternoon from a walk to find her mother dead in their room, having cut her throat with a carving knife.

In many ways this traumatic episode was the turning point in Dorothy's life; it freed her from the emotional demands of her family and allowed her to move to an independent life in London. As women writers always did, however, she paid dearly for her freedom. Her mother's suicide was first of all a warning, a hereditary hint that no daughter

[15] Rose Odle, "Some Memories of Dorothy M. Richardson and Alan Odle," November 18, 1957; unpublished ms., Dorothy Richardson Collection, Beinecke Library, Yale University.

[16] John Rosenberg, *Dorothy Richardson: The Genius They Forgot*, London, 1973, p. 8.

[17] Ibid., p. 17.

of an ardent Darwinian could ignore. More basically, it established a terrible precedent, a terrible contrast between the impregnable materialism and rationalism of men, secure with their built-in defenses, and the intuitive, involuntary, fatal sensitivity of women like her mother, defenseless against the deadly atmosphere of an indifferent culture. One sees this contrast stated most explicitly in *The Tunnel* (1919), the volume of *Pilgrimage* that describes Miriam Henderson's first years in London. Miriam's epiphany comes when she reads an insulting entry on "Woman" in an encyclopedia, and rebels against the futility of women's lives in an age controlled by science.[18]

At this moment of despair in the novel, Miriam, convinced that "life is poisoned for women, at the very source," can only recommend that, in protest, "all women ought to agree to commit suicide."[19] Suicide becomes a grotesquely fantasized female weapon, a way of cheating men out of dominance. Martyrdom and self-immolation are viewed as aggressive, as a way of inflicting punishment on the guilty survivors. This passage, with its suggestion that Richardson saw her own mother's suicide as a protest against her father, is extremely significant; it is a direct advocacy of the art of self-annihilation that is the hallmark of female aestheticism. At times Richardson recognized that suicide was just another form of power politics: "If women commit suicide in becoming partisan, what is the use of their entering party politics?" she wrote in her journal.[20] She would not choose the martyrdom of commitment because that was masculine. Instead she chose to live at the perilous borders of egolessness, in the female country of multiple receptivity.

[18] *The Tunnel, Pilgrimage*, II, London, 1979, p. 220. There is a very similar passage in *A Room of One's Own*, in which the narrator, doing research on women in the British Museum Reading Room, imagines a definitive male treatise on female inferiority. Virginia Woolf reviewed *The Tunnel* for the *Times Literary Supplement* (February 13, 1919): 81.

[19] *The Tunnel*, p. 221.

[20] Dorothy Richardson Collection, Beinecke Library, Yale University.

She risked self-destruction through psychic overload, ego death from the state of pure receptive sensibility that George Eliot had described as the roar on the other side of silence.[21]

Richardson saw this openness to psychological stimuli— we could also call it a form of negative capability—as the natural result of woman's position in the world, as "the human demand, besieging her wherever she is, for an inclusive awareness, from which men, for good or evil, are exempt."[22] One gets a clue in this passage to the sources of her lifelong sense of being embattled. Women's responsiveness to human demands had always kept them from becoming great artists, but Richardson thought she could see a way to turn this liability into an asset. Women had always been accused of a chameleon-like susceptibility to the ideas of their lovers. From her perspective, this openness merely demonstrated women's greater range, their comprehension of the timeless oneness beyond the ideological flux. "Views and opinions are masculine things," she wrote in *Revolving Lights*. "Women are indifferent to them really. . . . Women can hold all opinions at once, or any, or none. It's because they see the relations of things which don't change, more than things which are always changing."[23]

Richardson's view helped her make sense of her own fragmented life in London at the turn of the century. During the day she worked as a dentist's assistant; at night she immersed herself in books and radical societies. She attended meetings of the Fabian Society, contacted Anarchists, and met with suffragettes, Quakers, and Zionists. In 1906 the publisher Charles Daniel asked her to write reviews for his new periodical, *Crank*. Among the cranks on Daniel's staff, Mary Everest Boole most impressed Richardson. She was the wife of the mathematician George Boole

---

[21] *Middlemarch*, London, 1965, bk. II, ch. 20, p. 226.
[22] "Women in the Arts," *Vanity Fair*, May 1925.
[23] *Revolving Lights, Pilgrimage*, III, London, 1979, p. 259.

and mother of the novelist Ethel Voynich; she wrote with cabalistic intensity of epistemology and spiritualism and rated women's intuition high on the scale of human faculties. Richardson remained aloof in terms of committing herself to any of these groups or ideologies. Noncommitment itself became one of her ideals; she saw it as a characteristic attribute of feminine genius. Partisan politics, organized religion, and even personal relationships imposed false patterns on pure reality; women unsexed themselves by declaring any allegiance. The feminine mind, she wrote, "is capable of being all over the place and in all camps at once."[24] Her refusal as a novelist to structure consciousness came from this same refusal to impose any pattern or system on being.

But just as any novel *must* structure consciousness, whatever its pretensions to be pure, so Richardson's independence was a pose. She was much more easily swayed than she could ever bear to admit; the collective influence of London radicalism certainly affected her at this time. In the early 1900s she was particularly swayed by Fabian ideas. Much later she made fun of the doctrines of the Fabian Nursery, especially those of free love and the destruction of the nuclear family: "I recall a solemn discussion at a meeting of young women, on the desirability of selecting a suitable male, producing an infant, and going on the rates."[25] But in 1906, when she discovered that she was pregnant with H. G. Wells's child, she was determined to follow the Fabian gospel by raising the child completely on her own. Unhappily—for she had an intense maternal drive—she had a miscarriage in 1907, around Easter, shortly after visiting suffragette prisoners in Holloway. The whole affair brought her close to breakdown.

[24] Quoted in Sydney Kaplan, "Featureless Freedom or Ironic Submission," *College English* (May 1971): 917.

[25] Letter to Curtis Brown, January 16, 1950, Dorothy Richardson Collection, Beinecke Library, Yale University.

Wells, of course, cast his seed far and wide; in the recent biography of him by Norman and Jeanne Mackenzie, Dorothy Richardson is scarcely mentioned. She is simply part of the chorus, another Fabian groupie. In her biography, however, the Wells affair was a major event, both in personal and artistic terms. In the aftermath of this experience (Wells had moved on to Amber Reeves), she began to struggle with the first volume of her novel. I think we can assume that when she said that the novel came from her effort to "produce a feminine equivalent of the current masculine realism" it was chiefly Wells's realism she had in mind.[26] Richardson's first literary efforts to define the female artistic identity took the form of a dialectic; eventually she wrote the anti-Wellsian novel.

There were historical as well as personal reasons why Richardson should have had to define herself in opposition to Wells. Although they were almost the same age, they came from different literary generations. In the year that Richardson began serious work on *Pilgrimage*, Wells published his twenty-seventh book, *The New Machiavelli*. He was an Edwardian with Bennett and Galsworthy; she was a Georgian with Forster and Woolf. Thus Richardson's repudiation of Wells was also a repudiation of the Edwardian novel of external realism and accumulated detail. It is also clear that to Richardson and Woolf the Edwardians represented a male literary culture. And though male artists too have had to struggle against the influence of famous predecessors, only in rare cases have those celebrities been their lovers.

In fact it had been Wells who had first encouraged Richardson to write. Some idea of how she recalled his cheerful and businesslike eogism, and her own unyielding epistemology, may be gleaned from the dialogues in *Dawn's Early Light*:

[26] Foreword to *Pilgrimage*, New York, 1938. See also Caesar Blake, *Dorothy Richardson*, Ann Arbor, 1960, pp. 181–182.

"Perhaps the novel's not your form. Women ought to be good novelists. But they write best about their own experiences. Love-affairs and so forth. They lack imagination."

"Ah, imagination. Lies."

"Try a novel of ideas. Philosophical. There's George Eliot."

"Writes like a man."

"Just so. Lewes. Be a feminine George Eliot. Try your hand."[27]

Even though Richardson admired Wells and had been educated by him, she came to see him as an opponent, the quintessential male artist. Her name for him in *Pilgrimage* is "Hypo Wilson": Hypo (with its innuendos of hippoes and hypocrisy) actually means "less than, or subordinated to"; Wilson echoes "Wilkins," the name Wells used for himself as public figure in his own novels. Her Hypo is the public man, the figurehead, larger than life and slightly absurd.

Horace Gregory has commented on the debt that Richardson owed to Wells as a teacher; from him she learned conversational style, realistic observation, mimicry, and use of the novel as a medium for advanced ideas. Gregory also finds "undertones of Wellsian prophecy" in Richardson's feminism.[28] The debt is there, in the sense that any anti-novel pays tribute to its antagonist. But the antagonism, the dialectic, is much more important. Wells was concerned with the visionary and the Utopian; Richardson opted for the prosaic continual present. He chose a novel of ideas; she chose a novel of consciousness. He was politically engaged (and serially monogamous in his politics); she disdained any ideological or temporal division of the all-embracing female psyche. Wells constantly changed, shifted, developed, and exchanged old ideas for new; Richardson worked at *Pil-*

[27] *Dawn's Left Hand, Pilgrimage,* IV, London, 1979, pp. 239–240.

[28] Horace Gregory, *Dorothy Richardson: An Adventure in Self-Discovery,* New York, 1967, p. 113.

grimage for thirty years without any significant modification of her style, approach, technique, or ideas. In her serene lack of development, she was like the cello player in the joke who never moves his finger because he has found the note for which all the other cellists are searching.

On the personal level too, Richardson needed to free herself from the influence of Wells, whose exuberance and inventiveness had come close to taking over her personality. For Wells, possession was a challenge; he confided to a friend that "the more marked the individuality, the more difficult it is to discover a complete reciprocity."[29] Richardson cannot have been too difficult a conquest; Wells was only the most dominant figure in a series of male mentors, beginning with her father. Her efforts at psychological liberation came in middle age, and perhaps that is why they have something of the fanaticism of late converts to obscure religions. In her novels, if not in her statements to friends, she was able to analyze with considerable delicacy the process by which she discovered that Wells had transformed her into an extension of himself. Miriam becomes aware that she is seeing her own experience with Hypo's eyes and then betraying its integrity and complexity in an effort to entertain him. To reverse this process, which she understands as a feminist problem, the unconscious expression of her training in female subordination, she must deliberately and persistently oppose him. At the same time, she recognizes how round and firm and fully packed his personality is, and how wispy, tentative, and embryonic her own looks next to it. Defining an authentic self necessarily takes the form of "wide opposition" and negation for her; and, in this sense, she is still dependent: "The joy of making statements not drawn from things heard or read but plumbed directly from the unconscious accumulations of her own experience was fermented by the surprise of his increased attention, and the pride of getting him occasionally to accept an idea or to modify a point of view. It beamed

[29] Vincent Brome, *H. G. Wells*, London, 1951, p. 127.

compensation for what she was losing in sacrificing, whenever expression was urgent in her, his unmatchable monologue to her own shapeless outpourings. But she laboured, now and then successfully, to hold this emotion in subjection to the urgency of the things she longed to express."[30] Even honesty can become merely a tactic for pleasing a man; as long as Richardson worried about holding Wells's attention, the ideas themselves were secondary. As with the Fabian Society, it went against Richardson's grain to admit that she had been annexed, and she had to rationalize her own susceptibility by arguing that women remain basically themselves, despite shifting their allegiances with their men.

She also rationalized the problem of her "shapeless outpourings" by working out a theory that saw shapelessness as the natural expression of female empathy, and pattern as the sign of male one-sidedness. If a novel had symbolic form, that was because a man's truncated vision was responsible for it. Men could be tidy in their fiction because they saw so little. Richardson's battle with Wells became more than a battle of the books, or even a sexual skirmish. She was claiming that the entire tradition of the English novel had misrepresented feminine reality. In her letters to the poet and essayist Henry Savage, especially during the 1950s, when she was able to put it most positively, Richardson returned obsessively to her theories of the female novel: "Monstrously, when I began, I felt that all masculine novels to date, despite their various fascinations, were somehow irrelevant, and the feminine ones far too much infl. [sic] by magic traditions, and too much set upon exploiting the sex motif as hitherto seen and depicted by men."[31]

In pursuing a distinctively female consciousness, rather than attempting to explore female experience, Richardson was applying the ideas of the feminists, especially those of the social evolutionists and the spiritualists. She was fasci-

---

[30] *Revolving Lights*, p. 255.
[31] Quoted in Gregory, *Dorothy Richardson*, p. 12.

nated by idealist theories of language and by the mystic's claims to being superior to the artist. Spiritualism in its highest and lowest forms she found irresistible; sixty years after the event she still loved to tell friends about a female palmist who had read her hand at a garden party and whispered "Begin to write." The faculty of prophecy, she wrote solemnly to Savage, seems to be a female trait, "save in those countries, notably Tibet, where men specialize in esoteric research."[32] Women had a monopoly on the essences of being; men had a monopoly on the metaphors of being.

The distinction between consciousness and experience was an important determinant of the direction modernist women's writing took. The Victorian world had been sexually polarized by experience; the normal lives of men and women had scarcely overlapped. By 1910, however, advanced women like Dorothy Richardson could move freely in social atmospheres previously closed to them; they could enjoy a masculine range of sexual and professional experiences. But the possession of quantitatively more experience did not lead to picaresque or even naturalistic fiction. Instead women writers found the world sexually polarized in psychological terms. They had fought to have a share in male knowledge; getting it, they decided that there were other ways of knowing. And by "other" they meant "better"; the tone of the female aesthetic usually wavered between the defiant and the superior.

Women, Richardson thought, were wise in their ancient maternal suffering. If they were to keep their advantage, therefore, they must continue to monopolize suffering and refuse to benefit by the social changes that would permit them to share masculine consciousness. Conversely, men had to remain emotionally childish, or women would lose their power. Socialists had observed with distress that, in the political realm, Mrs. Pankhurst's initial motives, which had included personal ambition, gradually merged with a

[32] Ibid.

mystical self-destructive identification with the Cause. Similarly, the quest for the female consciousness, basically a liberating and fulfilling pilgrimage, could become a self-defeating rejection of all male culture, an end in itself, a journey to nowhere. In the case of Dorothy Richardson, I think, female consciousness became a closed and sterile world; thus she was an innovator who did not attract disciples.

When we try to get down to some hard definitions of female realism as Richardson understood it, we are faced with a difficult task. For one thing, her own antipathy to definitions and schools was an obstacle to, and an evasion of, any personal effort to sort out her ideas. In addition, her most enthusiastic critics and interpreters have tended to circle around her theories. The most troublesome problem has been isolating the qualities, if there are any, that make the writing female in an absolute sense. It is one thing to show that fiction before 1910 differed from fiction after 1910, and to label the differences metaphorically "male" and "female" (or "masculine" and "androgynous" or "bisexual"). It is another thing altogether to talk about female style when you mean female content. And it is the hardest of all to prove that there are inherent sexual qualities to prose apart from its content, which was the crucial point Richardson wished to make.

Like Joyce, Richardson had philosophical objections to the inadequacy of language; unlike Joyce, she regarded language as a male construct. Richardson maintained that men and women used two different languages, or rather, the same language with different meanings. As might an Englishman and an American, "by every word they use men and women mean different things." Typically, she never gives an example of these differences, and sometimes she seems to imply that women have a separate dialect, which they speak to each other.[33] Generally, she implies that women communicate on a higher level; in using the language—the

[33] *Oberland, Pilgrimage,* IV, London, 1979, p. 93.

"words," as she says—of men, they limit themselves the way an intergalactic race of telepathics would limit itself in using speech. Thus in all social interactions dependent on "words" women are disadvantaged—not as a deprived subculture forced to use the dominant tongue, but as a superior race forced to operate on a lower level. "In speech with a man," she wrote in *The Tunnel*, "a woman is at a disadvantage—because they speak different languages. She may understand his. Hers he will never speak or understand. In pity, or from some other motives, she must therefore, stammeringly, speak his. He listens and is flattered and thinks he has her mental measure when he has not touched even the fringe of her consciousness."[34] Similarly in law, art, systems of thought, religions, and even writing, women were merely participating in men's games. Arid intellect and egoism were the sources of all these foolish efforts; by becoming "women of letters," women risked spiritual sterility.

Such a philosophy would seem to preclude any successful competition with men in the fields of art, but Richardson argued that women's art was both qualitatively different and superior. It was the invisible art of creating atmosphere. Like mediums at the seance, women exhausted themselves in animating the inanimate, in creating harmony out of clashing personalities. Their preeminence in this art was the true source of emancipation. "It's as big an art as any other," Miriam assures Hypo in *Revolving Lights*. "Most women work at it the whole of the time. Not one man in a million is aware of it. It's like air within the air. It may be deadly. Cramping and awful, or simply destructive, so that no life is possible without it. So is the bad art of men. At its best it is absolutely life-giving. And not soft. Very hard and stern and austere in its beauty. And like mountain air. A woman's way of 'being' can be discovered in the way she pours out tea. . . . I feel the atmosphere created by the lady of the house as soon as I get on to the door step."[35]

34 *The Tunnel*, p. 210.   35 *Revolving Lights*, p. 257.

This whole approach to the female consciousness had affinities to spiritualism. Men might invent religions, but women were in touch with the Beyond. The utter paradox of this theory, however, was that, as Richardson ruefully admitted, "it would be easier to make all this clear to a man than to a woman. The very words expressing it have been made by men."[36]

The stream-of-consciousness technique (a term, incidentally, that Richardson deplored, and parodied as the "Shroud of Consciousness") was an effort to transcend the dilemma by presenting the multiplicity and variety of associations held simultaneously in the female mode of perception. Henri Bergson's hypothesis that the intensity of an emotion depended on the number of memories and associations awakened by an event was relevant to this undertaking, but in Richardson's version all events evoke the same number of associations and thus have the same intensity.[37]

Dorothy Richardson did not want to suggest intensity. As many critics pointed out, her lack of punctuation, use of ellipsis, and fragmented sentences, worked against the structural potential of the sentence in terms of wit and climax, and main and subordinate ideas. Virginia Woolf was sufficiently impressed by this technique to call it "the psychological sentence of the feminine gender, a sentence of a more elastic fibre than the old, capable of stretching to the extreme, of suspending the frailest particles, of enveloping the vaguest shapes. Other writers of the opposite sex have used sentences of this description and stretched them to the extreme. But there is a difference. Miss Richardson has fashioned her sentence consciously, in order that it may descend to the depths and investigate the crannies of Miriam

[36] *Revolving Lights*, p. 79.

[37] See Henri Bergson, *Time and Free Will*, London, 1971. Katherine Mansfield had no sympathy with this refusal to take hold. "Everything being of equal importance," she wrote of *Interim*, "it is impossible that everything should not be of equal unimportance" (*Novels and Novelists*, London, 1930, p. 137).

Henderson's consciousness. It is a woman's sentence, but only in the sense that it is used to describe a woman's mind by a writer who is neither proud nor afraid of anything she may discover in the psychology of her sex."[38]

Richardson may indeed have fashioned the woman's sentence, or at least the chosen sentence of the female aesthetic. But Woolf is seriously mistaken in calling it unafraid. It is afraid of the unique, the intimate, the physical. By placing the center of reality in the subjective consciousness, and then making consciousness a prism that divides sensation into its equally meaningful single colors, Richardson avoids any discussion of sensation itself, especially as a unified and powerful force. Just as she would not commit herself to ideologies, she would not discriminate among her experiences.

Most of all, Richardson's art is afraid of an ending. Looked at from one point of view, her inability to finish is a statement in itself, a response to the apocalyptic vision of Wells and Lawrence. If men were so obsessed by their sense of an ending that they could not understand the present moment, women were outside of time and epoch, and within eternity. But as Richardson grew older, her relationship to *Pilgrimage* became more obviously possessive and anxious. The book was an extension of herself; to complete it was to die. When Dent published an edition of *Pilgrimage* in 1938, Richardson was deeply upset to read that critics thought this was the whole book. From 1939 to 1951 she worked on a final section of *Pilgrimage*; after her death the manuscript (published as *March Moonlight*) was discovered among her papers; presumably, it was still unfinished. Her conception of the book as a continuous process was the myth that enabled her to publish at all; without such a sustaining illusion, Olive Schreiner, a novelist of very similar temperament, found herself endlessly writing and rewriting the same unfinished book. It is significant that in *March*

[38] Virginia Woolf, "Romance and the Heart," *Nation and Athenaeum* (May 19, 1923): 229.

Moonlight Richardson finally identified her obsession with the process of her own life as guilt: "If one could fully forgive oneself, the energy it takes to screen off the memory of the past would be set free."[39]

Pilgrimage can be read as the artistic equivalent of a screen, a way of hiding and containing and disarming the raw energy of a rampaging past. Richardson devised an aesthetic strategy that protected her enough from the confrontation with her own violence, rage, grief, and sexuality that she could work. The female aesthetic was meant for survival, and one cannot deny that Richardson was able to produce an enormous novel, or that Virginia Woolf wrote several, under its shelter. But ultimately, how much better it would have been if they could have forgiven themselves, if they could have faced the anger instead of denying it, could have translated the consciousness of their own darkness into confrontation instead of struggling to transcend it. For when the books were finished, the darkness was still with them, as dangerous and as inviting as it had always been, and they were helpless to fight it.

[39] *March Moonlight*, p. 607.

CHAPTER X

꽈꽈꽈꽈꽈꽈꽈꽈꽈꽈꽈꽈꽈꽈꽈꽈꽈꽈꽈꽈꽈꽈꽈꽈꽈꽈

Virginia Woolf and the Flight Into Androgyny

It needs little skill in psychology to be sure that a highly gifted girl who had tried to use her gift for poetry would have been so thwarted and hindered by other people, so tortured and pulled apart by her own contrary instincts, that she must have lost her own health and sanity to a certainty.—*A Room of One's Own*

If I were a woman I'd blow someone's brains out.—*The Voyage Out*

IN recent years it has become important to feminist critics to emphasize Virginia Woolf's strength and gaiety and to see her as the apotheosis of a new literary sensibility—not feminine, but androgynous. Caroline Heilbrun has described the members of the Bloomsbury Group as the first examples of the androgynous way of life; she demands that we recognize "that they were all marvelously capable of love, that lust in their world was a joyful emotion, that jealousy and domination were remarkably sparse in their lives."[1] Within this milieu, we are to understand, Virginia Woolf was free to develop both sides of her nature, both male and female, and to create the appropriate kind of novel for the expression of her androgynous vision.

The concept of true androgyny—full balance and command of an emotional range that includes male and female elements—is attractive, although I suspect that like all utopian ideals androgyny lacks zest and energy. But whatever the abstract merits of androgyny, the world that Virginia Woolf inhabited was the last place in which a woman

[1] *Towards a Recognition of Androgyny*, New York, 1973, p. 123.

could fully express both femaleness and maleness, nurturance and aggression. For all her immense gift, Virginia Woolf was as thwarted and pulled asunder as the women she describes in *A Room of One's Own*. Androgyny was the myth that helped her evade confrontation with her own painful femaleness and enabled her to choke and repress her anger and ambition. Woolf inherited a female tradition a century old; no woman writer has ever been more in touch with—even obsessed by—this tradition than she; yet by the end of her life she had gone back full circle, back to the melancholy, guilt-ridden, suicidal women—Lady Winchelsea and the Duchess of Newcastle—whom she had studied and pitied. And beyond the tragedy of her personal life is the betrayal of her literary genuis, her adoption of a female aesthetic that ultimately proved inadequate to her purposes and stifling to her development.

In Virginia Woolf's version of female aestheticism and androgyny, sexual identity is polarized and all the disturbing, dark, and powerful aspects of femaleness are projected onto maleness. Woolf deals with her most intimate experience through biographical essays on other women writers, including Jane Carlyle, Geraldine Jewsbury, Charlotte Brontë, and George Eliot. In her fiction, but supremely in *A Room of One's Own*, Woolf is the architect of female space, a space that is both sanctuary and prison. Through their windows, her women observe a more violent masculine world in which their own anger, rebellion, and sexuality can be articulated at a safe remove. Yet these narrative strategies, as in the novels of her predecessors Schreiner and Richardson, are ultimately unsuccessful. It is a man, of course, who speaks the line from *The Voyage Out* quoted above. The ambiguity of violence in Woolf's fiction is instructive; the vague target, the "someone" whom the sensitive woman is likely to destroy, is inevitably the woman herself. When we think about the joy, the generosity, and the absence of jealousy and domination attributed to Bloomsbury, we should also remember the victims of this emotional utopia: Mark Gertler, Dora Carrington, Virginia Woolf. They are the failures of androgyny; their suicides are one of Bloomsbury's representative art forms.

For the past fifty years, Virginia Woolf has dominated the imaginative territory of the English woman novelist, just as George Eliot dominated it the century before. "The woman writer is urged to be as 'Woolfian' as possible," according to Joyce Carol Oates[2]—that is, to be subjective, and yet to transcend her femaleness, to write exquisitely about inner space and leave the big messy brawling novels to men. A similar idealization and mystification of Woolf's life style is extending her sphere of historical influence to personal relationships. I think it is important to demystify the legend of Virginia Woolf. To borrow her own murderous imagery, a woman writer must kill the Angel in the House, that phantom of female perfection who stands in the way of freedom. For Charlotte Brontë and George Eliot, the Angel was Jane Austen. For the feminist novelists, it was George Eliot. For mid–twentieth-century novelists, the Angel is Woolf herself.

From the beginning of her life, Virginia Woolf found the achievement of a coherent and comfortable sexual identity an urgent problem. She saw her own life in sexually polarized terms, terms that her biographers and critics have invariably adopted. Quentin Bell repeats the familiar distinction between her maternal and paternal heredity, between the poetic, highspirited Pattles, and the rational, vulnerable Stephens. According to Bell, Woolf herself "believed that she was the heiress to two very different and in fact opposed traditions . . . these two rival streams dashed together and flowed confused but not harmonised in her blood."[3] Maleness and femaleness seemed like two distinct principles, which Woolf came to relate to the extremes of her own

[2] Review of Carolyn Heilbrun and Nancy Topping Bazin, *Virginia Woolf and the Androgynous Vision*, *New York Times Book Review* (April 15, 1973): 10.

[3] Quentin Bell, *Virginia Woolf: A Biography*, 1, London, 1972, p. 18.

personality. Nancy Bazin has convincingly shown that Woolf later related manic stages of her mental illness to her mother and the feminine vision of life, and depressive periods to her father and the masculine vision of life.[4] These arbitrary divisions of personality into sexual stereotypes were reinforced by her personal experience. The female model her mother represented led to self-annihilation, to what the Victorians called selflessness. The masculine model offered more opportunities for self-realization, but to choose it meant to renounce womanhood, to declare herself deficient in sexual and maternal energy. Thus Woolf's "androgyny" was a struggle to keep two rival forces in balance without succumbing to either. Full "femaleness" and full "maleness" were equally dangerous.

It is customary to make Leslie Stephen the heavy in Virginia Woolf's personal drama. Critics often refer to the entry that Woolf made in her diary in 1928, on what would have been her father's ninety-sixth birthday: "His life would have entirely ended mine. What would have happened? No writing, no books;—inconceivable." In his biography of Lytton Strachey, Michael Holroyd describes the dynamics of Virginia's relationship with her father as a kind of possession:

> However she might respect his various gifts and achievements objectively, she still felt in an organic sense that his dominating presence had squeezed the very lifeblood from her veins. Somehow he had taken away from her the ability to nourish her ravenous unappeased appetite for life. As she helped to nurse him through his long, last appalling illness she must already have known that her hopes of liberation, of spiritual release, centred upon his death. The consciousness of this had filled her with a dreadful sense of guilt, and in 1903, a few months before

[4] Nancy Bazin, *Virginia Woolf and the Androgynous Vision*, New Brunswick, 1973, pp. 6ff.

her father's death, she suffered a mental breakdown. . . . From him she had inherited a strong egoism together with a neurotic and demanding conscience; from her mother a fine, artistic delicacy and sensitivity. These diverse elements were not to be resolved, but waged within her a tangled and exhausting conflict. Her increasing obsession with death indicated a growing awareness that a part of her father still lived on in her. While she breathed, his alien spirit continued to enshroud her. She could not wash it off. So death became for her the ultimate release, the resurrection through patricide by *felo de se*.[5]

Holroyd's vision of Woolf's mortal combat with her father's shade is romantically compelling, and to see Stephen as the patriarchal villain also permits a feminist reading of her suicide as a triumphant overthrow of maleness. Examining the numerous accounts of Woolf's mental breakdowns, I am struck by the way in which critics have abstracted and mythologized her experience; almost without exception they have linked it to the conflict with her father or to an even more romantic artistic possession, a divine seizure by the muse. Considered from another perspective, however, her major breakdowns were associated with crises in female identity: the first occurred in 1895, after the death of her mother and the onset of menstruation; the second from 1913 to 1915, after Leonard decided that they should not have children. Her suicide in 1940 followed menopause; though less information about it has been published, it seems to have repeated elements of the earlier episodes. While I have no wish to substitute one magical explanation of her anguish for another, it is clear that most of the information we have about her comes from those most concerned to deny or repress their own complicity in her sicknesses. Leslie Stephen, safely dead since 1904, is a con-

[5] Michael Holroyd, *Lytton Strachey: A Critical Biography*, I, London, 1967, p. 401.

venient, even a reasonable, scapegoat. It is riskier, but more promising, I think, to ask how Virginia felt about people a little closer at hand.

Quentin Bell tells us that Virginia "forgot" all but the physiological symptoms of her breakdown after her mother's death. As she recalled them, her symptoms were a racing pulse, nervousness, depression, excitability, and excessive shyness: "She became terrified of people, blushed scarlet if spoken to and was unable to face a stranger in the street."[6] Although none of Woolf's biographers mention it, this breakdown must have coincided with the onset of menstruation, and its symptomatology is precisely that of female adolescent shame and anxiety. "Abnormal reactions to the first menses are extremely varied," writes Helene Deutsch. "Intensified excitability, feelings of discomfort, greater susceptibility to fatigue, and depressions are frequent manifestations of puberty as a whole; usually they increase during menstruation." Deutsch records numerous case histories of adolescent girls who feel unclean, who avoid going into the street, who blush violently, and who even attempt "suicide during menstruation because they were tormented by terrible fear of a painful disease." The death of her mother, and the death in 1897 of her half sister Stella, in her early pregnancy, further emphasized the connection for Woolf between femaleness and death. "With the onset of menstruation," writes Deutsch, "the associative connection between death and birth is particularly strengthened. . . . It is innate in the feminine psyche to bring blood, conception, birth and death into close connection with one another."[7]

Another symptom now understood as an aspect of female adolescent trauma is *anorexia nervosa*, or willful self-starvation. Helene Deutsch explains anorexia as an attempt "to

[6] Bell, *Virginia Woolf*, I, p. 45.

[7] Helene Deutsch, "Menstruation," *The Psychology of Women*, I, New York, 1973, pp. 169, 159, 183.

combat the evil" of menstruation and puberty; recently, physicians have defined the anorexic girl as one who "is trying desperately not to grow up. Her body is becoming a woman's, against her will. That's got to be stopped."[8] Anorexia was to become the most predictable accompaniment of Virginia Woolf's attacks. Leonard Woolf speculated about the symptoms: "It might have been said that she had a (quite unnecessary) fear of becoming fat; but there was something deeper than that, at the back of her mind or in the pit of her stomach, a taboo against eating."[9] One of Leonard's regular responsibilities during their marriage was to watch over her diet in health and spoon-feed her in sickness.

It was also during the period 1896–1897, according to Virginia, that she was sexually molested by her half-brother George Duckworth, then in his midtwenties. Fear, ignorance, shame and shyness kept her from confiding these incidents (Bell thinks they continued until 1904 or 1905) to anyone but Vanessa. Gordon Haight has suggested that Virginia's overheated adolescent imagination led her to invent these stories: "The slight evidence of his 'fondlings and fumblings' in the schoolroom and night nursery originates mostly in Virginia's confidences to women with whom her relations were decidedly queer."[10] Of course, it is impossible to know exactly what George did, but it is altogether reasonable to believe that his attentions were a terrifying sign to Virginia that people *knew* about her, that her changed state was a signal to men.

A famous story that Virginia told to the Memoir Club illuminates her adolescent sense of shame and the relief she

[8] Sam Blum, "Children Who Starve Themselves," *New York Times Magazine* (November 10, 1974): 68.

[9] *Beginning Again*, London, 1964, p. 163. Eleanor Marx was another late-Victorian anorexic. Until recently, *anorexia nervosa* was usually treated as a physical problem.

[10] Review of Quentin Bell's *Virginia Woolf: a Biography*, *Yale Review* (Spring 1973): 427.

felt when liberated from it. In the summer of 1908, she and Vanessa were sitting in their drawing-room when

> the door opened and the long and sinister figure of Mr. Lytton Strachey stood on the threshold. He pointed his finger at a stain on Vanessa's white dress.
>
> "Semen?" he said.
>
> Can one really say it? I thought & we burst out laughing. With that one word all barriers of reticence and reserve went down. A flood of the sacred fluid seemed to overwhelm us. Sex permeated our discussion. The word bugger was never far from our lips. We discussed copulation with the same excitement and openness that we had discussed the nature of good. It is strange to think how reticent, how reserved we had been and for how long.[11]

In fact Woolf was far from sexless; her view of the world seems to have been quite sensual, even erotic, until she was forced to translate her feelings into sexual events. And Bloomsbury set high standards on sexual performance. Copulation and buggery, to use the engaging Bloomsbury terminology, were suddenly fashionable. Despite her delight in this new verbal freedom, Virginia felt a new anxiety when she contrasted her life with that of her sister, Vanessa, a cheerful heroine of free love, marriage, and motherhood —a natural woman. Phyllis Rose has brilliantly analyzed Virginia's fear that writing was an act that unsexed her, made her an unnatural woman, and isolated her from the world of female fulfillment represented by her mother and Vanessa:

> A crude summary of the chain of causality might go like this: Everyone loved and admired her mother (and after her mother's death, her sister . . .). To be loved she must be like her mother. Committing herself to children of the mind over children of the body, art over people, is not

---

11 Bell, *Virginia Woolf*, 1, p. 124.

being like her mother. Therefore, after producing every work of art, she feels excessively unlovable; having reaffirmed her difference from her mother, she fears people will ignore or reject her, and so she needs excessive reassurance that she is loved and protected.[12]

Marriage to Leonard Woolf in 1912 seemed like a guarantee of love, security, and normalcy, although, as she wrote to him brutally, she felt "no physical attraction" for him.[13] Perhaps they hoped the honeymoon would solve their sexual problem; predictably, it did not. Undoubtedly Virginia was awkward, shy, and frightened of male passion; on the other hand, Leonard Woolf does not seem to have been a passionate man. At Cambridge his friends found him a "rather dry, nervously unemotional young man"; he was famous for his Puritanism.[14]

Their honeymoon, spent wandering about Provence and Spain, ended with a rough Mediterranean voyage on a Hungarian ship; it did not encourage sexual confidence and relaxation. When they returned, apparently disturbed by Virginia's "frigidity," they innocently sought Vanessa's counsel; she made the most of the opportunity. "They seemed very happy," she wrote to Clive, "but are evidently both a little exercised in their minds on the subject of the Goat's coldness. I think I perhaps annoyed her but may have consoled him by saying I thought she never had understood or sympathised with sexual passion in men. Apparently she still gets no pleasure at all from the act, which I think is curious. They were very anxious to know when I

12 Phyllis Rose, "Mrs. Ramsay and Mrs. Woolf," *Women's Studies*, 1 (Summer 1973): 212.

13 Bell, *Virginia Woolf*, 1, p. 185.

14 Michael Holroyd, *Lytton Strachey*, 1, p. 108. Leonard Woolf writes about himself that when he learned about sex at the age of twelve "it was only with the most heroic effort that I was preventing myself from being sick." *Sowing*, London, 1960, p. 66. He lost his virginity in Ceylon at the age of twenty-five.

first had an orgasm. I couldn't remember. Do you? But no doubt I sympathised with such things if I didn't have them from the time I was 2.''[15]

In short, after a mere six weeks' trial, Virginia was confirmed in her "frigidity" and encouraged to think of herself as a hopeless case. At the same time it was implied that *real* women—i.e., Vanessa—experienced these ecstasies instinctively, and that Leonard was much to be pitied. We know more now about so-called frigidity; perhaps Vanessa really had no better advice to give. Yet her cheerfulness in the face of Virginia's anxiety is unmistakable, as is the destructiveness of her "consolation" of Leonard. Perhaps Vanessa liked her role as the sensual woman and had no wish to share it with her sister. At any rate, the contemporary view of Leonard as a martyr and saint begins with their honeymoon; Elizabeth Hardwick considers Leonard's "endurance of Virginia's famous frigidity . . . altogether to his credit.''[16]

The inadequacy Virginia felt when she contrasted the sexual side of her life with Vanessa's was compounded by Leonard's decision that they should not have children. The sources of this decision are rather obscure. According to Quentin Bell, Virginia had happily anticipated having children and did not know of Leonard's misgivings until some time after they married. Her ill health in the fall of 1912 was the immediate source of Leonard's concern; it was not until later, however, that he became aware of the seriousness of her medical history. In January 1913 Leonard consulted a number of doctors, looking, it appears, for someone to lend medical authority to a decision he had already made. Quentin Bell describes his search: "Leonard talked to Dr. (now Sir George) Savage, and Sir George, in his breezy way, had exclaimed that it would do her a world of good; but Leonard mistrusted Sir George; he consulted

15 Bell, *Virginia Woolf*, II, p. 6.
16 "Bloomsbury and Virginia Woolf," *New York Review of Books*, (February 8, 1973): 16.

other people: Maurice Craig, Vanessa's specialist, T. B. Hyslop and Jean Thomas, who kept a nursing home and knew Virginia well; their views differed, but in the end Leonard decided and persuaded Virginia to agree that, although they both wanted children, it would be too dangerous for her to have them. In this I imagine Leonard was right. It is hard to imagine Virginia as a mother. But it was to be a permanent source of grief to her and, in later years, she could never think of Vanessa's fruitful state without misery and envy."[17]

Male critics have generally agreed that Leonard's decision was correct. Michael Holroyd, for example, maintains that "children with their wetness and noise would surely have killed off the novels in her: and it was about novel-writing that she cared most."[18] Behind this confident diagnosis are the old stereotypes about the incompatibility of childbearing and art, as well as a peculiarly English upper-class aversion to infantile squalor. Surely Virginia would have had nannies for her children; Cynthia Ozick (one of the few female critics who have lately challenged Leonard's authority and motives in this decision) reminds us that Vanessa had two.[19] Besides, it was Leonard who hated disorder, Virginia who worked amidst chaos. Leonard's view was that childbirth would endanger Virginia's health and precarious mental stability, and he may have been right. On the other hand, it is impossible not to suspect that he had much more complex unconscious motives: jealousy of prospective children, as Cynthia Ozick suggests, or possibly some deficiency in passion of his own.

Virginia was led to feel not only that she had renounced a primary female role, failed to accomplish the act that is woman's rite of passage into adulthood, but also that in marrying Leonard she had destroyed his opportunities to be a father. Soon after this decision, in the spring of 1913, ac-

---

[17] Bell, *Virginia Woolf*, II, p. 8.

[18] Review in the London *Times*, October 19, 1973.

[19] "Mrs. Virginia Woolf," *Commentary* (August 1973): 40.

cording to Leonard, Virginia suffered one of her most terrible attacks.

In this, as in all her attacks of madness, Virginia Woolf was treated by variations of the "rest cure," a therapy for neurasthenic people, particularly women, that had been developed by the American physician Silas Weir Mitchell. Dr. Mitchell specialized in cures of neurotic women through a drastic treatment that reduced them "to a condition of infantile dependence on their physician."[20] The ingredients of the rest cure were isolation, immobility, prohibition of all intellectual activity, and overfeeding, accompanied in some cases by daily massage. In the cases of American women patients like Jane Addams and Charlotte Perkins Gilman, the cure had nearly killed; Mrs. Gilman wrote a powerful short story, "The Yellow Wall-Paper" (1891), about a woman *driven* mad by her enforced confinement and passivity. Besides forcing a woman to stifle the drives and emotions that had made her sick with frustration in the first place and depriving her of intellectual outlets for their expression, the rest cure was a sinister parody of idealized Victorian femininity: inertia, privatization, narcissism, dependency. In particular, the weight gain that was considered an essential part of the cure was a kind of pseudo-pregnancy. Ann Wood, who has studied Mitchell's theories in the context of nineteenth-century attitudes toward female health and sexuality, argues that Mitchell was an outspoken misogynist, whose methods punished "deviant" and discontented women by forcing them into an allegedly therapeutic female role.[21]

Virginia's treatment was carried out in a nursing home "for female lunatics" in Twickenham, where she was re-

[20] Gail Parker, *The Oven Birds: American Women on Womanhood 1820-1920*, New York, 1972, p. 49.

[21] Ann Douglas Wood, " 'The Fashionable Diseases': Women's Complaints and Their Treatment in Nineteenth-Century America," in *Clio's Consciousness Raised*, ed. Mary S. Hartman and Lois Banner, New York, 1974, pp. 1-24.

quired to remain in bed in a darkened room, eating well, drinking milk in the daytime and mulled wine at night, and taking "Robin's Hypophospate." This was not her first trip to Twickenham; she had been sent there in 1910, and the experience of boredom, loneliness, and repression had nearly made her suicidal. Nonetheless she was sent there again in 1913 against her will. "A few miserable shaky pencil-written notes to Leonard survive from that time," writes Bell. "They make one think of a child sent away by its parents to some cruel school. Childlike, she burst out against the husband who had put her away in this awful place. But then, seeing his worn and distressed face, she was overcome with guilt and misery."[22]

The treatment itself left her shaky and desperate. When she came out she still seemed sick, and in the summer of 1913 Leonard insisted that she should return to the nursing home. Virginia insisted that she was perfectly all right. Leonard, having secretly consulted a new physician, suggested that they should go to a doctor and each present their case. He was delighted when Virginia suggested they visit the very physician he had consulted; predictably, the verdict was that she was ill and that she should enter the home. That night she attempted to kill herself.

In *Asylums*, Erving Goffman explains how the progress from home to hospital leads to a sense of betrayal for the mental patient:

> His next-of-relation presses him into coming to "talk things over" with a medical practitioner. . . . But typically the next-of-relation will have set the interview up, in the sense of selecting the professional, arranging for time, telling the professional something about the case, and so on. This move effectively tends to establish the next-of-relation as the responsible person to whom pertinent findings can be divulged, while effectively establishing the other as the patient. . . . Upon arrival at the office the pre-

[22] Bell, *Virginia Woolf*, II, p. 13.

patient suddenly finds that he and his next-of-relation
have not been accorded the same roles, and apparently
that a prior understanding between the professional and
the next-of-relation has been put in operation against
him.[23]

This is precisely the coalition Leonard (with the advice of
Vanessa) had arranged. Virginia was powerless to assert
herself against such massed authority. Having attempted
suicide, she was, of course, put under nurses' care. Later
that year she was sent back to Twickenham for more rest
cures. Thus Woolf became the real-life epitome of that
feminine archetype, the Mad Wife.

It was the illness of 1913–1915 that, in John Bayley's
words, "ratified" Leonard's doubts about having children.
In fact the outstanding symptom of this particular episode
of madness was fury toward Leonard. In 1915 Virginia's
expression of her anger was interpreted by Vanessa, among
others, as a sign of the severity of her illness: "She won't
see Leonard at all & has taken against all men."[24] The dynamics of this particular attack suggest that Virginia recognized the tyranny of Leonard's decision at the same time
that she was guiltily coerced into accepting it. Madness was
the role in which she articulated her resentment and rage,
and feeling rage against someone who loved her and
wanted to care for her redoubled her sense of guilt.

Woolf used this episode as a central theme of *Mrs. Dalloway* (1925), presenting her own experience through a male
character, Septimus Smith. She had emerged from the rest
cures of 1915 weighing 168 pounds; in *Mrs. Dalloway*, Septimus fights against the maddening therapy of "rest in bed;
rest in solitude; silence and rest; rest without friends, without books, without messages; six months rest; until a man

[23] Erving Goffman, *Asylums*, Harmondsworth, 1968, pp. 128–129.
[24] Bell, *Virginia Woolf*, II, p. 26. John Bayley reviewed the Bell biography in *The Guardian*, October 19, 1973.

who went in weighing seven stone six [104 pounds] comes out weighing twelve [168 pounds]."[25]

A great deal of her anger comes out in the portrait of Sir William Bradshaw, the Harley Street nerve doctor. Personal experience explains the inartistic lack of proportion most critics have noticed as a "flaw" in this fiercely vibrant section of the novel. When Sir William tries to talk Septimus Smith into going for a rest cure, he is clearly attempting to punish and imprison him: "Sir William had a friend in Surrey where they taught, what Sir William frankly admitted was a difficult art—a sense of proportion. There were, moreover, family affection; honour; courage; and a brilliant career. All of these had in Sir William a resolute champion. If they failed, he had to support him police and the good of society, which, he remarked very quietly, would take care, down in Surrey, that these unsocial impulses, bred more than anything by the lack of good blood, were held in control. . . . Naked, defenceless, the exhausted, the friendless, received the impress of Sir William's will. He swooped; he devoured. He shut people up. It was this combination of decision and humanity that endeared Sir William so greatly to the relations of his victims."[26]

She could hardly have expressed her feelings of victimization and rage more plainly. This passage is almost Kafkaesque in its sense of conspiracy and guilt; Sir William is a vulture backed by the authority of the state. Woolf's personal experience also dictated Sir William's insistence that Septimus should not have children; he "forbade childbirth, penalized despair, made it impossible for the unfit to propagate their views until they too shared his sense of proportion."[27] And the "relations of the victims"? There is no record that Leonard and Vanessa recognized themselves as collaborators, nor that in Sir William they detected Virginia's doctor, Sir George Savage. It is Savage's surname,

[25] *Mrs. Dalloway*, London, 1976, p. 89.
[26] Ibid., p. 91.   [27] Ibid., p. 89.

so appropriate, from Virginia's point of view, that generates much of the imagery surrounding Sir William. It is not even certain that Woolf acknowledged her own motives or felt relieved in exorcising some of this anger. The people who had most betrayed her were those to whom she owed the most. Her marriage, in some ways so admirable and fulfilling, placed her in a position of perpetual guilt and dependence; and, despite such covert protests as this one, she seems to have abdicated her right to make basic decisions in it.

In 1940, after the years at the uncannily named Monks House, there was a question of the rest cure again. Virginia made her woman physician promise that there would be no rest cure "ordered," but it was clear that no such promise would be kept. She killed herself the next day. Her three suicide notes express her guilt about spoiling Leonard's life; indeed, they exonerate Leonard so completely that Mrs. Ian Parsons felt it necessary in 1973 to present them to the British Museum as proof that Leonard had not made them up himself.[28] Nancy Bazin sees the suicide as "both an act of despair and an act of faith—despair that the androgynous whole would ever be established on earth but faith in the existence (in the timeless realm of death) of its mystical equivalent—oneness."[29] Woolf's suicide has thus come to represent an ultimate gesture of self-sacrifice and "feminine" nobility.

Yet to see Woolf's suicide as a beautiful act of faith, or a philosophical gesture toward androgyny, is to betray the human pain and rage that she felt; to see the suicide as a proof of her feminine neurosis is to condemn her in death

[28] "I am particularly anxious that it should be known that these letters are now in the British Museum because lately I have been disturbed by a rumour that Virginia never wrote the letters quoted by Leonard in the last volume of his autobiography, and that—incredible as this may seem—he had concocted them himself" (*Times Literary Supplement*, July 13, 1973).

[29] *Virginia Woolf and the Androgynous Vision*, p. 222.

to the stereotype that imprisoned her in life. The feelings of guilt and inadequacy as a woman that she had always struggled with, and often succumbed to, intensified in the mid-1930s, when she was going through menopause. In March of 1936 she had tried to describe her symptoms in her diary: "I wish I could write out my sensations at this moment. They are so peculiar and so unpleasant. Partly T[ime] of L[ife]. I wonder? A physical feeling as if I were drumming slightly in the veins: very cold, impotent and terrified. As if I were exposed on a high ledge in full light. Very lonely. L. out to lunch. Nessa has Quentin, don't want me. Very useless. No atmosphere around me. No words. Very apprehensive. . . . And I know that I must go on doing this dance on hot bricks till I die."[30] For a woman, and especially for a childless woman, menopause itself can be a kind of death. For Virginia Woolf, it meant facing the fact that her reproductive life was over, a life that Leonard, in some sense, had denied her. Vanessa's maternal fulfillment, even after the death of Julian Bell in the Spanish Civil War, was still a source of jealousy and torment.

I have not meant to attack Leonard's motives or his sincerity, nor to deny that he loved Virginia. We cannot penetrate the private mystery of their life together. It is clear, however, that his view of her has prevailed over her own to such a degree that some critics have outrageously concluded that his genius was dominant as well. Gordon Haight has said of Leonard, "It is not too much to say that to him we owe the whole of her contribution to English literature."[31] It is far too much to say, even with the kindest interpretation of Leonard's role; and it ignores the fact that there are ways in which love can usurp a woman's responsibility for her own life, cripple her, and destroy her.

[30] Bell, *Virginia Woolf*, II, pp. 190–199. John F. Hulcoop calls the menopause a "preoccupation or even obsession," in Woolf's writing ("McNichol's Mrs. Dalloway: Second Thoughts," *Virginia Woolf Miscellany*, [Spring 1975]: 4).

[31] Review of Quentin Bell's *Virginia Woolf, Yale Review* (Spring 1973): 429.

Woolf's illnesses had always had some source in female experience; they had taken the classic female forms of frigidity, depression, and suicide attempts, and had been treated in female asylums with a therapy intended to induce female passivity. It is the peculiarly poignant irony of female depression that it decreases the ability to express hostility. The guilt, which so puzzled Leonard, and which I have described as her feelings of female inadequacy and her immense internalized anger against him and against Vanessa, became so overwhelming in this last attack that only self-destruction seemed commensurate with her despair. On previous occasions, suicide attempts had been punished by more rest cures, more guilt. This time she would not risk recovery, would not face what Sylvia Plath called the "peanut-crunching crowd," the accusing faces that defined her eternally as weak, feminine, and dependent. Deprived of the use of her womanhood, denied the power of manhood, she sought a serene androgynous "oneness," an embrace of eternity that was inevitably an embrace of death. In recognizing that the quest for androgyny was Woolf's solution to her existential dilemma, we should not confuse flight with liberation.

Woolf's ideas about women's literature were closely connected to her personal struggle for self-definition. In 1918, in an anonymous review of R. Brimley Johnson's *The Women Novelists*, Woolf expressed her dissatisfaction with the feminine novelists, who wrote under "the tyranny of what was expected from their sex," and the feminist novelists, "the women who wish to be taken for women." "The change," she argued, "is hardly for the better, since any emphasis, either of pride or of shame, laid consciously upon the sex of a writer is not only irritating, but superfluous." In this early essay, Woolf was raising some of the problems that she dealt with in *A Room of One's Own*; she was attempting to find a way of talking about women's writing that would accept the continuity of the literary tradition, yet transcend what she described negatively as "the tyranny of sex." Woolf agreed completely with Johnson that the novels of women were special: "A woman's writing is always feminine; it cannot help being feminine; at its best it is most feminine; the only difficulty lies in defining what we mean by feminine." She believed the sex of a novel to be an elusive but unmistakable aura, at once a Zen mystery, like the sound of one hand clapping, and a matter of values, from which spring "not only marked differences of plot and incident, but infinite differences in selection, method, and style."[32] What she wanted was an impersonal and inconspicuous technique in which femaleness was neither flaunted nor renounced, a separate literary and sexual peace.

Much of Woolf's writing at this point was concerned with the external difficulties and obstacles of the woman writer—an emphasis connected to her own struggles to find a voice. In 1919 her second conventionally structured novel, *Night and Day* (dedicated to Vanessa), was not a success. She was in an anxious state of transition between two ways of writing; consequently, her view of the straitened possibilities for the woman artist was defensively pessimistic. She expressed this view in a good-humored exchange with "Affable Hawk" (Desmond McCarthy) in the *New Statesman*:

It seems to me that the conditions which made it possible for a Shakespeare to exist are that he shall have had predecessors in his art, shall make one of a group where art is freely discussed and practiced, and shall himself have the utmost freedom of thought and experience. Perhaps in Lesbos, but never since, have these conditions been the lot of women.[33]

Lesbos or not, London provided these conditions in 1920, and they were substantially the lot of Virginia Woolf. She was deeply aware of the female literary tradition and cog-

[32] *Times Literary Supplement* (October 17, 1918): 1183 (reprinted October 17, 1968).
[33] Letter, *New Statesman* (October 16, 1920): 45-46.

281

nizant of her own place in it. Her many affectionate essays about women novelists, poets, diarists, and letter-writers reveal her need to define her own literary identity in some real relationship to her predecessors. And whatever one might think of Bloomsbury, it was certainly a group in which art was freely discussed and practiced. But that last condition—freedom of thought and expression—she could not meet. Even in the moment of expressing feminist conflict, Woolf wanted to transcend it. Her wish for experience was really a wish to forget experience. In the 1920s, as her fiction moved away from realism, her criticism and her theoretical prose moved away from a troubled feminism toward a concept of serene androgyny.

The most famous of Woolf's statements about androgyny is *A Room of One's Own*. A. J. Moody is in the minority when he objects that "the title has enjoyed a fame rather beyond the intrinsic merits of the work" (Woolf's most conspicuous antagonists, the Leavises, found *Room* too flimsy to warrant their close attention).[34] What is most striking about the book texturally and structurally is its strenuous charm, its playfulness, its conversational surface. There is nothing here to suggest the humorless polemics of *Votes for Women* or the *Egoist*. The techniques of *Room* are like those of Woolf's fiction, particularly *Orlando*, which she was writing at the same time: repetition, exaggeration, parody, whimsy, and multiple viewpoint. On the other hand, despite its illusions of spontaneity and intimacy, *A Room of One's Own* is an extremely impersonal and defensive book.

Impersonality may seem like the wrong word for a book in which a narrative "I" appears in every third sentence. But a closer look reveals that the "I" is a persona, whom the author calls "Mary Beton," and that her views are carefully distanced and depersonalized, just as the pronoun "one" in the title depersonalizes, and even de-sexes, the subject. The whole book is cast in arch allegorical terms from the start:

34 Moody, *Virginia Woolf*, London, 1963, p. 41. See also Q. D. Leavis, "Caterpillars of the World, Unite," *Scrutiny* VII (1938): 205.

"I need not say that what I am about to describe, Oxbridge, is an invention; so is Fernham; 'I' is only a convenient term for somebody who has no real being." In fact the characters and places are all disguised or delicately parodied versions of Woolf's own experience. "Fernham" is Newnham College, Cambridge, where she had given the lectures that were the genesis of the book. Woolf's cousin Katherine Stephen was Vice-Principal of Newnham; she is the "Mary Seton" who explains to Mary Beton why the women's colleges are so poor. Her mother, "Mrs. Seton," has had thirteen children (actually Mrs. Stephen had seven). The narrator, Mary Beton, lives in a London house by the river. Before 1918 she made her living in the jobs open to untrained middle-class women: amateur society journalism, clerical work, and teaching. Then she inherited 500 pounds a year from an aunt, also named Mary Beton, who had fallen off a horse in Bombay. Woolf had inherited 2,500 pounds from her aunt Caroline Emelia Stephen, whose life was much less romantic.[35] The last Mary, Mary Carmichael, author of *Life's Adventure*, is probably also a parody or a composite figure.

The entire book is teasing, sly, elusive in this way; Woolf plays with her audience, refusing to be entirely serious, denying any earnest or subversive intention. As M. C. Bradbrook has written, "The camouflage in *A Room of One's Own* . . . prevents Mrs. Woolf from committing the indelicacy of putting a case or the possibility of her being accused of waving any kind of banner. The arguments are clearly serious and personal and yet they are dramatized and surrounded with all sorts of disguises to avoid an appearance of argument."[36] In the opening chapters, this defensiveness

[35] Aunt Caroline Emelia, called "The Nun" by Virginia and Vanessa, had been jilted by a young man who went out to India. At one point Virginia wrote a "comic life" of her aunt, but it has been lost. Bell, *Virginia Woolf*, I, pp. 6–7, 93.

[36] "Notes on the Style of Mrs. Woolf," in *Critics on Virginia Woolf*, ed. Jacqueline E. M. Latham, London, 1970, pp. 24–25.

leads to a rather unpleasantly Stracheyesque kind of in-
nuendo, as if the Cambridge setting had recalled the style
of the Apostles. An example is the appearance of a Manx cat
in the Oxbridge luncheon scene. Mary Beton is suddenly
convulsed with laughter at the sight of "that abrupt and
truncated animal. . . . I had to explain my laughter by point-
ing at the Manx cat, who did look a little absurd, poor
beast, without a tail, in the middle of the lawn. Was he
really born so, or had he lost his tail in an accident? . . . It
is strange what a difference a tail makes—you know the sort
of things one says as a lunch party breaks up and people are
finding their coats and hats."[37] This certainly sounds like a
feline swipe at Cantabrigian impotence.

In chapter 3, however, the narrative finally moves beyond
this kind of gamesmanship and focuses on the question of
women and fiction. Woolf insists that a woman must have
an independent income and a room of her own if she is to
write fiction, and that the mind of the artist should be
androgynous. Apart from the specific question of income,
to which Marxists object, these ideas are very nearly as
civilized and unabrasive as the style, and it is easy to get
caught up in the seductive flow. Who could possibly object
to the idea of androgyny? Even clinical psychology confirms
that "the really creative individual combines 'masculine'
and 'feminine' qualities";[38] indeed, since masculine and feminine personality qualities are stereotypes to begin with, it
is virtually a tautology to say that creative people are not
limited to one set. Woolf's selection of Shakespeare to exemplify the androgynous artist also provokes little disagreement, especially since we know so little about Shakespeare's
life; although there is no obvious connection between her
other examples—Keats, Sterne, Cowper, Lamb, and Coleridge—one could probably discover some similarities, perhaps in their attitudes toward fantasy and madness.

[37] *A Room of One's Own*, London, 1945, p. 15.

[38] Judith Bardwick, *The Psychology of Women*, New York, 1971,
p. 203.

Woolf, however, does not supply the connections; nor does she encourage the reader to pursue them very strenuously. If one can see *A Room of One's Own* as a document in the literary history of female aestheticism, and remain detached from its narrative strategies, the concepts of androgyny and the private room are neither as liberating nor as obvious as they first appear. They have a darker side that is the sphere of the exile and the eunuch.

Virginia Woolf was extremely sensitive to the ways in which female experience had made women weak, but she was much less sensitive to the ways in which it had made them strong. Filling in the outlines of her 1918 review, she wrote finely about the problems in the lives of several of her predecessors: their domestic responsibilities, their narrowness of range, and their frustration and anger. "We feel the influence of fear in it," she wrote of Charlotte Brontë's portrait of Rochester, "just as we constantly feel an acidity which is the result of oppression, a buried suffering smouldering beneath her passion, a rancour which contracts those books, splendid as they are, with a spasm of pain."[39] All of these passionate responses she deplored because she thought that they distorted the artist's integrity. She describes with compassion and scornful illustration how women writers were disadvantaged and harassed—an important and fully realized discovery. But in wishing to make women independent of all that dailiness and bitterness, so that they might "escape a little from the common sitting-room and see human beings not always in their relation to each other but in relation to reality,"[40] she was advocating a strategic retreat, and not a victory; a denial of feeling, and not a mastery of it.

We can see this withdrawal most plainly in the theory of androgyny presented in the last chapter of the book, which is the psychological and theoretical extension of the material reform implied in the private room. Woolf brings in

[39] *A Room of One's Own*, p. 74.
[40] Ibid., p. 112.

the discussion of androgyny in a characteristically low-keyed way, as if it were an afterthought; but it is central to her thinking not only in this book but also in her novels. The androgynous vision, in Woolf's terms, is a response to the dilemma of a woman writer embarrassed and alarmed by feelings too hot to handle without risking real rejection by her family, her audience, and her class. A room of one's own is the first step toward her solution; more than an office with a typewriter, it is a symbol of psychic withdrawal, an escape from the demands of other people. Mary Beton or Mary Carmichael would not, in entering that room, be liberated from the fear of what people might say or fortified to express her anger or her pain; instead, she would be encouraged to forget both her grievances and her fellows, and seek an underlying or transcendent meaning. Woolf had faith that the androgynous vision would express itself in uniquely feminine terms, but purely and unconsciously, as femininity's essence distilled in a new supple sentence and open structure, as a pervasive but inoffensive quality of perception, "that curious sexual quality which comes only when sex is unconscious of itself."[41] Stripped of its anger, femininity would spread out over fiction to become a smooth and absorbent surface.

In describing androgyny, Woolf goes a step further to imagine that the highly developed creative mind needs no such crutch as physical privacy to transcend the burden of sex consciousness. The passage in which she gracefully leads up to the idea intimates unmistakably that feminist awareness is a painful state of mind:

If one is a woman one is often surprised by a sudden splitting off of consciousness, say in walking down White-hall, when from being the natural inheritor of that civilisation she becomes, on the contrary, outside of it, alien and critical. Clearly the mind is always altering its focus, and bringing the world into different perspectives. But

[41] Ibid., p. 93.

some of these states of mind seem, even if adopted spontaneously, to be less comfortable than others. In order to keep oneself continuing in them one is unconsciously holding something back, and gradually the repression becomes an effort. But there may be some state of mind in which one could continue without effort because nothing is required to be held back.[42]

Despite a certain fluttering of indefinite pronouns here, I think that the less comfortable states of mind that Woolf refers to are the angry and alienated ones, the feminist ones, and that she would like to possess a more serene and thus more comfortable consciousness.

In Virginia Woolf's case, agitation was the first symptom of mental collapse, and the personal need for equanimity without repression is very close to the surface of these carefully abstract sentences. "Equanimity," said her physician in 1925, "practice equanimity." But how can one, if one is a woman, be serene in the face of injustice? There is an eerie hint that in the androgynous solution Woolf provides there lurks a psychological equivalent of lobotomy. Yet when she actually describes androgyny, Woolf uses a literal sexual imagery of intercourse between the manly and womanly powers of the mind:

If one is a man, still the woman part of the brain must have effect; and a woman also must have intercourse with the man in her. Coleridge perhaps meant this when he said that a great mind is androgynous. It is when this fusion takes place that the mind is fully fertilised and uses all its faculties. Perhaps a mind that is purely masculine cannot create, any more than a mind that is purely feminine.[43]

The minutely Freudian analogy with biological sexuality here, particularly in the last sentence, continues a few pages later in a passage of almost erotic revery:

[42] Ibid., p. 96.   [43] Ibid., p. 97.

287

Some marriage of opposites has to be consummated. The whole of the mind must lie wide open if we are to get the sense that the writer is communicating his experience with perfect fullness. There must be freedom and there must be peace. . . . The curtains must be close drawn. The writer, I thought, once his experience is over, must lie back and let his mind celebrate its nuptials in darkness. He must not look or question what is being done.[44]

Obviously Virginia Woolf had not looked at or questioned what she had done in this passage: made the writer male. In a book exquisitely in control of its pronouns, this is not a small thing. It suggests, I think, how unconsciously she had felt the soft, dead hand of the Angel in the House descend upon her shoulder, censoring even this innocent metaphorical fantasy, and transferring it to the mind of a male voyeur. How could any woman writer pretend to be androgynous—indifferent, undivided—in the grip of such inhibition? At some level, Woolf is aware that androgyny is another form of repression or, at best, self-discipline. It is not so much that she recommends androgyny as that she warns against feminist engagement: "It is fatal for anyone who writes to think of their sex. It is fatal to be a man or woman pure and simple; one must be woman-manly or man-womanly. It is fatal for a woman to lay the least stress on any grievance; to plead even with justice any cause; in any way to speak consciously as a woman. And fatal is no figure of speech; for anything written with that conscious bias is doomed to death. It ceases to be fertilised."[45] In many respects Woolf is expressing a class-oriented and Bloomsbury-oriented ideal—the separation of politics and art, the fashion of bisexuality. It is only fair to note that she found male writers ruined by exaggerated, or exacerbated, virility. But there is also more than a hint of fear in her warning. She had taken to heart the cautionary tales to be found in the lives of earlier women writers. She had seen

[44] Ibid., p. 103.   [45] Ibid, pp. 102–103.

the punishment that society could inflict on women who made a nuisance of themselves by behaving in an uncivilized manner. It seems like a rationalization of hei own tears that Woolf should have developed a literary theory that made anger and protest flaws in art.

The androgynous mind is, finally, a utopian projection of the ideal artist: calm, stable, unimpeded by consciousness of sex. Woolf meant it to be a luminous and fulfilling idea; but, like other utopian projections, her vision is inhuman. Whatever else one may say of androgyny, it represents an escape from the confrontation with femaleness or maleness. Her ideal artist mystically transcends sex, or has none. One could imagine another approach to androgyny, however, through total immersion in the individual experience, with all its restrictions of sex and anger and fear and chaos. A thorough understanding of what it means, in every respect, to be a woman, could lead the artist to an understanding of what it means to be a man. This revelation would not be realized in any mystical way; it would result from daring to face and express what is unique, even if unpleasant, or taboo, or destructive, in one's own experience, and thus it would speak to the secret heart in all people.

One can see the problem more clearly, I think, in a different context. Woolf disliked partisanship in fiction, and she interpreted it as broadly as possible. In a review of American fiction, she objected to the pervasive sense of national identity and compared it revealingly to the sexual identity of women:

Women writers have to meet many of the same problems that beset Americans. They too are conscious of their own peculiarities as a sex; apt to suspect insolence, quick to avenge grievances, eager to shape an art of their own. In both cases all kinds of consciousness—consciousness of self, of race, of sex, of civilization—which have nothing to do with art, have got between them and the paper, with results that are, on the surface at least, unfortunate.

289

It is easy enough to see that Mr. Anderson, for example, would be a much more perfect artist if he could forget that he is an American; he would write better prose if he could use all words impartially, new or old, English or American; classical or slang.

Nevertheless as we turn from his autobiography to his fiction we are forced to own (as some women writers also make us own) that to come fresh to the world, to turn a new angle to the light, is so great an achievement that for its sake we can pardon the bitterness, the self-consciousness, the angularity which inevitably go with it.[46]

I suspect that few readers will agree that the great flaw in American literature is its national consciousness, its insistence on exploring what is local and special in American culture, or its use of the language which that culture has generated. The sort of perfect artist who can forget where he comes from is a figure more pathetic than heroic. Similarly, the notion that women should transcend any awkwardly unorthodox desire to write about being women comes from timidity and not strength.

Virginia Woolf herself never approached the state of serene indifference she called androgyny; as shown in the quotation above, she was even able to appreciate the excellence of a partisan art. She did try, however, to get away from personal identity, from the claims of the self to be expressed. In terms of the female aesthetic, as I have shown, egolessness was associated with the highest form of female perception. Thus James Naremore, writing of the duality of Woolf's vision, says:

On the one hand is the world of the self, the time-bound, landlocked, everyday world of the masculine ego, of intellect and routine, where people live in fear of death, and where separations imposed by time and space result in agony. On the other hand is a world without a self—

[46] "American Fiction," *Collected Essays*, ii, London, 1966, p. 113.

watery, emotional, erotic, generally associated with the feminine sensibility—where all of life seems blended together in a kind of "halo," where the individual personality is continually being dissolved by intimations of eternity, and where death reminds us of sexual union.[47]

Naremore argues that both of these worlds are equal in Virginia Woolf's writing, except that the second is a little more equal. The chasm between them, however, is never bridged. Indeed, an extended residence in the world without a self is the worst possible preparation for a sojourn in the other world: skills atrophy, courage evaporates, and self-deception becomes habitual. Woolf's books show signs of a progressive technical inability to accommodate the facts and crises of day-to-day experience, even when she wanted to do so.

Woolf did change her ideas over a period of years. In 1928, androgyny, which she had also celebrated in the tedious high camp of *Orlando*, represented her ambivalent solution to the conflict of wishing to describe female experience at the same time that her life presented paralyzing obstacles to such self-expression. The novel, she wrote firmly, should not be "the dumping-ground for the personal emotions." Woolf seems to have been echoing the formidable Beatrice Webb, who had told the Woolfs in 1918 that "marriage was the waste paper basket of the emotions."[48] But where would female emotions and experiences find an outlet?

In the 1930s Woolf tried to deal with the problem by splitting her writing into "male" journalism and "female" fiction. David Daiches has noticed that the mannerisms of her fiction frequently disappeared in her criticism and biography: "The force and clarity of much of her occasional prose sometimes makes us wonder whether she would not

[47] *The World Without a Self*, New Haven, 1972, p. 245.
[48] "Women and Fiction," *Women and Writing*, p. 61. Leonard Woolf quotes Beatrice Webb's remark in *Beginning Again*, London, 1964, p. 117.

have made a brilliant political pamphleteer. For while in her fiction her prose tends to be subtle and lyrical, elsewhere she can write in a most forthright and virile idiom."[49] Woolf's most complex and candid analysis of her own inhibitions as a writer is found in the 1931 essay, "Professions for Women," in which she described the phantom of the Angel in the House, and her own self-censorship:

> I want you to imagine me writing a novel in a state of trance. I want you to figure to yourselves a girl sitting with a pen in her hand, which for minutes, and indeed for hours, she never dips into the inkpot. The image that comes to my mind when I think of this girl is the image of a fisherman lying sunk in dreams on the verge of a deep lake with a rod held out over the water. She was letting her imagination sweep unchecked round every rock and cranny of the world that lies submerged in the depth of our subconscious being. Now came the experience that I believe to be far commoner with women writers than with men. The line raced through the girl's fingers. Her imagination had rushed away. It had sought the pools, the depths, the dark places where the largest fish slumber. And then there was a smash. There was an explosion. There was foam and confusion. The imagination had dashed itself against something hard. The girl was roused from her dream. . . . To speak without figure, she had thought of something, something about the body, about the passions, which it was unfitting for her as a woman to say. Men, her reason told her, would be shocked. The consciousness of what men will say of a woman who speaks the truth about her passions had roused her from her artist's state of unconsciousness. She could write no more.[50]

There is much in this passage worth discussing at length —the shift from the first to the third person narrative, the

[49] *Virginia Woolf*, New York, 1963, pp. 150–151.
[50] "Professions for Women," *Women and Writing*, p. 51.

"figure" of fishing as an allegory of woman's failure to reach orgasm, the significance of the hard explosive somethings that rouse the girl from her dream, and the projection of responsibility at the end onto men. Here I wish to emphasize the last part, the most typical, I think, of the direction of Woolf's thought: it is men who mysteriously control these fantasies by judging them harshly. The sense of this judgment is plain enough, and true enough, to a point, but Woolf wished neither to accuse men nor to look very closely at her own capitulation and self-repression. On the other hand, she was much too honest and perceptive not to see the evasion in her own writing; even if she had not been, there was the composer Ethel Smyth to point it out to her. Smyth had been a co-performer at the Women's Service League when the paper was read, and she urged Woolf to try to write about her "experiences as a body." Woolf in turn suggested that Smyth attempt a novel about the sexual lives of women. At any rate, Woolf began to think in terms of a nonfictional work, "a sequel to *A Room of One's Own*— about the sexual life of women."[51] The fact that this work eventually turned out to be *Three Guineas* demonstrates that she was incapable of carrying out her plan.

Furthermore, the decade of the thirties brought Woolf into repeated contact with death and tragedy; the deaths of Lytton Strachey, Roger Fry, and her nephew Julian Bell were devastating. Julian's death in the Spanish Civil War seemed particularly senseless and tragic because of its associations with the male world of aggression, uniforms, and glory. At the same time she felt a kind of guilt about it; she could not understand his intensity and commitment, and she was forced to question her own attitudes. In a private memoir of her nephew written shortly after his death, she asked herself, "What made him do it? I suppose it's a fever in the blood of the younger generation which we can't possibly understand. I have never known anyone of my generation have that feeling about a war. We were all C.O.'s in the

[51] *A Writer's Diary*, pp. 158–159.

Great war. And though I understand that this is a 'cause,' can be called the cause of liberty & so on, still my natural reaction is to fight intellectually: if I were any use, I should write against it: I should evolve some plan for fighting English tyranny."[52] Here is the motive behind *Three Guineas*: an effort to write, for once, a serious, angry manifesto against war from a feminist viewpoint, partly as a gesture for Julian, partly as her own way of fighting tyranny.

Finally, throughout the latter part of the thirties Woolf was experiencing menopause. Still unable to ignore—much less transcend—the claims of female experience, and also unable to express them in her novels, she sought to evade them once more in a sexless secession from the male world. *Three Guineas* (originally called *On Being Despised*) was the book nobody liked—not even Leonard. Not only did it advocate an almost total withdrawal from male society, on the lines of *Lysistrata*, but it also refused steadfastly to be charming. To the question, How shall we prevent war? *Three Guineas* replies that women should found an "Outsiders Society," honorable, anonymous, indifferent, and self-sufficient, completely detached from the bloody patriarchy.

Whereas the tone and the repeated allusions to men hiding behind the curtains in *A Room of One's Own* show a controlled awareness of a male audience, *Three Guineas* is basically concerned with a female audience, "the daughters of educated men." And here Woolf was betrayed by her own isolation from female mainstream. Many people were infuriated by the class assumptions in the book, as well as by its political naiveté. More profoundly, however, Woolf was cut off from an understanding of the day-to-day life of the women whom she wished to inspire; characteristically, she rebelled against aspects of female experience that she had never personally known and avoided describing her own experience. Thus for all its radical zeal in linking war with patriarchy (Engels had made the same kind of point in

[52] Bell, II, pp. 258–259.

Origins of the Family, Private Property and the State), its careful research (there are 123 lengthy footnotes), and its courage, *Three Guineas* rings false. Its language, all too frequently, is empty sloganeering and cliché; the stylistic tricks of repetition, exaggeration, and rhetorical question, so amusing in *A Room of One's Own*, become irritating and hysterical.

Most of the flaws of *Three Guineas* were exposed in Q. D. Leavis's cruelly accurate *Scrutiny* review. Leavis addressed herself to the question of female experience, making it clear that from her point of view, Woolf knew damn little about it:

"Daughters of educated men" [she quoted] "have always done their thinking from hand to mouth. . . . They have thought while they stirred the pot, while they rocked the cradle. It was thus that they win us the right," etc. I agree with someone who complained that to judge from the acquaintance with the realities of life displayed in this book there is no reason to suppose Mrs. Woolf would know which end of the cradle to stir. Mrs. Woolf in fact can hardly claim that she has thus helped us to win the right, etc. I myself, however, have generally had to produce contributions for this review with one hand, while actually stirring the pot, or something of that kind, with the other, and if I have not done my thinking while rocking the cradle it was only because the daughters even of educated men ceased to rock infants at least two generations ago. Well, I feel bound to disagree with Mrs. Woolf's assumption that running a household alone and unaided necessarily hinders or weakens thinking. One's own kitchen and nursery, and not the drawing-room and dinner table where tired professional men relax among the ladies (thus Mrs. Woolf), is the realm where living takes place, and I see no profit in letting our servants live for us. The activities Mrs. Woolf wishes to free educated women from as wasteful not only provide a valuable discipline, they serve as a sieve for determining which values are important and genuine and which are conventional and contemptible.[53]

Despite its bias, this view is very persuasive. *Three Guineas* is often indignant, articulate, solid—even powerful—but the metaphor of an Outsiders Society is all too accurate a picture of Woolf's world.

In George Lukacs' formulation, the ethic of a novelist becomes an aesthetic problem in his writing. Thus it is not surprising to recognize in Virginia Woolf's memorable definition of life: "a luminous halo, a semitransparent envelope surrounding us from the beginning of consciousness to the end," another metaphor of uterine withdrawal and containment. Woolf's fictional record of the perceptions of this state describes consciousness as passive receptivity: "The mind receives a myriad impressions . . . an incessant shower of innumerable atoms."[54] In one sense, Woolf's female aesthetic is an extension of her view of women's social role: receptivity to the point of self-destruction, creative synthesis to the point of exhaustion and sterility. In *To the Lighthouse*, for example, Mrs. Ramsay spends herself in repeated orgasms of sympathy: "There was scarcely a shell of herself left for her to know herself by; all was so lavished and spent."[55] Similarly, Woolf herself was drained and spent at the conclusion of each novel.

Yet there is a kind of power in Woolf's fiction, that comes from the occasional intense emotion that resists digestion by the lyric prose. There is also a kind of female sexual power in the *passivity* of her writing: it is insatiable. There is a sexual ecstasy in Mrs. Ramsay's exhaustion: "She seemed to fold herself together, one petal closed in another . . . while there throbbed through her, like the pulse in a

[53] "Caterpillars of the World, Unite," *Scrutiny* (September 1938): 210–211.
[54] "Modern Fiction," *Collected Essays*, II, p. 100.
[55] *To the Lighthouse*, London, 1964, p. 45.

spring which has expanded to its full width and now gently ceases to beat, the rapture of successful creation."[56] The free-flowing empathy of woman seeks its own ecstatic extinction. For Mrs. Ramsay, death is a mode of self-assertion. Refined to its essences, abstracted from its physicality and anger, denied any action, Woolf's vision of womanhood is as deadly as it is disembodied. The ultimate room of one's own is the grave.

[56] Ibid., p. 45.

....

CHAPTER XI

Beyond the Female Aesthetic:
Contemporary Women Novelists

> In what way are you different? Are you saying there haven't
> been artist-women before? There haven't been women who were
> independent? There haven't been women who insisted on sexual
> freedom? I tell you, there are a great line of women stretching
> out behind you into the past, and you have to seek them out
> and find them in yourself and be conscious of them.—DORIS
> LESSING, *The Golden Notebook*

IT is easy to see why Virginia Woolf and her generation
tried to create a power base in inner space, an aesthetic that
championed the feminine consciousness and asserted its
superiority to the public, rationalist masculine world. At the
same time that it promised women an alternative source of
experience and self-esteem, however, the female aesthetic
uncannily legitimized all the old stereotypes; Woolf's disciples elevated passivity into a creed. But female aestheticism was only one phase of a tradition, and not its moment
of truth. Today women novelists are continuing a phase of
female self-discovery and self-scrutiny in forms and vocabularies very different from those employed by Woolf.

In the 1930s the Leavises and other contributors to *Scrutiny* attacked the refinement, incorporeality, and inaction
of Woolf's novels. Women novelists of the 1930s too rejected
much of the experimentation of modernism, although in
their descriptions of the artistic imagination, they were influenced by Woolf's definition of the artist as passive
consciousness. The influence is apparent, for example, in
Rosamond Lehmann's description of the creative act: "The
creator is *acted upon* . . . what is necessary is to remain as it

were actively passive, with mind and senses at full stretch, incorporating, selecting, discarding; in fact abandoned—not to sanctimonious looseness—but to every unbargained-for, yet acceptable, inevitable possibility of fertilization."[1] The heroines of women's novels in the 1930s are still passive and self-destructive, but in Lehmann's *The Weather in the Streets* (1936), and Jean Rhys's *Voyage in the Dark* (1939), *After Leaving Mr. Mackenzie* (1937), and *Good Morning, Midnight* (1939), there is a new frankness about the body and about such topics as adultery, abortion, lesbianism, and prostitution; there is a sardonic gallantry about women's sexual oppression that recalls the taut, painful stories of Katherine Mansfield. "Everyone knows England isn't a woman's country," the young gigolo in *Good Morning, Midnight* tells the heroine, Sasha. "You know the proverb—'Unhappy as a dog in Turkey or a woman in England.' "[2] A bittersweet resignation to woman's lot of unhappiness and insecurity pervades these novels, in which all the men seem to be hearty, married, and rich, while all the women are aging, single, and poor.

Feminists in the 1930s were already beginning to seem absurdly intense; Miss Jean Brodie in Muriel Spark's novel is one of "legions . . . who crowded their war-bereaved spinsterhood with voyages of discovery into new ideas and energetic practices in art, social welfare, education or religion," who taught their students about the menarche and the love life of Charlotte Brontë, who were fascinating, but lonely and increasingly eccentric.[3] Feminist protest seemed anachronistic; the suffragettes who lingered on were often, like the Pankhursts, embarrassing fanatics with new and less ennobling causes. With each decade up to the 1960s, feminism seemed more irrelevant to women who were per-

[1] "Rosamond Lehmann Reading," quoted in Sydney Janet Kaplan, *Feminine Consciousness in the Modern British Novel*, Urbana, 1974, p. 112.
[2] *Good Morning, Midnight*, London, 1969, pp. 131–132.
[3] *The Prime of Miss Jean Brodie*, Harmondsworth, 1965, p. 42.

suaded that in leading "emancipated" individual lives, they had overcome the limitations of the feminine role.

"Do you know what 'the feminine role' is?" Rose Macaulay asked her sister in 1954. "I am accused of rejecting it by a correspondent (a psychologist) who disagrees with me that men tend to be cleverer than women. She perceives evidence of this rejection in my novels. How does one reject it, I wonder? And what *is* it?"[4] In Macaulay's best novel, *The Towers of Trebizond* (1956), the woman narrator, Laurie, and her lover, Vere, are not identified by masculine or feminine pronouns until the end of the book. In some ways the novel is a *tour-de-force*, a demonstration of the universality of human emotions, but in other ways it is an evasion of the facts. Laurie and Vere (who is married but able to get away from his wife to travel with his mistress) are not identically free, as Macaulay hoped to persuade the reader (and perhaps herself).

This postfeminist conviction that the vote had canceled out differences between masculine and feminine roles, that major battles had been won, had a basis in the real differences in the opportunities enjoyed by women of Woolf's generation and women born in the twentieth century. Of women novelists born between 1900 and 1920, about 50 percent attended universities. Among women novelists born after 1920, one searches a long time to find one without a degree; in a representative group of ten, seven were educated at Oxford and Cambridge, two at London, and only one at home.[5] During the postwar period, it also seemed that the boundaries of the female subculture, still strong for working-class women, were not as rigid for a cultural elite.

4 *Letters to a Sister*, ed. Constance Babington-Smith, London, 1964, p. 159.

5 Nina Bawden, A. S. Byatt, Margaret Drabble, Cambridge; Christine Brooke-Rose, Brigid Brophy, Gillian Tindall, Jennifer Dawson, Oxford; Maureen Duffy and Penelope Gilliatt, London; Elizabeth Jane Howard was privately educated, but is one of the older members of this group (b. 1923).

Women writers educated like their brothers at Oxford and Cambridge were no longer likely to venerate masculine knowledge, like Dorothea Casaubon, or to reject it, like Lily Briscoe. Women allowed to express their own sexuality, albeit in very limited ways, were not so insistent on chastity for men. The differences in subject matter and tone between the works of English women novelists and their male contemporaries, such as Angus Wilson, Anthony Powell, C. P. Snow, and Graham Greene, were not as dramatic as the differences between English novelists generally and their more ambitious, explosive American counterparts.

The novels of the 1960s, particularly Doris Lessing's powerful *The Golden Notebook*, began to point out, in a variety of notes of disillusionment and betrayal, that the "free women" were not so free after all. Lessing's free women are Marxists who think they understand how the oppression of women is connected to the class struggle, who have professions and children, and who lead independent lives; but they are fragmented and helpless creatures, still locked into dependency upon men. In A. S. Byatt's *The Game* (1967), a brilliant novel that should be much better known, the glamorous novelist Julia Corbett, who seems to have everything, must make the immemorial choice of the woman artist from *Aurora Leigh* on, between love and art; she is punished when she chooses art. In a 1974 essay called "And They All Lived Unhappily Ever After," Rebecca West summarized the failure of feminist reform to change the fundamental ways in which women viewed themselves:

We have an elegant sufficiency of women novelists, and they give us a great deal of evidence which will enable us to make up our minds whether the feminist pioneers have been disappointed in their hope that, if women were admitted to the universities and the professions and commerce and industry and exercised the vote and were eligible for both Houses of Parliament, they would not only be able to earn their own livings and develop their minds

301

and live candidly, but might also be luckier in love than their mothers and grandmothers, and would take it better if they were unlucky. But this evidence is not forthcoming. After a course in Contemporary Women Novelists, it is as if one heard a massed female choir singing . . . "Oh, don't deceive me, oh, never leave me, how could you use a poor maiden so?"[6]

In trying to deal with this recognition of an ongoing struggle for personal and artistic autonomy, contemporary women writers have reasserted their continuity with the women of the past, through essays and criticism as well as through fiction. They use all the resources of the modern novel, including exploded chronology, dreams, myth, and stream-of-consciousness, but they have been profoundly influenced by nineteenth-century feminine literature, sometimes to the point of rewriting it. *The Game* builds on the Brontës' childhood narratives of Angria and Gondal; Jean Rhys's *Wide Sargasso Sea* (1966) retells the story of Bertha Mason; an anonymous Lady has even finished Jane Austen's *Sanditon*. Many contemporary women writers have produced biographies of nineteenth-century women novelists or edited collections of their letters. Gillian Freeman used the pseudonym "Eliot George" for the un-Victorian *The Leather Boys* (1961); Margaret Drabble and Doris Lessing are routinely compared by critics to George Eliot and George Sand.[7]

Contemporary women novelists are also feminine in their preoccupation with the conflict between personal relationships and artistic integrity. Victorian women novelists sometimes got around these issues by using pseudonyms, in order not to hurt their families or offend their friends by unconventional opinions. But in their use of material from life, they were in bondage to the feminine codes of love and

6 *Times Literary Supplement* (July 26, 1974): 779.

7 See, for example, Bernard Bergonzi's essay on Drabble in *Contemporary Novelists*, ed. James Vinson, London and New York, 1972, p. 359; and West "And They All Lived Unhappily Ever After," p. 779.

loyalty. In 1853, Charlotte Brontë asked Mrs. Gaskell how she coped with her conflict of interests: "Do you, who have so many friends—so large a circle of acquaintance—find it easy, when you sit down to write, to isolate yourself from all those ties and their sweet associations, so as to be your *own woman*, uninfluenced or swayed by the consciousness of how your work may affect other minds; what blame or what sympathy it may call forth?"[8] The distress of Sylvia Plath's mother over the "ingratitude" of *The Bell Jar* suggests how difficult it has been for women to transcend social and familial pressures to write only what is pleasant, complimentary, and agreeable. In Iris Murdoch's first novel, *Under the Net* (1954), Jake Donahue agonizes over publishing a book distilled from conversations with his dearest friend. (Anticlimactically, the book is a flop.) Rosamund Stacey, the heroine of Margaret Drabble's *The Millstone* (1965), discovers that her tenant and close friend Lydia is writing a novel about her in secret, but tolerantly accepts the situation. (Later the novel is destroyed—actually chewed up—by Rosamund's illegitimate baby.) In contrast to these comic renderings, when Julia Corbett (in Byatt's *The Game*) publishes a novel about her sister Cassandra, Cassandra's self-image is so traumatically shattered that she kills herself. Even when ironically distanced, or comically undercut, these concerns for the rights of the subject are unfashionable in an era that asserts the absolute title of the imagination and sets aside the raw material as irrelevant to the final, shaped transcendent work of art. Indeed, the violation of private affection, the public exposure of someone else's suffering, has become almost a rite of passage for male writers, a display of manliness that critics take as a sign of true artistic dedication. However old-fashioned and "feminine" the interest women take in the ethics of the novelist may be, these are not irrelevant or vulgar concerns, and it is to the moral credit of Murdoch, Byatt, Drabble, and Lessing that they continue to raise them.

[8] *Life of Charlotte Brontë*, ch. XXVII, p. 383.

Around 1970, the clever, dry tone of these novels, in which women guiltily confronted the collapse of their expectations, began to change to something much more urgent, angry, and unpredictable. In Penelope Mortimer's *The Home* (1971), Muriel Spark's Kafkaesque *The Driver's Seat* (1970), and Doris Lessing's *The Summer Before the Dark* (1973), we see a heroine at her absolute limits of endurance, filled with unexpressed rage. It is difficult to guess precisely how the female tradition will continue to develop in the English novel; Mortimer, Lessing, Drabble, Byatt, and Spark all seem to be moving into new phases in their writing. Feminine realism, feminist protest, and female self-analysis are combining in the context of twentieth-century social and political concern.

Of all the contemporary English women novelists, Margaret Drabble is the most ardent traditionalist. Her sense of connection to female tradition, "the sexual doom of womanhood, its sad inheritance,"[9] comes first of all from her own past. Drabble described her childhood at the annual meeting of the Brontë Society in 1974: "I was brought up in Sheffield, on the edge of countryside very similar to the country round Haworth. My family was of the same size and constitution as the Brontë family; my siblings and I were interested in writing, and in our childhood composed magazines and stories together."[10] Both Drabble and her sister A. S. Byatt have used material from the Brontë novels and legend as controlling myths in their own writing; Drabble has also written extensively about nineteenth-century women novelists, and about Virginia Woolf and Katherine Mansfield. Her full-length biography of Woolf's Edwardian literary adversary, Arnold Bennett, underlines her personal commitment to nineteenth-century social realism. "I don't want to write an experimental novel to be read by people in fifty years, who will say, oh, well, yes, she foresaw what

[9] *The Waterfall*, Harmondsworth, 1971, p. 154.

[10] "The Writer as Recluse: The Theme of Solitude in the Works of the Brontës," *Brontë Society Transactions* XVI (1974): 259.

was coming," she said in 1967. "I'm just not interested. I'd rather be at the end of a dying tradition, which I admire, than at the beginning of a tradition which I deplore."[11] The women in Drabble's novels are unselfconsciously named for the great Victorian heroines, as if the supply of women's names were, after all, very small: Rosamund, Clara, Emma, Lucy, and Jane. It is as natural for a character in a Drabble novel to gossip about nineteenth-century heroines as to discuss her own childhood; in fact, more so. Heroines rather reticent about their own sexuality will decide that "Emma got what she deserved in marrying Mr. Knightley. What can it have been like, in bed with Mr. Knightley?"[12]

For Drabble's heroines, at least up to Rose Vassiliou in *The Needle's Eye* (1972), there is a kind of peace in the acknowledgment of, and submission to, female limitation. In *The Millstone*, Rosamund Stacey, a Ph.D. candidate living in a posh apartment that her parents have loaned to her, becomes pregnant in a single encounter with a man she admires but has no claims upon. Rosamund is pretty, self-disciplined, and courageous; but, in bearing a child, she is brought to admit that she has lost control of her own destiny. She is humbled, first by her body, which forces a reluctant admission of femaleness upon her, then by the startling strength of her love for the child. In the maternity clinic, Rosamund feels her oneness with the shabby, exhausted women who wait with her to see the doctors: "I was one of them, I was like that too, I was trapped in a human limit for the first time in my life, and I was going to have to learn to live inside it."[13]

Children are the compensation for feminine surrender. Drabble is the novelist of maternity, as Charlotte Brontë was the novelist of the schoolroom. The interaction between

---

[11] Quoted in Bernard Bergonzi, *The Situation of the Novel*, London, 1972, p. 78.

[12] *Waterfall*, p. 58.

[13] *The Millstone*, Harmondsworth, 1968, p. 58.

mother and child, the love that comes unbidden like the operations of grace, is for Drabble the most instructive and surprising human relationship. For a Drabble heroine, a room of one's own is usually a place to have a baby, but it is at the same time a testing-ground for resilience and charity and wisdom. Thus Drabble finds a female resolution to the feminine conflict between biological and artistic creativity. Pregnancy is a way of knowing, a process of education that not only helps Rosamund work "with great concentration and clarity" on her thesis, but also makes real to her the abstractions of the human condition: "I had always felt for others in theory and pitied the blows of fate and circumstance under which they suffered; but now, myself, no longer free, myself suffering, I may say that I felt it in my heart."[14] Men, particularly successful men, are magnetically attracted to the company of these knowing women; in *The Waterfall* James is literally seduced by watching Jane convalesce from childbirth in a warm room at the top of an empty house.

Yet childbirth is not a victory; it is an acceptance of the compensations of giving in and giving up, of the "necessary pleasure of feeling from time to time the warm sense of defeat."[15] Drabble's heroines are well aware of the boundaries of their world, and wryly, distantly amused by their own futile efforts to escape. At the conclusion of *The Garrick Year*, Emma tells no one that she has seen a snake clutching at the belly of a sheep on a family picnic in Hertfordshire: "One just has to keep on and to pretend, for the sake of the children, not to notice. Otherwise, one might just as well stay at home."[16]

As the novelist, of course, Drabble always notices and proclaims the presence of the snake her heroines gamely pretend not to see. By the end of *The Needle's Eye* (1972), however, the gap between novelist and heroine has almost

[14] *The Millstone*, p. 68.
[15] *The Garrick Year*, London. 1966, p. 171.
[16] Ibid., p. 172.

closed; graceful resignation to feminine destiny, to the curse of Eve, has come to seem much more masochistic and despairing. Rose decides to live with a husband she despises, once more "for the children's sake"; but this time she feels that she has made a suicidal decision prompted only by duty, and that the "price she had to pay was the price of her own living death, her own conscious dying, her own lapsing . . . from grace."[17]

Drabble herself has speculated about the extent to which Rose's martyrdom is connected to her personal need to force the ideology of marriage on a fiction straining to go beyond it. "I haven't written a novel since Clive and I separated," she told Nancy Hardin in 1972, "and I'm very interested to see what comes out next. I wrote the whole of *The Needle's Eye* when we were still together. And I might not have made it end like it did if we had separated first. I might have allowed her her freedom."[18] A good deal of Drabble's strength and ability to grow comes out in the simplicity of this admission. Like her sister Antonia Byatt (now working on a four-volume novel), Drabble has been increasingly ambitious, serious, and open-minded; her work is the record of a feminine consciousness expanding and maturing. In some respects she has been clinging to a tradition she has outgrown. *The Needle's Eye* is evidently the end of a prolonged phase in Drabble's writing; perhaps she will now allow herself more freedom, more protest.

Drabble has called Doris Lessing "Cassandra in a world under siege,"[19] and, like Cassandra, Lessing seems to be a lonely and embattled figure on the contemporary scene. She has an extraordinary barometric sensitivity to the social climate, but she anticipates trends rather than capping them with a novel. Thus the encyclopedic study of intellectual,

[17] *The Needle's Eye*, Harmondsworth, 1973, p. 395.
[18] Nancy S. Hardin, "Interview with Margaret Drabble," *Contemporary Literature* XIV (1973): 277.
[19] Margaret Drabble, "Doris Lessing: Cassandra in a World Under Siege," *Ramparts* X (February 1972): 50–54.

political women in *The Golden Notebook* (1962), preceded, and in a sense introduced, the Women's Liberation Movement. Lessing's early fiction (that is, the novels up to *The Four-Gated City* in 1969), has many similarities to Victorian feminine and feminist writing. Olive Schreiner, another South African novelist about whom Lessing has written an enthusiastic essay, obviously influenced the first Martha Quest books. In her almost somnambulistic passivity, Martha also resembles Maggie Tulliver, "caught," as Walter Allen writes, "between the pressure to conform (not only to the local mores, but also, as it were, biologically, as a woman) and the urge, intermittent but increasingly insistent, to be free to make her own life."[20] Lessing's theories (in *The Golden Notebook*) of a male deficiency in the ability to love and of differences in the ways men and women use language powerfully extend the female aestheticist theories of Richardson and Woolf. Despite her heroine Anna's insistence that she and her friend Molly are completely new types of women, there is an explicit and implicit continuity between their experiences, emotions, and values and the "great line" of independent artist-women of the past.

The Golden Notebook is such a monumental achievement that it is tempting to see it as Lessing's ultimate statement about twentieth-century women and the female tradition. But her writing has since undergone a massive shift, away from female concerns, and most determinedly away from the social realism she admired in the late 1950s. Lessing now believes that we are heading for a global catastrophe, through germ warfare, nuclear warfare, or simply breakdown of civilization; sex and gender are irrelevant in terms of this human disaster. In the surreal *Memoirs of a Survivor* (1975), we hear from a woman on the other side of revelation, a woman who has escaped a crumbling society in which children have become cannibals and animals are sentient, a woman who has no relationships with men, who

20 Quoted in Kaplan, *Feminine Consciousness*, p. 153.

displays vestiges of maternal feeling, but is beyond sexual distinctions. Lessing calls this allegorical novel "an attempt at autobiography"; it is a form light-years away from the documentary autobiography of *The Golden Notebook*.

The change in Lessing's fiction from the individual to the collective, from the personal to the communal, from the female to the global, consciousness seems at first like an abrupt transformation. It has, however, been a systematic, willed process of escape from a very painful encounter with the self, with the anguish of feminine fragmentation. Almost since the beginning of her career, Lessing has struggled against the "feminine" elements in herself, especially as they have expressed themselves in narrative techniques. In the introduction to *African Stories* (1964), Lessing explained how she had deliberately rejected the style of a story called "The Trinket Box," with its Freudian intimations of a narcissistic, overelaborate femininity, for the more clumsy but authoritative style of a story severely titled "The Pig":

> *The Pig* and *The Trinket Box* are two of my earliest. I see them as two forks of a road. The second—intense, careful, self-conscious, mannered—could have led to a style of writing usually described as "feminine." The style of *The Pig* is straight, broad, direct; is much less beguiling, but is the highway to the kind of writing that has the freedom to develop as it likes.[21]

As Lynn Sukenick has shown in an outstanding essay, Lessing's aversion to the feminine sensibility has progressed from satiric asides in the early novels to a resolute stand against all emotion and irrationality. Even in her handling of dreams and insanity, Lessing is "practical, rational, and even mechanical," comparing her own engineering of her dreams to "a mathematician who supplied his brain with in-

[21] Quoted in Lynn Sukenick, "Feeling and Reason in Doris Lessing's Fiction," in *Doris Lessing: Critical Studies*, ed. Annis Pratt and L. S. Dembo, Madison, Wisconsin, 1974, p. 99.

formation and worked it like a computer."[22] For Lessing, the subconscious is a less tractable but potentially useful intelligence, which can be programmed and debriefed. Women's readiness to pay attention to these unconventional signals gives them an advantage in communication, which in the case of Lynda Coldridge and Martha Quest in *The Four-Gated City* is actually a form of extrasensory perception. Lessing does not, however, wish us to understand women's ability to manipulate the subconscious in terms of a stereotyped "feminine intuition." She presents women as being more practiced than men in interpreting inner space, but she chooses a male protagonist in *Briefing for a Descent into Hell* to emphasize the nonexclusivity of the gift.

The term "feminine" has class connotations for Lessing, as well as suggestions of weakness, affectation, and emotionality. The affliction of feminine sensibility is portrayed in *The Golden Notebook* in a parody of "a lady author" who notes in her journal how essential it is "to have clean linen on one's bed every day."[23] In an interview that came out at the time the novel was published, Lessing used similar language to describe Virginia Woolf:

> I've always felt this thing about Virginia Woolf—I find her too much of a lady. There's always a point in her books when I think, my God, she lives in such a different world from anything I've ever lived in. I don't understand it. I think it's charming in a way, but I feel that her experience must have been too limited, because there's always a point in her novels when I think, "Fine, but look at what you've left out."[24]

[22] Ibid., p. 113; Jonah Raskin, "Doris Lessing at Stony Brook: An Interview," *New American Review* VIII (January 1970): 172.

[23] *The Golden Notebook*, Harmondsworth, 1964, p. 431.

[24] Robert Rubens, "Footnote to *The Golden Notebook*," *The Queen* (August 21, 1962): quoted in Nancy Joyner, "The Underside of the Butterfly: Lessing's Debt to Woolf," *Journal of Narrative Technique* v (1974): 204–205.

There are, in fact, some interesting similarities between Lessing and Woolf; their worlds are not nearly as far apart as Lessing insists here. Both novelists have a fondness for fantasy, especially when they write about animals, but the affinities are deeper. Like Lessing, Woolf began with a contempt for sensibility, which came in part from her terror of her own anger and passion. She argued that the novel should be something more than "the dumping-ground for the personal emotions." Lessing presents the issue of sensibility as political rather than aesthetic; "the personal," explains Lynn Sukenick, "is by definition a private possession and may represent for the former communist a form of self-ishness, a capitalist hoarding of emotional territory."[25] In *The Golden Notebook* Anna finally convinces herself that the personal is political, that "if Marxism means anything, it means that a little novel about the emotions reflects 'what's real' since the emotions are a function and a product of a society."[26] But in Lessing's recent fiction, we are in a landscape that is the political, collectivized equivalent of Woolf's "world without a self." The feminine ego is merged for Woolf into a passive vulnerable receptivity; for Lessing, into a transmitter for the collective consciousness.

Lessing has also wished to minimize feminism, both as a historical and as a contemporary influence on her writing. *The Golden Notebook*, as Margaret Drabble says, is "a document in the history of liberation," the most complex rendering we have of the woman intellectual. But Lessing insists it is not primarily about women's liberation. I tend to agree with Ellen Morgan that Lessing has not yet confronted the essential feminist implications of her own writing, that she is alienated "from the authentic female perspective."[27] Even in *The Golden Notebook* there are evasive passages in which Anna or Ella absolutely deny the evi-

[25] Sukenick, "Feeling and Reason," p. 115.
[26] *Golden Notebook*, p. 48.
[27] "Alienation of the Woman Writer in *The Golden Notebook*," in *Doris Lessing: Critical Studies*, p. 63.

dence of their own bodies in favor of socially appropriate, fashionable, or mystical explanations of what is happening to them. One of these passages is the notorious celebration of the "real" or vaginal (as distinguished from the "inferior" clitoral) orgasm: "There is only one real female orgasm, and that is when a man, from the whole of his need and desire, takes a woman and wants all her response. Everything else is a substitute and fake, and the most inexperienced woman feels this instinctively."[28] This extraordinary insistence on blood-knowledge, instinct, and female submission has persuaded Kathleen Nott and Mark Spilka that Lessing was consciously writing a semiparodic "female counter-recrimination" to D. H. Lawrence.[29]

But Lessing's heroines systematically employ a semimystical, semipolitical theory of thought transference to avoid responsibility for their own sensations, their own feelings. The eleventh vignette in *The Golden Notebook* paraphrases R. D. Laing's hypothesis in *Sanity, Madness and the Family*, that "often it's the most 'normal' member of a family or a group who is really sick, but simply because they have strong personalities, they survive, while other, weaker personalities, express their illness for them."[30] When she breaks down in terror and self-loathing, Anna consoles herself with the thought that she is "expressing" someone else's anxiety-state, that "what I was experiencing was not *my* thought at all."[31] In *The Four-Gated City*, Martha and Lynda are "mad" only because they can tune in to other people's thoughts. Lessing herself in a recent interview has disclaimed anything unique or personal in her ideas and perceptions: "I don't believe anymore that I have a thought. There is a thought around."[32]

28 *Golden Notebook*, p. 213.
29 Mark Spilka, "Lessing and Lawrence," *Contemporary Literature* XVI (1975): 232; Kathleen Nott, *Time and Tide*, April 26, 1962.
30 *Golden Notebook*, pp. 526–527.
31 *Golden Notebook*, pp. 563, 600.
32 Raskin, "Lessing at Stony Brook," 173.

Taken out of context, these remarks sound more extreme than they are. Lessing's pessimism certainly articulates our vague collective *fin-de-siècle* despair; *Memoirs of a Survivor* is her version of H. G. Wells' *Island of Dr. Moreau*. But her dismissal of the sexual dimension of experience, her claim to have gone beyond the female tradition, rings very false. Lessing herself will have to face the limits of her own fiction very soon, if civilization survives the 1970s, which she has predicted it will not. Either she will have to revise her apocalyptical prophecies (like other millenarians), or confront, once again, the struggling individual. Kate Brown and the nameless "survivor" of the memoirs discard their female identities because they are unimportant in the face of impending doom. But this is not a solution; it is the equality that comes at the end of a gun.

The Women's Liberation Movement has not yet had the impact on English women writers that it has had in the United States and in France. Strongly socialist, the English movement has rejected the idea of hierarchy, and therefore there have been no charismatic feminist leaders, as there were for the suffragettes. The media in England have been slower to publicize the movement; one or two natural spokeswomen such as Germaine Greer have been sensationalized and discredited; radical feminists have tended to scorn newspapers and television, which, despite distortion and exploitation, have carried the messages of the new feminism with remarkable speed to small towns in America.

The English movement is beginning to catch up. Parliament has passed equal rights legislation; women's studies' courses have begun at major universities. A new wave of feminist energy has generated its own network of magazines, newsletters, and publishing houses, designed to promote and distribute women's literature. Most of these women's presses are in the United States: the Feminist Press in New York; Daughters, Inc., in Vermont; Alicejames Books in Massachusetts; Shameless Hussy Press in California. In 1975 Virago, a "feminist publishing imprint" in London, distributed its first catalog of nine books ranging from Angela Carter's study of *The Sadeian Woman* to *The British Woman's Directory*, which tells "how to get a solicitor, legal aide, a divorce, an abortion." As in the suffrage movement, a strong women's press encourages an autonomous literature.

Sheila Rowbotham, one of the leaders of the Women's Liberation Movement in England, has written that "the fortunes of the new feminism will depend on our capacity to relate to the working-class and the action of working-class women in transforming women's liberation according to their needs."[33] There is a female voice that has rarely spoken for itself in the English novel—the voice of the shopgirl and the charwoman, the housewife and the barmaid. One possible effect of the women's movement might be the broadening of the class base from which women novelists have come. "These pages are only fragments," Virginia Woolf wrote in 1930, introducing a collection of autobiographical essays by workers in the Women's Co-operative Guild. "These voices are beginning only now to emerge from silence into half articulate speech. These lives are still half hidden in profound obscurity."[34] As the women's movement turns to these silent women, they may find their voice at last; perhaps the next literary generation will be theirs.

Another effect of women's liberation has been the reopening of the long literary debate about the woman writer. What does "liberation" mean for her? What, as Mill and Lewes asked in the nineteenth century, does the literature of women really mean? Radical Marxist feminists believe that women's literature should dedicate itself to the forging of a new consciousness of oppression by developing cultural myths of women in struggle and women in revolution. The task of a radical women's literature should be to replace the

[33] *Hidden from History*, London, 1973, p. 169.
[34] *Life As We Have Known It*, ed. Margaret Llewelyn Davies, London, 1977, xxxxi.

secondary and artificial images women receive from a male chauvinist society with authentic and primary identities. Such a literature would be directed toward other women and would opt to describe revolutionary life-styles. It would challenge the sexist bases of language and culture. According to Adrienne Rich, it would be accompanied by "a radical critique of literature, feminist in its impulses," that "would take the work first of all as a clue to how we live, how we have been living, how we have been led to imagine ourselves, how our language has trapped as well as liberated us; and how we can begin to see—and therefore live—afresh."[35] In 1974 Rich and two black women poets wrote a collective acceptance speech for the National Book Awards, rejecting the idea of literary competition between women and relating their work to feminist revolutionary struggle; their statement is the first manifesto of women's literature:

> We, Audre Lord, Adrienne Rich, and Alice Walker, together accept this award in the name of all the women whose voices have gone and still go unheard in a patriarchal world, and in the name of those who, like us, have been tolerated as token women in this culture, often at great cost and in great pain. . . . none of us could accept this money for herself, nor could she let go unquestioned the terms on which poets are given or denied honor and livelihood in this world, especially when they are women. We dedicate this occasion to the struggle for self-determination of all women, of every color, identification or derived class: the poet, the housewife, the lesbian, the mathematician, the mother, the dishwasher, the pregnant teen-ager, the teacher, the grandmother, the prostitute, the philosopher, the waitress, the women who will under-

[35] "When We Dead Awaken: Writing as Re-Vision," in *Adrienne Rich's Poetry*, ed. Barbara Charlesworth Gelpi and Albert Gelpi, New York, 1975, p. 90.

stand what we are doing here and those who will not understand yet; the silent women whose voices have been denied us, the articulate women who have given us strength to do our work.

So far, English women writers have not become involved in the Women's Liberation Movement, or at least not with the openness, zeal, and intellectual vigor of American writers like Rich, Tillie Olsen, Erica Jong, Susan Sontag, Alix Shulman, and Marge Piercy. Despite a flourishing tradition of lesbian art, contemporary English women have displayed little enthusiasm for the descendants of Radclyffe Hall and Vernon Lee. In the United States, books like Jill Johnston's *Lesbian Nation* and Marge Piercy's *Small Changes* take the sisterly bonds of the female subculture to their sexual extremes. But English women novelists have responded coolly to "the new Amazonian female culture," and its literary forms in works like Monique Wittig's *The Lesbian Body*, which tries to invent a new language free of gender distinctions. In a review of this experimental novel, Antonia Byatt explained her own allegiance to a more moderate tradition: "I like change, not revolution. I like subtle distinctions within a continuing language, not doctrinaire violations."[36] Probably few English women writers, who are also involved in the caution and anti-experimentalism of the post-war British novel, will want to adopt the aesthetic policies of radical feminism; nonetheless, they can hardly avoid being sensitized and challenged by the new climate of feminist solidarity and by the discussions in art, as well as in literary criticism, of female iconography and female vision.

With the relaxation of taboos on the open discussion of female sexual experience, and with women's increased interest in themes of menstruation, masturbation, abortion, and childbirth, there has developed a critical backlash that insists that freedom for the woman writer means a mascu-

[36] "Give Me the Moonlight, Give Me the Girl," *The New Review* II (1975): 67.

line range of experience and subject. There has been a revival of the Victorian idea that female experience is narrow and insignificant, and that in deliberately opting to portray it the novelist diminishes her own potential and restricts herself to a cultural ghetto.

In the 1950s, Elizabeth Hardwick was convinced that women writers could never compete on an equal basis with men because of the absolute and immutable difference in experience:

> If women's writing seems somewhat limited, I don't think it is only due to these psychological failings. Women have much less experience of life than a man, as everyone knows. But in the end are they suited to the kind of experience men have? *Ulysses* is not just a work of genius, it is Dublin pubs, gross depravity, obscenity, brawls. Stendhal as a soldier in Napoleon's army, Tolstoy on his Cossack campaigns, Dostoevsky before the firing squad, Proust's obviously first-hand knowledge of vice, Conrad and Melville as sailors, Michelangelo's tortures on the scaffolding in the Sistine Chapel, Ben Jonson's drinking bouts, dueling, his ear burnt by the authorities because of a political indiscretion in a play—these horrors and the capacity to endure them are *experience*. Experience is something more than going to law school or having the nerve to say honestly what you think in a drawing room filled with men; it is the privilege as well to endure brutality, physical torture, unimaginable sordidness, and even the privilege to *want*, like Boswell, to grab a miserable tart under Westminster Bridge. . . . In the end, it is in the matter of experience that women's disadvantage is catastrophic. It is very difficult to know how this may be extraordinarily altered.[37]

But of course it *has* been extraordinarily altered. Equal rights legislation, the sexual revolution, and the counter-

[37] "The Subjection of Women," in *A View of My Own*, New York, 1962, pp. 180–181.

culture of the 1960s have all contributed to the change. Even in Hardwick's terms, it is now possible for women to have some of the violent male experiences she valued so highly as literary material, to write, if they wish, about war and torture. One may reasonably inquire whether even Boswell had more experience of the sordid than the "miserable tart" he picked up; until very recently women were the victims of such male experience, and not its privileged consumers. More importantly, we are discovering how much in female experience has gone unexpressed; how few women, as Virginia Woolf said, have been able to tell the truth about the body, or the mind.

The radical demand that would yoke women writers to feminist revolution and deny them the freedom to explore new subjects would obviously not provide a healthy direction for the female tradition to take. But the denigration of female experience, the insistence that women deal with "the real business of the world," is also destructive. In women critics' attacks on novelists who have failed so to direct their interests, one senses a rationalization of the old self-hatred of women. Their theories of the transcendence of sexual identity, like Woolf's theory of androgyny, are at heart evasions of reality.

The problem of autonomy that the woman novelist faces is, to name the extremes, whether to sacrifice personal development and freedom as an artist to a collective cultural task, or whether to sacrifice authenticity and self-exploration and accept the dominant culture's definition of what is important to understand and describe. George Eliot believed that women could write novels that were among the very greatest: "We have only to pour in the right elements— genuine observation, humour, and passion."[38] Virginia Woolf believed that, given economic independence and a room of one's own, given "the habit of freedom and the courage to write exactly what we think, . . . then the oppor-

[38] "Silly Novels by Lady Novelists," in *Essays of George Eliot*, ed. Thomas Pinney, London, 1963, p. 324.

tunity will come and the dead poet who was Shakespeare's sister will put on the body which she has so often laid down."[39] If the room of one's own becomes the destination, a feminine secession from the political world, from "male" power, logic, and violence, it is a tomb, like Clarissa Dalloway's attic bedroom. But if contact with a female tradition and a female culture is a center; if women take strength in their independence to act in the world, then Shakespeare's sister, whose coming Woolf asked us to await in patience and humility, may appear at last. Beyond fantasy, beyond androgyny, beyond assimilation, the female tradition holds the promise of an art that may yet fulfill the hopes of Eliot and Woolf.

[39] *A Room of One's Own*, 1945, p. 112.

CHAPTER XII

✳✳✳

Laughing Medusa

TWENTY-FIVE years ago, I wrote that "in the atlas of the
English novel, woman's territory is usually depicted as desert." Now, at the end of the twentieth century, the success of British feminist publishers and the explosion of
work from British and American feminist critics, literary
historians, journalists, and biographers has filled in many
of the blank spaces in the map of women's writing. Reference books like Joanne Shattock's *Oxford Guide to British
Women Writers* (1994) and Margaret Drabble's monumental *Oxford Guide to English Literature* (1992) have consolidated biographical information, so that the biographical
appendix that I compiled for the first edition of *A Literature of Their Own* is now outdated and unnecessary. TV
adaptations, paperback editions, and critical studies have
made scores of forgotten women writers newly accessible
and influential. If the female literary tradition in the English novel was once a lost Atlantis, it has now risen triumphantly to rule the waves.

Paradoxically, British women's writing at the millennium may also be coming to the end of its history as a
separate "literature of their own." In 1977, I predicted
that English women writers could not avoid "being sensitized and challenged by the new climate of feminist solidarity and by the discussions in art, as well as in literary
criticism, of female iconography and female vision." I did
not anticipate, however, that two decades of critical and
theoretical attention to women's writing would profoundly
alter the evolution of the woman's novel. Women writers'
postmodernist awareness of belonging to a literary tradi-

tion has made their fiction self-reflexive in a new way. From the early 1970s—when a number of British women novelists became involved in the issues of the women's movement and the development of feminist criticism— until today, the themes, metaphors, iconographies, paradoxes, and problems of women's fiction have become familiar to both readers and writers. Madwomen in the attic, female body imagery, mother-daughter relationships, father-daughter incest, lyric *écriture féminine*, the mother tongue, lesbian affiliations and romances, concentric form, embroidery and patchwork, jewelry and clothing, cooking and eating, anorexia nervosa, and the female masquerade are part of the literary repertoire of every first-time writer. Just as the heroine of a New Woman novel in the 1890s was likely to be an artist or writer, the heroine of a New British Woman novel in the 1990s is likely to be a feminist literary critic.[1]

Second, the insularity of setting and the consistency of

[1] This shift has not, of course, been unique to British women's writing. In the U.S., Gail Godwin's *The Odd Woman* (1974), somberly revised Gissing to show the psychological contradictions persisting in the life of Jane Clifford, a feminist critic of George Eliot who turns to Victorian literature for the psychological clarity, moral certainty, and sexual control she finds missing in her own life. In Carolyn Heilbrun's *Death in a Tenured Position* (1981), Professor Janet Mandelbaum is not actually a feminist critic herself, but rather a scholar of seventeenth-century English literature outraged by the idea that she should "rally to some woman's cause." Indeed, Professor Mandelbaum has been carefully selected for tenure in the Harvard English Department as a "woman professor who was perfectly safe on the subject of feminism and women's studies." Eventually, humiliated about the circumstances of her appointment, and defeated by the hostility and cynicism that surround her, Mandelbaum takes cyanide. The mystery of her death is solved by Kate Fansler, Heilbrun's feminist detective, who deciphers the clue of the book Mandelbaum is reading before her death: a biography of Karl Marx's daughter Eleanor, a feminist idealist, activist, and writer of the 1880s who committed suicide a century before. In France, novels like Julia Kristeva's *Les Samouris* are similarly self-reflexive.

style that made English women's fiction so homogeneous as a literary subculture twenty-five years ago have been radically transformed. The British women's novels I considered in 1977 showed virtually no awareness of American literature, and very little European influence. Now the situation is markedly different. A. S. Byatt has written the introductions to the Virago Modern Classic Edition of Willa Cather; Hermione Lee is writing a biography of Edith Wharton; both classic and contemporary American women's writing is widely available in paperback in the U.K. and taught at universities. The new generation of novelists are as likely to be influenced by Toni Morrison or Anne Tyler as by Mansfield and Woolf, and as likely to have visited San Francisco as Stratford.

Moreover, contemporary British women's novels are set all over the world, and reflect the international stylistic influences that come with a global culture and the new Europe. Complexity and diversity are no longer a national preserve, and a good thing too. With contemporary mobility and the popularity of travel writing, British women writers have abandoned Austen's two little inches of ivory for an international canvas ranging from the Middle East to the Antarctic. From Jean Rhys, Ruth Prawer Jhabvala, and Anita Desai to Arundhati Roy, Grace Nichol, and Buchi Emecheta, British women writers come from hybrid and multiracial backgrounds—African, Caribbean, Indian, and Asian.[2]

Finally, women's fiction is no longer restricted to the social and domestic. In 1977, I predicted that "as the women's movement takes on cohesive force, and as feminist critics examine their literary tradition, contemporary women novelists will have to face the problems that

[2] See Susheila Nasta, *Motherlands: Black Women's Writing from Africa, the Caribbean and South Asia*, London: The Women's Press, 1991; and Lauretta Ngcobo, ed., *Let It Be Told: Black Women's Writing in Britain*, London: Virago, 1988.

black, ethnic, and Marxist writers have faced in the past: whether to devote themselves to the forging of female mythologies and epics, or to move beyond the female tradition into a seamless participation in the literary mainstream that might be regarded either as equality or assimilation."

In fact, British women writers have both forged female mythologies and transcended them. Moreover, the boundaries between women's popular commercial fiction and high culture are less rigidly drawn. Mystery writers like P. D. James and Ruth Rendell are among the most honored contemporary writers, while the books of Joanna Trollope and Helen Fielding offer significant insights into the lives of British women in the late twentieth century. Women artists of the 1990s have found a genuine freedom to explore anger and adventure. Those in midcareer exult in the medical and technological advances that have prolonged youth and health, and added, as Margaret Drabble comments, "ten years to every plot."[3] Women novelists have joined the mainstream as postmodern innovators, politically engaged observers, and limitless storytellers.

CARTER COUNTRY

Angela Carter's influence on British women's writing was pivotal in this opening and transformation. Carter's familiarity with and enthusiasm for Japanese popular culture, American movies, Latin-American magical realism, French surrealism, perverse sexuality, and carnivalesque masquerade marked a totally new turn in the English female literary tradition. Since her premature death from lung cancer in 1992, Carter has become a cult figure in English letters, and her popularity is the subject of leg-

[3] Margaret Drabble, in an interview June 1996 with Elaine Showalter, for a BBC radio series on "Women of the 1990s."

end. As one critic notes, "the story goes, that among the requests for grants for doctoral study received by the British Academy in the academic year 1992–93, there were 40 proposals to study Carter's work, more—and this is the punch line—than the Council received for the entire eighteenth century."[4] Today the British women's novel is as likely to be set in decadent Carter Country as the decorous Home Counties.

Born in industrial south Yorkshire, Carter grew up in the neorealist fifties, in the era of austerity and conformity, and the "glum poetry of domestic complaint."[5] In contrast, she had begun to read the French Symbolist poets, Blake, Dada, the decadents, Baudelaire, James Joyce, and Nabokov. Her reading gave her a dim view of the English literary fashions of her youth: "Anybody who had a stiff injection of Rimbaud at 18 isn't going to be able to cope very well with Philip Larkin, I'm afraid. There must be more to life than this one says. It made the circumstances of my everyday life profoundly unsatisfactory."[6] Carter worked as a journalist and married at twenty-one before she attended Bristol University, specializing in medieval literature and reading widely in anthropology, sociology, psychology, myth, and folklore. In the 1960s, she was reading Melville and Dostoevsky, plus the camp fiction of Ronald Firbank, the fables of Isak Dinesen, and the surrealist fiction of Cocteau. She never identified with English nationalism: "I don't feel particularly English," she told Lisa Appignanesi in 1987.[7]

[4] Sarah Gamble, *Angela Carter: Writing from the Front Line*, Edinburgh: Edinburgh University Press, 1997, p. 1.

[5] Lorna Sage, *Angela Carter*, Plymouth: Northcote House, 1994, p. 2.

[6] Lorna Sage, "The Savage Sideshow," *New Review* 4, nos. 39–40 (July 1977): 54.

[7] *Writers in Conversation: Angela Carter*, London: Institute of Contemporary Arts, 1987, video. Lisa Appignanesi, herself a scholar of European literature and psychoanalysis, was Director of the ICA in the

As a thinker and writer, Carter was very much a product of the 1960s. She wrote three novels in three years, *Shadow Dance* (1966), *The Magic Toyshop* (1967), and *Several Perceptions* (1968); and in 1968, she won 500 pounds from the Somerset Maugham Award, a fellowship intended to allow young English writers to travel abroad. Later she would celebrate the revolutionary year of 1968 as a watershed in her political and feminist coming-of-age:

> [I]t felt like Year One, that all that was holy was in the process of being profaned and we were attempting to grapple with the real relations between human beings. So writers like Marcuse and Adorno were as much a part of my personal process of maturing into feminism as experiments with my sexual and emotional life and with various intellectual adventures in anarcho-surrealism. . . . I can date to that time and to some of those debates and to that sense of heightened awareness of the society around me in the summer of 1968, my own questioning of the nature of my reality as a *woman*.[8]

When Virginia Woolf had argued that women writers needed 500 pounds a year, she never would have imagined the use to which Carter put her prize. She left her marriage, traveled all across the United States, and then went to live in Japan, an experience which intensified her sense of being an outsider. In Japan, too, she "learnt what it is to be a woman and became radicalized."[9]
Carter was one of the first English women writers to engage openly with feminist criticism and the women's

---

1980s, and a secret writer of Mills & Boon romances. In the 1990s she began writing commercial popular fiction.

[8] Angela Carter, "Notes from the Front Line," in *Shaking a Leg: Collected Journalism and Writings*, ed. Jenny Uglow, London: Vintage, 1997, p. 37.

[9] Angela Carter, *Nothing Sacred: Selected Writings*, London: Virago, 1992, p. 28.

movement. "The women's movement has been of immense importance to me personally, and I would regard myself as a feminist writer," she wrote in "Notes from the Front Line," "because I'm a feminist in everything else and one can't compartmentalize these things."[10] She was well aware of belonging to a female literary tradition, but she also refused to sentimentalize women's writing or to share in any feminist myth of victimization. She had nothing but scorn for women writers like Elizabeth Smart who moaned about their love lives; "I began to plot a study of the Jean Rhys/E. Smart/E. O'Brien woman titled 'Self-inflicted wounds.'"[11] When she read Marilyn French's *The Women's Room* (1977), Carter was full of mischievous sympathy for the male characters: "they seemed to have awful lives surrounded by such dreadful women."[12] Her attitude toward Virginia Woolf typified her mix of admiration and irreverence; she wrote a libretto for an opera based on *Orlando*, and clearly followed Woolf's lead in writing about gender-crossing, but she also participated with zest in a TV program trashing Woolf, *J'Accuse*, in 1991.

Just as gaining control of publishing had been crucial for women novelists in the 1870s, Carter was especially sustained in the 1970s by the two most visionary feminist publishers of the century, Liz Calder and Carmen Callil. Now the head of her own house, Bloomsbury, Calder was working as an editor for Victor Gollancz when she commissioned the book that became *The Bloody Chamber*. In

[10] "Notes from the Front Line," p. 37.

[11] *Angela Carter*, p. 32. Doris Lessing had a similar reaction to Elizabeth Smart and other hand-wringing women writers of Soho bohemia in the 1960s: "Elizabeth Smart came to have lunch with me. She drank and wept and wept and drank from about midday to seven at night and was savagely witty about her life and the lives of women. I would not describe her as an advertisement for the *joie de vivre* of Soho." Doris Lessing, *Under My Skin*, London: Flamingo, 1995, p. 410.

[12] John Haffenden, "Angela Carter," in *Novelists in Interview*, London: Methuen, 1985, pp. 93-94.

1977, Callil, a young Australian feminist who had come to London to work in publishing, invited Carter to join the advisory board of a new press, Virago, which would become "*the* classic feminist success story."[13]

Carter's first feminist novel was *The Passion of New Eve* (1977), a fierce dystopian allegory of gender rebirth which she conceived as "a feminist tract about the social creation of femininity."[14] It has echoes of the French decadent writer Rachilde's *Monsieur Venus*, Villiers de L'Isle Adam's *L'Eve Future* and of the American Thomas Pynchon's *Crying of Lot 49*. Lorna Sage, who profiled Carter in the *New Review*, astutely noted that she was parodying and subverting popular genres of fiction in the interests of a meta-fictional project: "She has taken over the sub-genres (romance, spies, porn, crime, gothic, science fiction) and tuned their grubby stereotypes into sophisticated mythology."[15] The novel was influenced as well by Barthes, and his essay in *Mythologies* (1972) on Greta Garbo, who appears in the novel disguised as the transvestite love goddess, Tristessa St. Ange.

But 1979, the year Carter published *The Sadeian Woman* and *The Bloody Chamber* and Margaret Thatcher became Prime Minister, was the historical turning point. *The Sadeian Woman: An Exercise in Cultural History* was a truly shocking and avant-garde work for its moment. In a combination of scholarly exegesis, postmodernist theorizing, and analysis of popular culture, Carter defended pornography as an aesthetic genre and made the case for Sade as a prophet of female sexual emancipation. Anticipating the rise of French feminism, the book draws on the work of Barthes, Foucault, Bataille, Breton, and Lacan, and, most significantly, on Simone de Beauvoir's "Must We Burn Sade?" Carter also discusses the iconography of the

[13] Maureen Freely, "Sugar and Spite," *The Observer*, 13 June 1998, p. 4.
[14] "Notes from the Front Line," p. 38.
[15] "The Savage Sideshow."

blonde sex goddess from Garbo to Monroe. In her argument, Sade was one of the first philosophers to separate sex from reproduction, and thus to imagine woman's equality of sexual desire. In her "polemical Preface" to the book, Carter defined a writer she calls "the moral pornographer." Such a writer would be "an artist who uses pornographic material as part of the acceptance of the logic of a world of absolute sexual license for all the genders, and projects a model of the way such a world might work. A moral pornographer might use pornography as a critique of current relations between the sexes."[16]

When it appeared, the book startled and offended feminist readers who regarded pornography as the theory, and rape as the practice. Nicole Ward Jouve recalls on her first reading of the section on Sade's Eugenie that she was outraged: "Carter talks about de Sade's creativity in thus allowing a daughter to be indulged in her most aggressive drives against the censoring mother. Liberating. . . . Again that fucking business of fantasy and reality, I thought. All very well for that bitch to indulge herself."[17] It took another decade of French feminist theory before Jouve was able to accept Carter's position, and see her as a woman writer who actually killed the chaste monitory specter of Virginia Woolf's *Angel in the House*, by giving full play to a female sexuality that was polymorphous rather than androgynous. *The Bloody Chamber*, she recalls, was "the first Carter book I actually enjoyed. . . . I recognised a canny reader of Colette."[18]

Colette was only one of a number of unusual literary

[16] Angela Carter, *The Sadeian Woman: An Exercise in Cultural History*, London: Virago, 1979, p. 19.

[17] Nicole Ward Jouve, "Mother Is a Figure of Speech," in *Flesh and the Mirror*, ed. Lorna Sage, London: Virago, 1994, p. 140. See also Sally Keenan, "Angela Carter's *The Sadeian Woman:* Feminism as Treason," in *The Infernal Desires of Angela Carter*, ed. Joseph Bristow and Trev Lynn Broughton, New York and London: Routledge, 1997, pp. 132–48.

[18] "Mother is a Figure of Speech," pp. 161 and 144.

influences on Carter's fiction. As Margaret Atwood noted, *The Bloody Chamber* "may be read as a 'writing against' de Sade, a talking-back to him, and, above all, as an exploration of the possibilities for the kind of synthesis de Sade himself could never find because he wasn't even looking for it."[19] The stories rework traditional fairy tales to suggest both the violent and erotic subtexts of female desire and the subversive potential of the female imagination. In a postmodern reimagining of the red room of *Jane Eyre*, the gory gothic chamber in which Bluebeard pleasures and butchers his wives is also a metaphor of the womb, the bloody center of female sexuality and reproduction. Female mastery of the chamber's myths is empowering, and women's creativity comes out of cruelty and lust, as well as tenderness.

Indeed, Carter was not only experimenting with an avant-garde literary style, but also reflecting the classic female tradition of the Gothic back to *Jane Eyre*. In an introduction to an edition of *Jane Eyre* for Virago in 1990, Carter emphasized Jane Eyre's toughmindedness and independence, rewriting Brontë in order to make her an appropriate precursor for Carter herself. First of all, she emphasized Brontë's use of telepathic communication, "an element so pronounced that it gives the novel a good deal in common . . . with certain enormously influential, sub-literary texts in which nineteenth-century England discussed in images those aspects of unprecedented experience for which words could not, yet, be found." She also pointed out that *Jane Eyre* "fuses elements of two ancient fairytales, *Bluebeard* . . . and *Beauty and the Beast*." But Carter stressed Jane Eyre's modernity: "If Jane Eyre arrives, like Bluebeard's wife or Beauty, at an old, dark house, whose ugly fanciful master nourishes a fatal secret, she arrives there not as a result of marriage or

---

[19] Margaret Atwood, "Running with the Tigers," in *Flesh and the Mirror*, p. 120.

magic, but as the result of an advertisement she herself had placed in a newspaper. She has come to earn her own living, and the fairytale heroine, as she travels to the abode of secrets and the place of initiation, is specifically the product of history. 'Let the worst come to the worst,' she ponders, 'I can advertise again.'" To Carter, Jane Eyre "is only pretending to be a heroine of romance or fairy tale. . . . [S]he is not a romance figure at all, but a precursor of the rootless urban intelligentsia."

In Carter's re-reading, *Jane Eyre* is primarily about Charlotte Brontë's "unfulfilled desire," a sexual longing that has to be tamed in order to conform to Victorian realities. Rochester, whose name "irresistibly recalls that of the great libertine poet of the Restoration, the Earl of Rochester," is "libido personified." But in the fire that destroys Thornfield he is tamed; "after that, he ceases to be a cad and becomes . . . something else. A husband. A father. He loses the shaggy grandeur with which unfulfilled desire has endowed him."[20]

All of these elements show up in "The Bloody Chamber," in which the seventeen-year-old heroine marries a libertine Sadeian Marquis and goes to his remote castle. She responds passionately to his perverse sensuality, but defies his commands and unlocks all the doors to find his secret torture room of dead wives. Although the telephone wires have been cut, through telepathic communication, the heroine alerts her mother who comes riding to her rescue. The husband-monster is slain and the heroine marries a gentle piano tuner and lives a retired life with her mother, as tamed as Jane Eyre: "We live a quiet life, the three of us. . . . The castle is now a school for the blind, though I pray that the children who live there are not haunted by any sad ghosts looking for, crying for, the husband who will never return to the bloody chamber,

---

[20] Angela Carter, "Charlotte Brontë: Jane Eyre," in *Expletives Deleted*, London: Vintage, 1992, pp. 162, 163, 168, and 171.

the contents of which are buried or burned, the doors sealed."[21] Even a great-great-granddaughter of Jane Eyre, Carter suggests, cannot live every day in fulfilled desire.

THE 1990S

A few months after Carter's death, John Bayley contrasted Virginia Woolf's elegant modernist privacy with what he saw as Carter's politically correct postmodernist engagement. The difference between them could be spatially symbolized: "A room of one's own or a bloody chamber?"[22] The question offended feminist critics, but it sums up the extreme stereotypes of women's writing— chaste withdrawal into the psyche or militant and erotic feminist polemic. In 1977, I concluded that British women novelists had to resist both the temptation to "sacrifice personal development and freedom as an artist" by limiting themselves to writing about female experience, and the temptation to "sacrifice authenticity and self-exploration" by accepting the dominant culture's definition of important literary subject matter. A room of one's own, I believed, could be both a sanctuary and a prison. If it is an excuse for "feminine secession from the political world . . . it is a tomb." But if a room of one's own is a place to gather strength and conviction to act in the world, it is a place of birth.

The womb is a bloody chamber, but it is a necessary beginning. Younger writers cite Carter's daring variety as their example. In 1997, Michele Roberts praised Carter as a woman writer who "refused to fit into the categories offered to her. . . . [S]he's been a liberating example to

---

[21] Angela Carter, *The Bloody Chamber*, London: Victor Gollancz, 1979.

[22] John Bayley, "Fighting for the Crown," *New York Review of Books*, 23 April 1992, pp. 9–11. See the comments by Elaine Jordan and Hermione Lee in *Flesh and the Mirror*.

those of us who've come just after her."[23] Following Carter's influential work on Sade, women's novels in the
1990s explore the archetypal roles of slasher and victim,
sadist and masochist, male and female, that have increasingly become central obsessions of contemporary culture. For younger writers, including Jenni Diski, Helen
Dunmore, Sarah Dunant, Helen Zahavi, and Maureen
Freely, there is full access to every language, style, and
subject, including pornography, sexual fantasy, and the
boundaries of pleasure and danger. These writers use fictional technique as a shield to enter the subterranean,
freakish, and dangerous spaces of the modern city.

The fairy tale and the fable have provided a form for
women writers from a variety of class and ethnic backgrounds to explore their literary identities. Suniti Nam-
joshi's *Feminist Fables* (1981) is obviously influenced by
Carter, as is Jeanette Wintersons's *Sexing the Cherry* (1989).
In her eighth novel, *Impossible Saints* (1997), Michele Roberts juxtaposes two narratives: the Bildungsroman of Josephine, who leaves her convent to become a writer and
to found a utopian women's literary colony; and the lives
of eleven women saints. Along with linked tales that reflect Carter's writing, and images of female selfhood as
treasure chest, secret chamber, or dream house explored
in feminist literary criticism, Roberts's work also has a
violent Gothic subtext: images of mutilation, dismember-
ment, chopping, wounding, and biting. Her "saints" are
hunger artists, slicing into vegetables as if they were animals: Josephine cooks like Jack the Ripper, stabbing "the
thick violet skins of the aubergines," slashing their
"spongy, cream-colored flesh," packing spices into the
wounds, and stewing the "little corpses" in a pan. In Roberts's novels, women writers are voracious and omnivo-
rous, Balzacian in their creative appetites, but struggling

[23] Michele Roberts, in a publicity booklet for the relaunch of Virago
Modern Classics, summer 1997.

to limit themselves to domestic narrative spaces they have long outgrown, bursting from their female cocoons into monstrous butterflies, shaking out "great wet, dragging wings that were stuck together."

In another reflection of Carter's legacy, women writers have become more direct about using feminist literary criticism itself as part of the subject of their fiction. The heroine of Joan Smith's detective novels, Loretta Lawson, is a feminist academic working on a study of Edith Wharton. A. S. Byatt's Booker-Prize–winning novel *Possession* (1990) is dedicated to her friend Isobel Armstrong, professor of English at Birkbeck College and a distinguished scholar and critic of Victorian women's poetry. An academic herself, Byatt has so thoroughly absorbed feminist critical history of Victorian women's writing that she invents a whole canon of it in a brilliant literary tour de force. Not only does she create a pantheon of Victorian women poets and writers, and compose all their poetry, letters, stories, and journals; she also imagines, reproduces, and satirizes the feminist literary criticism written about them by British, American, and French female academics. *Possession* is explicitly about the battle for ownership of British literature between English and American scholars, traditional and feminist critics; but it is implicitly a statement that Byatt's imaginative possession of her literary heritage makes criticism superfluous, redundant, and absurd. When fiction so anticipates and exceeds a particular critical fashion, we have come to the end of an era.

Fay Weldon's *Big Women* (1998) is explicitly about the end of that era. From *Down Among the Women* (1971) on, Weldon has frequently used a group of women friends as choral heroines who reflect the issues and concerns of their historical moment. The "Big Women" are feminists who get together to start a publishing house called Medusa: "A small, vivid group of wild livers, freethinkers, lusters after life, sex and experience, who in the last decades of the century turned the world inside out and up-side down."[24] In a mixture of realism and caricature, Weldon traces the rise of Medusa to its moment of apo-theosis and assimilation, merged into another company: "Medusa's hair will in the end get washed and shorn; there's no help in it. It falls now in a silky cloud, no longer in a wreath of twisting snakes. How pretty Medusa looks, how unravaged her face . . . Medusa turns no one to stone; her power is gone; she is thoroughly approved of, upsets nobody and could be any gender at all."[25]

Weldon declares that she "knew almost nothing about Virago." She wanted to write a novel about feminism, and the history of Virago "more or less coincided with the rise and fall of feminism as a special case." But readers, reviewers, and the founders of Virago itself all noticed the parallels to the breakup of the original Virago in 1996, when it was sold to Little Brown for 1.3 million pounds. But in contrast to Weldon's unhappy ending, the Virago imprint continues to flourish and expand in its new home. Former Virago director Harriet Spicer says "I know it sounds weird but it's as if Virago always had a life of her own. As if she had decided the time had come and made the choice."[26]

Writing about the evolution of women novelists, I now understand, feminist literary critics were also writing about ourselves, and about our own relationship to the institutions of criticism. Like women novelists, women critics too have demanded and received acceptance in every genre and field. And we can now understand that the history of women's writing will never be finished. Its narratives will continue to be reimagined, rewritten, and revised in ever-expanding contexts. In her superb biogra-phy of Virginia Woolf, Hermione Lee concludes that no

[24] Fay Weldon, *Big Women*, London: Harper Collins, 1998, p. 1.
[25] Ibid., p. 345.
[26] "Sugar and Spite."

critic can have the last word on Woolf: "Virginia Woolf's story is reformulated by each generation. She takes on the shape of difficult modernist preoccupied with questions of form, or comedian of manners, or neurotic highbrow aesthete, or inventive feminist, or pernicious snob, or Marxist feminist, or historian of women's lives, or victim of abuse, or lesbian heroine, or cultural analyst, depending on who is reading her, and when, and in what context. In the quarter-century since Bell's biography, her status has grown beyond anything that even she, with her strong sense of her own achievements, might have imagined. And the debates she arouses—over madness, over modernism, over marriage—cannot be concluded, and will go on being argued long after this book is published."[27]

So I do not think that success has spoiled feminist criticism, or that moving into the world will tame the female literary imagination. In her great manifesto "The Laugh of the Medusa," Hélène Cixous says that it's only superstition that has made the Medusa—the woman intellectual, writer, or critic—into a mythical monster who turns men to stone. "If you look straight at her," writes Cixous, "you see that she's beautiful and she's laughing." Feminist scholars and critics have given women's fiction a critical room of its own in the house of literary history. Now we are free to come and go as we please, not in sorrow but in laughter.

[27] Hermione Lee, *Virginia Woolf*, London: Vintage, 1997, p. 769.

Biographical Appendix

THE 213 women writers and activists in this list are the most prominent literary women born in England after 1800; but there are many more who published novels for whom no biographical information is available. The data here were compiled from manuscript sources and library catalogues in England and the United States, from biographies and memoirs, and from the following major printed sources: *Dictionary of National Biography*; Frances Hays, *Women of the Day* (London: Chatto & Windus, 1885); Victor Plarr, *Men and Women of the Time* (15th ed., London: Routledge, 1899); Frederick Boase, *Modern English Biography* (6 vols., Netherton, Truro, 1892–1921, rpt. Frank Cass, 1965); Stanley Kunitz and Howard Haycraft, *British Authors of the Nineteenth Century* (New York: H. W. Wilson, 1936); Kunitz and Haycraft, *Twentieth Century Authors: A Biographical Dictionary* (New York: H. W. Wilson, 1950); and James Vinson, *Contemporary Novelists* (London and New York: St. Martin's, 1972).

The details provided are those most useful for sociological analysis. A complete listing includes the following information: pseudonym (s), birth and death dates, profession (s), place of birth, father's occupation, birth order and number and sex of siblings, religion, education, health, marital status, number of children, and date and title of first book-length publication. In some cases I have also listed travel, political and professional activities, and titles of well-known books.

In order to emphasize the changes from one generation to the next, and to show how women writers shared career orientations with other professional women of their generation, the list is organized chronologically by dates of birth. Readers wishing to locate information on a particular woman writer can consult the alphabetical listing in the index.

CATHERINE CROWE (1800–1876): Novelist. Born in Kent, née Stevens, educated at home, married an army officer in 1822, had one child. Interested in education reform, women's rights, and phrenology. Went mad in 1859. First novel, *Adventures of Susan Hopley* (1841). Also known for *The Story of Lily Dawson* (1847).

ANNA MARIA HALL (1800–1881): Novelist, journalist. Born in Dublin, née Fielding, married journalist S. C. Hall in 1824, no children. Interested in Temperance, women's rights, and needy governesses; was anti-suffrage. First book, *Sketches of Irish Character* (1829). Also conducted *Sharpe's London Magazine* from 1845, and *St. James's Magazine*, 1861.

CATHERINE SINCLAIR (1800–1864): Novelist. Born in Edinburgh, fourth daughter of a baronet. Church of England. Remained single. First novel, *Modern Accomplishments* (1836). Best known for *Holiday House* (1839), a children's novel.

CAROLINE CLIVE (1801–1873): Novelist. Born in London, second daughter of an M. P. Church of England, educated at home, married clergyman Archer Clive, had two children. Invalid. First book, *IX Poems by V.* (1840). Best known for *Paul Ferroll* (1855).

LAETITIA ELIZABETH LANDON (1802–1838): Poet, novelist. Born in Chelsea, oldest daughter of a businessman. Educated at school, married governor of the Gold Coast in 1838. First novel, *Duty and Inclination* (1838). Died under mysterious circumstances.

HARRIET MARTINEAU (1802–1876): Writer, journalist, novelist. Born in Norwich, sixth of eight children of a woolen merchant, did needlework to support family. Involved in Unitarian Movement, educated at home and school, remained single. Deaf; had no sense of smell or taste. First book, *Traditions of Palentine* (1830). Also known for *Deerbrook* (1839) and the nonfictional *Society in America* (1837).

Contributed to the *Edinburgh Review* and wrote over sixteen hundred articles for the *Daily News* (1851–1866).

SARA COLERIDGE (1802–1852): Poet and literary worker. Born in Keswick, daughter of Samuel Coleridge. Educated by Southey, married a lawyer 1829, had one son. Best known for *Autobiography* (1873).

EMMA CAROLINE WOOD, LADY WOOD (1802–1879): Novelist. Pseudonym, "C. Sylvester." First novel, *Rosewarn* (1866).

HARRIETT MOZLEY (1803–1852): Children's book writer. Eldest sister of J. H. Newman, sister-in-law of Anne Mozley. Married Rev. Thomas Mozley, a clergyman at Wiltshire and later a journalist for the *Times*, had one daughter. Wrote *The Fairy Bower* (1841) and *The Lost Brooch* (1841).

ROSINA, LADY BULWER-LYTTON (1804–1882): Novelist. Born in Ballywine, County Limerick. Married novelist Edward Bulwer-Lytton in 1827, separated in 1836. First novel, *Cheveley; or the Man of Honour* (1839).

SARAH FLOWER ADAMS (1805–1848): Poet and hymn writer. Born in Essex, daughter of a political journalist. Unitarian. Married an inventor at age 29, no children. Best known for "Nearer My God to Thee."

JULIA S. H. PARDOE (1806–1862): Poet, historian, novelist. Born in Yorkshire, daughter of an army officer. Precocious writer, published poems at age 14. Traveled to Portugal and Turkey. Remained single, received Civil List Pension in 1860. First novel, *The Romance of the Harem* (1832).

LADY EMMELINE STUART-WORTLEY (1806–1855): Poet, travel writer. Daughter of the Duke of Rutland. Married captain of Dragoons, widowed in 1844, three children. Edited *Keepsake* in 1837 and 1840. First book, *Poems* (1833).

GEORGIANA, LADY CHATTERTON (1806–1876); Novelist. Born in London, only child of a clergyman. Privately educated, married at age 17, later remarried. Converted to Catholicism in 1875. First novel, *Aunt Dorothy's Tale* (1837).

ELIZABETH BARRETT BROWNING (1806–1861): Poet. Born in Ledbury, oldest of twelve children of a businessman. Educated at home by tutors. Invalid. Married Robert Browning in 1846, had one son. First book, *An Essay on Mind* (privately printed, 1826). Best known for *Sonnets from the Portuguese* (1850) and *Aurora Leigh* (1857).

ANNE MANNING (1807–1879): Novelist. Born in Chelsea, oldest of five children of an insurance broker. Unitarian. Educated at home, remained single. Invalid. First novel, *Village Belles* (1833). Best known for *The Maiden and Married Life of Mary Powell, Afterwards Mrs. Milton* (1849).

JEMIMA, BARONESS VON TAUTPHOEUS (1807–1893): Novelist. Born in Donegal, née Montgomery, daughter of a landowner. Educated at home, married in 1838, lived in Germany. Husband and son died in 1885. First novel, *The Initials* (1850).

CAROLINE NORTON (1808–1877): Novelist, pamphleteer. Second daughter of an aristocrat, granddaughter of playwright Sheridan. Married to George Norton in 1827, divorced in 1836, remarried in 1877. Interested in divorce and child custody. First novel, *The Wife and Woman's Reward* (1835). Also known for *Lost and Saved* (1863) and pamphlets on legal status of women.

ANNE MOZLEY (1809–1891): Journalist. Only daughter (and middle child between two brothers) of a bookseller. Church of England. Privately educated, remained single. First book, *Church Poetry* (1843).

MARY COWDEN CLARKE (1809–1898): Novelist, journalist. Born in London, daughter of an organist. Married William Cowden Clarke in 1828. First novel, *The Iron Cousin* (1854). Best known for *The Girlhood of Shakespeare's Heroines* (1850–1852).

MARGARET GATTY (1809–1873): Novelist, children's book writer. Born in Essex, née Scott, youngest daughter of clergyman. Church of England. Educated at home, married a clergyman in 1839, mother of novelist J. Ewing. First book, 1839. Founded and contributed to *Aunt Judy's Magazine for Children* from May 1866.

ELIZABETH GASKELL (1810–1865): Novelist. Born in Chelsea, daughter of a Unitarian minister. Educated at home and school by an aunt in Cheshire. Married a Manchester clergyman in 1832, had four children. Interested in humanitarian reform and Unitarianism. First novel, *Mary Barton* (1848), others include *North and South* and *Ruth*.

SARAH ELLIS (1810–1872): Novelist, essayist. Born in Hull, née Stickney, daughter of a farmer. Quaker, later became a Congregationalist. Married missionary William Ellis in 1837, no children. Interested in Temperance, female education, and Christian missionaries; ran a girls' school, Rawdon House. First novel, *Pictures of Private Life* (3 sers. 1833–1837). Best known for *The Women of England* (1839) and its sequels *The Wives of England, The Daughters of England, The Mothers of England*.

JANE CROSS SIMPSON (1811–1886): Poet, religious writer. Pseudonym, "Gertrude." Born in Glasgow, daughter of an advocate. Presbyterian. Married in 1837, had one child. First book, *April Hours* (1838).

LADY GEORGIANA FULLERTON (1812–1885): Novelist. Born in Staffordshire, youngest child of Lord Granville Leveson-Gower; lived with her father in Paris. Educated at home, married, had one child. Anglican, converted to Catholicism 1846. Interested in convents and philanthropy. First novel, *Ellen Middleton* (1844).

GERALDINE JEWSBURY (1812–1880): Novelist, journalist. Born in Measham (Midlands), moved to Manchester at age 6; fourth of six children of a cotton manufacturer. Educated at school, remained single. First novel, *Zoë* (1845).

JULIA CECILIA [DEWINTON] STRETTON (1812–1878): Novelist. Born in Durham, second of fifteen children of a clergyman, acted as head of family. Church of England. Educated at home, married at age 19, remarried in 1858, had three children. First novel, *Woman's Devotion* (1855).

ANNA SWANWICK (1813–1897): Translator. Born in Liverpool, educated at home and in Berlin. Unitarian. Remained single. Member of Council in Queen's and Bedford Colleges, London. Assisted in foundation of Girton College, Cambridge.

EMMA ROBINSON (1814–1890): Novelist. Born in London, daughter of a bookseller. Remained single. Went mad. First novel, *Whitefriars; or, The Court of Charles II* (1844).

MRS. HENRY WOOD [ELLEN PRICE] (1814–1887): Novelist. Born in Worcester, daughter of a glove manufacturer. Educated at home, married in 1836, had a large family. Invalid. First novel, *Danesbury House* (1860). Best known for *East Lynne* (1861).

ELIZABETH MISSING SEWELL (1815–1906): Novelist, educator. Born on Isle of Wight, third daughter in family of twelve of a solicitor who died in debt. Educated at school, worked as governess, remained single, member of Oxford Movement. First novel, *Amy Herbert* (1844).

GRACE AGUILAR (1816–1847): Novelist. Born in Hackney, eldest child of a merchant. Educated at home because of frail health. Jewish. Remained single, traveled widely. First novel, *Home Influence* (1847). Also known for *The Mother's Recompense* (1851) and *Women's Friendship* (1851).

FRANCES BROWNE (1816–1879): Children's book writer. Born in Donegal, seventh of twelve children of a postmaster. Blind from childhood. Self-educated, left home at age 21 to write; went first to Edinburgh, then London. Belonged to the Religious Tract Society. Remained single. First novel, *The Ericksons* (1852).

CHARLOTTE BRONTË (1816–1855): Novelist. Born in Yorkshire, third daughter of a clergyman. Church of England.

341

Educated at school and in Brussels, worked as governess, married a clergyman, no children. First novel, *Jane Eyre* (1847).

EMILY BRONTË (1818–1848): Novelist. Born in Yorkshire, fourth daughter of a clergyman. Church of England. Educated at school and in Brussels, remained single. First novel, *Wuthering Heights* (1847).

ELIZA COOK (1818–1889): Poet. Born in London, youngest of eleven children of a brazier. Self-educated, remained single. Invalid. First book, *Lays of a Wild Harp* (1835). Edited *E. C.'s Journal*, 1849–1854.

GEORGE ELIOT [MARY ANN EVANS CROSS] (1819–1880): Novelist, translator, editor. Born in Warwickshire. Youngest daughter of an estate agent. Church of England; became an agnostic in 1842. Educated at school. Went to Germany with George Henry Lewes in 1854; lived with him in England until his death in 1878. Married J. W. Cross 1880. No children. First book, *Scenes of Clerical Life* (1858).

MARIA CHARLESWORTH (1819–1880): Children's book writer. Born in Blakenham Parva near Ipswich, daughter of a clergyman, had one brother. Church of England. Self-educated, remained single. Best known for *Ministering Children* (1854).

ANNE BRONTË (1820–1849): Novelist. Born in Yorkshire, youngest sister of Charlotte and Emily Brontë, daughter of a clergyman. Church of England. Educated at school, remained single. First novel, *Agnes Grey* (1847).

FLORENCE NIGHTINGALE (1829–1910): Nurse. Born in Florence, Italy, second daughter of a wealthy country gentleman. Church of England, later interested in mysticism. Educated privately in England and on the continent, remained single. First publication, *The Institution of Kaiserwerth on the Rhine for the Practical training of Deaconesses* (1851). Best known for *Notes on Nursing* (1860).

342

JEAN INGELOW (1820–1897): Poet, essayist. Born in Boston, Lincolnshire, oldest daughter of a banker, had one brother. Church of England. Remained single. Opposed Women's Suffrage. First book, *A Rhyming Chronicle* (1850).

ANNA SEWELL (1820–1878): Children's book writer. Born at Yarmouth, father poor. Mother was a children's book writer, famous for the ballad "Mother's Last Words." Quaker. Remained single, traveled in Germany and Spain. Invalid. Wrote the children's classic *Black Beauty* (1877).

MENELLA BUTE SMEDLEY (1820–1877): Novelist, poet. First book, *The Maiden Aunt* (1849), published anonymously.

ISABELLA VARLEY LINNAEUS BANKS (1821–1897): Novelist. Born in Manchester, daughter of a chemist. Church of England. Self-educated, married editor George Linnaeus Banks in 1846. Supported women's rights. First novel, *God's Providence House* (1865). Best known for *The Manchester Man* (1875).

DORA GREENWELL (1821–1882): Poet. Born in Durham, daughter of a country squire, had four brothers. Remained single. Invalid. Interested in prison-visiting, match-workers, Fenian group, anti-vivisection, suffrage, CD campaigns.

FRANCES POWER COBBE (1822–1904): Philanthropist and writer. Only daughter of Charles Cobbe of County Dublin. Interested in ragged schools, anti-vivisection, women's employment. Edited the *Zoophilist*.

ELIZABETH F. S. HARRIS (1822–1852): Religious novelist. Published *From Oxford to Rome* (1847).

ELIZABETH LYNN LINTON (1822–1898): Novelist, essayist. Born in Keswick, Cumberland, youngest of twelve children of a clergyman. Was 5 months old when her mother died. Church of England. Self-educated, learned French, German, and Italian. Married engraver W. J. Linton in 1858, separated in 1867. First novel, *Azeth the Egyptian* (1846). Best known for *The Girl of the Period* (1883).

CHARLOTTE M. YONGE (1823–1901): Domestic novelist. Born in Winchester, oldest of two children of a rich clergyman. Church of England [Oxford]. Educated at home, remained single. First novel, *Abbey Church* (1844). Best known for *The Heir of Redclyffe* (1853) and *The Daisy Chain* (1856). Edited and contributed to three journals: *Monthly Packet*, 1851–1894; *Monthly Paper of Sunday Teaching*, 1860–1875; and *Mothers in Council*, 1890–1900.

JULIA KAVANAGH (1824–1877): Novelist. Born in Thurles, Ireland, only child of M. P. Kavanagh, writer and linguist. Educated at home, cared for invalid mother, remained single. Traveled to Paris. First novel, *Madeleine* (1848).

LOUISA SHORE (1824–1895): Poet. Born in Bedfordshire, daughter of a clergyman. Church of England. Remained single, became a militant feminist. First book, *War Lyrics* (1855).

KATHERINE MACQUOID (1824–1917): Novelist. Born in London, née Gadsden, married a Yorkshire artist in 1851. First novel, *A Bad Beginning* (1862), published anonymously.

CHARLOTTE MARIA TUCKER (1825–1893): Children's religious book writer. Pseudonym, "A.L.O.E." ("A Lady of England"). Daughter of the chairman of the East India Company, had four sisters, five brothers. Church of England. Self-educated, remained single, became a missionary. First book, *The Claremont Tales* (1854). Over 140 published works.

[EMILIA] JESSIE BOUCHERETT (1825–1905): Feminist, editor. Born in Lincolnshire. Organized the Society for Promoting the Employment of Women, 1859. Founded and edited the *Englishwoman's Review*, 1866–1871.

ANNIE FRENCH HECTOR (1825–1902): Journalist, novelist. Pseudonym, "Mrs. Alexander." Born in Dublin, only child of a solicitor. Educated at home by governesses, married in 1858, had four children. Published 41 novels after the death of her husband in 1875. First novel, *Kate Vernon* (1854).

ANNIE KEARY (1825–1879): Children's novelist. Born in Yorkshire, daughter of a clergyman. Church of England. Remained single, traveled in Egypt in 1858. Collaborated with her sister, Eliza. First book, *The Heroes of Asgard* (1857).

ADELAIDE PROCTER (1825–1864): Poet. Born in London, daughter of the poet "Barry Cornwall." Converted to Catholicism. Educated at home, remained single. Interested in women's employment, also worked for women's refuges. Edited *Victoria Regia* (1861), an anthology of verse and prose.

DINAH MARIA MULOCK CRAIK (1826–1887): Novelist. Born in Stoke-on-Trent, daughter of a dissenting preacher, had two brothers. Church of England. Educated at school, married George Lillie Craik, editor for Macmillan, in 1864, had one adopted daughter. First novel, *The Ogilvies* (1849). Best known for *John Halifax, Gentleman* (1857) and *The Little Lame Prince* (1875).

BARBARA LEIGH SMITH, later BODICHON (1827–1891): Feminist activist. Born in Norwich, daughter of a radical M. P. Left motherless at an early age. Given yearly income of £300 by her father; married Dr. Eugène Bodichon in 1857. Campaigned for Married Women's Property Act. Author of *Brief Summary in Plain Language of the Most Important Laws Concerning Women* (1855), founder of the *Englishwoman's Journal* (1858). Endowed Girton College, Cambridge, 1891.

EMILY JANE [DAVIS] PFEIFFER (1827–1890): Poet and essayist. Married. Wrote *Poems and Stories* (1857) and *Women and Work* (1887).

LYDIA BECKER (1827–1890): Women's rights leader. Born in Manchester. Secretary of the Manchester Women's Suffrage Society, 1867; member of the Manchester School Board. Edited *Women's Suffrage Journal* 1870–1890.

ELIZABETH RUNDLE CHARLES (1828–1896): Novelist, poet. First novel, *Chronicles of the Schönberg-Cotta Family* (1864).

HARRIET PARR (1828–1900): Novelist. Pseudonym, "Holme Lee." Born in York, daughter of traveler dealing in silks and satins, remained single. First novel, *Maude Talbot* (1854). Best known for *Sylvan Holt's Daughter* (1858).

JOSEPHINE BUTLER (1828–1906): Feminist, leader of the campaign to repeal the Contagious Diseases Acts. Born Milfield, née Grey, seventh child of abolitionist and radical parents. Married in 1852 to George Butler, a professor who became principal of Liverpool College; had three children (the only daughter was killed in an accident at age 5). Tireless activist in rescue work, women's education, and social reform.

MARGARET OLIPHANT (1828–1897): Novelist, journalist. Born in Scotland, youngest of three children of a customs house clerk. Presbyterian. Educated at home, married 1852, had three children. First novel, *Passages in the Life of Mrs. Margaret Maitland* (1849).

EMMA MARSHALL (1830–1899): Novelist. Born in Norwich, youngest of seven children of a banker. Church of England. Educated at school, married a bank manager in 1854, had eight children. Promoted higher education for women. First novel, *The Happy Days at Fernbank* (1861).

ELIZABETH SHEPPARD (1830–1862): Novelist. Born in Kent, daughter of a clergyman. Church of England. Educated at school, remained single. First novel, *Charles Auchester* (1853).

CHARLOTTE BARNARD (1830–1869): Poet. Pseudonym, "Claribel." Privately educated, married at age 24. Wrote ballads.

ELIZA BRIGHTWEN (1830–1906): Naturalist. Born in Scotland, educated by her uncle Alexander Elder of Smith &

Elder. Presbyterian. Married in 1855, widowed in 1883, no children. First book, 1890.

CHRISTINA ROSSETTI (1830–1894): Poet. Born in London, daughter of a refugee teacher; brother, Dante Gabriel. High Church. Educated at home, remained single. Invalid. First book (poems), 1862.

FRANCES HOEY [MRS. CASHEL HOEY] (1830–1908): Journalist, novelist. Born in Dublin, first of eight children of a clerk. Self-educated, married in 1846, had two daughters. Began journalism career in 1853. Husband died in 1855. She went to London, remarried in 1858 to an Irish journalist, and was converted to Catholicism. Received Civil List pension £50 in 1892. Published 11 novels. First book, *House of Cards* (1868).

EMILY DAVIES (1830–1921): Pioneer in women's education. Daughter of Rector of Gateshead. Helped found Girton College, Cambridge. Published *Higher Education of Women* (1866).

ISA CRAIG (1831–1903): Published verse and fiction. Born in Edinburgh, daughter of a hosier. Married John Knox, iron merchant. Secretary of the National Association for the Promotion of Social Science, 1857. Won first prize for a Competition Ode recited at the Burns Centenary Festival, 1858. Books included *Poems* (1857).

ISABELLA BIRD BISHOP (1831–1904): Wrote travel books, founded hospitals. Born in Yorkshire, daughter of a clergyman. Church of England. Self-educated, married in 1880, widowed in 1885. First book written in the 1880s.

GEORGIANA CRAIK (1831–?): Novelist. Born in London, youngest child of a professor. First novel, *Riverston* (1857).

AMELIA B. EDWARDS (1831–1892): Novelist. Born in London, only child of an army officer. Church of England. Educated at school, received several honorary degrees, remained single. An Egyptologist, interested in travel. First novel, 1855.

347

MRS. J. H. RIDDELL [CHARLOTTE COWAN] (1832–1906): Sensation novelist. Pseudonyms, "R. V. M. Sparling," "Rainey Hawthorne," "Charlotte," and "F. G. Trafford." Born in Ireland, youngest daughter of the High Sheriff. Self-educated, married after her mother's death. First novel, *Zuriels' Grandchild* (1856).

SARAH SMITH (1832–1911): Children's religious novelist. Pseudonym, "Hesba Stretton" ("Hesba" comes from the initial letters of her siblings' names). Born in Shropshire, fourth of eight children of a bookseller. Church of England. Educated at school and by reading in her father's shop, remained single. Worked with prostitutes, interested in London S.P.C.C. First publication appeared in *Household Words*, 1859, received £5 from Dickens. Best known for *Jessica's First Prayer* (1867), which sold $1\frac{1}{2}$ million copies.

MARY ANNE HEARNE (1834–1909): Hymn writer, school teacher. Pseudonym, "Marianne Farningham." Born in Kent, daughter of a postmaster. Remained single. First book, *Lays and Lyrics of the Blessed Life* (1860).

ELIZABETH C. WOLSTENHOLME-ELMY (1834–1918): Militant suffragette and writer. Born in Eccles, daughter of a Methodist minister. First secretary of the Manchester National Society for Women's Suffrage. After her marriage to Ben Elmy known as Mrs. Wolstenholme-Elmy. As "Ellis Ethelmer," wrote *The Human Flower* (1895) and *Woman Free* (1893).

EMILY FAITHFULL (1835–1895): Novelist, publisher, essayist, women's rights activist. Born at Headley Rectory, Surrey, daughter of a clergyman. Remained single. Founded Victoria Press, where women did all the printing work. First novel, *Change Upon Change* (1868).

ISABELLA BEETON (1836–1865): Editor, cookbook writer. Brought up in Epsom, oldest of 20 children of two marriages; stepfather a printer. Married at twenty to journalist and editor Samuel Beeton; died of puerperal fever giving birth to her fourth child. Best known for editing the *Englishwoman's Domestic Magazine* and for *The Book of Household Management* (1861).

MATILDA BETHAM-EDWARDS (1836–1919): Novelist. Born in Westerfield, Suffolk, fourth daughter of a farmer, Christian Freethinker. Educated at school, traveled in rural France, remained single. Interested in anti-vivisection and cremation. First novel, 1857.

ANNE ADALIZA PUDDICOME (1836–1915): Novelist. Pseudonym, "Allen Raine." Born in Wales, oldest of four children of a solicitor. Educated at school, married a banker in 1872, no children. First book, *A Welsh Singer* (1897).

ELIZABETH GARRETT ANDERSON (1836–1917): Doctor. Born in Aldeburgh, daughter of Newson Garrett and sister of Millicent Garrett Fawcett. Qualified to practise medicine through the Society of Apothecaries in 1865, married J. G. S. Anderson in 1871.

MARY ELIZABETH BRADDON [MAXWELL] (1837–1915): Sensation novelist. Born in London, youngest daughter of a solicitor. Church of England. Privately educated, married in 1874, had five children. First novel 1854. Best known for *Lady Audley's Secret* (1862). Edited *Belgravia* from 1866, the *Belgravia Annual* from 1867, and *Mistletoe Bough* from 1878.

ANNE ISABELLA THACKERAY [LADY RITCHIE] (1837–1919): Novelist. Born in London, oldest daughter of William Thackeray. Married Richmond Ritchie in 1872, had one daughter. First novel, *The Story of Elizabeth* (1863).

LUCY BAXTER (1837–1902): Art critic. Pseudonym, "Leader Scott." Born in Dorchester, third daughter of poet William Barnes. Married in 1867, had three children. Published *The Cathedral Builders* (1899).

349

MARY F. CHAPMAN (1838–1884): Novelist. Pseudonyms, "Francis Meredith" and "J. Calder Ayrton." Born in Dublin. Educated at school. First novel, *Mary Bertrand* (1860).

OCTAVIA HILL (1838–1912): Housing reporter, philanthropist. Pioneered slum clearance, also involved in women's education, the National Trust, and the Poor Laws.

LADY AUGUSTA NOEL (1838–1902): Novelist. First novel, *Effie's Friends* (1865).

FLORENCE MARRYAT (1838–1899): Sensation novelist. Born in Brighton, youngest of eleven children of novelist Frederic Marryat. Spiritualist. Educated by governesses. Married in 1854, divorced in 1878; married again in 1879, had eight children. Wrote fifty-seven novels. First novel, *Love's Conflict* (1865).

MARIE LOUISE DE LA RAMEE (1839–1908): Sensation novelist. Pseudonym, "Ouida." Born in Bury St. Edmunds, daughter of a French teacher. Self-educated, remained single. First novel, *Held in Bondage* (1863). Best known for *Under Two Flags* (1867) and *Moths* (1880).

[MRS.] MARY LOUISE MOLESWORTH (1839–1921): Children's novelist. Pseudonym, "Ennis Graham." Born in Rotterdam, daughter of a major-general, had one sister. Calvinist. Privately educated, married a major, had five children, later divorced. Published over one hundred books. First novel, *Lover and Husband* (1870).

LADY ANNE BRASSEY (1839–1887): Travel writer. Born in London. Married in 1860 to a statesman, had five children, traveled with her husband. Published *A Voyage in the "Sunbeam"* (1878).

ALICE KING (1839–1894): Novelist. Born in Cutcombe, Somerset, daughter of a clergyman. Church of England. Educated by her mother, remained single. Blind from the age of seven. First novel, *Forest Keep* (1862).

ISABELLA HARWOOD (1840–1888): Novelist, dramatist. Pseudonym, "Ross Neil." Daughter of the editor of the *Saturday Review*. Remained single. First book, 1864.

SOPHIA JEX-BLAKE (1840–1912): Doctor. Daughter of Thomas Jex-Blake, Proctor of Doctors Commons. Founded the London School of Medicine for Women, 1874; gained legal right to practise, 1877.

CAROLINE ASHURST BIGGS (1840–1889): Women's rights activist and journalist. Born in Leicester, daughter of Joseph Biggs. Remained single. Edited the *Englishwoman's Review*, 1870–1889. Wrote *White and Black* (1864).

RHODA BROUGHTON (1840–1920): Novelist. Born in Staffordshire, youngest of four children of a clergyman, niece of the Irish novelist Sheridan LeFanu. Church of England. Educated at home by her father, remained single. As an adult, lived in Oxford. First novel, *Not Wisely But Too Well* (1867).

ROSA NOUCHETTE CAREY (1840–1909): Novelist. Born in London, second youngest of eight children of a shipbroker. Church of England. Self-educated, "delicate" health, remained single. First book, *Nellie's Memories* (1868).

JULIANA HORATIA EWING (1841–1885): Children's book writer. Daughter of Mrs. Gatty, father a clergyman. Married an army officer in 1867. First book, *Melchior's Dream* (1862). Best known for *The Brownies* (1870) and *Six to Sixteen* (1875). Assisted in editing *Aunt Judy's Magazine*, 1874–1876.

MATHILDE BLIND (1841–1896): Poet, biographer. Pseudonym, "Claude Lake." Born in Germany daughter of a banker; stepfather was revolutionary Karl Blind. Educated at home, remained single. Traveled widely. First book, 1867. Wrote biography of George Eliot (1883). Also known for *The Ascent of Man* (1889), on evolution.

351

AGNES MARY CLERKE (1842–1907): Irish scientific writer. Born in County Cork, daughter of a bank manager. Educated at home, remained single. Traveled in Ireland and Italy. First book, *A Popular History of Astronomy* (1885).

MARY MONTGOMERIE SINGLETON, afterwards LADY CURRIE (1843–1905): Novelist and poet. Pseudonym, "Violet Fane." Born in Sussex, daughter of an aristocrat. Church of England. Educated at home, married an Irish landowner in 1864, had four children; remarried to ambassador to Constantinople in 1894. Family disapproved of writing. First book (poems), *From Dawn to Noon* (1872).

SARAH DOUDNEY (1842–?): Children's novelist. Born in Portsmouth, educated at school, remained single. Began to write at early age; published at 18 with Dickens in *Churchman's Family Magazine.* Wrote 36 girl's novels. First novel, *Under Grey Walls* (1871).

MARGARET VELEY (1843–1887): Novelist, poet. Born in Essex, second of four daughters of a solicitor. Church of England. Educated at home and at Queens College, remained single. Began to write at 14. First novel, *"For Percival"* (1878).

ISABELLA FYVIE MAYO (1843–?): Novelist. Pseudonym, "Edward Garrett." Born and educated in London, married John Mayo in 1870 (he died in 1877). Wrote many articles and at least 16 books. First and best-known novel, (1868), *The Occupations of a Retired Life.*

ADA CAMBRIDGE (1844–1926): Novelist. Born in Norfolk, educated at home. Married a clergyman in 1870, had two children, lived in Australia. First novel, *My Guardian* (1878).

EMILY LAWLESS (1845–1913): Poet and novelist. Born in County Kildare, daughter of a baron. Educated at home, remained single. Some travel. First book, *A Chelsea Householder* (1882).

Mrs. Lucy Bethia Walford (1845–1915): Novelist. Born in Scotland, daughter of an author and aristocrat, had two brothers; niece of Catherine Sinclair. Scots Presbyterian. Educated at home, married a magistrate, had seven children. First novel, 1872, published anonymously.

Emily Hickey (1845–1924): Poet. Catholic. First book, *A Sculptor* (1881).

Annie Besant (1847–1933): Radical, feminist, spiritualist. Born in London, née Wood, second of three children of a doctor, who died when she was five. Educated by Ellen Marryat (daughter of Captain Marryat) in London, Bonn, and Paris. Married clergyman Frank Besant in 1867, had two children, separated in 1879. With Charles Bradlaugh circulated *The Fruits of Philosophy* (on birth control); tried for obscenity in 1877. Later became a Fabian (1885), then a theosophist active in the Psychic Society with Madame Blavatsky.

Millicent Fawcett (1847–1929): Constitutional suffragist. Born in Aldeburgh, daughter of Newson Garrett and sister of Elizabeth Garrett Anderson. Married Henry Fawcett, M.P., in 1867. Author of *Political Economy for Beginners*, a life of Queen Victoria, and a history of the Suffrage Movement.

Alice Thompson Meynell (1847–1922): Poet. Born in Barnes, second of two children of a Cambridge graduate and dilettante. Church of England, later converted to Catholicism. Educated at home, married Wilfred Meynell in 1877, had eight children. Traveled in France, Switzerland, and Italy. First book, *Preludes* (1875).

Mary Gleed Tuttiet (1847–1923): Journalist, novelist. Pseudonym, "Maxwell Gray." Born on Isle of Wight. Remained single. First novel, *The Broken Tryst* (1879).

Flora Annie Steel (1847–1929): Novelist, suffragist, member of W.W.S.L. Born in Harrow, sixth of eleven children of a sheriff's clerk. Educated by governess and at school, married an Indian officer, had one child. First book, 1884. Best known for *On the Face of the Waters* (1897).

MARY ELIZABETH HAWKER (1848–1908): Novelist, short story writer. Pseudonym, "Lanoe Falconer." Born in Aberdeenshire, oldest child of landed gentry. Educated at home, remained single. First book, *Mlle Ixe* (1890).

FRANCES HODGSON BURNETT (1849–1924): Children's novelist. Born in Manchester, one of six children of a manufacturer. After widowed, her mother began writing to support the family. Married a doctor in 1873, divorced, remarried in 1897, had two children. Involved in Christian Science, Theosophy, and Spiritualism. First book, 1877. Best known for *Little Lord Fauntleroy* (1886) and *The Secret Garden* (1905).

MRS. MARGARET HUNGERFORD (1850–1897): Novelist. Pseudonym, "The Duchess." Born in County Cork, daughter of a clergyman. Church of England. Educated at school, married twice (second time in 1883), had six children. Published 32 novels, usually anonymously. First novel, *Phyllis* (1877). Best known for *Molly Bawn* (1878).

JESSIE FOTHERGILL (1851–1891): Novelist. Born in Manchester, daughter of a cotton merchant; father died when she was young. Quaker. Educated at home, remained single. First novel, *Healey* (1875).

ELLA D'ARCY (1851–1939): Short story writer, novelist. Acted as assistant editor of *The Yellow Book*. Also known for *Monochromes* (1895) and *Modern Instances* (1898).

ADELINE SERGEANT (1851–1904): Novelist. Born in Derbyshire, second daughter of a Methodist missionary; her mother wrote poetry. Wesleyan, joined Church of England, later became Catholic. Educated at Queen's College, London, remained single. Interested in women's suffrage, member of Fabian Society. Wrote 75 novels. First book, *Poems* (1866).

MRS. [MARY AUGUSTA] HUMPHRY WARD (1851–1920): Novelist. Born in Hobart, Tasmania, oldest of eight children of Thomas Arnold, a teacher with religious problems. Niece of Matthew Arnold. Church of England (Oxford). Educated at boarding schools, married T. Humphry Ward, fellow of Brasenose College, had three children. Anti-Suffrage. First novel, *Miss Bretherton* (1884). Best known for *Robert Elsmere* (1888).

MARY KINGSLEY (1852–1931): Novelist. Used pseudonym, "Lucas Malet" because she did not want to profit by family name. Born in Devonshire, youngest daughter of a clergyman and writer, "muscular" Christian Charles Kingsley. Studied at Slade, married the minister William Harrison in 1876, later converted to Catholicism. First novel, *Mrs. Lorimer* (1882). Best known for *The Wages of Sin* (1891).

HELEN MATHERS [REEVES] (1853–1920): Novelist. Born in Somersetshire, one of twelve children of a gentleman. Church of England. Educated by governess and at school, married a surgeon in 1876, had one son. Deaf. First novel, *Comin' Thro' the Rye* (1875).

OLIVE SCHREINER (1855–1920): Novelist, feminist. Born in Basutoland, South Africa, ninth child of a Wesleyan missionary. Self-educated, married S. C. Cronwright-Schreiner in 1894, had one stillborn child. First novel, *Story of an African Farm* (1883).

[ALICE] MONA CAIRD (c. 1855–1932): Novelist, poet, feminist theoretician. Pseudonym, "G. Noel Hatton." Born on Isle of Wight, daughter of an inventor. Married J. A. Henryson-Caird in 1877. First novel, *Whom Nature Leadeth* (1883). Best known for *The Morality of Marriage and Other Essays on the Status of Women* (1897) and *The Daughters of Danaeus* (1894).

VIOLET PAGET (1856–1935): Novelist, essayist, critic. Pseudonym, "Vernon Lee." Born in Boulogne, only daughter of mother's second marriage, had one half-brother. Educated at school, remained single. First novel, *Ottilie* (1883).

MARGARET LOUISA WOODS (1856–1945): Novelist. Born in Rugby, daughter of G. G. Bradley, dean of Westminster. Married in 1879 to H. G. Woods, president of Trinity College, Oxford. First novel, *A Village Tragedy* (1887).

ADA ELLEN BAYLEY (1857–1903): Novelist. Pseudonym, "Edna Lyall." Born in Brighton, youngest of four children of a barrister. Church of England. Educated at home and school, remained single. First novel, *Won by Waiting* (1879).

LADY FLORENCE DIXIE (1857–1905): Feminist, novelist. Born in London, youngest of six children of Marquess of Queensbury. Church of England. Educated at home, married a baronet in 1875, had two sons. Interested in women's suffrage, Zulus, anti-Fenian. First book, 1880, on travel. Best known for *Gloriana, or the Revolution of 1900* (feminist utopia) (1890).

BEATRICE WEBB (1858–1943): Fabian socialist reformer, English diarist and political writer. Born and brought up in Gloucestershire, she was educated at home. Daughter of an industrialist, she had eight sisters (her only brother died in infancy). Married Sidney Webb in 1892, no children. With him devoted her life to the application of scientific method to social questions. In 1894 the couple published *A History of Trade Unionism*. Published political books and also extracts from her diary called *My Apprenticeship* (1926). Travelled extensively. Helped found London School of Economics and Political Science (1895) and the *New Statesman* (1913).

EDITH NESBIT BLAND (1858–1924): Children's novelist. Born in London, youngest daughter (sixth child) of a chemist. Educated at a convent, married Fabian socialist Herbert Bland in 1880, had four children; remarried in 1917. Received Civil List Pension of £60 in 1915. First novel, *The Story of the Treasure Seekers* (1899). Also known for *The Railway Children* (1906).

MARY CHOLMONDELEY (1859–1925): Novelist. First novel, *The Danvers Jewels* (1889). Best known for *Red Pottage* (1899).

MARY CHAVELITA DUNNE (1860–1945): Story writer and novelist. Pseudonym, "George Egerton." Born in Australia, grew up in Ireland, oldest of six children of an ex-army officer. Catholic. Educated at school, married twice, had one son. First book, *Keynotes* (1893).

MRS. DESMOND HUMPHREYS (1860–1938): Novelist. Pseudonym, "Rita." Born in Scotland, second child of a landowner, had two brothers. Spent childhood in Australia, educated at home and at Broughton and Mathers' School. Married twice. Founded the Writers Club for Women in 1902. Wrote *Sâba Macdonald* on suffrage.

EDITH OENONE SOMERVILLE (c. 1860–1949): Novelist. Born in Corfu, daughter of Lt.-Col. Somerville of County Cork. Remained single. Became president of the Munster Women's Franchise League; master of West Carberry Fox-hounds. Collaborated with her cousin Violet Martin; best known for *The Real Charlotte* (1894).

ELLEN THORNEYCROFT FOWLER (1860–1929): Novelist and poet. Daughter of Viscount Wolverhampton. Married A. L. Felkin in 1903. First book, *Verses Grave and Gay* (1891).

MARY COLERIDGE (1861–1907): Poet, novelist, critic. Born in London, oldest of two daughters of Arthur Coleridge, Clerk of the Assize and great-nephew of Samuel Taylor Coleridge. Taught working women at her home and at Working Women's College. Remained single. First book, *The Seven Sleepers of Ephesus* (1893).

AMY LEVY (1861–1889): Poet. Born in Clapham, daughter of an editor. Jewish. Educated at Brighton School and Newnham, remained single. Committed suicide. First book of poems, 1881.

357

KATHARINE TYNAN (1861–1931): Poet, novelist. Born in Ireland. Educated at Siena Convent, married barrister H. A. Hinkson in 1893, had three children. First book, *Louise de la Vallière* (1885); first novel, *The Handsome Brandons* (1898).

VIOLET MARTIN (1862–1915): Novelist. Pseudonym, "Martin Ross." Born in Galway, youngest daughter of eleven children of a laywer. Protestant. Educated at home and at Alexandra College, Dublin, remained single. Collaborated on books with her cousin Edith Somerville, including *The Real Charlotte* (1894) and *Tales of an Irish R. M.* (1899).

MARY KINGSLEY (1862–1900): Travel writer. Daughter of a physician, had an older brother. Self-educated, remained single.

FRANCES McFALL (1854–1943): Novelist. Pseudonym, "Sarah Grand." Born in Ireland, daughter of an army officer. Church of England. Educated at home and school, married at age 16 (husband died in 1898), had one son. First novel, *Ideala* (1888). Best known for *The Heavenly Twins* (1893).

ELIZABETH ROBINS (1863–1952): Actress, novelist, suffragette. Born in Kentucky, married George Parkes. Came to England as a widow in 1889. Founder of Women Writers Suffrage League. Acted in Ibsen plays. Best known for *The Magnetic North* (1894).

HELEN BANNERMAN (1863–1946): Children's book writer. Born in Edinburgh, daughter of an army chaplain. Married, had four children, lived in India. Best known for *Little Black Sambo*.

MAY SINCLAIR (1863–1946): Novelist. Born in Cheshire, had five brothers. Educated at Cheltenham Ladies College, remained single. Family went bankrupt and lived with her mother in reduced circumstances when parents divorced. Supported herself with reviews and translations, best-known

BIOGRAPHICAL APPENDIX

for her review in 1918 of part of Dorothy Richardson's *Pilgrimage*. Modernist writer, works include *The Three Sisters* (1914), *The Life and Death of Harriet Frean* (1922) and *The History of Anthony Waring* (1927).

ELINOR SUTHERLAND GLYN (1864–1943): Novelist. Born in Jersey, second daughter of a civil engineer, who died when she was four months old. Privately educated; married in 1892 to Clayton Glyn, sportsman and country gentleman, had two daughters. First novel, *The Visits of Elizabeth* (1900). Best known for *Three Weeks* (1907).

MARY MACKAY (1864–1924): Novelist. Pseudonym, "Marie Corelli." Born in Bayswater, youngest child of a lawyer. Spiritualist. Educated at school, remained single. First novel, *A Romance of Two Worlds* (1886).

BEATRICE HARRADEN (1864–1936): Novelist. Born in London, daughter of Samuel Harraden, ward of Mrs. Lynn Linton; remained single. Suffragette, active in W.S.P.U. First novel, *Ships That Pass in the Night* (1889).

ETHEL LILIAN VOYNICH (1864–1960): Novelist and political radical. Born in Cork, Ireland, daughter of mathematician George Boole and feminist philosopher Mary Everest Boole. Educated at school and in Berlin. Traveled in Russia. Married Polish patriot Wilfred Voynich in 1891; lived after 1916 in New York. First book, *Stories From Garshin* (1893). Best known for *The Gadfly* (1897), a Marxist novel of revolution.

ADELA NICHOLSON (1865–1904): Poet. Pseudonym, "Lawrence Hope." Born in Gloucestershire, daughter of a colonel. Educated at home, married a colonel in 1889, had one child. Committed suicide. First book *Songs From the Garden of Kana* (1901).

ISOBEL VIOLET HUNT (1866–1942): Novelist. Born in Durham, daughter of the artist Alfred Hunt and the novelist Margaret Hunt. Educated at school, companion of Ford

359

Madox Ford. Involved in suffrage movement. First novel, *The Murder's Progress* (1894).

BEATRIX POTTER (1866–1943): Children's book writer. Born in London, daughter of a barrister and clubman, had one brother. Church of England. Educated at home; married William Healis, a solicitor, in 1913, no children. First book, *Peter Rabbit* (1900).

PEARL CRAIGIE (1867–1906): Novelist. Pseudonym, "John Oliver Hobbes." Born in Chelsea, Massachusetts, one of four children of a businessman; moved to London. Roman Catholic convert. Educated at home, attended lectures at University College, London; married in 1887, divorced, had one child. First novel, *Some Emotions and a Moral* (1891).

KATHERINE MAUD MARSHALL DIVER (1867–1945): Novelist. Born in India, daughter of an Indian army colonel. Married a lieutenant-colonel. First novel, *Captain Desmond* (1907). Also known for *The Englishwoman in India* (1909, nonfiction).

MRS. HENRY NORMAN (1867–?): Writer on women. Pseudonym, "Ménie Muriel Dowie." Born in Liverpool, second daughter of well-to-do father. Raised in Highlands. Educated in Liverpool, Stuttgart, and France; married a newspaperman. Published *Gallia* (1895).

ALICE PERRIN (1867–1934): Novelist. Daughter of general of Bengal Cavalry. Married Charles Perrin in 1886, lived in India while husband was with Indian Public Works. Published 25 novels and some short stories.

MARIE BELLOC LOWNDES (1868–1947): Novelist. Daughter of a French barrister and Bessie R. Parkes. Catholic. Educated at a convent, married a *Times* journalist in 1896, had three children. First novel, *The Heart of Penelope* (1904). Wrote a two volume autobiography. Best known for novel *The Lodger* (1913), based on Jack the Ripper.

CHARLOTTE MEW (1869–1928): Poet. Born in London,

oldest daughter of an architect. Educated at Lucy Har-·rison's School for Girls, attended lectures at University College, London; remained single. Committed suicide. First book, *The Farmer's Bride* (1915).

MARGARET FAIRLESS BARBER (1869–1901): Poet, essayist. Pseudonym, "Michael Fairless." Born in Yorkshire, youngest of three daughters of a lawyer and antiquarian. Church of England. Educated at school, remained single. Both parents died when she was 21. Invalid. Became a nurse. First book, *The Gathering of Brother Hilarius* (1901).

ETHEL F. L. RICHARDSON (1870–1946): Novelist. Pseudonym, "Henry Handel Richardson," Born in Melbourne, Australia, daughter of a doctor. Educated at school and at the Leipzig Conservatorium. Married a professor at London University. First novel, *Maurice Guest* (1908).

FLORA MACDONALD MAYOR (1872–1932): Novelist. Educated at Newnham College, Cambridge. Lived in Hampstead. Fiancé died of typhoid, and she remained single. Wrote *Mrs. Hammond's Children* while in her twenties. Best known for *The Rector's Daughter* (1924).

DOROTHY M. RICHARDSON (1873–1957): Novelist, journalist and translator. Born in Berkshire, daughter of a tradesman, third of four sisters. Had affair with H. G. Wells in 1906, who was influential in her development as a writer; figured in her major work, *Pilgrimage*. Married Alan Odle in 1917, no children. Modernist writer.

RADCLYFFE HALL (1880–1943): Novelist and poet. Born in Bournemouth, educated for one year at King's College, London. Father died in 1898 leaving her financially independent. Never married. *Well of Loneliness* (1928) was largely autobiographical, her first attempt to deal with lesbian identity. Prosecuted for obscenity due to this.

ETHEL DELL SAVAGE (1881–1939): Novelist. Born in Streatham, younger daughter of an insurance agent. Educated at school, married in 1922. First novel, *The Way of an Eagle* (1912).

MARY WEBB (1881–1927): Novelist. Born in Shropshire, née Meredith, oldest daughter of a schoolmaster. Educated at home, married a schoolmaster 1912, no children. Interested in pantheism. Developed Grave's Disease, which her biographer attributed to overwork, at age 20. First novel, *The Golden Arrow* (1916).

ROSE MACAULAY (1881–1958): Novelist, poet, travel writer and critic. Born in Cambridge, second oldest of several children of a lecturer at Cambridge University. Anglo-Catholic family. Educated at Somerville College, Oxford, remained single. Works include, *Abbots Verney* (1906), *The World my Wilderness* (1950) and *The Towers of Trebizond*.

VIRGINIA WOOLF (1882–1941): Novelist. Born in London, younger daughter of editor Leslie Stephen. Privately educated, married Leonard Woolf in 1912, no children. Committed suicide. First novel, *The Voyage Out* (1915).

"ANNA WICKHAM" [EDITH ALICE MARY HEPBURN] (1884–1947): Poet. Born in Wimbledon, Surrey, daughter of a music-shop keeper and piano tuner. Studied singing in Paris, married Patrick Hepburn, a solicitor and president of the Royal Astronomical Society.

SHEILA KAYE-SMITH (1887–1956): Novelist. Born at St. Leonards-on-Sea, daughter of a physician. Educated at school, married Rev. T. Penrose Fry in 1924. Both became Catholics in 1929. First novel, *The Tramping Methodist* (1908).

I. A. R. WYLIE (1885–1959): Novelist. Born in Melbourne, Australia. Educated at Cheltenham Ladies' College. Traveled extensively in Germany and other parts of Europe. First novel, 1906. Known for *The Daughter of Brahma* (1912).

VIOLA MEYNELL (1886–1956): Novelist and poet. Born in London, daughter of Alice Meynell. Married in 1922, had one child. First novel, *Martha Vine* (1910).

WINIFRED ASHTON (1887–1965): Novelist and dramatist. Pseudonym, "Clemence Dane." Educated at school, attended the Slade School of Art. First novel, *Regiment of Women* (1917). Also known for *The Woman's Side* (1926).

KATHERINE MANSFIELD [MURRY] (1888–1923): Short story writer. Born in New Zealand, third daughter of a banker. Educated at Queen's College, London, married twice, no children. First book, *In a German Pension* (1911).

E. M. DELAFIELD (Edmee Elizabeth Monica de la Pasture) (1890–1943): Novelist, short story writer and journalist of French descent. Born in Monmouthshire, oldest daughter of Count Henri de la Pasture. Married an army officer in 1919, had two children. Writing is largely autobiographical and includes *The Pelicans* (1918), *The War Workers* (1918), *The Way Things Are* (1927) and her best-known work *The Diary of a Provincial Lady* (1931).

AGATHA CHRISTIE (1890–1976): Novelist, mystery writer. Born in Torquay. Educated at home. Married Col. Archibald Christie in 1914, divorced in 1928; married Max Mallowan, an archaeologist, in 1930, one daughter. First novel, *The Mysterious Affair at Styles* (1920).

GLADYS BERTHA STERN (1890–1976): Novelist and short story writer. Born in London. Jewish. Educated at school, attended the Royal Academy of Dramatic Art. Married Geoffrey Holdsworth, a journalist, in 1919. Wrote *Pantomime* (1914).

[MARGARET] STORM JAMESON (1891–): Novelist. Born in Whitby, Yorkshire, daughter of a shipbuilder. Educated at Leeds University and London, married twice, has one child. First book, *The Pot Boils* (1919). Wrote *The World Ends* under the pseudonym "William Lamb." Autobiography titled *Journey from the North* (1969).

363

Ivy Compton-Burnett (1892–1969): Novelist. Born in Pinner, educated privately, she went on to read classics at Royal Holloway Women's College, London. Remained single. Suffered from a long physical and mental breakdown during the early 1920s. Her works include, *Dolores* (1911), *Pastors and Masters* (1925), *Two Worlds and Their Ways* (1949), *A Heritage and its History* (1959), *Men and Wives* (1931), *Daughters and Sons* (1937).

Vita Sackville-West (1892–1962): Novelist, poet and biographer. Born at Knole Castle, Kent, only child of the third Baron Sackville. Married Sir Harold Nicholson in 1914, had two sons. Had an affair with Violet Trefusis and a close friendship with Virginia Woolf which inspired Woolf's *Orlando*. Poems include *The Land* (1927), *Solitude* (1938) and *The Eagle and the Dove* (1943). Best known for her novels *The Edwardians* (1930) and *All Passion Spent* (1931).

"Rebecca West" [Cicily Isabel Andrews] (1892–): Novelist and journalist. Born in London, daughter of an army officer. Freethinker. Educated at George Watson's Ladies' College, Edinburgh, married H. M. Andrews in 1930, has one child. Interested in women's suffrage. First novel, *The Return of the Soldier* (1918). Also known for *The Judge* (1922) and *The Harsh Voice* (1935).

Stella Benson [Anderson] (1892–1933): Novelist. Born in Shropshire, third child of a gentleman and niece of Mary Cholmondeley. Educated at home, married John Anderson in 1921, no children. First novel, *I Pose* (1915).

Dorothy L. Sayers (1893–1957): Mystery novelist. Born in eastern England, daughter of Rev. H. Sayers, headmaster of the Cathedral Choir School. Educated at Oxford. First novel, *Whose Body?* (1923).

Jean Rhys (1894–1979): Novelist. Born in the West Indies, educated at Royal Academy of Dramatic Art. First book, *The Left Bank* (1927). *Wide Sargasso Sea* (1966) tells the Jane Eyre story from the viewpoint of the mad wife.

PHYLLIS BENTLEY (1894–1977): Novelist. Born in Yorkshire, youngest child and only daughter of a textile manufacturer. Educated at London University. First novel, *Pedagomania* (1918). Best known for *Inheritance* (1932), a chronicle of families associated with the textile industry in Yorkshire over a century.

WINIFRED BRYHER (1894–): Novelist. Born in Kent. Educated at school. Married Robert McAlmon in 1921, divorced in 1926; married Kenneth Macpherson in 1927, divorced in 1947. First novel, 1920. Known for *The Key to Artemis*.

MARGARET KENNEDY (1896–1967): Novelist. Born in London. Educated at Oxford, married David Davies, a barrister, in 1925, had three children. First novel, *The Ladies of Lyndon* (1923). Best known for *The Constant Nymph* (1924).

NAOMI MITCHISON (1897–): Novelist. Born in Edinburgh, daughter of Professor J. S. Haldane. Educated at Oxford, married Richard Mitchison, a lawyer, in 1916, has six children. First novel, *The Conquered* (1923). Others include *The Bull Calves* and *Cloud Cuckoo Land*.

VERA BRITTAIN (1893–1970): Novelist. Born in Staffordshire, oldest child of a paper mill owner. Church of England. Educated at Somerville College, Oxford, married George Catlin in 1925, had two children. First novel, *The Dark Tide*.

WINIFRED HOLTBY (1898–1935): Poet and novelist. Born in Yorkshire, younger daughter of a gentleman farmer. Educated at Oxford. First book, *My Garden and Other Poems* (1911); first novel, *Anderby Wold* (1923). Best known for *South Riding* (1936).

ELIZABETH BOWEN (1899–1973): Novelist. Born in Dublin, only child of a barrister. Educated at Downe House School, Kent, and in Ireland and Europe, married Alan Cameron in 1923. First book, *Encounters* (1923). Best known for *The House in Paris* (1935) and *The Death of the Heart* (1938).

ANTONIA WHITE (1899–1980): Novelist, translator, journalist. Born in London. Educated at a convent, attended the Royal Academy of Dramatic Art; married in 1930, had two children. Wrote autobiographical first novel, *Frost in May* (1933). Also wrote *The Lost Traveller, The Sugar House, Beyond the Glass, The Hound and the Falcon* and *Three in a Room.*

ENID BAGNOLD (1889–1981): Novelist. Educated in Paris, married, had four children. First book, 1917.

ROSAMOND LEHMANN (1900–): Novelist. Born in Bourne End, Buckinghamshire, daughter of an M.P. and contributor to *Punch*, sister of actress Beatrix Lehmann and writer John Lehmann. Educated at Girton College, Cambridge; first marriage to Leslie Runciman, divorced; second marriage to Wogan Phillips, a painter, in 1928, had one daughter (deceased) and one son. First novel, *Dusty Answer* (1927). Also wrote *Invitation to the Waltz* (1932), *A Note in Music* (1930), *The Ballad and the Source* (1944), *The Swan in the Evening* (1967), *A Sea-Grape-Tree* (1976), *The Gypsy's Baby* (1946) and *The Weather in the Streets* (1936).

PENELOPE MORTIMER (1918–): Born in North Wales, daughter of a clergyman. Church of England. Educated at London University. Married in 1937 (divorced in 1949), married John Mortimer in 1949 (divorced in 1972), has six children. First novel, *Johanna* (1947).

DORIS MAY LESSING (1919–): Novelist. Born in Kermanshah, Persia, née Tayler, daughter of a farmer. Grew up in Southern Rhodesia. Educated at a convent school. Married Frank Charles Wisdom in 1939, two children, divorced in 1943. Married Gottfried Lessing in 1945, has one child, divorced in 1949. First novel, *The Grass Is Singing* (1950).

IRIS MURDOCH (1919–): Novelist and philosopher. Born in Dublin. Educated at Badminton School, Bristol, and

Somerville College, Oxford. Worked with U.N.R.R.A. in London, Belgium, and Austria. Married in 1956 to John Bayley, don and novelist. First novel, *Under the Net* (1954). Died in 1999.

BRIGID BROPHY (1929–): Novelist. Born in London. Educated at Oxford. Married Michael Levey in 1954, has one child. First novel, *Hackenfeller's Ape* (1953).

EDNA O'BRIEN (1936–): Born in County Clare. Attended pharmaceutical college in Dublin; married Ernest Gebler in 1962 (divorced), has two children. First novel, *The Country Girls* (1960).

A. S. [ANTONIA SUSAN] BYATT (1936–): Born in Sheffield, sister of Margaret Drabble. Educated at Cambridge. Married I. C. R. Byatt in 1959 (divorced), married Peter J. Duffy in 1969, has three children. First novel, *Shadow of a Sun* (1964).

MARGARET DRABBLE (1939–): Born in Sheffield, sister of A. S. Byatt. Educated at Cambridge. Married Clive Swift, an actor, in 1960 (divorced), has three children. First novel, *A Summer Bird Cage* (1963).

Şelected Bibliography

THE purpose of this bibliography is to present the most useful sources for studying nineteenth- and twentieth-century English women novelists. General histories of the English novel, general critical studies, and fiction have not been included.

I. BIBLIOGRAPHIES AND SURVEYS OF RESEARCH MATERIALS.

Houghton, Walter E., ed., *The Wellesley Index to Victorian Periodicals, 1824-1900.* 2 vols. Toronto: U. of Toronto Press, 1966, 1970.

Kanner, Barbara S. "The Women of England in a Century of Social Change: A Select Bibliography." *Suffer and Be Still: Women in the Victorian Age.* Ed. Martha Vicinus. London: Methuen University Paperbacks, 1980.

McGregor, O. R. "The Social Position of Women in England, 1850-1914: A Bibliography." *British Journal of Sociology,* VI (1955), 48-60.

Showalter, Elaine and Jean L'Espérance. "Notes from London: Research on Women." *Women's Studies,* I (1973) 223-233.

Showalter, Elaine. "Literary Criticism: A Review Essay." *Signs: Journal of Women in Culture and Society,* I (1975), 435-460.

Watt, Ian. *The British Novel: Scott through Hardy.* Northbrook, Illinois: AHM, 1973.

Wiley, Paul. *The British Novel: Conrad to the Present.* Northbrook, Illinois: AHM, 1973.

II. BOOKS ON WOMEN AND THE NOVEL, VICTORIAN WOMEN, THE WOMEN'S MOVEMENT, INDIVIDUAL NOVELISTS.

Adburgham, Alison. *Women in Print.* London: George Allen and Unwin, 1972.

Allott, Miriam, ed. *The Brontës: The Critical Heritage.* London: Routledge & Kegan Paul, 1974.

Altick, Richard. *Victorian Studies in Scarlet.* New York: Norton, 1970.

Babington-Smith, Constance. *Rose Macaulay.* London: Collins, 1972.

Baker, Ernest A. *The History of the English Novel.* 10 vols. London: Witherby, 1924–1939.

Bald, Marjory A. *Woman Writers of the Nineteenth Century.* Cambridge: Cambridge U. Press, 1928.

Basch, Françoise. *Relative Creatures: Victorian Women in Society and The Novel.* London: Allen Lane, 1974.

Bazin, Nancy Topping. *Virginia Woolf and the Androgynous Vision.* New Brunswick: Rutgers U. Press, 1973.

Bergonzi, Bernard. *The Situation of the Novel.* Harmondsworth: Penguin, 1972.

Black, Helen C. *Notable Women Authors of the Day.* Glasgow: David Bryce & Son, 1893.

Branca, Patricia. *The Silent Sisterhood: Middle Class Women in the Victorian Home.* London: Croom Helm, 1975.

Brightfield, Myron. *Victorian England in its Novels.* 4 vols. Los Angeles: U.C.L.A., 1968.

Byatt, Antonia S. *Degrees of Freedom: The Novels of Iris Murdoch.* London: Chatto & Windus, 1965.

Caird, Mona. *The Morality of Marriage.* London: Redway, 1897.

Carroll, David, ed. *George Eliot: The Critical Heritage.* London: Routledge & Kegan Paul, 1971.

Coghill, Mrs. Harry, ed. *Autobiography and Letters of Mrs. M. O. W. Oliphant.* London: Blackwood, 1899.

Colby, Robert A. and Vineta. *The Equivocal Virtue: Mrs. Oliphant and the Victorian Literary Market-place.* Hamden, Conn.: Archon, 1966.

Colby, Robert A. *Novels With a Purpose.* Bloomington: Indiana U. Press, 1967.

Colby, Vineta. *The Singular Anomaly: Women Novelists of the Nineteenth Century.* New York: New York U. Press, 1970.

Colby, Vineta, *Yesterday's Women: Domestic Realism in the English Novel.* Princeton: Princeton U. Press, 1974.

Corelli, Marie. *Free Opinions.* London: Archibald Constable & Co., 1905.

Cornillon, Susan Koppelman, ed. *Images of Women in Fiction: Feminist Perspectives.* Bowling Green, Ohio: Bowling Green U. Popular Press, 1972.

Cott, Nancy F. *Root of Bitterness.* New York: E. P. Dutton, 1972.

Courtney, Janet. *The Women of My Time.* London: Lovat Dickson, 1934.

Courtney, William L. *The Feminine Note in Fiction.* London: Chapman & Hall, 1904.

Craik, Dinah M. *A Woman's Thoughts About Women.* London: Hurst & Blackett, 1858.

Cruse, Amy. *The Victorians and Their Books.* London: Allen & Unwin, 1935.

Davidoff, Leonore. *The Best Circles: Society, Etiquette and the Season.* London: Croom Helm, 1973.

Edel, Leon, ed. *The Diary of Alice James.* London: Hart-Davis, 1965.

Ellmann, Mary. *Thinking About Women.* London: Virago, 1979.

Elwin, Malcolm. *Victorian Wallflowers.* London: Cape, 1934.

Ewbank, Inga-Stina. *Their Proper Sphere: A Study of the Brontë Sisters as Early-Victorian Novelists.* London: Edward Arnold, 1966.

Gaskell, Elizabeth. *Life of Charlotte Brontë.* London: Dent Everyman Paperback, 1973.

Gawsworth, John, ed. *Ten Contemporaries.* London: Ernest Benn, 1932.

Gettman, Royal A. *A Victorian Publisher: A Study of the Bentley Papers.* Cambridge, England: Cambridge U. Press, 1960.

Gornick, Vivian and Barbara K. Moran, eds. *Woman in Sexist Society.* New York: Basic Books, 1971.

Graham, Kenneth. *English Criticism of the Novel, 1865–1900.* London: Oxford U. Press, 1965.

Griest, Guinevere. *Mudie's Circulating Library and the Victorian Novel.* Bloomington: Indiana U. Press, 1970.

Gunn, Peter. *Vernon Lee: Violet Paget, 1856–1935.* London: Oxford U. Press, 1964.

Haight, Gordon S., ed. *The George Eliot Letters,* 7 vols. New Haven: Yale U. Press, 1954–1955.

Haight, Gordon S. *George Eliot: A Biography.* London: Oxford U. Press, 1968.

Hamilton, Catherine J. *Women Writers: Their Works and Ways.* London: Lock, Bowden and Co., 1892.

Hamilton, Cicely. *Marriage as a Trade.* London: Women's Press, 1981.

Hartman, Mary S. and Lois Banner, eds. *Clio's Consciousness Raised: New Perspectives on the History of Women.* New York: Harper & Row, 1974.

Haweis, Mary. *Words to Women: Addresses and Essays*, Ed. Rev. H. R. Haweis. London: Burnet & Isbister, 1900.

Heilbrun, Carolyn G. *Towards a Recognition of Androgyny: Aspects of Male and Female in Literature*. London: Gollancz, 1973.

Hinkley, Laura L. *Ladies of Literature*. New York: Hastings, 1946.

Howe, Susanne. *Geraldine Jewsbury*. London: Allen & Unwin, 1935.

Hunt, Violet. *The Flurried Years*. London: Hurst & Blackett, 1926.

Ingelow, Jean. *Some Recollections of Jean Ingelow*. London: W. Gardner, Darton & Co., 1901.

Ireland, Mrs. Alex, ed. *Letters of Geraldine Jewsbury to Jane Welsh Carlyle*. London: Longmans, Green, 1892.

Jameson, Storm. *Journey From The North*. London: Collins, 1969.

Johnson, R. Brimley. *Sone Contemporary Novelists (Women)*. London: Leonard Parsons, 1920.

Johnson, Wendell Stacy. *Sex and Marriage in Victorian Poetry*. London: Cornell U. Press, 1975.

Jones, Enid Huws. *Mrs. Humphrey Ward*. London: Heinemann, 1973.

Kaplan, Sydney Janet. *Feminine Consciousness in the Modern British Novel*. Urbana: U. of Illinois Press, 1974.

Laski, Marghanita. *Mrs. Ewing, Mrs. Molesworth, and Mrs. Hodgson Burnett*. London: Barker, 1950.

Layard, G. S., ed. *Mrs. Lynn Linton: Her Life, Letters, and Opinions*. London: Methuen, 1901.

Linton, Mrs. Lynn.. *My Literary Life*. London: Hodder and Stoughton, 1899.

Maison, Margaret M. *The Victorian Vision: Studies in the Religious Novel*. New York: Sheed & Ward, 1961.

Mansfield, Katherine. *The Letters of Katherine Mansfield*. Ed. J. Middleton Murry. London: Constable, 1930.

Marder, Herbert. *Feminism and Art: A Study of Virginia Woolf*. Chicago: U. of Chicago Press, 1968.

Martineau, Harriet. *Autobiography*. Ed. Maria Weston Chapman. London: Smith, Elder & Co., 1877.

Masefield, Muriel. *Women Novelists from Fanny Burney to George Eliot*. London: Nicholson and Watson, 1934.

Maxwell, Christabel. *Mrs. Gatty and Mrs. Ewing*. London: Constable, 1949.

Meynell, Viola. *Alice Meynell: A Memoir*. London: Jonathan Cape, 1929.

Mill, John Stuart and Harriet Taylor Mill. *Essays on Sex Equality.* Ed. Alice S. Rossi. Chicago: U. of Chicago Press, 1970.

Miller, Betty, ed. *Elizabeth Barrett to Miss Mitford.* London: J. Murray, 1954.

Mitchell, Juliet. *Woman's Estate.* Harmondsworth: Penguin Books, 1971.

Moers, Ellen. *Literary Women.* London: The Women's Press, 1978.

Moore, Doris Langley. *E. Nesbit: A Biography.* London: Benn, 1967.

Needham, G. B. and R. P. Utter. *Pamela's Daughters.* Berkeley: U. of California Press, 1936.

Papashvily, Helen White. *All The Happy Endings.* New York: Harper, 1956.

"Paston, George" (Emily Symonds). *At John Murray's 1843–1892.* London: J. Murray, 1932.

Pinney, Thomas, ed. *Essays of George Eliot.* London: Routledge, 1963.

Pollard, A. and J. A. V. Chapple, eds. *The Letters of Mrs. Gaskell.* Manchester: Manchester U. Press, 1966.

Raeburn, Antonia. *The Militant Suffragettes.* London: Michael Joseph, 1973.

Ray, Gordon N. *H. G. Wells and Rebecca West.* London: Macmillan, 1974.

Reed, John R. *Victorian Conventions.* Athens: Ohio U. Press, 1975.

Richards, John Morgan. *The Life of John Oliver Hobbes.* London: John Murray, 1911.

Riley, Madeleine. *Brought to Bed.* London: Dent, 1968.

"Rita" (Eliza M. Humphreys). *Recollections of a Literary Life.* London: Andrew Melrose, 1936.

Rogers, Katherine M. *The Troublesome Helpmate: A History of Misogyny in Literature.* Seattle and London: U. of Washington Press, 1966.

Rosen, Andrew. *Rise Up, Women!* London: Routledge & Kegan Paul, 1974.

Rosenberg, John. *Dorothy Richardson: The Genius They Forgot.* London: Duckworth, 1973.

Rowbotham, Sheila. *Women, Resistance and Revolution.* London: Allen Lane, 1972.

Rowbotham, Sheila. *Hidden From History.* London: Pluto Press, 1973.

Rowbotham, Sheila. *Woman's Consciousness, Man's World.* Harmondsworth: Penguin, 1973.

Sadleir, Michael. *Things Past.* London: Constable, 1944.

Schlueter, Paul. *The Novels of Doris Lessing.* Carbondale: Southern Illinois U. Press, 1973.

Schmalhausen, Samuel D. and V. F. Calverton, eds. *Woman's Coming of Age.* New York: Liveright, 1931.

Sewell, Eleanor C. *The Autobiography of Elizabeth M. Sewell.* London: Longmans, 1908.

Shorter, Clement. *The Brontës: Life and Letters.* 2 vols. London: Hodder and Stoughton, 1908.

Spacks, Patricia Meyer. *The Female Imagination.* London: Allen and Unwin, 1976.

Sprigge, Elizabeth. *The Life of Ivy Compton-Burnett.* London: Gollancz, 1973.

Stang, Richard, *The Theory of the Novel in England, 1850–1870.* London: Routledge, 1959.

Stebbins, Lucy Poate. *A Victorian Album: Some Lady Novelists of the Period.* New York: Columbia U. Press, 1946.

Stephens, Winifred, *The Life of Adeline Sergeant.* London: Hodder and Stoughton, 1905.

Stevens, Michael. *V. Sackville-West.* London: Michael Joseph, 1973.

Stone, Donald. *Novelists in a Changing World.* Cambridge, Mass.: Harvard U. Press, 1972.

Strachey, Ray. *The Cause.* London: Virago, 1978.

Thomson, Patricia. *The Victorian Heroine: A Changing Ideal.* London: Oxford U. Press, 1956.

Tillotson, Kathleen. *Novels of the Eighteen-Forties.* London: Oxford U. Press, 1954.

Tompkins, J. M. S. *The Popular Novel in England 1770–1800.* London: Methuen, 1932.

Trevelyan, Janet Penrose. *The Life of Mrs. Humphry Ward.* London: Constable, 1932.

Vicinus, Martha, ed. *Suffer and Be Still: Women in the Victorian Age.* London: Methuen University Paperbacks, 1980.

Walbank, Alan. *Queens of the Circulating Library.* London: Evans, 1950.

Wandor, Michelene, ed. *The Body Politic: Writings from the Women's Liberation Movement in Britain, 1969–1972.* London: Stage 1, 1972.

374

Ward, Mrs. Humphry. *A Writer's Recollections*. London: Wm. Collins, 1918.

Webb, Beatrice. *My Apprenticeship*. Harmondsworth: Penguin, 1971.

Welsh, Alexander. *The City of Dickens*. London: Oxford U. Press, 1971.

White, Cynthia L. *Women's Magazines, 1693–1968*. London: Michael Joseph, 1972.

White, Terence de Vere. *A Leaf from the Yellow Book*. London: The Richards Press, 1958.

Winnifrith, Tom. *The Brontës and Their Background: Romance and Reality*. London: Macmillan, 1973.

Wood, Charles W. *Mrs. Henry Wood: A Memoir*. London: Bentley, 1895.

Woolf, Virginia. *Collected Essays*. II. Ed. Leonard Woolf. London: Chatto & Windus, 1967.

Woolf, Virginia. *A Room of One's Own*. Harmondsworth: Penguin Books, 1945.

Woolf, Virginia. *Three Guineas*. Harmondsworth: Penguin Books, 1977.

Woolf, Virginia. *Women and Writing*. Ed. Michèle Barrett. London: The Women's Press, 1979.

Yonge, Charlotte et al. *Women Novelists of Queen Victoria's Reign*. London: Hurst & Blackett, 1897.

III. Articles in nineteenth-century periodicals, listed chronologically.

"The Education of Women—Madame Roland," *Westminster Review*, XXX (1831), 69–89.

"Miss Martineau's *Monthly Novels*," *Quarterly Review*, XLIX (1833), 136–152.

[E. G. Bulwer-Lytton]. "Cheveley: or the Man of Honour," *Fraser's*, XIX (1839), 618–629.

[Venables, G. S.]. "Miss Martineau," *Blackwood's*, XLVII (1840), 177–188.

"A Batch of Novels," *Fraser's*, XXVII (1843), 520–535.

[Eastlake, Elizabeth]. "Lady Travellers," *Quarterly Review*, LXXVI (1845), 98–136.

[Lewes, G. H.]. "The Condition of Authors in England, Germany and France," *Fraser's*, XXXV (1847), 285–295.

[Eastlake, Elizabeth]. "*Jane Eyre* and *Vanity Fair*," *Quarterly Review*, LXXXIV (1848), 153–185.

[Whipple, E. P.]. "Novels of the Season," *North American Review*, LXVII (1848), 354–369.

"Jane Eyre," *Christian Remembrancer*, XV (1848), 369–409.

"An Evening's Gossip on New Novels," *Dublin University Magazine*, XXXI (1848), 608–614.

[Lorimer, James]. "Noteworthy Novels," *North British Review*, XI (1849), 255–265.

[Phillips, C. S.]. "Miss Strickland's *Queens of England*," *Edinburgh Review*, LXXXIX (1849), 435–462.

[Greg, W. R.]. "Mary Barton," *Edinburgh Review*, LXXXIX (1849), 402–435.

[Charles Kingsley]. "Recent Novels," *Fraser's*, XXXIX (1849), 417–432.

[Lewes, G. H.]. "Currer Bell's *Shirley*," *Edinburgh Review*, XCI (1850), 153–173.

"Vivian" (G. H. Lewes). "A Gentle Hint to Writing Women," *The Leader*, I (1850), 189.

"Puseyite Novels," *Prospective Review*, VI (1850), 512–534.

[Taylor, Harriet]. "The Enfranchisement of Women," *Westminster Review*, LV (1851), 289–311.

[Lewes, G. H.]. "The Lady Novelists," *Westminster Review*, n.s. II (1852), 129–141.

"The Progress of Fiction as an Art," *Westminster Review*, LX (1853), 342–374.

"The Lady Novelists of Great Britain," *Gentleman's Magazine*, n.s. XL (1853), 18–25.

[Greg, W. R.]. "Recent Novels: Agatha's Husband," *Edinburgh Review*, LXCVII (1853), 474–491.

[Lewes, G. H.]. "Ruth and Villette," *Westminster Review*, LIX (1853), 474–491.

[Ludlow, J. M.]. "Ruth," *North British Review*, XIX (1853), 81–94.

[Stephen, Fitzjames]. "Guy Livingstone," *Edinburgh Review*, CVIII (1853), 532–540.

"Heartsease," *Fraser's*, L (1854), 489–503.

"The Author of *Heartsease* and the Modern School of Fiction," *Prospective Review*, X (1854), 460–482.

"Belles Lettres," *Westminster Review*, n.s. VII (1855), 275–291.

[Oliphant, Margaret]. "Charles Dickens," *Blackwood's*, LXXVII (1855), 451–466.

[Oliphant, Margaret]. "Modern Novelists—Great and Small," *Blackwood's*, LXXVII (1855), 554–568.

[Eliot, George]. "Silly Novels by Lady Novelists," *Westminster Review*, LXVI (1856), 442–461.

"Aurora Leigh," *National Review*, IV (1857), 239–267.

"The Professor," *Saturday Review*, III (1857), 550.

"Our Library Table," *Athenaeum*, VII (1857), 881.

"Belles Lettres," *Westminster Review*, LXVIII (1857), 296–314.

[Dallas, E. S.]. "Currer Bell," *Blackwood's*, LXXXII (1857), 77–94.

[Kaye, J. M.]. "The Employment of Women," *North British Review*, XXVI (1857), 157–182.

[Patmore, Coventry]. "Mrs. Browning's Poems," *North British Review*, XXVI (1857), 237–247.

[Roscoe, W. C.]. "Miss Brontë," *National Review*, V (1857), 127–164.

[Stephen, Fitzjames]. "The License of Modern Novelists," *Edinburgh Review*, CVI (1857), 124–156.

[Hutton, R. H.]. "Novels by the Authoress of 'John Halifax,'" *North British Review*, XXIX (1858), 254–262.

"Adam Bede," *Westminster Review*, n.s. XV (1859), 486–512.

"Parsons and Novels," *Saturday Review*, VII (1859), 708–709.

[Anne Mozley]. "Novels by Sir Edward Bulwer-Lytton," *Bentley's Quarterly Review*, I (1859), 73–105.

[Anne Mozley]. "Adam Bede and Recent Novels," *Bentley's Quarterly Review*, I (1859), 433–472.

"Queen Bees or Working Bees?" *Saturday Review*, VII (1859), 576.

"Novels and Novelists," *British Quarterly Review*, XXX (1859), 443–469.

[Collins, W. Lucas]. "Adam Bede," *Blackwood's*, LXXXV (1859), 490–504.

[Greg, W. R.]. "The False Morality of Lady Novelists," *National Review*, VII (1859), 144–167.

[Martineau, Harriet]. "Female Industry," *Edinburgh Review*, CIX (1859), 293–336.

[Norton, Caroline]. "Adam Bede," *Edinburgh Review*, CX (1859), 223–246.

"The Mill on the Floss," *Saturday Review*, IX (1860), 470–471.

"The Mill on the Floss," *Westminster Review*, LXXIV (1860), 24–33.

"Novels of the Day: Their Writers and Readers," *Fraser's*, LXII (1860), 205–218.

Bagehot, Walter. "The Novels of George Eliot," *National Review*, XI (1860), 191–219.

[Collins, W. Lucas]. "The Mill on the Floss," *Blackwood's*, LXXXVII (1860), 611–683.

[Robertson, James Craigie]. "George Eliot's Novels," *Quarterly Review*, CVIII (1860), 469–499.

[Craik, Dinah]. "To Novelists—and a Novelist," *Macmillan's*, III (1861), 441–448.

[Massey, Gerald]. "Last Poems and Other Works of Mrs. Browning," *North British Review*, XXXVI (1862), 271–281.

[Oliphant, Margaret]. "Sensation Novels," *Blackwood's*, XCI (1862), 564–584.

[Rae, W. Fraser]. "Sensation Novels: Miss Braddon," *North British Review*, XLIII (1863), 92–105.

[Mansel, Henry]. "Sensation Novels," *Quarterly Review*, CXIII (1863), 481–514.

"Romola," *British Quarterly Review*, XXXVIII (1863), 448–465.

"Novels with a Purpose," *Westminster Review*, LXXXII (1864), 24–49.

"Clara Vaughan," *Saturday Review*, XVII (1864), 539–541.

Lewes, G. H. "Never Forgotten," *Fortnightly Review*, I (1865), 253–254.

Trollope, Anthony. "On Anonymous Literature," *Fortnightly Review*, I (1865), 491–498.

[Arnold, Thomas]. "Recent Novel Writing," *Macmillan's*, XIII (1866), 202–209.

[Lancaster, H. H.]. "George Eliot's Novels," *North British Review*, XLV (1866), 103–120.

[Morley, John]. "George Eliot's Novels," *Macmillan's*, XIV (1866), 272–279.

[Oliphant, Margaret]. "The Great Unrepresented," *Blackwood's*, C (1866), 367–379.

[Taylor, Harriet]. "Women and Criticism," *Macmillan's*, XIV (1866), 335–340.

"Wives and Daughters," *Saturday Review*, XXI (1866), 360–361.

"The Author of John Halifax," *British Quarterly Review*, XLIV (1866), 32–58.

[Oliphant, Margaret]. "Novels," *Blackwood's*, III (1867), 257–280.

"George Eliot," *British Quarterly Review*, XLV (1867), 141–178.

"The Works of Mrs. Gaskell," *British Quarterly Review*, XLV (1867), 399–429.

"Women's Heroines," *Saturday Review*, XXIII (1867), 259–261.

[Mozley, Anne]. "Clever Women," *Blackwood's*, CIV (1868), 420–427.

[Oliphant, Margaret]. "Mill's *Subjection of Women*," *Edinburgh Review*, CXXX (1869), 572–602.

[Mozley, Anne]. "Mr. Mill on the Subjection of Women," *Blackwood's*, CVI (1869), 309–321.

"Works by Mrs. Oliphant," *British Quarterly Review*, LXIX (1869), 301–329.

Allan, James Macgrigor. "On the Real Differences in the Minds of Men and Women," *Journal of the Anthropological Society of London*, VII (1869), cxcv–ccix.

"The Subjection of Women," *Westminster Review*, XCIII (1870), 63–89.

Linton, E. Lynn. "The Modern Revolt," *Macmillan's*, VIII (1870), 142–149.

"Belles Lettrés," *Westminster Review*, XCV (1871), 272–290.

"Goodby, Sweetheart," *Saturday Review*, XXIV (1872), 586.

[Milnes, R. Monckton]. "Middlemarch," *Edinburgh Review*, CXXXVII (1873), 246–263.

[Collins, W. Lucas]. "Mrs. Oliphant's Novels," *Blackwood's*, CXIII (1873), 722–739.

Smith, G. Barnett. "Miss Thackeray's *Old Kensington*," *Edinburgh Review*, CXXXVIII (1873), 166–186.

"Belles Lettres," *Westminster Review*, CII (1874), 574–590.

[Cowell, Herbert]. "Sex in Mind and Education," *Blackwood's*, CXV (1874), 736–764.

Maudsley, Henry. "Sex in Mind and Education," *Fortnightly Review*, XV (1874), 466–483.

[Smith, George Barnett]. "Elizabeth Barrett Browning," *Cornhill*, XXIX (1874), 469–490.

[Smith, George Barnett]. "Mrs. Gaskell and Her Novels," *Cornhill*, XXIX (1874), 191–212.

379

"American Women: Their Health and Education," *Westminster Review*, n.s. XLVI (1874), 456–499.

[Morley, John]. "Harriet Martineau," *Macmillan's*, XXXVI (1877), 47–60.

[Oliphant, Margaret]. "Harriet Martineau," *Blackwood's*, CXXI (1877), 472–496.

"Women's Newspapers," *Englishwoman's Review*, LXVI (1878), 433–440.

"Charlotte Brontë," *Westminster Review*, CIX (1878), 34–56.

[Oliphant, Margaret]. "New Novels," *Blackwood's*, CXXVIII (1880), 378–404.

Salmon, Edward. "What Girls Read," *Nineteenth Century*, XX (1886), 515–529.

Craik, Dinah M. "Concerning Men," *Cornhill*, n.s. IX (1887), 368–377.

"An Appeal Against Female Suffrage," *Nineteenth Century*, XXVI (1889), 781–788.

Allan, Grant. "Plain Words on the Woman Question," *Fortnightly Review*, LII (1889), 448–458.

Linton, E. Lynn. "Literature: Then and Now," *Fortnightly Review*, LVI (1890), 517–531.

Bulley, Amy. "The Political Evolution of Women," *Westminster Review*, LXXXIV (1890), 1–8.

Caird, Mona. "A Defense of the So-Called Wild Women," *Nineteenth Century*, XXXI (1892), 811–829.

Crawford, Emily. "Journalism as a Profession for Women," *Contemporary Review*, LXIV (1893), 362–371.

Noble, James Ashcroft. "The Fiction of Sexuality," *Contemporary Review*, LXVII (1895), 490–498.

Sykes, A.G.P. "The Evolution of the Sex," *Westminster Review*, CXLIII (1895), 396–400.

Crackenthrope, Blanche A. "Sex in Modern Literature," *Nineteenth Century*, XXXVII (1895), 607–616.

[Oliphant, Margaret]. "The Anti-Marriage League," *Blackwood's*, CLIX (1896), 135–149.

Hogarth, Janet. "The Monstrous Regiment of Women," *Fortnightly Review*, LXVIII (1897), 926–936.

Coghill, Annie L. "Mrs. Oliphant," *Fortnightly Review*, LXVIII (1897), 227–285.

IV. ARTICLES IN TWENTIETH-CENTURY PERIODICALS, LISTED ALPHA-
BETICALLY BY AUTHOR.

Altick, Richard. "The Sociology of Authorship," *Bulletin of New York Public Library*, LXVI (1962), 389–404.

Cunningham, A. R. "The 'New Woman Fiction' of the 1890s," *Victorian Studies*, XVII (1973), 177–186.

Drabble, Margaret. "Doris Lessing: Cassandra in a World Under Siege," *Ramparts*, X (1972), 50–54.

Drabble, Margaret. "The Writer as Recluse: The Theme of Solitude in the Works of the Brontës," *Brontë Society Transactions*, XVI (1974), 259–269.

Fahnestock, Jeanne Rosenmayer. "Geraldine Jewsbury: The Power of the Publisher's Reader," *Nineteenth Century Fiction*, XXVIII (1973), 253–272.

Fernando, Lloyd. "The Radical Ideology of the 'New Woman'," *Southern Review*, II (1967), 206–222.

Gordon, Linda. "Voluntary Motherhood: The Beginnings of Feminist Birth Control Ideas in the United States," *Feminist Studies*, I (Winter-Spring 1973), 5–22.

Gorsky, Susan. "Old Maids and New Women: Alternatives to Marriage in Englishwomen's Novels, 1847–1915," *Journal of Popular Culture*, VII (1973), 68–85.

Greer, Germaine. "Flying Pigs and Double Standards," *Times Literary Supplement* (July 25, 1974), 784–785.

Hardin, Nancy S. "Interview with Margaret Drabble," *Contemporary Literature*, XIV (1973), 273–295.

Hardy, Barbara. "The Image of the Opiate in George Eliot's Novels," *Notes and Queries*, CCII (Nov. 1957), 487–490.

Harrington, Henry R. "Childhood and the Victorian Ideal of Manliness in *Tom Brown's Schooldays*," *Victorian Newsletter* (Fall 1973), 13–17.

Harris, Wendell V. "Egerton: Forgotten Realist," *Victorian Newsletter* (Spring 1968), 31–36.

Harrison, Brian. "Underneath the Victorians," *Victorian Studies* X (1967), 239–262.

Hartman, Mary S. "Murder for Respectability: The Case of Madeleine Smith," *Victorian Studies*, XVI (June 1973), 381–400.

Hartman, Mary S. "Child Abuse and Self Abuse: Two Victorian Cases," *History of Childhood Quarterly* (Fall 1974), 221–248.

Hartman, Mary S. "Crime and the Respectable Woman: Toward a Pattern of Middle-Class Female Criminality in Nineteenth-Century France and England," *Feminist Studies*, II (1974), 38–56.

MacKendrick, Louis K. "The *New Freewoman*: A Short Story of Literary Journalism," *English Literature in Transition* (1972), 180–188.

Maison, Margaret. "Adulteresses in Agony," *The Listener*, XIV (Jan. 1961), 133–134.

Mitchell, Sally. "Lost Women: Implications of the Fallen in Works by Forgotten Women Writers of the 1840's," *Papers in Women's Studies*, I (June 1974), 110–124.

Ozick, Cynthia. "Mrs. Virginia Woolf," *Commentary*, LXVI (Aug. 1973), 33–44.

Raskin, Jonah. "Doris Lessing at Stony Brook," *New American Review*, VIII (Jan. 1970), 166–179.

Rich, Adrienne. "Jane Eyre: The Temptations of a Motherless Woman," *MS* (Oct. 1973), 68–71, 98, 106–107.

Rose, Phyllis. "Mrs. Ramsay and Mrs. Woolf," *Women's Studies* (1973), 199–216.

Sage, Lorna. "The Case of the Active Victim," *Times Literary Supplement* (July 26, 1974), 803–804.

Showalter, Elaine. "Dinah Mulock Craik and the Tactics of Sentiment: A Case Study in Victorian Female Authorship," *Feminist Studies*, II (1975), 5–23.

Sinclair, May. "The Novels of Dorothy Richardson," *The Egoist*, v (April 1918), 57–59.

Smith-Rosenberg, Carroll. "Puberty to Menopause: The Cycle of Femininity in Nineteenth-Century America," *Feminist Studies*, I (1973), 58–72.

Smith-Rosenberg, Carroll. "The Female World of Love and Ritual: Relations Between Women in Nineteenth-Century America," *Signs*, I (Autumn 1975), 1–30.

Stansell, Christine and John Faragher. "Women and Their Families on the Overland Trail," *Feminist Studies*, II (1975), 150–166.

Stark, Myra C. "*The Clever Woman of the Family* and What Happened to Her," *Mary Wollstonecraft Journal*, II (May 1974), 13–19.

Stern, Jennifer. "Women and the Novel: A Nineteenth-Century Explosion," *Women's Liberation Review*, I (1973).

Stone, Donald. "Victorian Feminism and the Nineteenth-Century Novel," *Women's Studies*, 1 (1972), 65–91.

West, Rebecca. "And They All Lived Happily Ever After," *Times Literary Supplement* (July 26, 1974), 779.

Wolff, Robert Lee. "Devoted Disciple: The Letters of Mary Elizabeth Braddon to Sir Edward Bulwer-Lytton, 1862–1873," *Harvard Library Bulletin*, XII (Jan. 1974), 5–35; and (April 1974), 129–161.

Wood, Ann Douglas. "The 'Scribbling Women' and Fanny Fern: Why Women Wrote," *American Quarterly*, XXIII (Spring 1971), 1–24.

Wood, Ann Douglas. "The Literature of Impoverishment: The Woman Local Colorists in America, 1865–1914," *Women's Studies*, 1 (1972), 1–45.

Wood, Ann Douglas. "Mrs. Sigourney and the Sensibility of the Inner Space," *New England Quarterly*, XLV (June 1972), 163–181.

Index

abortion, 221, 299, 316
Acton, Dr. William, 120
Allan, Grant, 184–85
Allan, James Macgrigor, 77
Allen, Walter, 308
Altick, Richard, 39, 41
Amazon utopias, 4–5, 29, 191–92
androgyny, 34, 206, 263–64, 284,
    286–87, 289
Angel in the House, 14, 28, 109,
    113, 117–18, 165, 205–06, 265,
    288, 292; frigidity of, 190, 207.
    See also feminine ideal
anger, 35, 180, 213, 262, 263–64,
    277–78, 280, 285, 311
anorexia nervosa, 268–69
anti-suffragists, 217, 225–26
Athenaeum, 95, 177
Atwood, Margaret, 329
Austen, Jane, 3, 7, 18, 29, 74, 87,
    101, 102, 302, 305
autonomy, 318

Bagehot, Walter, 123
Bainbridge, Beryl, 5n, 35
Baker, Ernest, 5
Banks, Isabella, 47, 139
Barber, Margaret, 58, 72
Bardwick, Judith, 64, 284
Barrett, Elizabeth, *see* Elizabeth
    Barrett Browning
Bazin, Nancy, 266, 278
Becker, Lydia, 155
Bell, Currer, *see* Charlotte Brontë
Bell, Quentin, 265, 268, 273–74
Bennett, Arnold, 33
Benson, Stella, 237, 244–45
Bentley's, 38, 49, 156, 159, 177

Bentley's Quarterly Review, 123
Bergonzi, Bernard, 5
Bernikow, Louise, 36
Besant, 67
birth control, 191
Blackett, Henry, 31, 51
Blackmore, R. D., 91
Blackwood, John, 20, 31, 93, 105
Blind, Mathilde, 58, 62, 186
Bodichon, Barbara, 94, 155
Boole, Mary Everett, 63
Bradbrook, M. C., 283
Braddon, Mary, 28, 157, 163–64;
    on Brontë, 154; and Brough-
    ton, 173n; and Bulwer-Lytton,
    164; and Collins, 164, 166; and
    Eliot, 154, 171; and Gissing,
    158; and H. James, 156; and
    Paget, 160–61; and Reade, 157,
    164; *Lady Audley's Secret,* 163–
    68
Bradley, Katherine, 30n, 183
British Quarterly Review, 148
Brontë, Anne, 96
Brontë, Charlotte, 3, 7, 23, 46,
    55, 58, 59, 329; legend of, 106–
    07; 150–52, 304; on woman's
    man, 133; on women's suf-
    frage, 216
    and women writers: Austen,
    102, 103–14; Braddon, 154;
    Brontë sisters, 135; Byatt, 302;
    Craik, 139; Drabble, 304; Eliot,
    93–94, 105, 117, 122, 124–25;
    Gaskell, 106, 132, 303; Jews-
    bury, 141; Lessing, 124; Linton,
    105; Martineau, 92; Norton,
    140; Oliphant, 106, 122; Rhys,

385

Craik, Dinah Mulock, 16, 20, 45,
46, 61, 66; on vocation, 144; on
housekeeping, 86; rev. by Hutton, 88; rev. by James, 156; *Head
of the Family*, 50; *John Halifax,
Gentleman*, 51, 127, 136; *Little
Lame Prince*, 33; *Noble Life*,
38; *Ogilvies*, 50; *Olive*, 28,
50
Craik, George Lillie, 52
cripples, 127, 150, 200
Croker, Mrs. B. M., 67
Crowe, Catherine, 41

Daiches, David, 291–92
Dallas, E. S., 73, 79, 82
daughters, 15
delicacy, 95
Deutsch, Helene, 268
Dickens, Charles, 39, 66, 80, 153,
156, 163; as "feminine" novelist,
88
Diver, Maud, 67
divorce, 67, 122, 160, 172–73
Dixie, Florence, 191
Dixon, William Hepworth, 95
domestic realism, 20
double, 28, 125–26
double colonialism, 204
Dowie, Ménie Muriel, 194
Drabble, Margaret, 35, 320, 323;
and Brontës, 304; comp. to Eliot,
302; on Lessing, 307; on Mansfield, 247; and marriage, 307;
The Garrick Year, 306; *The Millstone*, 303, 305; *The Needle's Eye*,
306–307; *The Waterfall*, 131–32,
306
dreams, 309
Dublin University Magazine, 133
"The Duchess," *see* Margaret Hungerford
Dunne, Mary Chavelita, *see* George
Egerton

Edgeworth, Maria, 18, 56, 74, 101
Edinburgh Review, 59
education, 40, 41, 42, 90, 95
Edwards, Amelia, 154
Egerton, George, 31, 58, 189, 194,
210–15
Egoist, 235–36
Eliot, George, 3, 5, 6, 7, 9, 13, 18,
19, 29, 43, 46, 58, 60, 73, 76, 77,
95, 153, 180, 318; attacks on, 95;
cares for father, 64; on cultured
woman, 104; on female brain,
78; housekeeping, 66; legend of,
107, 111; in novels by Collins,
163–64; by Robins, 108–110; by
Wilford, 150–52; self-censorship,
96; on women's suffrage, 217.
and women writers: Austen, 104,
105; Blind, 186; Braddon, 104,
154; Brontë, 105, 117, 125; Cholmondeley, 108; Chopin, 131;
Craigie, 110–10; Craik, 104,
108n, 130n; Drabble, 131–32,
302n; Linton, 105, 107–08;
Oliphant, 104, 105, 107, 135;
Richardson, 254; Schreiner, 200–
01; Ward, 110; Wharton, 131;
Woolf, 111
works of: *Adam Bede*, 25, 91; re-
ception of, 93–95; *Daniel De-
ronda*, 171, 207; *Felix Holt*, 142;
Middlemarch, 25, 42, 171, 194;
Mill on the Floss, 41, 149–50, 161,
200–01, 232n; analysis, 125–32;
Romola, 24, 214; "Silly Novels by
Lady Novelists," 42, 45, 96–97
Ellis, Havelock, 195
Ellis, Sarah, 16, 22, 65
Ellmann, Mary, 7–8
Emerson, Ralph Waldo, 199
Englishwoman's Review, 38, 155
Erikson, Erik, 9
Ethelmer, Ellis, 149, 191
euphemisms, 116